Praise for *Shadow*

"Offers us a gripping overview o[...] unstoppable evolution from primit[...] the rapacious bureaucrat in charge of civic planning in y[...] neighborhood today."   —Elizabeth Lowry, *Wall Street Journal*

"If you told me that British historian Matthew Green was some kind of delightful English Calvino who'd conjured up an odd fictional encyclopedia of disappeared cities, lost towns, and ghostly villages, I'd still want to read this book. . . . [I]t is worth spending a little time with history's stark examples of time's dominion over us all."   —Jonny Diamond, *Literary Hub*

"An eloquent tour of lost communities."   —PD Smith, *Guardian*

"Through these slices of British history, Green has woven a moving exploration of impermanence, memory, and the hypnotic allure of the past."   —*Library Journal*, starred review

"Full of evocative imagery and fascinating lore, this vibrant account eulogizes the past and issues a stark warning for the future."   —*Publishers Weekly*

"A beautifully written, intelligent book, and it is offered as a warning as well as a memorial."   —James McConnachie, *Sunday Times* (UK)

"Startling. . . . Often playful in tone, *Shadowlands* nonetheless has a serious purpose. . . . [It] offers an urgent reminder of what may lie ahead as a result of climate change and rising sea levels."   —Miranda Seymour, *Financial Times* (UK)

"Gripping. . . . *Shadowlands* is both meticulously researched and vividly imagined. The author has a novelist's gift for bringing the past alive."   —Fiona Rintoul, *Herald* (UK)

"Consistently interesting [and] thought-provoking. . . . Green's passion and historical vision bursts from the page, summoning up the past in surround sound and sensual prose."
—Cal Flyn, *Times* (UK)

"This is an outstanding book, bursting with fascinating information. It's unobtrusively poignant and gently philosophical."
—Jake Kerridge, *Mirror* (UK)

"Superb. A beautifully written atlas of Ghost Britain, a summoning of places lost to memory, and a deft excavation of the void underlying myths of national identity."
—William Atkins, author of *The Immeasurable World*

"A haunting, lyrical tour around the lost places of Britain."
—Charlotte Higgins, author of *Under Another Sky*

"An exquisitely written, moving, and elegiac exploration of the dead ends and lost causes of history—a book to savor and cherish."
—Suzannah Lipscomb, author of *The King Is Dead: The Last Will and Testament of Henry VIII*

"A beautiful book, truly original. *Shadowlands* is poetic history written with great literary flair, inqusitiveness, soul-searching, and humanity. . . . It is a marvelous achievement."
—Ian Mortimer, author of *The Time Traveller's Guide to Medieval England*

"A haunting work of resurrection, stinging in a perpetual present. Shamanic consciousness for the borderlands of memory."
—Iain Sinclair, author of *The Last London*

MATTHEW GREEN

SHADOWLANDS

A Journey Through Britain's Lost Cities and Vanished Villages

W. W. NORTON & COMPANY
Celebrating a Century of Independent Publishing

For information about permission to reproduce selections from this book,
write to Permissions, W. W. Norton & Company, Inc., 500 Fifth Avenue, New York, NY 10110

For information about special discounts for bulk purchases, please contact
W. W. Norton Special Sales at specialsales@wwnorton.com or 800-233-4830

Manufacturing by Lakeside Book Company

ISBN 978-1-324-06449-7 pbk.

W. W. Norton & Company, Inc., 500 Fifth Avenue, New York, N.Y. 10110
www.wwnorton.com

W. W. Norton & Company Ltd., 15 Carlisle Street, London W1D 3BS

1 2 3 4 5 6 7 8 9 0

For my father

CONTENTS

ILLUSTRATIONS

Protest during the official opening ceremony of Llyn Celyn, Tryweryn, 28 October 1965 (Geoff Charles/National Library of Wales) 285

MAPS

INTRODUCTION

There is something thrilling about a lost city or ghost town, something that draws us in. I remember the moment in 2016 when I heard about a drowned medieval city off the coast of Suffolk, called Dunwich. Built on a cliff, much of it was swept into the sea by two ferocious storms in the thirteenth and fourteenth centuries, precipitating a process of erosion that claimed much of the rest of it over the succeeding centuries. It is frequently branded as 'Britain's lost Atlantis' even though we know exactly where fragments of its ruins languish on the ocean floor. All that remains today is a lonely priory and graves. The notion of a city falling off a cliff – literally 'going under' as W. G. Sebald puts it in *The Rings of Saturn*[1] – was instantly poignant, not just prescient of climate change but an emblem too of the turbulent political mood of the day, with the vote to leave the European Union in Britain and the election of Donald Trump in the United States representing a new era of uncertainty: a sense of everything melting down and changing form.

The years that followed would be a time of turbulence in my own life, too; I split up with my wife and lost my father, which contributed to a period of great emotional turmoil and psychological despair. Ambushed by memories, with the past hanging like a pall in the air, the present seemed so thin as to barely to exist at all; the future was too terrifying to contemplate. Could these lost cities – I hoped there was more than one – provide me with perspectives that would allow me to move forward? The sunken medieval metropolis began to sound like a salutary tale, and I was determined to discover how our country has come to be shaped by absences, just as my life had come to be defined by what was no longer there.

Dunwich's demise was by no means a freak historical occurrence. Britain, as it turned out, was a great reservoir – sometimes literally – of vanished places. A map of Britain in 1225 would show thousands of settlements – not just villages but towns and cities too – that do not appear on today's charts, or which exist only as a shadow of their former selves. Even a 1925 map shows dozens of settlements that lie forlorn and abandoned today. This, then, is the untold story of Britain's lost cities, ghost towns and vanished villages, the places that slipped through the fingers of history. From the stone cottages of Skara Brae in Orkney, Europe's most complete Neolithic village, to the lost city of Trellech in the Welsh Marches where England dissolves uneasily into its conquered neighbour Wales, the landscape of Britain is scarred with the relics of vanished places, their haunting and romantic beauty so often at odds with the violence and suddenness of their fate. I wanted to dig up not just the physical remains of Britain's shadowlands but the extraordinary stories of how those places met their fate, evoking a cluster of lost worlds, animating the people who lived, worked, dreamed and died there, and showing how their disappearances explain why Britain looks the way it does. And I found out just how easy it was for cities, towns and villages to fall foul of the historical process and sink into oblivion. Yet if history had taken an ever-so-slightly different path, it's feasible that some of these vanished places might very well still be thriving today.

I wanted to see them with my own eyes, to *feel* them. I recall my first journey vividly, waiting for eight listless hours in Aberdeen, finally boarding the night ferry to Orkney, standing on the deck, little pellets of rain tearing my face, as the port slowly faded from view and the ship coursed into the glittering black. On board, television sets beamed news into deserted corridors; a lonely cafeteria served meals to passengers who, shuffling gently to their tables, ate chips smothered in ketchup and stared out into the black waves; and, in the heart of the ferry, a cinema played to no one. I embraced the tilting of the boat as sleep came to my pod, before staggering into the cold, sea-sprayed air with wild, remote bells ringing in a charcoal sky. I walked up a dual carriageway towards the city of Kirkwall ahead of my trip to an abandoned Neolithic settlement – the oldest in Europe – the next day. It was the first of many journeys that would take me to the margins, to the shadowlands of Britain. In time, I would sail to an Outer Hebridean island of rock in the remotest part of the British Isles, peer into a lonely reservoir in the dying light in rural Gwynedd, and roam past ghost churches in Norfolk's golden heathland and in the upland splendour of the Yorkshire Wolds.

The remains of disappeared places, wherever they are to be found, are deeply affecting. A priory standing forlorn on a cliff while the rest of the city moulders beneath the grey waves of the North Sea. The former streets and alleys of a plague village, scorched into lonely fields. A village sunk in a reservoir, its slimy carcass revealed in times of drought. A city gate stranded in an overgrown field of nettles. A street in a once-flourishing village now a heap of bullet-riddled ruins. The incongruity between the settlements in their prime and in the quiet misery of their ruin conveys the transience of all earthly things – a truth so pat in words yet powerfully, in-effably, manifested in shrunken structures or total absence.

I came to realise that much of this timeless fascination with lost cities stems from their metaphorical and symbolic resonance, whether with Roman Pompeii's artefacts and buildings exquisitely preserved under volcanic ash and pumice for seventeen hundred years, the gold-rush towns of California left to rot in the desert, or, more recently, the inner-city prairies of Detroit. What were once vast monuments of human endeavour look, in their decay, like victims of hubris. Places like these can be soothing and uplifting, too, putting one's own troubles in perspective. Lost in a spiral of self-doubt staring at the battered remains of the church tower in a village wiped out following the Black Death in Yorkshire, I felt able to make peace with that doubt, and persist. The vanished place is a white-washed canvas on to which we can project.

As an author and social historian originally specialising in the history of London, I have always striven to make the past live – and live vividly. For almost a decade now, I have been leading immersive whirlwind tours, mainly through the City of London, powered by such things as 'bitter Muhammedan gruel' (seventeenth-century coffee), 'creator of the world's happiness' (medieval wine) and of course 'mother's ruin' (gin!). These tours are primarily to places and spaces that no longer exist: to the convivial, candlelit coffee-houses of the eighteenth century; medieval anchorite cells where living men and women were willingly entombed in a tiny, coffin-like space to bring them closer to God; Elizabethan bear pits and Victorian pornography shops. These are all places that, though their original buildings have long since crumbled away, helped shape the mentality of each successive age, and left their mark on the social life of the city, as well as the odd mournful remain. And so from lost London to lost Britain, I sought to chart Britain's shadow topography, highlighting the fragility and fluidity of our twenty-first-century map, and revealing the continued impact of these unseen places on both the landscape and imagination of Britain.

It felt urgent to do this now, as the planet heats and parts of society are ravaged by the coronavirus pandemic. As is well known, if carbon and other greenhouse gas emissions are not dramatically lowered within the next thirty years, catastrophic heatwaves, floods, storms, other extreme weather events, famines and social unrest stemming from refugee crises and a global fight for scarce resources, not to mention the extinction of entire animal, insect and plant species, will wreak havoc upon our land. Many of Britain's coastal communities are already vanishing into the sea, and one recent estimate puts more than four thousand villages at risk of fatal flooding over the course of the next two decades. It is predicted that much of London could be underwater by the end of the twenty-first century.[2] Covid-19 has, at the time of writing, already killed more than 130,000 people in the UK alone. And this may not even be the worst of it. It is thought that the destruction of natural habitats, bringing animals into closer proximity to humans, heightens the risk of further pandemics as pathogens leap across species.[3] Global warming is far from a new phenomenon. My itinerary of destruction includes two medieval cities that were swept into the sea by ferocious sea storms that coincided with the Medieval Warm Period, which saw temperatures and sea levels rise in western Europe, leading to the loss of hundreds of towns, villages, parishes and even islands between the eleventh and sixteenth centuries, and over 1.5 million lives. Medieval climate change was not man-made but the fates of the two sunken medieval cities encountered here, Old Winchelsea and Dunwich, nonetheless serve as an awful premonition of what lies ahead for some of our own homes as a direct result of climate change that *is* man-made.

As I toured Ghost Britain, I encountered settlements laid low by natural phenomena, territorial aggression, war and plague, economic paradigm shifts (such as from hunter-gathering to agriculture), industrialisation, technological and medical advances, changes in governance, and more – mediums of oblivion familiar to us today. By exploring Britain's history through this unusual prism I discovered places that had to be sacrificed so that the country could take the form it does today: tiny villages fed to industrial behemoths to allow for continued expansion; commandeered places vital in honing military strategies to help Britain defend herself; boom towns left to rot as a result of territorial conquests, still evident on maps today; the areas hollowed out to ensure that the incomes of landowners did not suffer in the aftermath of plague epidemics; the everyday life of remote communities irrevocably disrupted by intellectual curiosity. An end is not always a complete end, however, and one of the most surprising revelations of my journey is how places seemingly consigned to oblivion can be reanimated centuries later, if only in the imagination.

By focusing on the false starts, dead ends and lost causes of history, I hope to give a truer sense of the progress of time, foregrounding the forgotten. Often what we think is lost or failed can be relative, and the stories ahead bring home the importance of perspective in our sense of finality. To the Anglo-Saxons who arrived from the fifth century AD in the wake of the Roman withdrawal, much of Britain seemed like a graveyard of towns and cities: the abandoned city of Londinium was a ghost town, overgrown with brambles, infested with wolves and Viking invaders. They leave us a poem, *The Ruin*, composed possibly as early as the eighth century, and collected in a tenth-century codex of poems and riddles, though rather fittingly about a fifth of it is itself in ruins, the manuscript having become slightly singed.[4] The poem magnificently evokes the faded grandeur of a ruined Roman city by contrasting its fallen state with its historic majesty –

Bright were the buildings, halls where springs ran,
high, horngabled, much throng-noise;
these many mead-halls men filled
with loud cheerfulness.

– but it is a quivering image because we know it will not last, and the description of its downfall is almost incidentally tacked on: '. . . Weird [fate] changed that'. Then came war, pestilence, the death of heroes: 'where they stood to fight, waste places'; 'and on the acropolis', we learn, 'ruins'. We hear that 'the work of the Giants, the stonesmiths, mouldereth'. It describes 'snapped roof-trees, towers fallen'. Of those who built such wonders 'earthgrip holds them – gone, long gone', the once-powerful walls hacked away by weapons, and the skilled furnishings now encompassed in 'loam-crust'. Though it could defeat enemies, the city itself was no match for nature. In the eyes of the Anglo-Saxon poet, the city was a lost cause, fallen to ruin, itself awaiting the cold grasp of the earth. And yet, it is still with us today. It is almost certainly Bath.[5] Shadowlands sometimes hide in plain sight.

This book is very far from being an encyclopaedia or atlas of Britain's vanished places. It is intended as a curated journey and I hope my selection will inspire people to follow in my footsteps and feel their ghostly presences for themselves.[6] Part of the poetic beauty of the lost city and ghost town, and much of the spell they cast over us, lies in the haunting juxtaposition with what little remains. I have not explored former Roman towns which, after the influx of Germanic invaders and the rise of the Anglo-Saxon kingdoms from the fifth century AD, would go on to become the nuclei of prominent English cities, like Bath, or Verulamium, or the embryonic villages that would later merge into the great industrial behemoths of Liverpool, Manchester and Leeds in the eighteenth and nineteenth centuries.[7] Although the resultant town or city might bear little physical resemblance to its progenitor, aside from the ruins that surface occasionally in its streets, they went on to shape or inform these places as foundations for urban success. Instead, this book is written in the minor key, more concerned with squandered potential, with failed or even *quailed* – in the Middle English sense of 'wasting away, coming to nothing' – places. I am interested in what fails, not what succeeds; in imploding – not exploding – topographies.

I have tried to rely upon primary sources wherever possible, and have spent years immersed in archival chronicles, state papers, parish records, plans, diaries, letters, newspapers, early photographs, even postcards, and in some instances have conducted first-hand interviews, always moved by how these sources bring forgotten voices and stories to life. I am indebted to an immense number of professional archaeologists, geographers and local enthusiasts who have written on lost villages, towns and cities in highly detailed and specialist ways. I have tried to illustrate diversity – chronologically (from the fourth millennium BC to AD 2021), geographically, topographically, and in terms of how these various places disappeared. However, I also want to explore the ways in which they were physically and mentally resurrected years later, investigating how these fallen stars continue to shape Britain today, both in the sense of how we conceive of our history, and, most poignantly, how we should contend with her future.

A 'shadowland' can be defined as 'an indeterminate borderland between places or states, typically represented as an abode of ghosts and spirits'; the word captures the haunting quality of these zones. The stations on my trail of oblivion are forever shadows of their former selves, or in the shadow of further annihilation. Shadowlands are also mysterious, secretive, of an uncertain identity or nature, and sometimes very difficult to reach. My first lay in one of the remotest corners of Scotland.

CHAPTER ONE

THE HOUSES BENEATH THE SAND: SKARA BRAE

There was blood in the ocean. In late November 1850, the British Isles were rocked by one of the worst storms in decades, a furious tempest that howled across the land and made dark mountains of the sea as it crashed upon the shore. Off the Cornish coast, a vessel from Cardiff was wrecked with the loss of all ten hands; a brig bound from Sydney to London vanished somewhere off the coast of Ramsgate, the first sign of it, the next morning, a copy of the *Sydney Morning Herald* floating across the waves; and off the Irish coast at Kilkee, a ship containing five hundred people off to start a new life in New York foundered in the darkness, the grinding and cracking of the hull against the Black Rock a terrible accompaniment to the shrieks and groans of the ninety-six who drowned, the blood from their battered heads and limbs swirling into the icy sea, corpses found floating the next day in only their nightclothes. Across the land, roofs were ripped from houses, spires from churches, and, in the cities, the horse-bus networks were brought to a sorry halt. The inhabitants of coastal villages lay in their beds at night in terror, listening to the sea's shrill hiss, a fire that blazed black.[1]

The storm that would claim two hundred lives reached its zenith of destruction on the night of Tuesday 20 November. It ravaged one of the remotest parts of the British Isles: a barren, virtually treeless, gently undulating landscape kissed by the midnight sun in midsummer, yet which at that time of year had some of the longest nights in the whole country. The archipelago was a relatively new addition to the United Kingdom, having been annexed from Norway in the late sixteenth century; Orcadian Scots still had a Norwegian lilt. Most strikingly, it was peppered with extraordinary prehistoric remains, a veritable Neolithic nirvana.[2] On the island of Mainland, the largest in Orkney, the storm blasted without cease for two full days, aided by the near-absence of trees. In a reversal of the usual order of things, the wind's destructive force also proved an impetus of discovery – or rediscovery. For when it was finally safe to go out, some of the villagers who lived on the western coast of the island discovered at the Bay of Skaill that the beach had been conspicuously reconfigured. There, the wind had scoured away the grassy veil of a high dune known as *Skerrabrae*, revealing a considerable chunk of what no one had been expecting to see: a five-thousand-year-old settlement miraculously preserved in the sand – just as Pompeii had been in ash and pumice – sunk in primeval muck.[3] The earth had been forced to give up her secrets, and what had lain concealed for millennia turned out to be amongst the oldest built structures anywhere on the planet – older than the Egyptian pyramids, older than the temples of Mycenae, and older, certainly, than Stonehenge.

———

As Professor Vere Gordon Childe stepped on to the night ferry at Aberdeen, his suitcase bulging with books, his mind flitted over the challenge that lay ahead, and, as so often, the cold beauty of the Marxist programme. It was the summer of 1928[4] and he had only recently been appointed Professor of Prehistoric Archaeology at the University of Edinburgh, so he was impatient to explore some ancient structures, structures of mysterious provenance. But by the time he got to Kirkwall, the chief and indeed only city on Orkney, a note of apprehension had crept into his thoughts. What was he doing here? He hated fieldwork. He liked books and was an accomplished archaeologist, writing for both academic and popular audiences. He didn't like going outside but he would have to spend the next couple of years shovelling sand on a beach – not a gorgeous Australian bay of fine white sand beneath a hot sun, but an abysmal Scottish one, assisted by men with cold, gloomy accents and of meagre cheer who wouldn't appreciate his spontaneous quotation of the Classics, nor his Roman arithmetic, and buttressed at all times by a glacial wind that would chill him to the bone.

The Australian professor was just the kind of eccentric, visionary, perhaps slightly ill-adjusted kind of creature that seems drawn to lost places. Childe, as his closest colleagues testified, was not the best-looking of men. He spoke seventeen languages and was hoping to learn an eighteenth before the year was out. He could do long division in Roman numerals (as anyone who went to one of his dinners discovered to their cost). He was astringent and hurtful, with an abrupt and alarming manner that almost everyone, including his closest colleagues, found objectionable. His moustache was a force unto itself, concealing his smirks, and he was thin as a rake with no chin to speak of. Once, in a single evening, he addressed his assembled company in six different languages, pontificated upon Bronze Age datings, and roamed over the entire gamut of European literature, quoting liberally.[5] *Examination* was his whole life; suspecting he had cancer, aged sixty-five, he took his own life in Australia's Blue Mountains, realising his long-held ambition not to get old and become a burden on society.[6] He grated the mind and sapped the energy from the room. His habits may have been peculiar (he liked to drink half-pints of rum and milk[7]), but no one could deny his colossal intellect. The trouble was, he was worried no one was going to appreciate it on Orkney.[8] How could he have known that, during the course of the two seasons he spent there, he would have an idea that would make his name and trigger an intellectual earthquake in the field of archaeology? On a bleak Scottish beach lay the key to unlocking the mystery of what kind of society our prehistoric ancestors lived in and of how civilisation began to take root in these isles.

It was not before time. The site up until that point had received woefully little attention. In the aftermath of the storm of November 1850, some residents of Skaill discovered two submerged houses, roofless, and the contours of a lost settlement in the sand. The local laird William Watt, who lived in a seventeenth-century mansion called Skaill House overlooking the site, launched an amateur excavation but ran out of steam after finding four houses. The mysterious settlement attracted the attention of Orcadian antiquaries[9] but remarkably, although a trickle of people travelled to see 'the Weem of Skara Brae' in the late Victorian period, correctly understanding them as 'one of the most remarkable series of primitive dwellings known',[10] no one attempted any further investigations (documented investigations, at least) for another fifty years and even then the site was hardly treated with the reverence it deserved. In 1913, a group of semi-drunken guests, after a dinner party at Skaill House, casually dug the site with shovels and emerged with a welter of historically significant artefacts, many of which were never seen again.[11] In December 1924, *another* violent storm washed away one of the houses, ramming home – a shameful seventy-five years after the site's discovery – the urgency of protecting, and documenting, the site. Who knew when the sea might come to swallow the site whole? So a sea wall was built (much-fortified since) and a decision taken by His Majesty's Commissioners of the Works to excavate the houses properly, at long last. A team of workmen from Kirkwall set to work in 1927 clearing sand, debris and the refuse of millennia, but it soon became clear that they needed a professional archaeologist to remove and document all the artefacts and archaeological deposits that were surely of such rich importance.

'When I reached the site,' wrote Childe in 1931, 'Skara Brae appeared as a grass-grown sand-dune from the seaward side of which protruded the ruinous walls of five huts and some sections of a connecting passage.'[12] Although he observed that 'a gigantic sand dune has embalmed a whole complex of huts and lanes', Childe quickly realised that the layer of sand was only superficial. 'On removing a couple of feet of it', he wrote, 'we would come upon a very tough clay-like soil, full of broken bones, shells, potsherds, and implements – a deposit that we shall term the midden.' He immediately recognised the importance of Skara Brae: 'The ruins and relics throw an exceptionally vivid light on the life of prehistoric man in these islands.' The 'reconstruction of commonplace scenes of prehistoric life' was no longer 'a work of pure imagination'. After two arduous seasons' work, Huts – he always called them 'huts', never 'houses' – 7 and 8 had been unearthed, along with some subterranean passages. By autumn 1929, a full eight houses had emerged from the tomb of sand and, his job done, Childe set his Mars-sized mind to other things and began writing up his findings. These were published two years later as *Skara Brae: A Pictish Village in Orkney* but, as the title suggests, he initially misdated the site – *Picti* was what the Romans called the hostile tribes who marauded beyond the Antonine Wall in the unwelcoming north of Britain, and they are first mentioned around AD 300, significantly later than the Neolithic Age. It would be courteous to remember, however, that Childe had been unable to remove and examine structural remains at Skara Brae properly; the remit of the dig was solely to clear out the structures and describe them. It was not until the mid-1950s that the archaeologist Stuart Piggott convincingly dated the site to the Neolithic age,[13] by which point Childe had long since embraced its Stone Age provenance. Yet bafflingly, another twenty years would pass before meticulous and empirically valid excavations involving radiocarbon dating were undertaken. These revealed the existence of a 'long-lived, settled community' in the late Neolithic period, beginning around 3100 BC and mysteriously disappearing around 2500 BC.[14]

I set off for Skara Brae as dawn broke over Orkney like drawn-out lightning. Like Childe, I had caught the ferry to Kirkwall, the islands' little city. The bus that was supposed to go there did not; but another, which wasn't, did. I was the sole passenger aboard with a streaming, panoramic view of the landscape, as though I were being carted along in my own private aquarium. Through the windows I saw distant promontories beneath smashed silver skies; patches of sea tinctured in fugitive sunlight; heathland, farmhouses and electricity pylons; flashes of Neolithic ruins and, far in the distance – with no trees, I could see for miles – a rainbow firing out of a lake into a vast, billowing, mushroom-shaped cloud.

At first glance Skara Brae looks like a crazy golf course, an endlessly curving helter-skelter of grass which, as you get closer, discloses a series of stone caverns as though the world underneath were made of stone. It looks odd, a mutation of nature, as though the grass is being gently boiled by some cavernous demon below. The sunken cocoons are connected by a trench-like passageway that bores through the ancient settlement like a giant writhing worm, making the whole a hotchpotch of humps and hollows, a

tiny eruption of prehistoric Britain in one of the remotest corners of the United Kingdom. From the viewing platform, it is clear that what lies below is much more than just the forlorn skeletons of Neolithic houses; their original contents, in some, lie untouched, and they come replete with furniture. The dressers, bed-frames, storage cells and hearth-places are almost identical to how they would have appeared five thousand years ago. It was in these wonderfully insulated cocoons, nestling in the shallows of the earth, that Neolithic Orcadians kept the cold, wind, rain, sleet and snow at bay, where they lay low when unidentified vessels or perhaps marauders passed by. It convulses the mind to consider just how long this ancient wonder has lain dormant – here, beneath a quilt of sand, as prehistoric man discovered bronze and iron, as the great civilisations of antiquity rose and fell, as waves of invaders rolled across the British Isles establishing rival kingdoms, as Christianity took hold, as England, Wales and Scotland warred, as the *United* Kingdom rose to become the foremost industrial power in the world, spreading its tentacles across the globe – here, mummified for over four thousand years in millions of grains of sand until the wind so rudely ripped off its veil, it slept.

In a blazing turquoise sky, clouds streamed towards Skaill House like the jet plumes of a Concorde. From a certain angle, the mansion almost makes a shadow of the Neolithic settlement, the house's crisp, triangular, perfectly symmetrical form a striking contrast to the wacky, concentric maze that is Skara Brae, so sensible and grave against the ancient circular marvels. Beyond, the Bay of Skaill was unerringly smooth like the side of an ice cube. It extended a gentle tongue towards the pebbles on the beach, almost licking the knoll in which Skara Brae nestles. The immediacy of the sea lends a sense of dramatic isolation and vulnerability to the settlement, belying Orkney's significance as a centre of prehistoric trade and worship. During its four-hundred-year lifespan, the true aquatic frontier was almost a mile further out – creeping inwards year upon year – the grey sheet of water in front of me then a duned lagoon, a watery desert of shellfish and trout.

The impression of completeness is deceptive; what I was in fact looking at was two different versions of the same village, one superimposed on top of the other.[15] The earlier one, consisting of a series of circular houses, was built around 2900 BC, from which only the lower ranges of stonework survive; Houses 9 and 10, which are still clearly visible, hail from this period.[16] The rest of this earlier village is buried beneath the final, ultimately deserted village whose remodelled houses went up – slightly bigger, rectangular in shape with rounded edges – a hundred years later. These later dwellings survive, incredibly, to roof height. The settlement's size is deceptive too; it was originally marginally bigger. It is thought that a couple of houses – and perhaps a burial ground – were lost to the sea before the site's rediscovery in 1850, and virtually all of House 3 was swept away in the storm of December 1924, which persuaded the government to take the threat to Skara Brae seriously.

The site is a palimpsest of prehistoric domesticity. Traces of walls, pottery, tools and hearth-places have been found about eight feet below the earliest visible houses, betraying an *older* settlement, now invisible. The same terrain was part of a farming settlement whose buildings lay elsewhere, but which have not yet been discovered. There were four distinct phases of occupation, with never at any one time more than a dozen houses. This means that there was never a population of more than a hundred, and the average may have been closer to fifty. Owing to a dearth of native timber on Orkney, the houses were built from a notoriously delicate sandstone called Devonian Old Red, which was easily hacked away with antler picks into smooth, flat slabs called flagstones. This was a considerable boon for archaeologists; had the buildings been made from perishable wood, which was the more usual practice, the settlement would almost certainly have faded into oblivion long ago. Out of this versatile sandstone the Orcadians built their houses and virtually everything inside.

Skara Brae has the appearance of an underground village but it only began to take on this aspect later. The original village was built on top of a mound of organic waste from the pre-existing, agrarian settlement. This midden continued to grow around it, a mulch of the Orcadians' own organic waste, fortifying their houses and insulating them against the cold, wicked winds. It consisted, for the most part, of refuse that rotted down like compost – flesh from animal bones, dung, human excrement, hearth ashes, decaying plant matter – but was studded with less perishable material that remained in its original form when it was excavated in the twentieth century: broken animal bones, fragments of stone, shells, and shards of discarded artefacts; the mulch, in other words, of millennia.[17] Thick, waterproof and, when mixed with sand, taking on the tenacity of hard clay, the midden soil made a superb and plentiful insulator and it was accordingly stuffed between the inner and outer walls of the houses and packed into the spaces between the buildings themselves, conjoining the whole settlement in vast swaddling cloth of muck. Imagine in the twenty-first century dumping all domestic waste outside your house rather than putting it in rubbish bins for removal, for decades on end, until it formed a protective, insulating cocoon. In the beginning, the Orcadians' houses were free-standing but, as the infill thickened, they gradually became engulfed and, as the midden amassed – as each new generation continued to smear their waste around their walls and dump it outside their huts, and the load of centuries took their toll – they became semi-subterranean; sunk, we might say, in their own shit.[18]

It can be hard to appreciate the importance of the midden as the 'skin' of the settlement since it is now covered by smooth turf, but the warren of passages are another matter. These snaking underground passageways, parts of which are still very visible, didn't come into existence until the last hundred years of the village's existence, bored beneath the great dung-hill which by then had absorbed so much of the village. They were a perfect way of navigating the subterranean world of Skara Brae; they would have been redundant when the settlement was more 'above ground'. Narrow, twisting, and never more than a metre high – you had to stoop or crawl – they integrated every single house into their dark labyrinth, the main tunnel running from the south-west of the settlement, through the centre, to the north-east, by what is now the sea. A number of separate passages fed off, and led back into it, debouching eventually outside the settlement. They had a stone roof and haphazard pavement (isolated stretches of which survive) so perhaps underground streets or alleys – albeit incredibly cramped ones – feels more appropriate. It is the roofed passages (or 'roofed streets' as Childe calls them) that make Skara Brae unique – they are not to be found in any other surviving Neolithic settlements in Orkney[19] – and they transform the relationship between the houses, making them less autonomous, self-contained units, more members of a wider collective; the arteries of the organism to the midden's flesh. Their existence has implications for privacy and power and may well help us to unlock (or at least conjecture felicitously) the mystery of the settlement's true nature. It also meant, of course, that you could pay visits to your neighbours without stepping outside to have your face excoriated by the wind.

Despite minor variations, the interiors of all the houses followed the same blueprint, maximising the space available for many of the very same domestic activities familiar today. Each has two bed-frames, a central hearth-place, a number of little tanks sunk into the ground, shelves, alcoves, drains and, presiding over it all, a tall dresser. The houses are bigger than we might expect: in the final village each family had a floor space of thirty-six square metres, which would fit nine king-sized beds today; the houses from the earlier village were only slightly smaller. Originally the beds were recessed into the walls, but in the last village they projected inwards towards the fire, with their frontal slab doubling up as a seat;

the upper edge sometimes has very faint decorative carvings, as though they have been scrubbed away by friction. The women, it seems, slept in the bed to the left of the fire, the discovery of beads and paint pots betokening a female presence; the men, in slightly larger beds on the other side. They lay on comfortable layers of straw, heather and feather, snug beneath blankets of sheep or deer skin; a stump at the front of the bed-frame may have been used to erect canopies of fur. At the centre of each house lay the hearthplace for the fire that had allowed civilisation to come into existence in the first place. It consisted of four narrow slabs forming a space of around five square metres, with a hearthstone behind. Here was the main source of warmth and light. Excavations reveal that the inhabitants burned heather, bracken, dried seaweed, whalebone and dung. Looming over the fire was the stone dresser at the back, consisting of a single shelf on which valued artefacts were displayed – grooved pots and jars with jellyfish-shaped rims, beads, curious stone balls etched with circles, polished stone axes, and more – all conferring a sense of personal identity and bringing a flush of pride to their owners. We should not be too quick to discount the idea that it may have served as an altar or shrine too, just like those to Vesta, goddess of the hearth, in classical Roman households, displaying mementoes of – or votive offerings to – Neolithic gods who have long since turned their backs on humanity.

In the corners of each house are a handful of sunken stone boxes, their joints carefully sealed with clay, making them watertight. The obvious conjecture is that these were tanks to store live shellfish and preserve dead ones – not unlike a modern-day fridge, particularly, given their great abundance in the midden, limpets. Perhaps they ate these chewy molluscs, but probably only as a last resort; there was quite an abundance of food at Skara Brae, as we have seen. It is more likely they were used as fishing bait. Some of these boxes, however, have underfloor drainage, raising the possibility

that they could have been a kind of Neolithic urinal.

The door – a stone slab, naturally – could be locked from the inside via a sturdy bar made of whalebone or wood which slid into holes in the doorjambs. These attest to a concern for the family's security, and perhaps privacy too. We find small cupboards above the beds and beehive-shaped cells towards the back of the houses, reachable in places by crawling beneath the dressers. Some of these were evidently latrines since they have sloping drains leading off, but others were predominantly for storage and one, in the west wall of House 1, resembles a veritable treasure trove. Here, in 1929, were discovered around three thousand bone beads along with a whale-vertebra dish with the residue of red pigment, some shards of pottery, and an exquisite pendant made from walrus tusks or perhaps the teeth of a killer whale. Were these abandoned possessions, hidden treasures or even votive offerings to demanding pagan deities? Mystery, similarly, surrounds how Orcadians kept out the elements. Conspicuously, none of the original roofing survives, an absence which allows visitors the privilege of peering into lost domestic worlds. Since virtually everything else *did* survive, this inclines many to believe they were of a perishable material: driftwood from America, perhaps, or the hides of local animals or the bones of stranded whales. Stone slates (like some structures built at a similar time at the Ness of Brodgar, a ritual landscape in the middle of the island) are a more remote possibility. Whatever the material, it is likely that it was thatched with eel-grass (a reed with long, ribbon-shaped leaves drawn from nearby marshland), turf, straw or seaweed.

The best-preserved house, House 7, is shut off to the public, although there is a beguiling reconstruction of it near the museum. The Office of Public Works foolishly foisted a glass roof with concrete base upon it in the 1930s to try to make it more presentable to the public, but this compressed the walls and increased the humidity inside, causing the walls to buckle and crack; today it has a turf roof and the doorway is sealed to prevent further decay. The house was in existence, it is thought, for the final three phases of Skara Brae's existence, and it is perhaps the oldest surviving building. Like other houses it has beds, a dresser, three sunken tanks, a sump and storage space, but it differs in several key respects: it is detached from the rest of the village, accessible only via a side-passage exclusive to the house, and is built directly on virgin soil rather than the refuse of earlier settlements (this makes it the lowest settlement). Ominously, it could only be locked from the outside, and, most intriguingly of all, the right-hand wall of the house was built *on top of* an ancient coffin containing the skeletons of two women along with some everyday objects – two flint flakes (known as Skaill knives) and some limpet shells; excavations in 1928 confirmed that these pre-dated the erection of the house. Because the stone cist is conspicuously decorated with carvings we might conclude that the interment of the two women was of some spiritual significance.

Their presence could articulate the ancient belief that spirits could be harnessed to sustain the walls of buildings (collapsing houses was a not totally uncommon cause of injury and death as late as the eighteenth century); in the Old Testament Joshua's curse upon Jericho, that any one impertinent enough to defy God's will and rebuild the destroyed city 'shall lay the foundation thereof in his firstborn, and in his youngest son shall he set up the gates of it'[20] could well be a translation of this same belief into a new context. As Professor Childe speculates, the ghosts of the two women may well have been charged with sustaining House 7, and perhaps keeping a vigil over the occupants. Hopefully they were buried there after death, but we cannot entirely rule out the possibility that they were sacrificed or even buried alive, as seems to have been the tradition in other prehistoric cultures, the limpets and knives constituting a dreadful last supper.[21] Set apart from the rest of the community and lockable only from the outside, what was House 7? A prison? An anchorites' cell? A transformative space where the dead were prepared for the next life mediated, perhaps, by the two women's' souls? A ritual space for births, marriages and deaths? A magicians' lodge? The joy is in the guessing.

Houses 7 and 8 were the first to be fully excavated. While House 7 may not have been a conventional house, the so-called

'House 8' certainly was not. It seems shorn of any domestic function whatsoever. It has no beds, no tanks and no dresser. In their place are alcoves and a partitioned-off recess in the wall. The structure is pear-shaped not pebble-shaped, and free-standing rather than submerged in midden. It has thicker walls, a flat stone pavement, and entry was via a porch. The structure may have had an open roof since the roof space was found choked with loose midden embedded with pottery fragments and implements, and it certainly had a large hearth. There are telltale signs that this was a place of manufacturing and possibly commercial exchange. When the site was excavated in 1929, the floor was bespattered with fragments of dark chert, a glass-like rock which, when clamped between hot igneous rock, can be fashioned into tools (lumps of just such a rock were found on either side of the building). At the coastal end of the building is a gap in the wall, facing into the prevailing wind. Too narrow for a doorway, it is entirely plausible that this was a flue to fan the flames of the fire when the rock was being heated.[22] All around the probable flue are recesses full of fire-cracked stones. The obvious conjecture is that this was a workshop for the manufacture, storage and perhaps exchange of tools wrought of chert when, towards the end of the settlement's life, supplies of the more versatile material of flint were depleted. Could this have been where all other artefacts that litter Skara Brae were wrought – the strange little spiky balls whose purpose and significance is baffling, the fine pendants, the beads? Other archaeological features muddy the waters, however. If this was a 'workshop' or 'industrial cell', as it is frequently called, why would it need to be so extensively and intricately decorated with carved patterns on the walls? These could have been expressions of identity but they hint at a more communal function. Could it in fact have been a meeting place, where all the inhabitants gathered to make collective decisions, doled out justice when required, performed betrothal ceremonies, funerals and other religious rituals, and, in the twilight of the settlement when the political structure of society changed, received orders from an overlord? Or was it some sort of cross between a workshop, showroom and marketplace?

And the walls that radiated from the south-east corner of House 8 – what were they for? They do not seem to have been defensive; more likely is that they were shields from the furious south-westerly winds, or lingering remains of corrals or cattle yards, since cows, pigs and sheep would have needed shelter through the winter. The prehistoric warren may have looked solid and stable, having survived for so many thousands of years, and yet it offered so little certainty – about its use but also about the wider society of which it was a part. It was a strange and enigmatic piece of abstract art.

I was never satisfied with the description of Skara Brae as a village, a word that would not be coined for another three thousand years and which originally meant the populated hinterland of a *villa* or country house. But Skara Brae did not tremor to the diktat of any imposing mansion. It was its own centre of gravity, a tiny beehive of activity bored into the earth, a commune. The idea that it was remote, too, is problematic. To the best of prehistorians' estimates, Britain had a population of just 250,000 by 2000 BC,[23] so virtually everywhere, we might say, was rather remote; any signs of life, even back then, were rare and exciting. The almost identical nature of the houses still extant must have brought a sense of order to what we might assume was a turbulent, precarious world; and their air of gentle domesticity allows us to transcend the remoteness of the time period, bringing a flicker of familiarity through the abyss of millennia. The departed seem only just out of reach.

The Orcadians bent their material environment to their will masterfully, and in a way that seems infinitely resourceful to our modern manufactured age. Skara Brae had grooved ware pottery – flat-bottomed earthenware vessels decorated with grooves and chevrons that are quintessentially Neolithic – for preparing drink and cooking food, and a number of prehistorians and archaeologists go so far as to claim that the entire tradition of making this type of vessel originated on Orkney.[24] Tools were made from stone, bone, horn and wood. Polished stone axes are very much in evidence at Skara Brae, debris from chert scattered across the floor of House 8, the probable workshop. Out of animal bone came needles, pins, knives and picks. Carved-stone objects were sculpted from volcanic rock, tools made out of antlers, and beads from cows' teeth, the root cavity serving as a perfect hole for the thread of necklaces. There were shovels gauged from the shoulder blades of cows, pickaxes from dogs' bones, and awls and smoothers from yet other types of bone for leather-working: truly it was the bone age as much as the Stone Age. Implements for more elaborate work were fashioned from oak trees, but woodland on Orkney was much too sparse to allow carpentry to flourish. Skaill knives, a term coined by Professor Childe, abound. These were made by splitting pebbles into oval segments with a sharp edge and thickened back. Crude yet effective, these were sometimes incised with motifs identical to those found on the interiors of the houses, suggesting how visual forms could confer a shared sense of identity. These – along with other strange-looking implements – were used to slaughter animals, it seems, rather than enemies. Remarkably, no remains of anything resembling a viable weapon have been found, nor is there any trace of a defensive ditch or rampart.[25] Contrary to one of the most prevailing mental pictures of the age, of primitive, scantily clad humans waging a desperate war for survival against the ferocity of both nature and brutal, axe-wielding enemies, Skara Brae seems to have been fundamentally peaceful. So slight was the population – not just on Orkney but across the British Isles – that there was not much competition for land. At least, not yet.

None of which is to say that Skara Brae was hermetically sealed from the island community nor the wider world. There were interactions with both; they seem, as far as we can tell, to have been largely non-violent. Orkney was a significant power centre with many sea routes connecting it to other regions, especially the Boyne Valley in Ireland, and what would become mainland Scotland and southern England.[26] Another Neolithic village on the Orcadian island of Rousay, Braes of Rinyo, was discovered in the decade following Professor Childe's excavations, and it is likely that there were many more scattered throughout the archipelago – by no means all the same tiny size. Skara Brae was no anomaly; marriage alliances with other settlements were surely necessary to sustain inter-generational health, and bartering for specific materials must have taken place too – the blood-coloured stone haematite, from the isle of Hoy, for example, has been discovered around Skara Brae. The erection of immense religious monuments at Brodgar and Stenness in the middle of Mainland would have required some kind of power structure or, at the very least, a sense of mutual obligation to corral the requisite craftsmanship, labour and resources needed to build them. It would be perverse to rule out the idea, given its proximity, that Skara Brae contributed to some extent.

The ubiquity throughout the British Isles of grooved ware pottery – if it did originate in Orkney – is testament to the islanders' influence; there are striking similarities in the patterning of stones in Skara Brae with the tombs along the River Boyne in eastern Ireland; and there is also the Orkney vole, unknown elsewhere in Britain and yet not native to the archipelago, coming most probably from France or Spain. And there must have been an awareness of lands that none of them had ever visited – the driftwood that floated across the Atlantic from North America must have conjured images of strange and faraway places.

What was Skara Brae? It does seem unique, within its context. The majority of settlements that have survived from prehistoric Britain are single farmsteads.[27] Skara Brae, along with other, less excavated settlements on Orkney –Rinyo on Rousay (1937), Barnhouse on Mainland (1980) and Pool on Sanday (1990) – was the polar opposite, a swarming beehive of a settlement, once again underlining how unique Neolithic Orkney was. The unusually high level of conformity between the houses is highly revealing too; one would normally expect more of a disparity in the size, quality and positioning of buildings; a certain organic haphazardness bespeaking a lack of directing authority. Could Skara Brae, with its uniform and relatively (by the standards of the day) commodious houses perhaps have been home to a priestly elite – or even a cluster of magician priests, as has been suggested[28] – foreshadowing the monastic settlements of Catholic Europe?[29] The decorated stones, beads and spiky balls lend credence to this idea, if we assume they were offerings to deities or even subjects of worship in their own right rather than something more mundane, like playing pieces.

It is perhaps telling that in the village's twilight, a long path led straight to the vast religious monuments in the heart of the island,[30] but Skara Brae vastly pre-dated their erection. Or was the settlement where the craft workers who manufactured the tokens, relics and sacrifices – in House 8 – lived? On this reading, Skara Brae becomes a colony of manufacturers; a factory, even. Could all the beads, tusks and carved balls have been bartered for the items lodged in the midden? Or perhaps the profusion of what appear to be religious monuments elsewhere on Orkney blinds us to the truth that Skara Brae was, in fact, home to a community who lived in an egalitarian commune, in houses whose identical nature mitigated against the prospect of egotism and greed undermining the solidarity of the group. This was the view of Professor Childe, chiming as it did with his Marxist beliefs and commitment to communism. Or could it have been home to a secular elite? On this reading, all the well-crafted artefacts could have been tributes to this ruling elite, or symbols of their power. Is a combination of these theories not fairly plausible? Or was it something else altogether? Lost places can be all things to all people.

———

Skara Brae's snug domesticity perhaps blinds us to how it was, in its day, a striking manifestation of a radical new trend, one which cut against the grain of 2.5 million years of humanity's past and came to be the defining feature of our daily existence today.[31] Preserved in the sand for so long, Skara Brae foretold a new domestic world.

When the first houses went up in Skara Brae, around 3200 BC, the idea – in these islands – of successive generations inhabiting the same built structures, burying their dead nearby, and living cheek-by-jowl with neighbours was positively revolutionary; in other parts of the isles, it had gained no traction at all. This is because, for 99 per cent of our existence, humans have been nomadic hunter-gatherers. Virtually the entire thrust of human endeavour was channelled into the fundamentals of surviving and procreating in what could be a relentlessly hostile environment. During the first phase of the Stone Age, lasting 2.5 million years, and which we call the Palaeolithic Age, *Homo sapiens* eclipsed Neanderthal man, spread beyond the shores of Africa to populate much of the landmass of the world, and survived an ice age lasting tens of thousands of years. Britain, a warm and humid landmass orbited by islands of various sizes on the periphery of Europe, was first populated around 13,000 BC. The landscape was very different from today's. Red deer, elephants and macaque monkeys flashed through forests, marshes and open grasslands, along with wolves and voles. Packs of humans – perhaps twenty-five apiece, or even more – snaked through the landscape, gathering leaves and berries, attacking their prey with wooden spears, with flint heads and axes made of reindeer bone, and grabbing slithering fish from the water. Woodland was slashed and burned to expedite hunting. Stone was used to make weapons and tools. As far as we can tell, settlements were temporary, and soon abandoned, more rightly described as camps;[32] the notion, at this stage, of a settled community like Skara Brae would have seemed completely outlandish. Evidence has been found in Britain of several lightweight Mesolithic shelters propped up by tree poles, covered in hides, and staked to the ground – a sort of prehistoric tent – and, on a much bigger scale, at Star Carr in East Yorkshire, a seasonally occupied encampment for hunters (probably of red deer) from around 9000 BC, which, since it has produced evidence of carpentry, jewellery and even fixed settlements bordering a lake, was a harbinger of the future.[33] The population at that time was unfathomably small, probably around just two thousand,[34] and the main landmass, what we call Great Britain today, was originally connected to Continental Europe via a vast plain of lakes, marshes, forest and woodland: Doggerland.

Millennia passed. Eventually the ice began to thaw, then went into full retreat, but not before Britain's landmass had been sculpted by coursing glaciers forming the valleys and hills that are still with us today. The second phase of the Stone Age, the Mesolithic, began as the climate warmed, around 8500 BC. Then – 'then' because vast stretches of unrecorded time can be folded into a single word without too much compunction – around 6000 BC, Doggerland began to disappear, possibly following an initial tsunami, but more likely over a two-thousand-year period as forested swamp turned to lake, and it became inundated by the southern North Sea, permanently severing Britain from Continental Europe. Thereafter, all new arrivals to Britain would be by boat, which is how settlers first reached Orkney.

About the same time, in the most imperceptible of increments, the entire landscape was transformed in a way which, by the time the process was complete (around 2000 BC), would till the soil – quite literally – for new settlements like Skara Brae, settlements that would have been unrecognisable to earlier humanity. Put simply, people in the British Isles began to farm particular fields instead of hunting and gathering. They remained fixed instead of forever marauding around. They settled. Thus began the Neolithic Age, the closing chapter of the Stone Age, which became synonymous with this new way of living.

The transition from a food-gathering to a food-producing economy can justifiably be described as one of the most consequential and far-reaching changes in social evolution that has ever taken place, second only, perhaps, to the domestication of fire.[35] It had far-reaching consequences that would dramatically transform the experience of humanity and go on to shape the socio-economic system we still have in place today, paving the way for the emergence of towns, villages and cities. It is thought that farming began in Britain just before 4000 BC,[36] a thousand years before Skara Brae was built, so the Orcadian settlement is not one of the *earliest* per se but rather the earliest to survive in such complete form.

Britain was relatively late to the game. Wheat was first cultivated in Asia around 8500 BC, just as the Ice Age was ending, and by 7000 BC agricultural communities were widely dispersed across the Near East, Palestine and Turkey. It took another millennium for crops to sprout in Europe; villages of farmers could be found in Greece by 6000 BC, but the practice did not reach the shores of Britain with any definitive consequences for another two thousand years. Academics have expended much energy trying to establish whether farming first reached Britain as an idea, in time adopted by some of the islanders, or as an alien practice imported by overseas settlers (though it doesn't seem beyond the realms of possibility that both could have happened at once: as a reality in some parts of the isles and an idea elsewhere). In any case, forests and woodland were cleared, wheat and barley cultivated and strange, exotic beasts – the pig, the sheep, the cow, the goat – brought over in boats, none being native to Britain, and reared for the slaughter and the plough.

The inhabitants of Skara Brae were practitioners of this new art, or at least aspects of it – farming probably arrived in Orkney by 3500 BC. The layers of midden around the houses are full of the bones of cows, calves, sheep, lambs, and, in much smaller numbers, pigs. Regarding crops, the picture is less certain. The seed grains of barley (for animal feed, not, it is thought, brewing), oats (for fodder) and wheat (for bread) are to be found in the oldest layers of midden, suggesting that the fields surrounding the site of occupation were put to agricultural use, but only before the houses were built.[37]

Farming brought about a self-perpetuating cycle: a higher population – it is easier to have, and bring up, children when you are fixed in one place; such children become economic assets as they are put to work in the fields, whereas the opposite can be the case if you are forever roaming. So farming itself precipitated an intensification and enhancement of agricultural practices. The population of Britain in 3000 BC was perhaps around twenty thousand; a thousand years later, it was probably closer to 250,000; if such figures are reliable, that is a mushroom-shaped population boom.[38] Just two hundred years after houses first sprouted at Skara Brae, all the land in the isles favourable to farming had been carved up into modest rectangular fields, marked out by fences and ditches, and some of these prehistoric boundaries can still be seen, at dusk, deeply grooved into the earth, as the earth tilts against the sun. Thick woodland and forests were cleared, bringing into existence moors and heaths and other open space on which wheat and barley were cultivated and pigs, cattle, goats and sheep grazed.

The idea of earthly permanence itself represented a fundamental shift in the Neolithic world view, making Skara Brae and settlements like it all the more radical. Earlier Neolithic forms that girdled open space have been described as causewayed enclosures. They generally consisted of circular trenches interspersed with natural 'earth bridges' leading to a central meeting place, whether for the purpose of trade, social solidarity, dispute mediation or religious practice – or, as is likely, all four. One of the most famous is Windmill Hill, in Wiltshire, and they were sometimes the seeds of the more famous ritual landscapes like those around Stonehenge or Avebury.[39] They contained, furthermore, skulls of revered ancestors, along with valuable objects at the butt of the trenches, thrown in, then covered up. The archaeologist Francis Pryor has observed and concluded that in many instances the ditches seem to have been dug, covered over, and re-dug: potentially by each new generation of a particular family or clan. These seem to have been constructed and reconstructed so frequently 'that we now believe that in many instances their construction *was* their use'.[40] To early Neolithic peoples, perhaps, the present may have seemed so thin and transient, which is why entire landscapes – cairns in the distance, long barrows marking agricultural holdings, the skulls in the trenches – conveyed a deep reverence for one's ancestors and why their monumental chambered tombs so often aligned with sunrays and moonbeams at certain times of year, dignifying such meagre human lifespans with a cosmic significance. It must have seemed at times that only the ephemeral was truly permanent. Skara Brae was of course remodelled four times, as its various layers show, but only on average every 175 years, not every generation, and only then, it seems, out of practical necessity. It was a sign of the future.

Peering into the surprisingly capacious prehistoric caverns, or experiencing the reconstructed House 8 with its crackling fire, straw mattresses, colourful decoration, beds and cupboards, it's hard not to wonder what caused places like Skara Brae – permanent agrarian settlements – to come into existence in the first place. It is a question that has preoccupied academic minds for many centuries and there is still no consensus – rather the opposite. There is a seductive argument that farming was brought about because of a new spiritual desire to live near the corpses of relatives, and it is certainly true that some of the earliest and sometimes largest structures, like long barrows and chambered cairns, were built to house not the living but the dead. On this reading, agriculture developed to facilitate 'stationary' living; it was not its first cause. Other theories abound – over forty, in fact – one involving beer.[41] What is most telling, however, is that different parts of the world – regions for which any kind of meaningful shared contact seems essentially inconceivable – embraced aspects of farming at around the same time. The birth pangs of agriculture were perceptible in the eastern Mediterranean in 9500 BC yet it took another six thousand years for it to be adopted in the Americas. Yet when we consider the first part of the Stone Age lasted 2.5 million years, even this seems quick.

This uncanny convergence lends much credence to the idea that the widespread and successful adoption of farming, which gave rise to permanent settlements like Skara Brae, had everything to do with a worldwide climate change in the centuries following the Ice Age. From around 10,000 BC, notwithstanding a millennia-long relapse into ice-age conditions, natural global warming rapidly set in, and 'almost everything we have done as advanced beings has been done in this brief spell of climatological glory'.[42] When we take the long view, we see that global warming can be a uniquely creative force bringing whole new modes of existence into being, as well as a sometimes devastating medium of oblivion in the Middle Ages and our own time.

Even if it cannot be said with absolute confidence why agriculture came about, there can be no doubt of its far-reaching consequences. Settlements like Skara Brae portended the coming of civilisation. The practice of building structures, putting down roots and becoming self-sufficient – the birth of domesticity, no less – allowed for the development of what we would recognise as essential ingredients of a new phase of human existence. It spurred the 'Neolithic Revolution', a term that was coined in a book called *Man Makes Himself* (1936). It argues that a mobile hunter-gathering lifestyle was ultimately replaced by a much more fixed, agricultural one. The process was incremental and had many false starts, but at its heart lay the cultivation of certain plant species, the husbandry of animals and the ownership of domestic property – all signature features of Skara Brae; such changes, it argued, facilitated a second, 'urban revolution'.[43] The book was penned by a certain professor of ancient archaeology who claimed to have had the idea as he was excavating none other than a mysterious settlement on west Mainland: Skara Brae; his research into other societies corroborated this. Professor Childe's theory became so influential it can be said that the whole intellectual edifice of how we conceive our post-Ice Age history was informed by the dips and grooves that had so captured my imagination above that windy Scottish beach.

———

A number of settlements in the British Isles, some once fairly significant, met their end – and in some cases salvation – in that antithesis of form, sand. Just like Skara Brae, these can ironically find themselves unusually well preserved. Kenfig, on the south coast of Wales, was once a prosperous farming community, founded in the twelfth century. It had a small port on a river sheltered by dunes. But, as intensive grazing of cattle dislodged the sand, and the climate became cooler and more tempestuous as the Medieval Warm Period came to an end, these dunes crept ever closer until, by the fourteenth century, many of its fields and buildings were inundated.[44] By 1650, the sorrowful settlement had been completely abandoned, by now totally shrouded in sand. But, as Professor Childe tells us, there was nothing gradual about the entombment of Skara Brae. The inhabitants were powerless to resist when, as he hypothesises, their entire settlement was buried in a tsunami of sand during a particularly ferocious storm that buffeted the coast of Orkney in the middle of the third millennium BC. Abandoning their possessions, he tells us, they ran away at full pelt, barely able to see further than a couple of inches ahead as the blizzard ripped off roofs and came down upon them. Clearing away the sand from House 7 for the first time, Professor Childe recorded a scene of 'abrupt desertion'.[45] There were two large cooking pots still containing animal bones and, in the left-hand bed, a midnight snack of a calf's head. Another cooking pot lay crushed by the hearth; a cracked whalebone basin next to the bed. Everyday objects like Skaill knives, pots, axe-heads, mortars, shovels and even a dish of pigment lay strewn about the floor and, more tellingly, items of exquisite craftsmanship too – a fine walrus-tusk pendant, ivory beads and the obligatory spiky stone ball. The whole house, he observed, had lain frozen in time for over forty centuries, ever since its occupants beat a hasty retreat that terrible day. The threat, he writes, was immediate and overwhelming. One woman was in such a rush to escape that she broke her cherished necklace – presumably by clasping it in terror or catching it on a surface – as she bundled herself through the low, narrow doorway leaving a trail of ornamental beads in her wake.

There is an agreeable symmetry to this dramatic account of the demise of Skara Brae, the apocalyptic storm of 2500 BC serving as a foil to the revelatory one four thousand years later, the original medium of oblivion – sand – becoming a medium of preservation, and this was perhaps somewhere at the back of Professor Childe's mind as he penned his evocative yet, it transpires, highly flawed account of the demise of Skara Brae. It *is* possible for entire urban or rural settlements, or substantial portions of them, to be swept away in a single, devastating stroke. These were the fates of some of the lost places I was yet to visit. But it is very rare, in Britain at least, for entire places to be abandoned in such a startling, Pompeian fashion. There are a number of plot holes in the professor's apocalyptic vision. First, all the evidence shows that the residents of Skara Brae had to contend with near-incessant sand-blow[46] and it seems improbable they would have capitulated after a single storm, however dramatic. Even if it had been the mother of all terrifying storms, the villages' structures evidently survived and nothing would have prevented the inhabitants from simply digging the sand out – excavations show that the deposits in House 7 were no more than half a metre deep – and the walls were several metres high.[47] We should not entirely discount the possibility the Orcadians believed the site was somehow cursed or that the storm had an especial, spiritual significance. Another possibility is that the flight was precipitated by a human rather than environmental threat: sworn enemies, a marauding band of looters or the appearance of hostile vessels. But again this seems unlikely as there is no evidence whatsoever of damage to the houses, which is precisely what one would expect in the aftermath of a raid, and we have already noted the conspicuous lack of defensive earthworks and battlements at Skara Brae, which very much distinguishes it from later lost settlements (although this could of course have made it more vulnerable to a sudden and unexpected eruption of violence). And then there are the beads. Childe claims that 'definite evidence of a hasty flight is . . . afforded by a trail of beads picked up in the doorway and along passage C to the left'; yet, if this were as pivotal as he claims, it seems odd that the exact position of the beads was never documented.[48] The real cause and manner of Skara Brae's abandonment is likely to have been less dramatic and more gradual, a slow but inexorable decline, not a hammer-blow to the head.

Environmental changes, it seems, were instrumental to the decline of Skara Brae, but it is likely that they bled the life from the settlement over a much longer period of time than Professor Childe would have us believe. The advancement of the sea towards the settlement is likely to have covered the fields in salt spray, making the land less fecund, and making the Orcadians more reliant upon birds. It was harder to grow crops and, as the pastureland turned to salt marsh, the farming of animals – the predominant form of economic activity, as we have seen – increasingly became a fool's errand. The salt-water lagoons, where the Orcadians liked to fish, slowly disappeared beneath the ocean, and the midden – that rich archive of gastronomic habits – shows that in the twilight of

Skara Brae, as the coast drew near, the inhabitants increasingly took to eating birds. The climate, too, took a turn for the worse around 2500 BC, becoming chillier and damper, much more like the spot it has become today, and the red bream that had proved such a lucrative source of food slowly vanished from the sea.[49] Perhaps a collective decision was taken to leave and resettle on more fertile lands, away from the menace of the sea. Or – as the experience of other doomed settlements shows – it is highly plausible that the younger, more able-bodied members of the community drained away, sucking the life from the colony. Those that remained withered and died as the fields were abandoned and the fisheries dried up. Then, after four hundred years of continuous habitation, the settlement fell quiet, House 7 degenerating for a while into a shelter for passing deer-hunters,[50] a little like the Mesolithic encampments of old, and gradually became entombed in layers of peat, drifting sand, and a coffin-lid of grass.

It is also hard to believe the erection of monumental stone henges and tombs that aligned with the seasons and stars at Brodgar, Stenness and Maeshowe, in the centre of the archipelago, in the final decades of Skara Brae's occupation, can be entirely coincidental, especially given the path that connects them to Skara Brae. It has been argued that the appearance of these spectacular, cosmically aligned monuments attests to the ascendancy of an Orcadian political elite who could corral the obedience, resources and labour needed to erect such gargantuan monoliths.[51] This, so the argument goes, rendered close-knit, autonomous villages increasingly obsolete as people became part of – whether willingly or through coercion – larger, more dispersed communities under the heel of powerful tribal or religious leaders. People no longer needed to seek safety in numbers by huddling together in hives; they could live in individual farmsteads under the protection of these leaders in exchange for allegiance, labour, prestige and perhaps tribute.

It is potentially significant, too, that the abandonment of Skara

Brae around 2500 BC coincides more or less with the beginning of the Bronze Age. If, as seems indisputable, Orkney was part – or even the fulcrum – of a widespread network of trade, obligation and kinship, the almost complete absence of surviving bronze weapons and ornaments is flummoxing. One possible explanation is that the religious leaders, tribal chieftains and village leaders – as far as they existed – failed to embrace the practical utility and social cachet of the wondrous new metal that made so much more effective and stylish tools and weapons and which was discovered in Britain by the middle of the third millennium BC in the twilight of Skara Brae's existence, falling in the esteem of overseas chieftains for their neglect.[52] Say Skara Brae were more dependent upon trade than has so far been realised, this could have been a further ingredient in its demise.

But if this confluence of factors – or anything like them – really were behind the abandonment of Skara Brae, how do we explain all the items of value that were left behind – the furniture, bone beads and walrus pendant in House 1, for example, as well as the alleged broken necklace and meat joints, and all the other artefacts and tools discarded in all the other houses? If the inhabitants believed the settlement to be cursed in some way, it is conceivable that what we see in House 7 is evidence of a last supper. It is also possible – and again, conjectures abound – that Skara Brae met a relatively abrupt end in the form of one of the infectious diseases that jumped across from livestock. There are plenty of contenders: flu from pigs and fowl, measles and smallpox from sheep and cows, anthrax from horses and goats, not to mention all the little scuttling creatures that could act as vectors of pestilence and disease. Living at such close quarters with each other, and their animals, the Orcadians would have been acutely susceptible. The absence of corpses casts doubt on this theory but then the burial ground, archaeologists posit, may well have been washed away by the sea. Or perhaps it was the custom, as with the Comanche and the Arapaho, and indeed perhaps like Professor Childe himself, for the elderly to wander off and die alone.[53] Even if nothing this dramatic happened and the inhabitants drained away in search of better prospects, it doesn't seem particularly odd that they left their furniture, pots and tools behind and their walls intact when versatile stone was so readily available elsewhere on the island. The treasure trove of beads may well have been a votive offering to a deity, or simply the hidden treasure of someone who died before they could recover it. Or perhaps the final generations of older residents remained in situ until they died off one by one, explaining why the houses that became buried were still furnished as Skara Brae became a ghost settlement.

Skara Brae was of course just one of hundreds, possibly thousands, of settlements in Neolithic Britain – many of those in southern Britain, it is thought, leave no archaeological trace because they and their furniture were made of perishable timber and perhaps because temporary encampments endured for longer than in northern Britain. The number of known settlements in Orkney itself, or anywhere in the British Isles, is only a fraction of the total: the remains of many Neolithic houses have been discovered (particularly in Scotland) in recent decades;[54] others lie underground, yet to be discovered, some effaced by later settlements;[55] the traces of others have been destroyed by much later intensive agriculture; or had their building material recycled for later settlements. Most were built from wood and have not survived – the dearth of wood goes a long way to explain the unusual preponderance of Neolithic domestic remains on Orkney. Yet through the intercession of millennia and despite its long hibernation, there is still a direct and irrevocable connection between Neolithic Skara Brae – as a synecdoche for all its vanished counterparts – and modern Britain. This tiny, wind-buttressed settlement on the west of the Orkney's Mainland that endured for over seven hundred years informed the idea of permanence.

Through historical accident it manifests uniquely, vividly the transformation of the experience of humanity within these isles and helps to explain why a map of Britain looks the way it does today; indeed, explain why there can be a map – in the sense of a constellation of fixed settlements – at all. Some seventeen hundred years after it blazed a trail at Skara Brae, the furnished roundhouse established itself as the quintessential domestic structure, centred upon a hearth, surrounded by fields for growing and grazing, and demarcated by barrows of the community's dead and ancestors. Without permanent settlements like Skara Brae, it is hard to imagine the development of ideas of property ownership, commercial exchange and social hierarchy that come with an unequal possession of wealth, let alone claims to territorial dominion which are the fuel of conflict, diplomacy and politics. Without them, too, it is hard to imagine the emergence of a new type of permanent settlement that would have been completely unfamiliar to the early farmers at Skara Brae, yet one that their new way of life made plausible, places indeed where 84 per cent of the UK's population live today,[56] not to mention more than half of the world's population: towns and cities.

Near Wales's border with England, on a plateau overlooking the Forest of Dean, stand three monoliths. They were originally part of a bigger stone circle dragged there at almost exactly the time Skara Brae was abandoned, at the beginning of the Bronze Age. We do not know how continuously the site was occupied after that, if at all, but eventually these three stones would stand in the shadow of an extraordinary town, even a city, that lay hidden for over five hundred years, one whose rediscovery was perhaps even more extraordinary than Skara Brae's. It was called *Tre-llech*, place of the three stones.

CHAPTER TWO

THE LOST CITY OF TRELLECH

One spring day in 2002, a farmer noticed something odd about the molehills in his fields.[1] They seemed to be speckled with something; they looked like mouldy crushed strawberries. On closer inspection, he saw that the 'seeds' were more like bits of old pottery – chinks of light, as he came to perceive it, from a vanished world.

The farmer, Jonathan Badham, from the village of Trellech in south-east Wales, dutifully brought his observations to the attention of the Monmouthshire Archaeological Society; he was aware, as were many others, of the controversial theory of the society's treasurer, Julia Wilson, that somewhere to the south of the village, buried beneath the fields, was a medieval city that had been lost for over five hundred years.[2] The Trellech Jonathan Badham knew was just a small village on a plateau beyond the Forest of Dean but, the Society claimed, this was just a forlorn relic of what had once been an expansive *city* – for a time, indeed, the biggest in Wales – a powerhouse of industry that had played a definitive role in the protracted wars that had forged medieval Britain and left a permanent mark on the landscape. But there was a hitch. No one could say with absolute authority where the carcass of this great medieval city lay; rival theories had been posited. Could moles boring blind into the earth have succeeded where humans had failed, turning up fragments of the lost city?

It was a delicious proposition, too poetic almost to be true: a second reclamation of the city by the forces of nature. The news reached the ears of a young archaeology graduate called Stuart Wilson, who lived in the nearby town of Chepstow. Wilson was working as a tollbooth operator on the Severn Bridge between

England and Wales, policing the crossing between two nations with very different histories. He *was* a local history aficionado; ever since he had finished his undergraduate degree at the University of York he dreamt of being a professional archaeologist, but it hadn't happened. He was familiar with Julia Wilson's theory that the medieval city lay to the south of the present-day village towards Catbrook, a theory that the moles' haul would seem to corroborate, and turned up on Jonathan Badham's doorstep quite out of the blue one day. Let me dig, he said, just some test trenches at first to see what, if anything, I can turn up. Within minutes Farmer Badham had been won over to the proposition. Wilson could proceed. A little dig could go ahead. Within a mere ten minutes, Wilson claims, he had found evidence of melted walls which aligned nicely (though not conclusively) with written evidence of devastating attacks in 1291 and 1295 that had razed much of medieval Trellech to the ground.[3] Further artefacts were found. The lost city, in Wilson's view, was stirring from the earth. He dug for two more seasons until Jonathan's elderly mother, disturbed by the noise of the machinery, the constant comings and goings, all the *palaver*, put a stop to the whole operation. It was ruining her sleep.

That might have been the end of it, were it not for an extraordinary twist of fate. In early 2005, Wilson noticed that livestock had been moved from an adjacent field (one where, he had noticed, moles had also turned up potsherds). When he enquired, he found that the landowners were planning to sell it. There was something strange about the field, thought Wilson. It consisted of rigid, square plots that seemed slightly out of keeping with the landscape. To Wilson's eyes, it seemed probable that the square plots were a footprint, and the field's usage as pastureland reinforced this idea – could there be something underneath that was preventing crops from growing? Most auspiciously, to Wilson's mind, it had a road frontage, which he took as a clue that this had once been part of a high street. *The* high street. Beneath this field, he intuited, lay the core of the lost city of Trellech, its buried medieval heart. Perhaps, then, all was not lost.

The field came up for auction. What the moles had turned up was suggestive not definitive, and he was effectively ploughing ahead as blindly as they, driven by the strength of his convictions. Yet he was determined not to squander this potentially once-in-a-lifetime opportunity. The auction, as it turned out, was a fraught and close-run thing; also bidding was a developer who'd had the land in his sights for some time. The asking price was £12,000. But within minutes it had leapt to £32,000. This was unnerving for a twenty-six-year-old who had £20,000 in savings from his job, but wasn't quite sure where the rest was going to come from. Seeing his son flounder, Wilson's father bid on his behalf, and, eventually, they won. Wilson got his field, but for £36,000 – almost three times the asking price. There would be consequences, sacrifices. As he filed out of the county hall in stunned silence the young man knew that the trajectory of his entire life had, in the rap of a hammer, spun off in a completely different direction from virtually everyone he knew; he hoped his victory would not prove false.

No one could have predicted that the moles' retrieval of the little shards of pottery from the ground would trigger a protracted archaeological conflict that would establish one of the longest-running and most democratic digs in British history,[4] engaging the attention of the British and American mass media, and, for some, betraying the otiose irrelevance of academia. There have been moments in this drama when it has all become a little unpleasant and vitriolic, with reputations smeared and entire decades of work casually dismissed on glowing smartphone screens, a controversy played out not just in the rustic fields of Trellech but in the mud-slinging coliseum of Twitter, in the orderly pages of peer-reviewed journals and the headlines of tabloid newspapers, on television, radio, and in the vituperative comments of newspaper websites. It shows no sign of abating.

———

After buying the land, Wilson began to dig. At first he employed a small team of local volunteers but before long people were pouring in from all over the country, and even the world, to contribute each summer. What had once been lonely pasture was now gouged into rectangular pits overlooked by rows of tents, supervised by Wilson.

From the outset, by Wilson's account, the dig was remarkably successful. In the first season alone Wilson reported that he had discovered the foundations of a large stone manor house with a series of courtyards and a defensive round tower; it was not long before they stumbled upon the remains of a cobbled pavement, drains, fireplaces, wells and defensive ditches. It was quintessentially medieval, born of a war-torn world; the idea of building a settlement without any defences, on the model of Skara Brae over four thousand years earlier, would have been practically suicidal in this part of thirteenth-century Wales. A pleasing range of artefacts was recovered too, some highly evocative of the mental world of the medieval occupants – a roof finial to stave off witches, a gorgeous pilgrim's flask, a mummified cat. The earth has also disclosed pouches of silver coins, sharpening knives, and a jewel-encrusted plant pot. The more he dug, the more justified Wilson felt in his assertion that there was indeed a lost world beneath his feet.

The media got wind of these seemingly miraculous finds in the Monmouthshire soil soon after Wilson began his dig. In 2006, Radio 4 put out a programme called 'The Boy Who Bought a Field'.[5] The press embraced Wilson's lost city with especial gusto. 'Man finds ancient medieval city on border of England and Wales' declared the *Independent* in 2017; a 'history fan' has been 'proved right' after excavating 'a lost medieval city' announced the *Daily Mail*. The *Telegraph* wrote of Wilson's field as 'home to a medieval city' – 'the industrial heart of Wales', no less – and according to BBC News, Trellech was 'once Wales's largest city'. (We should bear in mind, however, that sub-editors, not journalists, tend to come up with headlines for stories and there is an obvious imperative to arrest the reader's attention.) Local papers struck a very similar tone, as have numerous websites, whether dedicated to nature, history or amateur archaeology. The media, it seems, accepts Wilson's dramatic account and is doing what it can to engrain medieval Trellech in the public imagination as that most alluring of things – a lost city in, of all places, a field in Wales.

There was only one slight problem. Wilson was not the first person to have gone in search of medieval Trellech. Archaeologists had in fact been on the trail long before he bought his field, publishing their findings in academic journals between 1990 and 2005.[6] Far from a visionary graduate, some of these professionals took him to be a roguish amateur bypassing the rigours of academia and feeding his findings to the clickbait media, undermining long, hard years of serious scholarship, and sometimes even tarnishing the reputations of his academic rivals who have had to do all the heavy lifting away from the glamour of the limelight. For all his claims, Stuart Wilson, they argue, is peddling a myth; he cannot possibly be digging up a 'lost city' for the very good reason that medieval Trellech was nothing of the sort, and nothing that he has turned up to date proves otherwise. He is not digging up a city in the earth, they say, but building castles in the air.[7]

———

I talk to Stuart Wilson at twilight one Hallowe'en. There is nothing weird or obsessive about him – nothing of the Balzacian monomaniac about his manner, no trace of Professor Childe's aloof eccentricity – and I feel a little foolish for expecting there to have been. He is broad, gym-trim, and, with his bellowing laugh and unbounded passion for Trellech, immediately likeable. This is a relief – going on some of the comments about him online, he may as well be the devil incarnate. He seems grounded; why then, I ask, did he decide to spend his entire life savings on a field that may or may not have contained the ruins of a lost medieval city? Was that not the most extraordinarily reckless of gambles?

'No, it wasn't really that much of a gamble, not financially,' he says. 'It's true I had to use my life's savings and take out a loan of £16,000 but it's not as though no one would have wanted the field if it had turned out to be a dud.' He tells me there were developers at the auction, and that it probably would not have been that difficult to sell it on (although, ironically, they may well have had to fund an archaeological survey to proceed, meaning qualified archaeologists would likely have excavated the spot anyway). But there must have been sacrifices? He tells me yes; he had to move back in with his parents in his mid-twenties, but it wasn't a problem. The biggest sacrifice, it soon becomes clear, was, and is, time. Wilson could quite easily have spent the best part of his life digging and found nothing. Happily, that was not the case. But it *is* clear he expects it to be his life's work. 'What we have discovered so far is just a tiny fraction of what is down there. To excavate the rest, or even part of the rest, may well take half a century or more' – certainly the rest of his life.

How can he be so sure? I mention the professional academics and archaeologists who have disparaged his description (or, more cynically put, branding) of Trellech as 'a lost medieval city' as a canny way of eliciting media attention. He moves his chair a little closer to the table. 'Look,' he says, clearing his throat, 'medieval Trellech, at its peak, contained at least five hundred buildings housing at least ten thousand people.' When, I ask? '1288.' His tone is stolid; I suspect he has rehearsed this speech many times. 'So it was bigger than Monmouth, bigger than Chepstow, bigger, almost certainly, than Cardiff. It was roughly the same physical size as the City of London and very nearly as populous as the city of Winchester.' And that, he adds, was just *within* the walls. 'Thousands more citizens – perhaps tens of thousands – may have dwelled outside, beyond the perimeter bank in the suburbs.' When I ask what archival evidence all these claims are founded upon, he refers amongst other things to medieval tax assessments, describing them as 'detailed' and 'conclusive' proof that Trellech was indeed a city, and one that was in all likelihood, for a time, the biggest in Wales. He does not set great store by the idea that a city must contain a cathedral, dismissing this Norman qualification as pedantic; as long as its population was the same size as other places that were officially cities, and as long as it was perceived by contemporaries as a city, it counts. (For me, though, there would need to be a discernible street layout, a certain density of population, shared communal spaces (like marketplaces or yards), services (like rubbish collection), some kind of municipal authority and perhaps even a sense of civic identity, too, before I could feel absolutely confident in the term.)

The excavation of Trellech is a golden opportunity, he tells me, and so rare. This is because normally the remains of cities, all the structures and artefacts, are buried beneath publicly or privately owned land or buildings. 'You can't just dig beneath homes and office blocks, schools, warehouses, hospitals and playgrounds.' It's hard enough – as he discovered – to dig relatively lightly in a field belonging to a friendly farmer. 'But here, there are no restrictions.' The core of an entire city was begging to be explored. His only obstacle was time, and, he adds, eyelids slightly aflutter, 'the professional archaeologists'.

By this, he of course means the archaeologists who have been digging up Trellech since the 1990s, albeit under much more restrictive conditions. He finds them and much of what they stand for objectionable: sour professionals who have been digging in the wrong place for the best part of twenty years, 'turning up hardly anything of consequence. Just rubbish and dirt, for the most part,' as he put it bluntly in an earlier newspaper interview (although he concedes this is what archaeologists dig up around ninety per cent of the time). Their mistake, he explains to me, was to situate medieval Trellech between the church and motte (on which the Norman fort had once stood), not to the south of the present-day village, towards Catbrook, just like people had suspected for some time. He tells me that he snuck on to their dig one night to prove that what they thought were medieval walls were actually parts of a drainage ditch. They are closed-minded people, he adds, working at a glacial pace, refusing to admit when they are wrong, and publishing their faulty findings in lofty jargon-filled journals which hardly anyone actually reads. He chuckles and slides his chair back. 'They don't realise the world has moved on.'[8]

For anyone who has ever met him, it is clear that the more Wilson digs, the more vindicated he feels. But the more *I* dug, the more complex the picture became. Historian and heritage consultant David Howell remembers dusting down and cleaning medieval pots from Trellech as a child in the 1990s. They had been excavated by students of his father, Ray Howell, a professor of archaeology at the University of Newport who had devoted a significant part of his academic career to an archaeological exploration of Trellech; when Ray retired, his historian son David continued to investigate the settlement. In the dozen or so scholarly articles Ray Howell published, medieval Trellech is described, with a very careful use of language, as 'a medieval urban settlement'.

'We don't believe it is a city,' David Howell said in an interview in 2017, 'but if it is – we discovered it twenty years before [Wilson] did.' It is certainly true that most journalists, with the notable exception of a *Washington Post* correspondent,[9] have been quite happy to write the Howells out of the picture, relegating them to the role of formal archaeologists who did things by the book but were apparently looking in the wrong place, as a foil to Wilson's (and the moles') sensational discovery.

'What is coming out of the ground is potentially of tremendous significance,' concedes David in the same *Washington Post* article, 'but it simply cannot bear the associations of being described as a city.' Leaving aside for a moment their strong reservations about Wilson's method and professionalism, why are they so quick to dismiss the possibility? What about medieval tax records? What about other archival evidence? David Howell wonders why on earth you would have a city on a damp landlocked plateau miles away from the nearest river. For him it beggars belief. 'Exactly,' he declared on Twitter in response to an architectural historian's post that if Trellech had been a city then he looked forward to the discovery of its cathedral, '#notacity #notagodamncity.'[10]

Wilson operated his 'people's dig' just five minutes away from where the Howells' professional digs had taken place, but they were worlds apart in other regards. Whereas the official digs had to abide by strict government regulations for the excavation of land around the church, forever replacing the topsoil and limiting how far and for how long they could dig, Wilson, in his field, had *carte blanche*. Of all Wilson's claims, the one they find the most egregious is that they were somehow 'looking in the wrong place' for fifteen years. If the Howells had had the liberty to churn up the fields till kingdom come, David argues, 'we can say with confidence there were more buildings'.[11] As things stood, however, the university funding dried up, the project expired in 2008, and the Howells moved on to pastures new, just as Wilson's rival dig was picking up pace and garnering media attention. To see decades of rigorous research 'casually dismissed' in a series of newspaper articles and elsewhere clearly stung. Ray Howell cannot talk of Trellech any more, will not do interviews. It is still too raw.

———

Given that so much of the disagreement over medieval Trellech has played out online, it is little wonder that the public have taken sides. The responses reveal much about what lost cities mean to people: as 'empty' spaces, they can quickly fill with emotional preoccupations and present-day concerns, especially where these involve or indeed revolve around harking back to a 'lost' era. Going on the comments below the line in a *Guardian* article of 2017, the vast majority of readers champion Stuart Wilson over the professional archaeologists (if they even know who they are), gunning for the rogue outsider, this 'Welsh Indiana Jones' who ignored the 'experts', had faith in the strength of his own convictions and ultimately discovered a lost world hiding in plain sight, proving them completely and utterly wrong. In this championing of the underdog, the troubles in Trellech captured something of the zeitgeist of the age.[12]

Many of these *Guardian* commenters found the whole story, as presented to them, inspiring. Wilson is hailed as a kind of Welsh hero, a man who sacrificed a normal life with a house and a proper job for a bloody-minded pursuit of his passions, and, against all the odds, succeeded; if he had invested his savings in a mortgage, no one would have heard of him, but he dared to dream. Many of the responders framed events – very much guided by the articles themselves – as an epic, if quirky, contest between heroes and villains.[13] And naturally, there is the inevitable slew of jokes about Wilson being the real expert in his field.

Occasionally, a discordant note is heard. A reader of the *Washington Post* boldly yet baselessly proclaims that sooner or later Wilson is going to be caught faking something. Such a smear could not go unanswered, with Wilson himself popping up in the comments section to direct the sceptical reader towards the Historic Environment Report of Monmouthshire which attests to the objective reality of his finds (if not his theories).[14] Like the Howells, some were troubled by his qualifications – his undergraduate degree gave him only limited fieldwork experience, it was noted, and he was not being supervised on the site, while one reader darkly invokes the memory of Heinrich Schliemann, the archaeologist who blew up some of the remains of Troy with dynamite.

Other readers were understandably perplexed by the timescale of the city's appearance and disappearance. How could a city of ten thousand people, purportedly the largest in medieval Wales, realistically have developed from scratch in fifty years? Even eight hundred years, for another reader, seemed a remarkably brief window of time for an entire city to 'fall down and get buried'.

It was becoming clear to me that I needed a more profound understanding of what medieval Trellech actually was – its size, population and purpose – for this seemed to lie at the heart of all the contention. The more I investigated this particular hilltop settlement – both in person, and in the archives – the more certain I became that its location within Wales was key to uncovering the mystery of its appearance, disappearance and reappearance. For medieval Trellech makes no sense in isolation. It was forged in the furnace of conflict between the nations of England and Wales. It was one of a remarkable cluster of a new type of settlement, very different from Skara Brae yet at the same time a logical expansion of its central premise of settled domesticity albeit in a new context of perpetual war, which came to fruition in the Middle Ages. Trellech's story conducts us into a turbulent world of rival warlords, border fires, midnight raids, and an appalling cycle of violence, and helps to explain how parts of Britain settled into their current form. Trellech was one of the most promising – and important – of them all, and it lay in the Marches.

———

The Marches between England and Wales were an area of luscious natural beauty, teeming with life. Deer flashed past trees in the Forest of Dean, grayling slithered in the River Wye, and mud-loving eel clambered the banks of Brecknock Mere, whose birds, according to tradition, would all burst into song when ordered to do so by the rightful, Welsh, ruler of the land.[15] On the River Usk, surrounded by woods and meadows, could be found the 'diminished antiquity' of Caerleon, the site of a considerable Roman settlement. By the Middle Ages it was a mournful spectacle, with the ruins of immense palaces with gilded gables, a military amphitheatre, baths and temples within crumbling brick walls,[16] and a deserted harbour without, and 'other vestiges of its one-time splendour'. These remains can still be seen today but were especially poignant reminders, in the Middle Ages, of Britain's past as an imperial colony at a time when its largest and most powerful part – England – was actively subduing her neighbours in Wales and Ireland, underlining the transformation from colony to colonist.

Derived from Anglo-Norman *marche*, boundary, the Marches were a murky borderland between England and Wales freshly carved into the domains of rival Norman lords. To consolidate his authority and trumpet his warlike credentials, William I sought to bring his western neighbours to heel in a way the Anglo-Saxon kings had never really managed; it would not do to have a nest of vipers biting at the heels of his new kingdom. He gave territories to the Marcher lords, as they came to be known, in exchange for loyalty and service. However, they were under no obligation to uphold English law, or even respect it. They governed their 'regalities' (a term frequently associated with Marcher lordships) like kings, often tyrannically so.

Fragmented into rival kingdoms, Wales, by 1066, was a very different cultural and political entity from the freshly conquered and already unified realm of England, and this would have profound implications for the nature of the settlement now beneath the Monmouthshire soil. Although, during the Roman occupation, there had been a significant amount of cross-fertilisation with Roman society and culture, there remained enough of a connection with the original pre-Roman civilisation (and indeed that of early agriculturalists) to warrant the description of these kingdoms as British or Brythonic (meaning 'British-speaking'), or, at least for a while, Romano-British. We might conceive of it as a kind of 'transposed Britain', shrunk and smashed into pieces and never quite able to coalesce into a single political unit as England had. After the collapse of Roman rule in the fifth century, Cymru, as it was known, emerged as a patchwork of princedoms – twenty-two at their peak – which in time would evolve into half a dozen bigger kingdoms. They were divided by war but united by language, law and culture.

Wales would eventually come to see itself as the last stand of the British, the 'original' civilised inhabitants of the isles, the only surviving Brythonic kingdoms, realm of the legendary King Arthur who had routed the Germanic barbarians, its existence a totem of resistance and independence. 'Wales' was the English word for 'alien' and to be called such a thing was a gross affront – 'barbarous words brought in by the Saxons when they seized the kingdom of Britain', thought Gerald of Wales in 1188 – because Wales contained the only surviving Brythonic kingdoms in a world of Anglo-Saxon dominion, Scotland excepted. By 1066, the various warring princedoms of Wales – eighteen at their peak – had coalesced into the four kingdoms of Gwynedd, Powys, Gwent and Deheubarth. Yet unlike England, which came together under a single ruler, Athelstan, in the tenth century, Wales was never a united polity. Some Welsh princes came close, but its essential fragmentation made it all the more vulnerable to Norman aggression.

William the Conqueror and his successors, who were very keen to continue his project, sought to buttress and expand the border zone, thrusting it westwards to protect England from raids and even invasions launched from the 'savage' alien domain. So William parcelled out land to the west of Offa's Dyke – much of which lay between the mouths of the River Dee in the north and River Severn in the south but also westwards along the south coast – to his principal magnates, the Marcher lords. It was the first chapter in the sorry history of English colonisation (the

English invasions of Ireland would begin a little later, in the mid-twelfth century, under Henry II) and this land-grab in Wales would have devastating consequences. In fact, it would still be obliterating settlements almost a thousand years later.

There were ultimately as many as one hundred and fifty Anglo-Norman Marcher lords, but the borderland was dominated by the vast sweeping earldoms of Shrewsbury, Hereford and Chester. To make Wales quiescent, William encouraged some similar methods to what had been so grimly effective against his rebellious northern subjects when he laid waste to much of Yorkshire and neighbouring shires in the cruel winter of 1069–70:[17] obedience through fear, consolidation through annexation, and fortification. The Marcher lord Robert of Rhuddlan, according to one chronicler, harried the Welsh for fifteen years, chasing them through woods and marshes and over hills and mountains, seizing their lands, and subduing them through violence. 'Some he slaughtered mercilessly on the spot like cattle,' he reveals, 'others he kept for years in fetters, or forced into a harsh and unlawful slavery.'[18] It was all most unchristian, he thought.

The landscape was transformed. Hundreds of motte-and-bailey castles rose up. These were virtually impregnable forts elevated on a mound of earth looming over a banked encampment with timber palisade; lacking the grandeur, permanence and majestic panoramas of some of the old Iron Age hillforts yet erected at an astonishing pace, they were highly effective at subjugating conquered settlements, providing the Norman troops with a redoubt to which they could retreat should they be attacked. It was the architecture of oppression, and the remains of one can be seen to this day at Trellech.[19] Ancient Welsh houses were effaced by *arrivistes* like the Carews, Baskervilles and Mortimers; a harsh form of feudalism was imposed and many free men found themselves enslaved. By 1100, a quarter of Wales had been infected by these aggressive Anglo-Norman tumours which only kept growing and mutating as lords married, died, attacked one another, and seized land from Welsh princes; they had subsumed great swathes of the ancient kingdoms of Powys and Gwent in eastern and southern Wales, and, audaciously, little islets elsewhere.

The Welsh, as one might expect, were none too enamoured with alien lordships incising deep into the belly of their nation. 'Passionately devoted to their freedom and the defence of their country' is how the chronicler Gerald of Wales described the Welsh in his *Journey Through Wales* (1191). Vivid, readable and gently humorous, Gerald's *Journey* along with his *Description of Wales* (1194)[20] describes, almost in diary form, the journey taken through Wales of his companion Baldwin, Archbishop of Canterbury, in 1188, to recruit archers for a pilgrimage to the Holy Land. His writings provide the earliest surviving detailed impressions of the British landscape and are a deliciously revealing social history too, describing miracles, folklore and nature. He gives a glimpse into the everyday lives of ordinary Welshmen – what they did, ate and wore, and how they could resist the English. And there was, of course, a great deal of resistance. With their fistfuls of arrows, spears and thin, puny shields, they sometimes seemed hopelessly ill-equipped against the Anglo-Norman military machine with its sleek armour and caparisoned steeds; sometimes, in desperation, they went completely unarmed. But although pitched battles were not their forte, the Welsh excelled in 'harassing the enemy by their ambushes and night attacks', capitalising upon their strength and agility that came from not being unencumbered by heavy armour. 'In a single battle they are easily beaten,' observed Gerald, 'though they are difficult to conquer in a long war.' They crouched in ditches, hid in thickets, perched in trees, and even disguised themselves in flocks of baying sheep, biding their time like coiled springs.

Gerald of Wales recalls a world of groaning portcullises and summary execution, of half-built towns and leaves fluttering against fortress walls; it was a world too of siege and torture, of chains wrapped tight around ribcages; of the midnight theft of cattle, corn and women, of Marcher lords rampaging up and down their earldoms' bounds, ravaging and torturing.[21] Here the heads of Welsh houses are summoned to Norman castles and there slaughtered,[22] pigs root for apples in Cistercian garths, and minstrels lie hacked to pieces on lonely trackways.[23] This was the world into which Trellech was born. For the Marches were originally a war zone, the Wild West of Britain.

———

The leading Marcher family was the de Clares, originally Norman warlords. Richard de Clare had been involved in planning the Conquest, perhaps even accompanying William across the Channel;[24] certainly he was soon one of the ten richest laymen in England. The family gained lands in Suffolk around the market town of Clare, after which the family took their name,[25] but this was just the beginning. Through territorial aggression, tactical marriages and military service – if not unwavering loyalty – to the Crown, the de Clares managed to carve out a territorial empire which by the twelfth century stretched all the way from East Anglia to the west coast of Ireland. Their most extensive, and significant, domains lay in the earldoms of Hertford (c.1138–1314) and Gloucester (1217–1314), both key to controlling the borderlands, and in the Welsh Marches. They received the lordship of Glamorgan, in the southernmost part of Wales, in 1217, and Usk in 1246, and would acquire more throughout the century so that by 1270, the family's territories comprised a vast swathe of southern Wales from the river Neath in the west to the river Wye in the east, including Cardiff, the future capital. Warlike, 'very bold in defence of their rights',[26] and possessed of a great pragmatism (sometimes mistaken for turncoatism) in a fluid political age, by the time Trellech rose to prominence in the mid-thirteenth century, the de Clares had emerged as one of the richest and most powerful dynasties in the realm at a time when land meant power. As such, they played an important – sometimes pivotal – role in the bloody sphere of England's medieval politics during the power struggles of Henry III's long and troubled reign which covered much of the thirteenth century, and as key allies in his son Edward I's masterplan to expand his authority over Wales and Scotland. Edward harnessed the full force of England's military might in the 1280s, shrinking the frontiers of the Welsh princes' domains, until Gwynedd, the hostile heartland in the north-west, fell to the English. The sense of perpetual war, and the need to provide resources, would come to define Trellech.[27]

The de Clares were the cream of Plantagenet society: violent, aggressive and hungry for power. Gilbert de Clare (1262–95) was the most renowned of the family, and a key lieutenant of the bellicose Edward I. Known as Gilbert the Red, or sometimes the 'red dog', after his blazing hair, he was 'the most outstanding of the noble magnates of the realm because of his eminence and incomparable range of his power', according to the chronicler Thomas Wykes.[28] It was on his watch that Trellech blossomed into a major urban entity. Some of Trellech's status can be explained by Gilbert the Red's elite connections and the pivotal role he played in England's politics. He helped to secure a peaceful end to the civil war in the 1260s, sat at Henry III's deathbed in 1272, and was even considered by Edward I to be the most lucrative match for his daughter, Joan of Acre.[29] He was one of only three people who could appoint people to the Council of Nine,[30] and Edward I gave Gilbert the Red special gilded leather armour, by no means a favour he extended to everyone. Gilbert the Red's son, another Gilbert de Clare, even served as regent while Edward II was away warring and treating in Scotland and France. You couldn't find much bigger players than the de Clares. And Trellech was a nerve centre of their power.

Here they claimed the right to hear all pleas, wage war, conclude peace and wring as much rent and tribute money to consolidate their hold over their little Welsh empire and advance their – and the king's, usually – interests elsewhere.[31] But the 'regalities' were under constant threat of attack, particularly in the mid-thirteenth century as Trellech was making its presence felt, requiring robust and near-continuous defence. These threats came from three overlapping quarters. Firstly, the Marches were rendered structurally unstable by the rulers of Gwynedd, the explosive, querulous kingdom in the north-west; secondly, the 'princes of Wales' who periodically claimed jurisdiction over all of Wales, and who expected the local Welsh princes to rise up in support; and finally, the feuding between rival Marcher lords (who sometimes enlisted the help of Welsh princes and even forged marriage alliances with them on occasion).[32] This further destabilised the region with raids and counter-raids – to the extent that Edward I was moved to try to ban private warfare altogether in the borderlands.[33]

To meet all these threats, there was then an urgent and persistent need for troops, weapons and structures for subjugation and defence, and it was this impulse that came to define the landscape. In England, a 'licence to crenellate' was required to erect castles, but in the Marches, magnates could build to their hearts' content – and did, on a scale that still impresses today. Some, like Caerphilly Castle near Cardiff, were positively avant-garde, with layers of fortifications arranged like Russian dolls where advancing invaders could be trapped in killing grounds; others were built in a more traditional mould. The castles were catalysts for the growth of something else, something which had not been seen in Wales since the collapse of Roman authority some seven hundred years earlier, something which the de Clares were at the forefront of conjuring into existence: towns and cities.

The efflorescence of new towns and cities between the Norman Conquest (1066) and the Black Death (1348–9) was one of the single biggest developments in the shaping of the British landscape since the establishment of permanent domestic settlements like Skara Brae at the end of the Stone Age.[34] By 1300, at least 120 new towns had appeared in England and 77 in Wales, and around 60 more would sprout before the Black Death. Some absorbed pre-existing communities, others were newly planted. A parallel process of lightning-fast urbanisation happened in Scotland, under David I in the early twelfth century; these were the first true Scottish towns.[35] Centres of commerce, justice and spirituality, these were the precursors of the towns and cities that are still with us today.[36] There had been forerunners, of course: *oppida*, the fortified Iron Age settlements and the Anglo-Saxon *burhs* (developed as a form of defence against Danish invaders in King Alfred's time). But it was in the Middle Ages, just as Trellech flourished, that for the majority of Britain's inhabitants towns lost their alien quality and ultimately became naturalised within, rather than imposed upon, the landscape. They still *looked* defensive, defined by fortified walls, crenellated gates and usually a castle, but increasingly developed sophisticated economic functions, many with guildhalls. Sanctioned by royal charter, they achieved a measure of self-determination.[37] And architecturally, they were more imposing than ever before, with cathedrals, multiple storeys, stone manors and timber-framed houses for the better sort, public latrines, massive marketplaces; even, at Chester, a raised street to allow shoppers to gaze down into shopfronts. And their populations swelled. Many of these places have been continuously occupied since the Middle Ages and still exist – thrive, even – all over the country today. Many, but not all.

———

Perched on a landlocked plateau, Trellech's topography seemed to inform against it; unlike many of Wales's other new medieval towns and cities – places like Cardiff, Chepstow and Monmouth – it was neither a river nor a coastal port, and there was seemingly little economic impetus to expand. Yet this is precisely what happened, furiously, during the regality of Richard de Clare, who came into possession of Trellech in 1246. On his watch, Trellech gained a market and a mayor, and he accorded it borough status, as was his Marcher lord right.[38]

What happened next can be pieced together from rental assessments, which appear at semi-regular intervals from the mid-thirteenth century onwards. These were carried out by the reeves of the de Clare family, who were charged with collecting the maximum possible rent, and, less regularly, by royal officials, who calculated what tax was owed to the king on the death of a de Clare (calculated as a share of the annual rent). These inquisitions post mortem are a major source of knowledge about the size of medieval towns and cities – essentially they show us what was taxable within the town, from which we may extrapolate the approximate population and number of buildings, and compare them with other urban settlements.

The originals are stored in the National Archives in London, and paging through the parchment and ink is like a shot of espresso to the imagination.[39] It is exciting to think that materials in the archives are beginning to manifest themselves in the artefacts and structures dug up by Wilson each summer as the lost settlement slowly rears from the earth.

A burgage was literally a 'slice of *burh*' or a 'unit of town'. Measured in perches of five metres, burghs were the economic building blocks of medieval towns and their value – or *landgable* – was payable in cash. This was something of a watershed: traditionally in England and Wales, where the vast majority of people lived in small rural communities, rents were paid in agricultural or military service: they would till the fields for a landlord and perhaps fight for them too. Burgage tenures, on the other hand, represented a landowner's desire to maximise the revenue from their land, and a desire on the part of residents to live in closer quarters, somewhere with more life and amenities. The trend towards carving land into burgage plots from the mid-thirteenth century represents a shift towards a more modern kind of urban society in which tenants were freed from compulsory agricultural and military labour, less socially, economically and politically beholden to their landowners' interests, and freer, therefore, to pursue a wider range of work.

Topographically, burgage plots were long, narrow strips culminating in a house – or some sort of shanty or shack – at right angles to the street; frontage was at a premium because it maximised the possibilities for passing trade; the most expensive plots faced on to main streets or a marketplace. The land behind the house could be used for grazing livestock, growing vegetables, cultivating herbs or, occasionally, just staring up at the sky and dreaming. Alleyways allowed people to walk from the dwelling house to the back of the plot without going through the land; to this day they often run the length of old burgage plots. The *landgable* was assessed solely upon the extent of one's territory, so tenants were free to erect as many buildings as they liked – an outhouse here, a workshop there, even perhaps a small dwelling to sublet. Burgages could be sold, bequeathed and, as the populations of towns thickened, amalgamated into less symmetrical, Tetris-shaped blocks. The tenants were called burghers or burgesses (it had nothing to do with the sex of the plot-holders). Burghers had to be freemen – that is, entitled to practise a trade in the town rather than being yoked to the fields. Ever have towns and cities been places of especial freedom and opportunity.

When Richard de Clare acquired Trellech in 1246 it was just a splatter of dwellings along a high street in the shadow of a motte-and-bailey castle. It had a dated wooden church, Wednesday market and sprinkling of holy wells – it was, in other words, what we would call a village. One imagines there would have been very few burgage plots. Yet the rental assessments of 1288, carried out by the reeves of the de Clares, record no fewer than 378.[40] The implications of this – if the evidence is to be taken at face value – are astonishing. It means that in the space of forty years a tiny hamlet had grown into the second biggest city in Wales. It had more burgage plots than Chepstow (308), and Usk (300) in Monmouthshire; Haverford West (360) and Pembroke (227½) in Pembrokeshire; Carmarthen (281) in Carmarthenshire; and Kenfig, not yet quite lost to the sands (142), in Glamorganshire.[41] Only Cardiff, built in Glamorganshire from 1081, was ever so slightly bigger, with 380 burgages in 1281 (the same decade as Trellech reached 378), growing to 421 plots by 1296. There are no overall rental assessments for Trellech in the early 1290s but this has not stopped a number of historians and journalists flirting with the idea that, assuming Trellech continued to grow at the same pace between 1288 and 1296 and increased its size by 10 per cent, it may have enjoyed a brief spell as the biggest city in Wales, which naturally heightens the mystery of its disappearance no end.[42]

Trellech's meteoric rise is perplexing. Extrapolating population figures from burgage plots is far from an exact science, as it relies upon assumptions about the number of houses per plot and average family sizes. Wilson deduces, reasonably, that 'at least five hundred buildings' stood on the 378 plots in 1288, and that (much more controversially) Trellech may have housed as many as ten thousand people.[43] That figure would put it on a par with some of England's biggest cities outside London, almost the same size as Winchester (eleven thousand residents in 1300),[44] Southampton or York, and around one-eighth the size of medieval London (eighty thousand).[45] Burgages were calculated by area, not occupancy; if the burghers of Trellech built more houses than we expect and threw themselves into subletting, or if the population consisted of high numbers of extramural burgesses – that is, people who lived outside the limits of Trellech, in suburbs – Wilson maintains the population may have been yet higher still. But leaving aside for a moment the extent of the population, it is the *pace* of urbanisation that is truly remarkable.

An urban population of ten thousand would necessitate, on average, 26.5 occupants per plot at a time in which even the most generous historians place the average family size at no more than five people. There must have been some serious subletting going on or some exceptional reason why Trellech was so populous. Considering that it took London – the capital and so, one would imagine, the most dynamic turbine of population growth – a hundred years to increase its population by ten thousand, growing from ten thousand (in 1100) to twenty thousand (in 1200), and, after the Black Death of 1348–9, 150 years to grow by another ten thousand, from forty thousand to fifty thousand – then the expansion of a landlocked town from hardly anything to five thousand or ten thousand within the space of forty years seems truly incredible.

Perhaps it *is* incredible. Might there be an argument to be more critical of burgage assessments? A research project at the University of Winchester to digitise inquisitions post mortem along with other evaluative literature has recently concluded that, whether the 'taxmen' were working on behalf of the Crown or the local landowners, they were susceptible to pressure, even bribery by the occupants of burgages in relation to the figures, and sometimes they were lazy and just parroted past assessments without revision.[46] The current consensus is that in the vast majority of cases, if assessors were prone to massage the figures at all, it would in all likelihood be to *diminish* rather than exaggerate the true population of medieval towns and cities.[47]

Urban historians tend to view burgage assessments as superior evidence for gauging population levels than measuring, say, the surface area within the walls.[48] So the 'professionals' whom he sometimes disparages do, in this instance at least, agree that Stuart

Wilson is on the right track. And if Trellech did mushroom so quickly then, as Wilson maintains, it can only have been a boom town.

———

When a new or small settlement undergoes an 'inorganic' growth spurt, we call it a boom town. There are myriad reasons why such places have come into existence: the fixation of a new trading route, an influx of refugees, the establishment of a royal court, the commissioning of a great public work, or the arrival of a major industrial employer, to name a few.[49] But the most powerful catalyst by far has been the exploitation of freshly discovered or urgently needed natural resources, buried in the earth or sea. California had its gold rush, Detroit the automobile boom, Manchester grew to wealth through textiles; Kimberley had its dream-craters of diamonds; Kalgoorlie its quarries of gold; North Dakota its oil fields. Out of these precious natural resources entire worlds have been born. They have been the rocket fuel for urban growth.

That iron was mined in medieval Trellech we can be in no doubt thanks to the labours of professional archaeologists, particularly Ray Howell, who discovered the scale and sophistication of the process in the early 1990s when digging into what had traditionally been assumed to have been the main part of the town, near the modern-day church. The findings, faithfully filed in the obscure *Monmouthshire Antiquary*, are fascinating.[50] The main excavation of this site revealed a continuous occupancy of a single burgage plot, articulating a dynamically evolving economy and a fluid topography that could adapt itself to the region's tempestuous politics.

Like the excavation of Skara Brae, the digs near the church revealed four distinct phases of occupation, preserved between the layers of the earth. Except these spanned sixty, not seven hundred, years. We can date them fairly precisely thanks to an abundance of potsherds – that is, shards of pottery – which can be carbon-dated. Depth is a measure of antiquity and, buried deepest, we find the residue of a timber-framed house. It had a central hearth, compacted clay floor, and indents left, it seems, by a chest or trestle table, or perhaps by tumbling beams since the whole structure – almost certainly the modest dwelling of a burgher and his family – was destroyed by fire around 1245. It is likely, conjectures Ray Howell, that the house was built when Richard de Clare acquired Trellech in 1242, precipitating a spurt in house-building as he sought to establish Trellech as a centre of de Clare dominion. In looks they are not dissimilar from Skara Brae's roundhouses, and yet these medieval townsmen saw the world in such different colours.

Excavations of the layer immediately above reveal that by the middle of the thirteenth century the site had been put to a very different use. Now there was a slag pit and furnace. So iron was smelted here, even though this was probably on a small, ad hoc scale, in a domestic environment even. It may well have been what we would describe as a 'live–work unit' for a blacksmith and his family. The third phase, a little higher up, is the most puzzling. Dating from around the 1270s, possibly a little earlier, it retains traces of iron manufacturing, but with all the hallmarks of a storehouse. Of all the dug-up dishes and jugs, the vast majority have been found here, implying that it may have been a living quarters for those engaged in extracting and fashioning iron: the miners, smelters and blacksmiths who comprised so much of Trellech's population. Both the second and third phases of occupation, in the 1250s, 1260s and 1270s, coincided with a period of heavy fighting in the Marches, with the de Clare lands under siege, at various points, from both native Welsh princes and rival Marcher lords.

The problem became more acute for Gilbert the Red in the 1270s and early 1280s as his persistent enemy Llywelyn ap Gruffudd launched what was almost a nationwide rebellion against

English colonisation and rule. It was at this point that Trellech seems to have hit its industrial peak, and this brings us to the fourth layer of excavations dating from around 1270 to 1290, where we find an upgrade from the earlier, more makeshift workshop. Ray Howell makes the convincing case that the more sophisticated purpose-built forge with a bloomery furnace in this layer attests to the aggressive campaigns of Gilbert the Red at a time when Edward I, his overlord, was attempting to subjugate Wales. Iron was needed for castle-building, too, so this sort of sophisticated enterprise may also, Ray Howell speculates, have helped facilitate the building of the de Clares' crowning achievement, the magnificent Caerphilly Castle, twenty miles to the south-east of Trellech. Trellech, Ray Howell argues, was prized as a 'sophisticated and large-scale iron production centre' because, built on a plateau in the eastern Marches, reassuringly close to the border with England, it was considered more secure than other towns under their control, and less vulnerable to Welsh attack. (Never mind that events would often prove the de Clares wrong.) It was the ideal spot, therefore, for a vast weapons factory. Trellech flourished in large part, therefore, because it was a turbine of war.

I set off for Trellech from a beautifully quiet hut in Monmouth on a hot afternoon in what seemed like an endless summer of sun. It was an eight-mile journey through the Forest of Dean and when I told the landlady that I would be going down by bike, she just laughed and said I wouldn't be going *down* anywhere. I would be going up. And up I went, up a helter-skelter of country lanes, with the forest's immense cascade of trees to my left and lorries swinging by to my right, until my heart became a punchbag. Once or twice I ventured off the road, into the forest, to catch my breath. The top of the pines floated in the wind, lofty and conspiratorial, the faint path pathetic against their might. After what seemed like hours a sign in the undergrowth announced: 'Trellech'. It was almost comically inconspicuous, like a home-made sign for a cake stand at a village fête.

Just outside the village I saw three stones, like arrows fired from outer space, in the belly of a field. About twice my height, they lurched sideways, dominoes on the brink of collapse. These megaliths, although formed of stone, sand and gravel, are the colour of rust, and appropriately so as they were placed here in the Bronze Age – at just the time Skara Brae was vanishing so far to the north – probably for ceremonial purposes (since they trace the curvature of the midwinter sunset). According to one legend they were thrown thirteen miles here by a giant, Jack of Kent, across rivers, valleys and hills in a rage at Satan, who had failed to express sufficient admiration for the giant's leap off Sugarloaf Mountain. That would make them emissions of rage and superhuman strength, a meaning that would prove portentous. The stones' presence is suggestive of a Bronze Age community, either here or nearby, but we

cannot claim with any confidence that it was the progenitor of today's village. They do, nonetheless, lend it its name – *tri* (three); *llech* (stone).

I went through a couple of gates, past some farmhouses, and found the site of a vanished castle. It once sat on a Norman motte, now just a grassy hump with paths leading up to the top, surrounded by gently swaying foliage. It reminded me of an execution site. Once, the fort loomed over an encampment of soldiers' huts surrounded by a palisade. The castle provided a stronghold to which the Normans could retreat when under siege, and it stamped a sense of Norman authority upon the village. Now, however, it was moribund, contributing to the sense of loss and absence that flowed through Trellech. From the top of the mound arose a fir tree with endlessly criss-crossing branches and, mid-way down, I saw a restless horse which from afar looked like it hovered in mid-air – in time it would trot over, thrust its snout through the fence, and bare its teeth at me.

I went on, into Trellech. There were fine stone houses, little hedge-framed alleyways squirrelling off from the main road, and a crisp, thirteenth-century church which serves as a giant roundabout for occasional traffic. The church is a fusion of various building materials – uneven brick from the late Middle Ages and stone added in a more orderly fashion later, alongside Normanesque rounded archways and a pleasingly cylindrical spire – but the whole edifice seemed woefully out of proportion with the rest of the village. Almost all of the shops were closed but the village's convivial pub was open, and inside I drank icy cider after my long cycle through the forest.

Banked in plumes of tilting wheat, I beat a path across a wooden bridge over a stream and, on my left, in the sunlight, I saw a wishing well. Dedicated to St Anne – who was associated with a Celtic mother-goddess, and so associated with healing and fertility – it resembled a mini amphitheatre and had stone benches to give rest, as the notice board put it, to the weary traveller. By now the sun shone low and hot in the sky, a blazing eyeball upon me as I squelched across the slabs with a sense that they could give way at any second. I sat, at last, in the shade. There were flies doodling about and green slime on the underside of the chipped stone. Far off I could hear dogs barking, the moans of cows, a silk breeze in the leaves, and a gurgling in the throat of the well. A white ribbon was flying in the wind – just one token of tens of thousands of votive offerings swallowed by the well over the last two thousand years. It is believed by some, still to this day, that wellsprings are portals to supernatural worlds inhabited by gods or guardian spirits who have the power to intervene in humanity's affairs. They have traditionally been repositories for wishes (to cure ailments or win the affections of a would-be lover) and for curses (where a token is thrown down the well; the number of bubbles rising to the surface, and the speed with which they do so hold of prognostic significance). At St Anne's Well, or the Virtuous Well as it is known, the presence of iron in the springs is believed to have curative properties, discharged by the three lurching stones from beneath which it flows. So this epochal metal, iron, was not just the substance of slaughter but a means of healing, too.

Everything Trellech had become, everything it had shrunk to, seemed quite at odds with what the sources tell us it once was in its prime: a weapons factory, a mint of mayhem and slaughter, the forge of de Clare dominion. It helped to power their whirlwind of bloody activity in all four nations of Britain, providing resources to conquer new territories, crush insurrections, and enforce the king's will (when they felt like it). But what did that actually mean in practice?[51] Trees felled in the Forest of Dean were smouldered into charcoal, which was then used to smelt iron ore. Then, in hissing smithies and spark-showered anvils, blacksmiths hammered out munitions that could inflict the most devastating of injuries, and tilt entire wars to the de Clare advantage. Here were made battleaxes to crack the skulls of the Welsh and knives to gauge out their eyes; manacles to pin back the arms of captives so that their ribs could be cracked one by one for the pleasure of the dungeon-master, and chains for the prisons. From the anvils of Trellech came swords to plunge into the hearts of enemies.

Out of Trellech came the war hammer's spike that could break a horse's gallop, flinging its rider to the ground; prick spurs to galvanise warhorses; battering rams; pincers to pull out tongues and knives for castration too; hand-axes like those that felled thousands of trees when Gilbert the Red's men chopped a road through the Forest of Dean in the summer of 1287, troops and their baggage trains passing like a great slithering worm to Dryslwyn Castle to crush the rebellion of the Welsh insurrectionist Rhys ap Maredudd; caltrops, those little iron spiders placed on battlefields to send horses yowling to the ground; and all the spears and javelins that were so necessary to the campaigns.

Defensive munitions were churned out too, so vital in the 1280s when the incorrigible Morgan ap Maredudd burst forth, seizing castles and corroding the de Clares' power base in Glamorgan: out came shields and the iron spikes for the bases of portcullises, the vertically sliding gates that kept besiegers at bay and trapped them in killing grounds where they could be torn to pieces by a blizzard of arrows streaming from murder holes; and the batons and spears with which the burghers tried to defend themselves as their towns and cities were burned to the ground. Though it was their stone façades that impressed and cowed, without a plenteous source of worked iron the de Clares would never have been able to embark upon such an ambitious programme of castle-building. Likely the smithies of Trellech were forever churning out crampettes for joining together stones, bolsters and hoops for fastening drawbridges to their axles, bars for windows, pins to fasten frightening bestial sculptures above gateways, clicket locks to hem in prisoners and fetterlocks to restrain gyrfalcons and hawks, as well as a bewildering variety of nails from the giant *braggenayls* and *spikenayls*, used for fixing planks, to *lathnails* for roofing, and *doublenails*, *spykings* and greater *spykings* for various other purposes.[52]

More than anything Trellech was a giant factory of armour for the breastplates, visors and chain-mail coats for the three thousand infantry and one hundred crossbowmen whom Gilbert de Clare commanded alongside Edward II's favourite Piers Gaveston in their campaign against the Scots in 1310, say, and for the thick breast plates, shin-protecting greaves, gauntlets and full chain-mail suits for warriors of nobler stock. It is even possible that Trellech manufactured the armour that immobilised the twenty-three-year-old Gilbert de Clare, the last of his house, in the abattoir of crushed bodies at Bannockburn in 1314, when (perhaps because in his haste he had forgotten to put on his distinctive surcoat with the de Clares' heraldic three chevrons, which would have marked him out as a potentially valuable hostage) he was picked off and slaughtered; hoist, we might say, by his own petard.

It may not have been the vast metropolis it is sometimes made out to be, but Trellech helped the de Clares sustain their primacy amongst the aristocratic dynasties in the realm.

———

The boom town, unable to sustain the furious pace of its early growth, so often becomes the foredoomed town, a totem of capitalist overreach or of man's greed, hubris or disrespect for nature; reduced to a shadow, a ghost town. When their lifeblood – be it gold, oil, iron or the capacity for large-scale production – is depleted, or the economic or political confluences that had allowed such a place to come into existence in the first place disjoin, the town goes into free fall, leaving it acutely vulnerable to misfortunes other towns are able to weather. An over-reliance upon one particular resource would die hard as a powerful medium of oblivion, hollowing out and destroying other towns and villages in industrial and post-industrial Britain many centuries later, including dying coal-mining villages in County Durham ominously labelled 'Category D' by the local council – doomed to 'decline and disappear'.[53] If Trellech's raison d'être was to mine iron and forge munitions for the de Clare family, it is little wonder it became obsolete with the extinction of the dynasty in 1314.

It was already in free fall. When Gilbert the Red's estates were surveyed in the inquisition post mortem of 1295, 102 burgage plots were marked as void – burned to the ground. This coincided with the insurrection of Morgan ap Maredudd, the southern ally of the Prince of Wales, so in a twist of poetic justice, the colonisers' forge was itself ransacked. The confidence of the town was shattered, many of its buildings lay in ruins, and, twenty years later, Trellech had lost a third of its population. It was now only the eighth largest town in Wales,[54] and, without its de Clare patrons from 1314, the town's awkward location and extreme economic specialisation began to conspire against it, and so the settlement became a sitting duck for the devastating plague epidemics that followed. By the mid-fourteenth century, there were forty-eight empty burgages – conceivably, the bulk of the town by then. Forty years later, they lay wild and fallow. After that there is no evidence anyone ever bothered to assess Trellech again. The *coup de grâce* may have been the further violent political unrest of the early fifteenth century; certainly, in later centuries, its fallen nature seemed to become its most distinguishing feature. In 1695, a Welsh botanist and antiquarian described Trellech as 'reduced to a poor inconsiderable village',[55] a sentiment reflected in the *Hereford Journal* and *Gloucester Journal*, which also labelled it a village.[56] It had lost its fire.

And so, robbed of its purpose from 1314, and much beleaguered, Trellech bled life, lay unwanted, and slowly sank beneath the soil.

CHAPTER THREE

THE OBLITERATED PORT: WINCHELSEA

The shingle spit had been breached before, but this was the first time the Monday Market had flooded and now the waters were amassing outside St Thomas's Church, striking at the heart of the beleaguered medieval port. Soon, the high altar would be a rudderless raft, bobbing like cork, and the angels would drown. In the guildhall on the other side of town an emergency session of the grand council was in session, and a vague if controversial consensus was emerging: they would beg for the king's help. They had been sending petitions to Westminster for forty years, and now the king was tantalisingly close, at Battle Abbey.[1]

Edward I – Longshanks, Hammer of the Scots, King of England – was not popular in Winchelsea. Many of the older townsfolk remembered how, ten years earlier in 1265, Prince Edward had slaughtered many of the principal citizens;[2] punishment, he claimed, for their treacherousness against his father[3] and for their rampant piratical activity in the Narrow Seas too, plundering ships – whether English or foreign – and flinging their crew overboard.[4]

But Edward *was* a builder *par excellence* and God only knew the number of towns and cities that had sprouted on his watch, in England, Gascony, even Gwynedd in the furthest reaches of Wales. So now, in 1276, if anyone could stop the rising of the waters, it was he.

Or so they desperately hoped. Founded by 1031,[5] Winchelsea was a once-flourishing port with a population of around four thousand: more than Southampton (with 2,800 residents at the beginning of the fourteenth century), more than the neighbouring hilltop port of Rye, but smaller than Bristol and York (around eighteen thousand apiece), and much smaller than London with its eighty thousand souls.[6] It was situated on a vast shingle spit off the East Sussex coast running from the cliffs of Fairlight to the promontory of Dungeness, a spur accreted by longshore drift, the process whereby sediment is deposited when a headland suddenly changes course. The firmest of foundations it was not but the spit was expansive, more like a bank or island, covered in stabilising dunes on which vegetation grew, and it gave the fishermen, merchants and tradesman unparalleled access to that highway of commerce, the sea.[7] There was indeed a cluster of towns on the shingle promontory (rather than the spit): Lydd, Hythe, Broomhill, Dymchurch and the freshly minted port of New Romney where the River Rother met the sea. The name Winchelsea (*gwent-chesel-ey*) is Middle English for 'shingle island on the level', or perhaps Old English (*wincel-ēg*) 'island on a bend', not, as it was later sometimes claimed, from *wind chills sea*.[8] Topographically, it was a crooked course of twisting streets and narrow alleys parcelled in seawater. Behind it lay extensive salt marshes; to the west lay the Weald, a hilly forest stretching from western Sussex into central Kent, and to the east the fishermen's port of Rye. There were fisheries and dockyards, storehouses and hospitals, several monasteries and a leper colony. It received its charter in 1191, provided significant revenue to the Exchequer, and seems to have risen to prosperity by at least 1200. This did not go unrecognised. Since the thirteenth century the 'ancient town' had become a senior member of the Cinque Ports, a confederacy of Sussex and Kent towns enjoying extensive trading privileges and political liberties in exchange for ship service to the Crown since there was not, at that time, a royal navy.[9] So valuable and well located a port was Winchelsea that Henry III took it for himself in 1247, by compulsory exchange from its owner, the Benedictine abbey of Fécamp in Normandy.

Winchelsea's fortunes, then – economic and existential – were for ever bound by the ebb and flow of the tide. It was near the narrowest crossing between England and France, and the Weald made land transportation difficult, reinforcing the importance of coastal and overseas trade. In a typical month on its quayside could be seen ships unloading cloth from Flanders and wine from Gascony, tin from Castile and woad for blue dye from Venice, salt from the North Sea and fish from the English Channel, copper cups from Scandinavia, and mirrors and garlic from San Sebastian. A one-fifteenth tax on merchants at seaports shows that by the turn of the thirteenth century, Winchelsea was third only in importance to London and Southampton as a south-eastern port; its merchants yielded considerably more to the king's coffers than Rye's.[10] Its prosperity depended on a continual flow of traded commodities and goods packed high on ships, the same craft that were now, in the 1270s, ferrying off the architecture of people's lives as they fled the rising waters: the timbers that had once propped up their wattle-and-daub houses, their thatches too; their furniture; and their locks, weapons and cooking pots. Wearily, they looked on. This time the exodus seemed permanent. The higher the waters, the shriller their pleas.

Longshanks could quite easily have let Winchelsea go under; medieval England was, after all, full of decayed Roman towns and cities, abortive Anglo-Saxon *burhs*, and Norman false starts. Even some of the king's new-planted towns were destined to wither on the vine only to be excavated by Welsh archaeology graduates many hundreds of years later. But Winchelsea was important. Edward valued it as an entrepôt of wine and cloth, and a bounteous source of ships for his wars (the town was one of the largest contributors of ships to royal fleets), and he wanted to see for himself if anything could be done. And so, in July 1276, he embarked upon a fact-finding mission.[11]

Word soon reached Winchelsea that the king was coming to town. The townsfolk were determined to receive him with *élan*. We can imagine that a new coat of whitewash was lathered on the city gates, a cavalcade of tumblers, jugglers and minstrels whirring to life, apple-sized meatballs imprisoned in great mounds of jelly laid out on silver platters in the feasting hall alongside elaborately coloured boars' heads,[12] and white goshawks with their metre-long wings were paraded through the streets on the wrists of prominent family members,[13] while the poor clustered at the town's gates. Messengers were sent to keep watch on the hill of Iham, and as the king's retinue appeared on the horizon, an abundance of malmsey wine – the strongest, sweetest and most exotic wine in the world, imported from the Peloponnese mountains in Greece – was poured into tin jugs engraved with the town's coat of arms.[14] They would be drunk on the spot by the king and his retinue as a token of respect but also a kind of votive offering for their deliverance. For even in its beleaguered state, if there was one thing Winchelsea could do well, it was wine, the very wine that fuelled so much of its prosperity.

Edward, seeing the hopelessness of Old Winchelsea, resolved to save it. The man loved town planning, loved the machismo kick of arranging timber, wood and muck into well-ordered streets, and would even, twenty years later, summon a colloquium at Harwich in Essex on how best to 'devise, order and array' new towns. He had a team of no fewer than twenty-four town planners forever seeking out new sites for 'the greatest profit of Ourselves and of merchants'.[15] Seeing Winchelsea founder made him think of his fearsome crenellated towns that were working so well in Wales and of his English foundations too. But most of all, he thought of his *bastides* in Aquitaine, his superb sun-drenched hilltop towns, fortified to the core, which protected his overseas domains so magnificently; no, Winchelsea must be saved. Like a precious relic in a cathedral, it would be *translated*.

Edward instructed his commissioners to find a suitable location and in 1282 they reported back: the new town would be built on the hill of Iham, a thickly wooded peninsula rising above low-lying countryside, riddled with rabbit warrens. It was about three miles inland and its northern cliff was washed by the Brede Estuary, a broad stretch of water that would bring in ships from all over Europe. It would be a two-tier town, with the river port down below and the buildings of the town behind it, on the cliff. This lofty new Winchelsea would be safe from the ravages of the sea, but, thanks to the tidal harbour it shared with Rye, it would maintain its booming overseas trade. What was not to like?

There were a few logistical difficulties. The hill was already home to a tiny village in the north-west corner with a modest church, St Leonard's. The rest of the site was occupied by a manor house with courtyards and gardens; with fields of wheat and barley, and pastureland; with a quarry, coppice and hill slopes for the livestock. And there was a potential spanner in the works – the hilly territory already belonged to various landowners including the abbots of Battle and Fécamp in Normandy. No matter – these were purchased or exchanged without too much fuss.[16] Overall, the king acquired 150 acres on the hill, including the entire manor of Iham, keeping twelve for himself (the future King's Green on the edge of town), and sequestering the Abbot of Fécamp's little village of St Leonard's behind a wall, rather ingloriously. The following year, Edward proclaimed that he was going to found a new settlement on the hill 'in lieu of our town of Winchelsea, which is in great part submersed by the inundations of the sea', and his commissioners began to pinpoint sites up on the cliff for the churches of St Thomas and St Giles, laying out the streets and lanes.[17] Edward had saved Winchelsea once before, from the rebellious barons, and now he would save it from the bloodthirsty waves.

It was unwelcome news to the villagers whose hill was about to be turned into a massive building site, a once-secluded woodland community, absorbed into England's newest town, not to mention the rabbits – a writ from 1283 mentions that before it was developed the Hill of Iham 'had been called a rabbit-warren'. Yet Edward's intervention could not have come at a better time.

Winchelsea had been sliding into the sea for decades, but now it was teetering on the brink of oblivion.

On an eerily quiet morning, five years later, a straggle of men, women and children inched their way down a wooded hill, stones cutting their bare feet. They'd managed to survive the night unharmed – they had relatives in Fairlight, beyond the Weald – but nothing could prepare them for what awaited them downhill, a scene that would be seared on to their minds for ever. Across a broad dyke, through a thin mist, they saw their town dissolved in the sea, a ruin of roof beams and battered hulls, sunken windmills and fallen walls, drowned pigs and drifting firewood, dogs, hawks, rubbish and hay, and the corpses of the townspeople, all revolving in a great muddy swirl; it was, as one chronicler put it, a 'pitiful waste of people, cattle and houses in every place'.[18]

It wasn't as though they hadn't been warned. A storm in 1250 – the first of a trio that would ultimately destroy Old Winchelsea – was so cataclysmic that it attracted the attention of some of England's finest chroniclers including the Benedictine monk Matthew Paris, who could evoke everything from crusaders' castles in Jerusalem to elephants galumphing up the Pilgrim's Way to London with a charm and humanity that cuts through the centuries. The first, fateful storm, he recalls, began in the early hours of 23 April and whorled towards the coast with unabated fury. Such violent, wanton destruction could only be a sign of God's wrath – upon what, no one was quite sure – but Paris wasted no time in summoning the very spirit of the apocalypse: 'On the first day of the month of October, the moon being in its first quarter, there appeared a new moon, swollen and red in appearance, as a sign of coming tempests.'[19] Within a week, a dense mist had descended, the wind flinging trees through the air, the sea swept inland. The roar of the ocean terrified old men in their beds and the surface glowed with fire. 'The disturbed sea transgressed its usual bounds, the tide flowing twice without any ebb,'[20] he says; waves 'battled' one another, and large vessels foundered and sank. At Winchelsea more than three hundred houses 'with some churches' were 'thrown down by the impetuous rise of the sea' along with bridges, mills, salt sheds and fishermen's cottages, alongside the mass of shingle on which they had formerly stood.

This was just the beginning. Just over a year later, in 1252, Paris described another tempest that struck England 'in the octaves of the Epiphany' – that is, in the month of January – slicing spires from churches, ripping roots from ancient oak trees, and sinking the mightiest ships in the narrow seas. At Winchelsea – 'a port of great use to the English and especially to the people of London' – the waves 'as if indignant and enraged at being driven back on the day before' surged into mills and houses, 'and drowned and washed away a great many of the inhabitants'.[21]

Though Winchelsea had been receiving grants to improve its sea defences on an almost annual basis since 1244, it seems that these storms critically breached the shingle bar on which it stood, permanently undermining the town's foundations, and exposing it to the full horrors of the south-westerly winds torpedoing in from the Atlantic, effectively sealing Old Winchelsea's fate.[22] And so the sea gushed in. By the end of the 1250s the tides were penetrating as far as Appledore, a quagmire eight miles to the north, and over the next few decades much of the town was swept into the sea in devastating increments. In the winter of 1271, the quay on the south side of St Thomas the Martyr's had been 'carried away by the floods and tempests of the sea' clawing away some of the church and gravely imperilling the rest of it;[23] between 1272 and 1273, the tolls of the port fell by two-thirds;[24] in July 1276, the king approved a land grant to one Matthew de Horne of Winchelsea to build a quay loaded with ballast 'for the defence of his house against inundation of the sea'; perhaps Edward had seen the poor man's plight for himself when he visited Winchelsea the day before.[25] But such things were to no avail. By 1280, four years after his appearance in Winchelsea, even the king realised the game was up. He issued a writ declaring 'the greater part of Winchelsea was drowned and the sea prevailing more and more against it that the rest is *hopeless long to stand*'[26] – haunting words, in their time and ours.

Three devastating storms delivered the *coup de grâce* to the disappearing town between 1287 and 1288. The chronicle of Gervase of Canterbury describes how, on 4 February 1288, 'the sea flooded so greatly that all the walls were broken down and almost all the lands covered from the great wall of Appledore towards the south and the west as far as Winchelsea'.[27] The sun vanished from view, the sky turned black, and the entire town was destroyed by the waves. The cracking of timbers, the levelling of churches, water gushing through houses, beams become battering rams, the drowning of men, women, children – all were encompassed in the sea's primal roar, and it was an abysmal scene that greeted the survivors that morning in 1288. The marshes were inundated, the coastline dramatically transformed, the towns of Dymchurch, Lydd and Bromhill lost to the waves; the port of New Romney choked with shingle and beached half a mile inland, forsaken by the River Rother. The sea, without its shingle restraint, now swept far, far in, producing a broad bay between the Hill of Iham and Rye. And with that, Winchelsea – or Old Winchelsea, as it was soon to be known – was destroyed.

It was not alone. The storms that laid waste to Old Winchelsea coincided with a period of unusually tempestuous weather in northern Europe. It has been claimed that at least 286 towns, villages and parishes, and many islands in western Europe were drowned between 1099 and 1570, with the loss of over 1.5 million lives.[28] It has also been claimed that around the time Old Winchelsea was foundering at least a hundred thousand people died along the Dutch and German coasts in four ferocious storm surges (in 1200, 1216, 1287 and 1362).[29] If anything, these obliterative storms only grew worse in the fourteenth and fifteenth centuries, putting paid to much bigger cities than Winchelsea. Tantalisingly, there is very little evidence of any major flooding along the medieval British coastline *before* Winchelsea began to suffer in the early thirteenth century.

The subject is not without contention but the demise of Winchelsea took place as the Medieval Warm Period (*c.*900–1200), characterised by the warmest and most stable weather since the thawing of the last ice age, gave way to the Little Ice Age (*c.*1300–1900), which, most climatologists and historians agree, was more turbulent and trying by far.[30] The perilously cold winter that afflicted Eastern Europe in 1215 was a harbinger of doom: in Poland and Russia parents resorted to selling their children into slavery and eating pine bark, so horrendous was the frost and crop failure, and a hundred years later Europe would experience the Great Famine (1315–19), which killed tens of thousands all across the continent, with 1316 being the worst cereal harvest of the entire Middle Ages. In the middle of the century, a mass of ice that normally floated at least a hundred kilometres out to sea came so close to Iceland that polar bears from Greenland slinked ashore.[31]

We know that it was not brought about by human activity but, beyond that, the causes of the Little Ice Age are contested; historians, archaeologists and climatologists do at least agree that one of the main effects of its onset was increased flooding and storms.[32] Professor Lamb suggests that the cooling Arctic strengthened the thermal gradient around the North Sea 'leading to increased incidence and severity of storms';[33] the archaeologist Dr Fraser Sturt explains that Old Winchelsea was the victim of an 'environmental double whammy', blaming not just climate change but also 'a thousand-year cycle in sea temperatures';[34] the geographer Basil Cracknell points to the surplus of water and accompanying storms and flooding brought on as a cumulative effect of the Medieval Warm Period;[35] and archaeologist Brian Fagan points to a pattern of vigorous depressions in the northern Atlantic between the Azores High and Icelandic Low (to which climate change potentially contributed) which generated mighty westerly winds as cold air thrust hot air above it, rearing the increased mass of seawater into deadly waves that pummelled fragile coastlines.[36] The worst manifestation of this deteriorating climate was the *Grote Mandrenke* (Great Drowning of Men) of 1362, the greatest North Sea disaster in history which saw up to thirty thousand dead and almost half the population of the marshland districts along the Jutland coast drowned, not to mention the inundation of substantial chunks of the city of Dunwich and the port of Ravenserodd on the North Sea coast of England. It is haunting to think that the storms that finished off Old Winchelsea are just the kind of extreme weather events that are becoming more common in our own time as a result of *man-made* climate change, much worse than anything the thirteenth or fourteenth centuries could dream up.[37]

The doomed port makes its final appearance in the historical record in 1292,[38] before vanishing for good. It was the first major town in Britain to drown since the beginning of recorded history. It would not be the last.

————

Today, the drowned town is largely forgotten. Medieval Winchelsea appears on later maps as a blotch several miles out to sea, a shadowy underwater presence. I went in search of Old Winchelsea myself one grey August afternoon in the last days of summer. I walked past solitary suburban houses and a lonely pub without seeing so much as a soul. By the shore was a long deposit of shingle – the shingle on which Old Winchelsea had once stood. For five thousand years before the town was washed away, it kept the open seas well to the south of the present Rye Bay. I clambered over, on to the beach. The sea was calm. The headland of Dungeness soaked up the day's residual sunbeams and I could just make out the black nuclear power station on its tip. Across the bay lay the cliffs of Fairlight, and St Andrew's Church. I wondered whether the bell-ringers of the old, medieval church could ever see the drowned city emerging from the tide.

It was in this very stretch of water – some six hundred years after the disappearance of Old Winchelsea – that fishermen 'often anchored their boats on the ruins of the old city' and it was exciting to imagine it all out there in the dying light – the towers, tomb-stones, bells and well shafts – mouldering beneath the waves.[39]

But this was just a flight of fancy. Because it was built on shingle, Old Winchelsea – what wasn't salvaged, at least – was dispersed in a hundred directions and lost to the waves. It was not like, say, the lost Egyptian city of Thonis-Heracleion, where soil liquefied in the third century BC after an earthquake, sending columns, urns and vast statues of animal gods fluttering to the ocean floor; nor, like Venice, doomed gradually to subside into the sea.[40] No tower tops or spires ever poked out of the sea at low tide, and geographers and archaeolo-gists believe it is unlikely any meaningful remains will ever be found because of the speed at which the spit disintegrated and the extent of coastal changes, although no one, it must be said, has attempted any deep-sea dives, unlike at certain other of Britain's drowned cities. Perhaps they would be futile anyway; one theory suggests that the stub of the old town lies *inland*, since the waters that overran Old Winchelsea would eventually become reclaimed marshland.[41] I might even have trampled over it on my way to the shore.

Yet, in some respects, it has not been *entirely* lost. Usually, when a town, city or village disappears, it either vanishes completely, becomes a ghost town or wilters to a shadow of its former self (like Trellech), or even assumes a completely different identity (as battle villages sacrificed to the war effort would in the mid-twentieth century). But Winchelsea didn't do any of these things. It was salvaged, transposed to a new site, and resurrected. Remarkably, this wasn't quite unprecedented. Some sixty years earlier, the Norman royal hilltop city of Old Sarum, in Wiltshire, 'became' the valley-bottom New Sarum, in fields three miles away. Old Sarum straddled the site of an Iron Age hillfort, with a cathedral and castle within the ancient earthworks, and its streets without. It seems the hilltop city was racked with social tension: a protracted dispute between the clergy and townsmen of Old Sarum culminated in the dean and canons receiving permission – from the Pope himself – to transfer the cathedral from the hill to the Avon meadows, where it stands to this day.[42] Henry III dished out market and fair charters and, from 1227, the cathedral on the hill was dismantled to build the new one and the old town became an economic ruin as the new city in the valley grew and flourished; its fortunes, one might say, went quite literally downhill.[43] The ghostly outline of its streets can still be made out today, etched into its abandoned hill, and New Sarum continues to prosper – as Salisbury.[44]

Today, if you turn your back to the sea at Winchelsea Beach you can just make out, several miles inland, a plateau to the left of Rye. The dense foliage can't quite obscure a tall gate and a big church. These were amongst the principal features of New Winchelsea, the town that came back from the dead. Although the body of the new town looked different in its new setting – bigger, stronger, flasher – it still beat with its old heart.

———

The locals had been up since before sunrise. It was refreshing to be free of the curfew. How could there be a curfew? There were no fortifications, no gates. Nor were the houses finished – people were still lugging beams from Icklesham, Pett and Fairlight, not to mention the watery grave of Old Winchelsea, erecting shanties in their allocated plots. These ramshackle homes probably would not stay up long – but they needed somewhere now, while they raised the money for the skilled carpentry for houses that would last. The commissioners' palisades marked the course of future streets. Livestock wandered through the building site, pigs jabbing their snouts into cauldrons of molten plaster, and rabbits were trapped underground after their warrens were covered in streets.[45] On the periphery of the hill there were still trees standing, but the centre was clear, freshly chopped. The future inhabitants of this embryonic city milled about the building site – the bereft fishermen, the salts with their leathery faces, the merchants in their green and red doublets, the Alards and their gyrfalcons in their finest silk hoods and even, at a safe distance, the lepers with their yellow cloaks and bells. There was perhaps a sense of pride in the air. Winchelsea had overcome the forces of nature and now, at a safe remove from the sea, was set to rise again as the greatest Cinque Port.

The new Winchelsea was forged to a grid plan. Its arrow-straight streets cut through each other at right angles forming a chequerboard of blocks, or 'quarters'. These, in turn, were subdivided into burgage plots for the citizens to build their houses, one for each family. The foundation rental list of 1292 is an extraordinarily detailed and precise document.[46] It bears some similarities to the burgage assessments of medieval Trellech, which were drawn up at almost exactly the same time, except here the king owned New Winchelsea directly whereas the de Clare scions were in possession of Trellech (although only in exchange for loyalty, military service and financial dues to the king, who technically, under feudalism, owned all land).

The main section, entitled 'rental of the burgage plots, 1292', begins: 'The following are the plots allocated, handed over, and rented out in the newly built town of Winchelsea' and goes on to show the name of each tenant (often the head of a family), the size of their plot (in *virgae* or perches), its location, and their annual rent.[47]

It is incredibly rare to find such a comprehensive portrait of a new town or city anywhere in medieval documents and so this affords us a striking and privileged insight into perhaps the most extraordinary of the hundreds of new towns and cities in medieval Britain; the meticulousness here stems from Winchelsea's unique circumstances and topography – the pressing need to fill a whole new city at top speed, for the king to maximise his revenue, and the chequerboard layout that allows us to reconstruct the city's geography. Many plots, at the time of assessment in 1292, would have been only semi- or shoddily built upon; as with Trellech it was the *land* that was being assessed, not the buildings (or eventual buildings) on them. The rental lists show that the thirty-nine quarters were divided into 802 plots: 723 on the hill and seventy-nine harbour plots along the Strand. Some new towns took their time to attract inhabitants; others faltered almost immediately. But the plots at New Winchelsea filled as though with water. The residents of Old Winchelsea could have moved away – to Rye, Fairlight, Southampton or even London. But that was a daunting, risky prospect. It was far easier to move up the hill and carry on with their lives, a proposal made attractive, no doubt, by Edward's promise to waive rents for the first seven years, even if the slippery monarch did renege after four years.[48] Extrapolating population figures from rental assessments is no easier for Winchelsea than it was for Trellech, with most historians positing between four thousand and six thousand people, and some later sources describe it as a city. This was substantial and Winchelsea's fabric was much more than just a blanket of residences – with guildhall, quayside, gallows, mansions, watchtowers and hospitals it contained a set of public buildings that gave the town status and scale, and landmarks that conferred a common identity upon its inhabitants. It had presence.

There were practical reasons why New Winchelsea looked the way it did. Planted towns – chief amongst them this one – may have been becoming commercially more sophisticated than the

Alfredian *burhs* that were their predecessors, but they never lost their defensive function, and here the grid came in useful. Straight thoroughfares were easier to defend than crooked streets and alleys. They were easier to keep watch over, too. Both were advantages because, lying on the southern coast, New Winchelsea would become something of a lightning rod for assaults by both domestic and overseas enemies. And notwithstanding the challenges of the hilly landscape, a chequerboard layout was the easiest way to parcel out land equally, though of course some plots were much more coveted than others, certain families took hold of multiple plots and amalgamated them, and what people could afford to build on them varied wildly. But the desirability, even genius, of the grid-plan layout transcends mere practicality. Ever since the emergence of the earliest civilisations, topography has been a powerful medium of expression. Old Winchelsea had not been dictated from above. It had, like many Anglo-Saxon ports, emerged organically, growing outwards as trade expanded, subject to no design but the passage of time, the lie of the shingle (and sea), and the daily rituals and needs of its people. Its streets sprawling over the shingle bank manifested a lack of centralised power at its inception; everyone used their topography as they saw fit. The layout of New Winchelsea, in contrast, was rich in meaning.

It was obviously, in some senses, a retort to the tyranny of nature, a display of orderliness against the chaos and caprice of the sea. Perched on a hill, New Winchelsea was untouchable, its steady rhythm of wide, criss-crossing streets a flexing of muscle against the wild and untameable forces that had laid its predecessor low. In this, the town planners were hubristic; nature was playing the long game.

But although a grid-plan topography connotes a natural egalitarianism, New Winchelsea's was predominantly an assertion of *political* power, of the muster and wherewithal needed to transform hilly woodland into rows of well-ordered streets, and in this

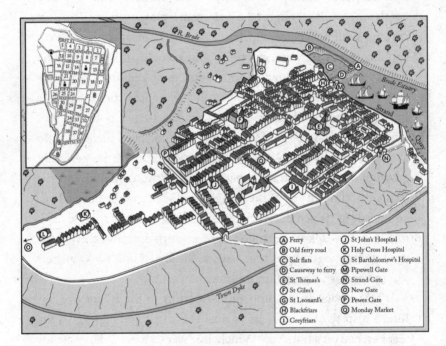

Ⓐ Ferry	Ⓙ St John's Hospital
Ⓑ Old ferry road	Ⓚ Holy Cross Hospital
Ⓒ Salt flats	Ⓛ St Bartholomew's Hospital
Ⓓ Causeway to ferry	Ⓜ Pipewell Gate
Ⓔ St Thomas's	Ⓝ Strand Gate
Ⓕ St Giles's	Ⓞ New Gate
Ⓖ St Leonard's	Ⓟ Pewes Gate
Ⓗ Blackfriars	Ⓠ Monday Market
Ⓘ Greyfriars	

New Winchelsea c.1325

Based on a model by W. M. Homan, 1941

sense New Winchelsea was but the latest incarnation of an age-old tradition. The Greeks loved grid-plan cities: they gelled with their notion of 'worldly order created out of variety'; for the Romans, too, it suited their love of military discipline and assimilatory tendencies.[49] Meticulously planned urban units were instrumental in subsuming new colonies into the empire. With the disintegration of the empire, even the most regimented cities and towns fell into disorder, and the grid-town vanished, only to be revived with the resurgence of trade, central authority and planning in the early Middle Ages. A few Anglo-Saxon *burhs* had grid-like street plans, in some cases drawing upon Roman topographies; Winchester, capital of Wessex (and eventually for a while Anglo-Saxon England) was laid out along a grid of sorts when it was revived after its post-Roman decline, without being beholden to symmetry, by the early tenth century.[50] But the first city since Roman times to be laid out with orthogonal exactitude, as far as the landscape allowed, was New Sarum, from 1219. New Winchelsea, at the end of the century, was an intensification of this urban trend. In time, the epic chequerboard would become the street-plan of choice for Baroque rulers and New World colonists who wanted to expand pre-existing cities. Some were spectacular: Salt Lake City, 'a monumental chequerboard sheltered by mountains',[51] was designed to receive Christ at the Second Coming and had a layout that allowed it to grow exponentially as the army of believers amassed.

The saviour whose power was being projected in Winchelsea was of course its founder, Edward I, and his blueprint was undoubtedly the *bastides* in his duchy of Gascony in south-west France. From the French *bastir* – to build – these were new fortified towns established by both French and English rulers to advance their economic and political interests in Aquitaine. Usually built on reclaimed forestland, *bastides* were invariably defined by thick walls, a dense swarm of houses, and most of all a grid layout. The direct inspiration for New Winchelsea was, in all likelihood, Monségur in the lowlands of rolling vines, upriver from Bordeaux.[52] Founded in 1265 by Eleanor of Provence, the wife of Henry III of England, to protect the wine trade with Gascony in south-west France, its name can be translated literally as 'hill of safety', and that's exactly how New Winchelsea was conceived as well. The link with the French *bastides* is clear – one of the commissioners appointed by Edward I to survey the site of New Winchelsea, a Gascon, was highly experienced in *bastide*-building. Another had been mayor of Bordeaux.[53] But there were *bastides* closer to home. After Edward I brought Wales to heel with the help of the Marcher lords, the ring of fortified towns he built in the most fiercely hostile districts – for example, Flint, Rhuddlan and, most magnificently, Conway – almost exactly replicated the French model, with arrow-straight streets, garrisoned castles and walls.[54] It was while he was establishing his Welsh *bastides* in the 1280s, and as Old Winchelsea slid ever further into the waters, that Edward decided to build his first English *bastide*. But this time, the enemy was as much the sea as a military aggressor (although recent research has shown there was probably a castle[55]). So Edward was able to give free rein to his urban auteur's instincts. He would do the same in the 1290s when he purchased and developed Wyke (later Kingston upon Hull)[56] to compensate for the precarious port of Ravenserodd, which, unlike Old Winchelsea, would take 130 years to vanish completely.[57]

What the inhabitants of New Winchelsea made of the grid plan is hard to say. Some no doubt admired the uniformity of the streets while others may have resented this alien structure that the king had foisted upon them; some, missing the familiarity and intrigue of Old Winchelsea's cluttered and labyrinthine streets, might perhaps have 'given the world for a crooked street', as Charles Dickens said of his reaction to 'distractingly regular' Philadelphia in 1842[58] – we simply do not know as such mindsets are not captured in the sources that survive. We can recreate a sense, however, from rent rolls, chronicles (such as that of the Anglo-Norman monk

Nicholas Trivet), later maps, royal ordinances and the natural land-scape, along with a little imagination, of what it would have been like to experience England's newest town at the turn of the thir-teenth century, of the gridded mounted citadel as it whirred to life in the late 1280s.

The way to get to New Winchelsea, for maximum visual splen-dour, and convenience, was by ferry. Visitors would have surren-dered to the ferryman's hand, falling into the downy cushions as the wherry listed a little, then glided slowly across the water. One's attention would have been drawn to the river's broad, tidal waters dissolving into Rye Bay on the horizon as ships sailed in from France, Scandinavia, the Low Countries, Castile and Portugal. A penny into the palm of the wherryman, a slippery causeway over salt ponds with their glistening white crystals, and there it was.

Winchelsea loomed over each new arrival 'from a cliff of rug-ged height', as Nicholas Trivet puts it.[59] The Strand was reached by walking up a well-rutted track, past a lonely well where ema-ciated beggars sat, to a row of private jetties and fishermen's huts, and tanners roasting hides; it may well have been the smell that first hit travellers – singed animal skin, fish, smoke, rotting en-trails, faeces and oak all interlaced with the sea's mincing breeze into a miasmic concoction. At high tide ships bobbed up and down in the anchorage, gulls swirling about their masts. Further down could be found the public quay, thronged with vessels, and the grunts and groans of workmen operating the semi-rotten wooden crane unloading, swivelling and thwacking down hogs-heads of wine torturously slowly. On the odd sorry occasion could be seen barrels plunging from the rope and crashing to the ground to the cries of merchants and ships' captains standing nearby, streams of pink-tinted wine gushing down the quayside, the cask a bloody mess.

The path up to town would not have been easy. It was so steep that had it not zigzagged with sinuous bends it would have forced 'people descending it to go headlong because of the great steepness, or people ascending it to creep up using their hands rather than to walk'.[60] It is fair to say that Winchelsea was not exactly welcoming; entrance, from seaward, was through a stately gate with a double portcullis and a siege engine on the roof, usually stocked with three hundred or so round stones to dash out the brains of any invaders. Iced in whitewash, it really *gleamed* – visible miles out to sea – and one's eye may well have been drawn to the finely carved architectural features painted brightly and colourfully (although the effect may have been ruined by watchmen's eyeballs peeping out of the murder holes). Beckoned through, fresh arrivals would have found themselves in a tiny alleyway barely wide enough to roll a barrel, wedged between the backs of houses and a clifftop rampart. In the crenellations between the earthenware rampart lay acres of glistening sea; to the left, Greyfriars' precinct where the lucky visitor may have been afforded a glimpse of the eagle they kept in captivity, sometimes tethered to the very altar.[61]

Around the next corner, the novelty and bravura of the new city would be laid bare. The nave and spire of the vast Gothic structure that greeted each new visitor would have made a mockery of the dwellings below, soaring resplendently into the sky, its transepts spread wide like the wings of an eagle. More impressive still would have been the ability to see straight down entire streets and out the other end. So often medieval streets were narrow, crooked and serpentine but here, as would have been immediately apparent, they were dead straight. Looking left, from the corner of the church, one would have been able to see into Winchelsea's southern quarter and here, as well, it would have been possible to see straight out into the Blackfriars' monastery on the edge of town and, beyond the dyke, into sheep-dotted pasture. A medieval visitor would have felt the capaciousness of the streets, the sense of order and regularity, as though someone had taken a red-hot grille and lowered it on to the town's confused medley of houses, melting them into shape like butter. One later visitor, in a report to the Privy Council, marvelled at 'the most excellent proportion thereof: being divided in to thirty-nine quarters the most part square, with streets very large and broad, all straight as the same were laid by a line'.[62] The east–west streets were simply known as 1st Street, 2nd Street, 3rd Street, like a medieval New York, and looking down them you would have been able to see for miles around: into the dark Weald, Rye, the harbour down below, or simply the sea and the sky. The sense of order, of panorama, of man's assertion over nature, would have struck even the most impassive of observers.

New Winchelsea contained a rather peculiar mixture of houses. A little saunter through the streets would have taken in vast stone mansions like 'Firebrand', built for the prominent Alard family, overlooking St Thomas's Church, but also meaner dwellings for labourers, many slipshod and dangerous (though no evidence of buried bodies whose sprits would prop up the walls), hurriedly built with very limited resources and expertise as the old town vanished, a stark manifestation of the splendour and squalor that was such an intrinsic feature of medieval urban life. A visitor arriving in 1292 could have paid a visit to, amongst others, Andrew of the Monastery in quarter 7; William Half-herring in quarter 10; Johanna Petronilla in quarter 18; and, in quarter 13, Richard Blobbere. John Death, for his part, could be found biding his time in quarter 4. One might even have been asked to share a goblet of wine with Dionysus Mares, the pretentiously christened occupier of a suitably fine house in quarter 18.[63]

The biggest houses by far were to be found in quarters 8 and 19, flanking St Thomas's Church, some long and thin with imposing frontages straddling the width of their entire plot; some occupying only a portion of it; others still occupying corner spots, much coveted, being less hemmed in, with two magnificent street facades.

The meanest dwellings were in the extreme north and south of the town, and around the odoriferous Monday Market, a medley of raucous wooden stalls selling meat, fur, dyes, copper and shoes, and burbling with the cry, 'What do ye lack?' Here could be found, amongst other things, livestock slaughtered in makeshift abattoirs and dairymaids milking, selling their produce in sheep's bladders; cats, in the shadows, sinking their teeth into rotting entrails; from a shed, a man in a dirty cassock touting tickets to the shrine of Santiago de Compostela in Galicia (clarifying that ships leave once a month and that it would be an idea to purchase some indulgences too, for, depending on the will of God, you never know when you will be thrown overboard). To the west of town could be seen, at a certain hour, farmers' wives from Icklesham streaming in with baskets of fruit balanced on their heads, and, to the south, where the pace of life was slower, three hospitals, a leper colony and a gallows. Between the wind-shaken lattice slits of the squalid dwellings on the southern side of the square could be caught the odd glimpse of women in striped cloaks caressing their hair, and trying to make eye contact with anyone who walked by. With so many sailors and pilgrims flooding into the town, they had no shortage of custom.[64]

It was possible to walk to the south-west of town to leave a votive offering beneath the altar of a dainty church, St Giles's, with its lovely green and spacious graveyard. A visitor could also have ventured to the north-west corner of the cliff if they wished to see the original settlement of Iham, including another parish church, St Leonard's with its fenced-off priest, and, indeed, the castle beyond.

The new city held great promise. If someone had paid a visit just a couple of years after it was founded they would have sensed life about the place, a real pulse, seething as it was with thousands and thousands of people – fishermen, pilgrims, merchants, gentry, priests, limners and swineherds, all trying to make a living in their self-contained hilltop world. On 1st Street, by the edge of the cliff overlooking the harbour, was a wall of clumped earth. Here, between the battlements at low tide, a visitor might have seen cogs and galleys in the harbour below, their sails furled, beached in the mud. From the yard masts flew the flags of blue shields with three golden lions, and smaller ones from the ship's castles at their bow and stern. It was from that very spot that Edward I nearly came to a sticky end as he inspected the fleet through the crenellations of the rampart when his horse, spooked by a noisy windmill, bounded over the battlements. The king's entourage and the crowd 'stood completely thunderstruck, with no one believing anything other than that the king, not appearing on the steep slope, had perished in the leap'. The people rushed forward to peer over the wall, only for the king to ride triumphantly back in through the gate a few minutes later, resurgent – the horse's fall had been broken by the soft mud. This spot was christened King's Leap.[65]

An inviting sight – almost on every street corner in the northern part of New Winchelsea – was that of the little stone doors projecting into the street. They led down to cellars. On hot summer nights, these doors were flung open as dancing shadows spilled out from within, along with chattering, clinking, laughter and lute music wafting into the streets.

These grottos were not big, about thirty square metres each, but full to the brim with hogsheads of wine – easily over a hundred in each. In some, one would have seen a series of arches connected by chamfered ribs, and every so often the flickering candlelight would have revealed the face of a gargoyle carved into a corbel. Such conspicuous architectural detailing suggests that such places were not just storage vaults but salesrooms and snug wine-tasting taverns too. Medieval wine lovers would have been delighted to find around seventy[66] of these wine caves in New Winchelsea, particularly in the wealthier, northern blocks between St Thomas's Church and 1st Street – block 8, for example, which was virtually monopolised by the Alards, who had buildings fronting on to all four sides of the quarter, had eight wine cellars, whereas there were almost none at all in the town's less salubrious southern quarters.[67] At the front of the vault could be found merchants or tradesmen – not just native vintners, but sometimes merchants in less familiar doublets and hose and with different shades of tan and mysterious accents, vintners from such places as Bruges, Ghent, Ypres, Dieppe Abbeville, Bayonne and Saint-Omer, not to mention all the visiting Gascon vintners who rented and sometimes lived in their cellars[68] – roaring and seizing barrels of wine, and, from a dramatic height, holding it over a silver-edged mazer as a rich, light-pink liquid gushed out and the customers lurched forward. New Winchelsea was an entrepôt of many goods and commodities. But wine was of key economic importance; it was wine that fuelled so much of its prosperity along with its piracy, wine that so poisoned relations with European rivals, and wine that had such a formative influence on New Winchelsea's topography; the wine that each spring gushed from an enormous wooden vat in the rich, rural heartland to the south of the Gironde estuary in France, where barefooted men and women squelched black grapes into a pulp under a scorching Bordelais sun, taking regular breaks so their sweat didn't ooze too much into the must.

Wine was one of the most widely traded valuable commodities in medieval Europe.[69] King Edward didn't just rule rain-laden Wales and windswept Northumberland but sun-kissed Aquitaine and Gascony too, where in places vines spread as far as the eye could see. Wine was the oxygen of Gascony's economy especially, and the vineyards required peace and stability to prosper.

Gascony and Aquitaine had been possessions of the Plantagenet house since 1152, when Henry Plantagenet (the future Henry II) married Eleanor of Aquitaine. Gascony was not, at first, a major source of England's wine; it was too far away for that, which made the vineyards of Normandy a much better prospect. But that changed with the collapse of English power in Normandy in the twelfth century. By the thirteenth century, Gascon wine had captured the English market – of the 348 casks taken as import duty by the king in 1212–13, 80 per cent hailed from Gascony[70] – and the transformation of the province's economy was extreme. Vineyards multiplied, spreading over more and more of the countryside. Villages, farms and entire forests were cleared to make way for the grape. They crept up close to the very walls of Bordeaux, capital of Aquitaine, erupting into the city itself. In time, hardly any other crop was being grown. The Bordelais had become a vine monoculture – bare essentials like cloth, timber and meat now had to be shipped in from England, including from Winchelsea, further tightening the ties between the two lands. More expensive sweet wines – malmsey, rumney, vernage, tyre, muscadel or Greek wine – were still imported from the Mediterranean region, but thanks to the English demand, Gascony emerged as one of the biggest wine-producing regions in the world and, just as New Winchelsea's wine cellars were being built, England entered a golden age of wine. With the outbreak of the Hundred Years War in 1337, it would be a long while before it flowed so cheaply and abundantly again.

Following fermentation, the wine was decanted into wooden casks, loaded on to cogs, and transported across the high seas to the ports of northern Europe. Oxygen is wine's worst enemy and in a world yet to discover the wonders of cork (which was used mainly for the soles of shoes, not preserving wine), or any kind of foolproof airtight container, good wine was new wine, or at least that year's wine. There was no concept of 'a good vintage', no one lusting after a bottle of *1284*, for example, and year-old wine was halved in price as soon as the new shipment arrived, or sometimes just poured away.

Fermentation complete, the sooner the wine could be transported and stored somewhere cool and dry – like one of Winchelsea's seventy cellars – the better. But the journey could be perilous. English merchants had to brave the swirling, sandy currents of the Gironde estuary, the law-starved settlements strung out along its banks, and the tempestuous waters of the Bay of Biscay; there was hardly any shelter for ships between the Gironde estuary and La Rochelle. Many never made it back. But not, usually, because of shipwrecks. It was the fate of so many poorly defended vessels to spot the dark silhouette of enemy cogs rearing from the mist like floating crucifixes. Soon after this, all hands would be dead, thrashing and drowning in the waves, as the pirates looked on and treated themselves to some delicious plundered wine. The men of Winchelsea were amongst the worst of them. In 1387, they were part of a fleet that overcame sixty ships off the Flemish coast, capturing over nine thousand tuns of wine. Frequently, wine intended for Southampton, for Bruges, for Cologne, for Gothenburg would instead gush into Winchelsea. No thought was spared for how, exactly, it had been procured. Among those who eagerly bought up barrels of wine raided from a Nantes merchant at a later date were Lady Popham of Buckland, Oxfordshire, and the Abbot of Tavistock, a notorious drunk, who bought 4,500 gallons.[71] When the cogs finally dropped anchor, the casks – obtained legally or illicitly – were unloaded, rolled up the hill and delivered to the cellars, for tasting. And what exactly did they taste, the vintners, or indeed the townsfolk of Winchelsea, in their dark, candlelit vaults?

Assuming it hadn't degenerated into a foul vinegary guck, they experienced a very light red wine – soft, with a bit of an afterkick. Fresh-tasting, it was more like modern-day rosé than claret – though confusingly it was called *clairet*. Mature citizens who'd grown up in Old Winchelsea would have found the wine's tint an exciting novelty; the old wines from Normandy had invariably been white and, in the best cases, 'clear as a sinner's tears'.[72]

If it *did* taste repugnant, the vintners had a number of tricks up their sleeves to hoodwink buyers. They liked to make bitter or sour wines appear sweet by persuading people to eat liquorice, nuts, strong salty cheese or spicy snacks before they drank. They might add pitch, wax and 'other horrible and unwholesome things' to spoiled wine to disguise the taste, and one of their oldest tricks was to soak a vessel in good wine – to accrue the right smell – then fill it with bad wine. These observations are from the fourteenth-century treatise *Liber Vinis*, which provides the first genuinely medieval perspective on wine, written at precisely the time New Winchelsea's star was rising.[73] It features a wealth of further advice for the rightly cautious buyer. You can tell if wine's been diluted, he says, by putting a pear into it – if it floats, the wine is pure, if not, you should take the vintner to a piepowder court for trial. Spit out any wine that feels 'slimy in the mouth' immediately. Wine may have been precious, fragile and easily corrupted but it was also a mysterious elemental force: never to be decanted beneath a full moon; thunder and lightning would ruin it, even in its cask (unless you stuff rye dough into the bunghole, that is); and ideally it should be tasted in a midday autumn wind, when wines are at their most changeable, never a north wind.[74]

The casks – corrupted or not – were eventually sold to the agents of various monasteries, mansions and sometimes the royal court itself. The remainder found its way into the town's priories, grand households and taverns. But not the peasant hovels. In Winchelsea, as in much of northern Europe, wine was confined to the social elite. It was the drink of knights and gentlewomen, clergy and scribes, falconers and tradesmen. This was unequivocally not the case elsewhere. In southern Europe, where vineyards prospered in abundance, wine was habitually drunk by the entire social spectrum. A tax return from the Provençal town of Carpentras, for instance, shows that nine in ten inhabitants stored wine in their houses; in Tuscany, builders and labourers could legally refuse to work if no wine was forthcoming; and in Florence the people drank, on average, 270 bottles of wine a year.[75] And not just the adults. An Italian medical tract from 1275 has the following, alarming sentence: 'When the time comes that the child is half a year or a year old . . . the wet-nurse should wean him off wine as much as possible,' something it concedes may well be impossible perhaps because, as another pamphlet advises, babies should be given wine along with breast milk;[76] another regimen directs mothers to feed their babies 'wine soup', it being 'very good' for their nourishment and growth, claiming that this was common practice amongst poor women in Italy.[77] There were no scenes remotely like this in Winchelsea. Owing to its cooler climate and somewhat less abundant sunlight, England, in common with much of the rest of northern Europe, had a far less prodigious viticulture. At the time New Winchelsea was built, there were some vineyards, attributable to the slightly more favourable temperatures in the Medieval Warm Period – forty-two manors are listed as having them in the Domesday Book – but they were never much of a commercial concern, and they dwindled dramatically as the Little Ice Age descended, and were all gone by 1400. In the first decade of the new town's existence, a gallon of *clairet* bought in bulk cost between 3d and 4d; by the cup in a tavern, ½d or 1d. At a time when a building labourer would earn, on average, just 2d a day, that was a serious extravagance. That is not to say profligate labourers *never* indulged. But ale was the labourer's drink.

Every time anyone, whoever they were, had a glug of wine in New Winchelsea, they were participating in a ritual that stretched back to antiquity, where wine was worshipped for its creative, philosophical and merrymaking properties. In the Middle Ages, wine was seen as a gift from nature to take the edge off life's miseries. In 1303, just a decade after the residents of New Winchelsea first took up their leases, a horticulturalist from Bologna described wine as something that 'comforted the body and rejoiced the heart' and 'took away sorrow from the soul';[78] with its 'sweet scent', 'attractive colour' and 'delicious flavour that lingers sweetly on the tongue', another, later writer described it as 'the creator of the world's happiness'.[79] It was a creative muse, inspiring 'genius and poetical fury'[80] and a notable prophylactic too, 'carrying goodness through all the members of the body with delectation'.[81] In the cellars you may well have been able to try ox-tongue wine which 'heals the insane and the demented'; 'wine in which gold has been quenched' which 'preserves youth'; 'eyebright wine' to keep the memory sharp; 'sage wine' to treat lung disease; and the wonderful purgative that was 'winter-cherry wine' which precipitated an irrepressible urge to urinate.[82]

Wine, whether in the Roman Empire or medieval Christendom, was spiritually charged. Jesus liked wine. Noah's first act after the flood was to plant a vineyard, showing he had got his priorities absolutely right. It lay, in fact, right at the heart of Christian doctrine and liturgy. In the Roman world, wine-drinkers believed they were physically ingesting the spirit of Bacchus (which was what made them merry); Christians believed they were ingesting the body and blood of Christ every time they received the Eucharist, redeeming them in the eyes of God. Medieval wine, then, held the keys to salvation but it presented dangers too. Wine could be, as Chaucer put it, 'the tomb of a man's wit and judgement and discretion';[83] too much, wrote another, could 'betray secrets, the very preparative to a thousand rapes and murders'.[84]

A fabulous quantity of wine was imported into New Winchelsea. In 1306–7 alone, it received nearly six million pints – 737,000 gallons to be precise – in twenty-one shipments; and that was just on Winchelsea ships.[85] The amount of wine gushing in swelled significantly after 1278, when the Cinque Ports were exempted from the royal duty or *prise* on wine, in gratitude for their naval service. The sheer number of wine cellars testifies to the extraordinary fecundity and profitability of the wine trade, predominantly with Gascony but also Spain, the Low Countries, Germany and Italy. Only the cities of Southampton, Norwich, Chester – all much bigger places – and of course London had more. Even the king sometimes hired vaults here, unsurprising since New Winchelsea was a frequent point of muster for his annual expeditions to Gascony – in 1297 it provided one-third of the naval force, including many of the biggest ships; this is part of the reason Edward, and Henry II before him, were so concerned with preserving the town's fortunes. And so, compared to other English ports of comparable size, Winchelsea was awash with wine. In wine it found its prosperity, in wine it found its status, and in wine it found its swagger.

———

On Southampton beach a throng of onlookers craned their necks to get a good look at the menacing ships – seventeen in number – drifting towards the shore. It was 30 September 1321. Most, eventually, ran. A patter of pebbles filled the air; it was a special Winchelsea barbarity to hang their enemies' corpses from the masts of their ships next to dead dogs, like butchers' meat in the wind, feet kicking paws, heads knocking snouts. Southampton was one of Winchelsea's main commercial rivals and, accordingly, they hated it, and were delighted to attack it without much compunction. The mayor of Southampton gave the aggressors two of the finest boats in the port in an effort to pacify them, but instead they burnt fifteen boats, including the pair they had been given. They then sailed off.[86]

It is likely that it had been Gervase Alard's idea to terrorise the port of Southampton to ensure that it would not dare – or be in a position – to encroach upon Winchelsea's maritime trade. Royal punishment was always too weak to deter such acts of piracy and the king was keen not to alienate the Cinque Ports who provided him with so many ships. The marauding crews rarely had any sense of national loyalty, unless it suited them to do so.

Gervase Alard was the latest scion of a long dynasty of Winchelsea magnates. Since the inception of New Winchelsea, they had occupied Firebrand, one of the impressive stone mansions in the town, occupying a prime position in quarter 25 right opposite the Monday Market. The Alards were frequent holders of the annually elected mayoralty, although it's fair to say their 'election' didn't come without quite a degree of coercion. Once they were in power – and even when they weren't – they excelled in the art of piracy. It wasn't as though piracy was illegal – in fact, there was no real distinction between legitimate and illegitimate trade, and kings shared in the bounty of plundered ships, at times actively encouraging piracy. Anyone in a ship was potentially a pirate.

As this shows, a surprising feature of medieval England is how readily English towns were prepared to attack one another – and savagely – on land or at sea, even during times of relative national political stability. Many of the coastal towns of Hampshire, Sussex and East Anglia, such as Southampton, Dunwich, Norwich and indeed Winchelsea, were especially guilty. In the Middle Ages the king's power was highly decentralised, compelling him to rely upon provincial magnates to enforce his authority; even the most peripatetic of kings couldn't hope to assert his rule in person. But the magnates weren't seriously brought (or bought) to heel until Henry Tudor took the throne in 1485 and subsequently enmeshed them in a web of recognisances and bonds, guaranteeing their lawful conduct. Thitherto, private armies, over-mighty magnates and power-hungry town and city corporations were the order of the day. Commerce and political self-interest could often undermine dynastic loyalty. The struggle for dominion of the North Sea herring trade, say, could easily trump the magnates' responsibility to uphold the king's law, particularly when royal authority was weak. So while coastal towns like Winchelsea and Southampton weren't technically at war, they existed in a near-perpetual state of commercial rivalry that sometimes erupted into violence. It occasionally suited the monarchy to define these affronts to royal authority as piracy, and this was precisely what 'strong kings' like Edward I periodically punished Winchelsea for. Nonetheless, if the 'pirates' of Winchelsea had so few qualms about attacking English ships, it's not hard to imagine what they did to hostile foreign forces.

Wine fuelled war. In 1349, the Castilian pirate Don Carlos de la Cerda, goaded by the French, captured some English vessels bringing back wine from the Bordelais and hurled the crew overboard, watching them drown in glee. Edward III (Longshanks's grandson) took his revenge the next year, spurred on by further acts of piracy in the Channel and by de la Cerda's outrageously hubristic pledge (perhaps made after drinking a cask or two) to 'destroy the English fleet, obtain dominion over the English sea, and then invade England and exterminate its people'.[87] Calculating that the Castilian fleet would have to return from Flanders before the equinoctial gales, Edward ordered a mass mobilisation of divine support to be delivered by his archbishops, commandeered thirty-five vessels from Kent and Sussex, impressed hundreds of seamen, and sailed to the most strategically advantageous spot: Winchelsea. Assuming command of his flagship, the cog *Thomas*, carrying 360 men, he lay in wait.

According to the chronicler Froissart, Edward III prepared for his engagement with the enemy flotilla, which on strength of numbers alone seemed destined to win, by drinking heavily. 'He was as joyous as he had ever been in his life,'[88] we are told, 'and ordered his minstrels to play before him a German dance', glancing up at the small castle in the mast from time to time, where he had installed a watch. He had taken on board with him four folding seats, pillowcases of fine linen and a featherbed, and was dandily clad in a black velvet jacket and a beaver-skin hat ('which became him much'). It was a clear summer's day. He and his men continued to guzzle down delicious wines, dancing to the music, priming themselves for the bloodshed ahead. When a watchman shouted, 'Ho! I spy a ship, and it appears to me to be a Spaniard,' the minstrels screeched to a halt and the watchman was asked how many ships he could see. 'I see two, three, four,' came the answer, 'and so many that, God help me, I cannot count them.' In total, there were forty-five, ten more than the English, all much bigger, sturdier and better armed. The king, emboldened by wine, ordered every single vessel under his command on a direct collision course with the Castilian fleet, an expression of bacchanalian fury against the people who counted de la Cerda amongst their number. Trumpets blasted, the ships assumed battle formation, and the king ordered yet more wine for him and his knights – against such appalling odds, they probably needed it. With the wind in their favour, the Castilians could quite easily have avoided 'speaking with the English' as Froissart puts it, 'but their pride and presumption made them act otherwise'.

The queen, Philippa of Hainault, safe in a convent nearby, de-manded an hourly report from the battlefront; there was every chance she would never see her husband again, nor her son, the Black Prince, nor even her ten-year-old grandson who had been taken along for the ride.[89] Shielding their eyes from the sun and staring out into the horizon, it's hard to imagine her emissaries could have gleaned anything of consequence in the first couple of hours. And indeed the tiny specks coming together on the hori-zon, silently, could give no sense at all of the barely imaginable horrors unfolding out at sea.

As the Castilian flagship approached the *Thomas* at full pelt the king screamed, 'I will have a tilt with him!' Froissart tells us the col-lision was 'like the crash of a torrent or tempest', knocking the fight-ing platform at the tip of the Castilian vessel's mast into the sea, where all its defenders drowned. The cog *Thomas* then grappled an-other Castilian vessel with chains and hooks and the two crews fired arrows at one another, a recipe for instant mass death. Rocks were hurled from fighting tops, dashing sailors' brains out, and large stones and iron bars bored holes in their decks, allowing water to surge in. Bags of quicklime were thrown into the faces of the enemy to blind them. Limbs flailing, they fell into the sea to drown. The mini-castles balanced on the bow and stern of medieval cogs were designed to add height to the deck, facilitating the boarding of enemy vessels (via the 'bridge') – according to Froissart, this is where the English had the advantage. Repeatedly, English crews boarded Castilian vessels, engaged in gallant hand-to-hand combat and then threw the crews overboard. The Black Prince only survived the battle after the duke of Lancaster surreptitiously boarded a Castilian vessel that had grappled the prince's own ship and single-handedly overpowered its defences, allowing the prince and his men to step on board as their own cog sank.

By nightfall, the Castilians had lost fourteen ships. The rest had fled. The trumpeters sounded a retreat and the victorious fleet returned to Winchelsea harbour. After the battle there was much rejoicing, much whoring and much minstrelsy, and a lavish feast was held. The vanquishers were treated to such things as hunks of meat which they devoured, stuffed dormice and endless red wine – some

no doubt imported from the land of their would-be destroyers – as though they were gurgling down the blood of their enemies. The revelries continued late into the night, and, drunk as they were on their success, songs were sung, no doubt, about their glorious victory at the Battle of Winchelsea. Some old banqueters may have remembered the genesis of New Winchelsea in 1292, and that sense of optimism, of promise, must have seemed to have been realised by 1350. Winchelsea was now the chief of the Cinque Ports. It had the honour of being a muster ground for royal naval campaigns. It had more stone mansions than most of the largest English towns. Its pirates were feared all over the land and not unheard of on the Continent. In physical size, it wasn't much smaller than the City of London, and conditions were ripe for rapid population growth. It could continue to flourish in a way that Trellech had never managed. Those who felt the girth of its streets, those who sipped sweet muscat of a summer evening and witnessed a royal muster, those who took in its cosmopolitan aura and sense of uncoiled potential could only feel, quite justifiably, that Winchelsea was set to become one of England's major commercial towns – or cities.

———

The journey from London to Winchelsea takes about an hour by train. On the platform is a large white sign announcing that Winchelsea is an 'ancient Cinque Port'. But it doesn't really have a station, this port of grand historic importance. You just step across the rail on to a raised platform. It takes about twenty-five minutes to reach the town, a pleasant walk through Ferry Fields, where cows and sheep graze. The ferry itself, though, as the name suggests, is long gone, and the stream-like River Brede is a pathetic parody of the broad, tidal estuary where ships from all over Europe once anchored. There is no Strand – only Tanyard Lane, no doubt a reference to the old waterfront tanneries – and the harbour plots are now occupied by suburban houses with sprawling gardens. After about twenty minutes I reached a lonely canal with an old timber-framed house overlooking it, Strand House, where I was staying. It had once stood next to the public quay where pilgrims set sail, and was more latterly a brothel, then a workhouse. The proprietor couldn't quite accept that I'd come to spend the weekend in the 'village' of Winchelsea as she disconcertingly kept calling it, dispensing all sorts of wisdom about Rye instead and never quite answering my questions about the ancient Cinque Port.

The minute I arrived in the main part of the town I could see why. I walked up the steep hill, through Strand Gate – now hollow and dull grey, open to the sky – on to what was once 3rd Street, now the high street. It was a Saturday afternoon but there were hardly any signs of life, just a couple of silent drinkers staring into space in the village's one pub (no Gascon rosé on sale), a genial old man taking his dog for a walk on St Leonard's cricket ground, and someone in a high-vis jacket that said 'speed watch', pointing a camera at non-existent cars.

Winchelsea today is a spectral echo of its former self, at its core a series of pleasant-looking houses around a semi-ruined church, which, even with its skeletal transepts and vanished spire, seems absurdly out of proportion with the rest of the village. The medieval grid is still in evidence but everything feels *slow*. With its wide, spacious streets and striking hilltop location, panoramic views of the marshland and ocean beyond, it's the perfect place for a stroll; is in fact the quintessence of tranquillity – not a drunk pirate wiping his mouth on the altar cloth nor a homicidal king in sight.

Some of the medieval stone mansions still survive, or at least their architectural carcasses do, since they have been much renovated over the centuries: Firebrand on the High Street where the Alards once dwelled; the Court Hall, further down the same street, now a fascinating museum with a large-scale model of Winchelsea at the height of its powers in 1325, where a retired oil executive volunteering for the day enthused about the city in all its medieval bravura; and the Armoury on Castle Street. But all the timber-framed houses have gone and it's impossible to get anywhere near the remains of Greyfriars' Monastery, despite its being reckoned one of the finest examples of monastic architecture in the country by as esteemed an architectural critic as Nikolaus Pevsner. The tradition of keeping a live eagle in captivity survived the Dissolution of the Monasteries in the early sixteenth century; there was one squawking in the ruins of the chapel until at least the late eighteenth century.[90] The other houses are either mainly brick-fronted Georgian (purchased or rented by the garrison of five hundred soldiers stationed here during the Napoleonic Wars, as attested by the place names Barrack Square, the Armoury, Cooks Green and Magazine House[91]); stuccoed Victorian, or more recent builds, all respectable, some handsome, dating from the post-war period when Winchelsea grew into a bucolic retreat for London commuters and well-off retirees, the new houses neatly marshalled into the town's still-impressive grid. One house in the north-eastern corner of town overlooking the motionless marshland below is called King's Leap. And most conspicuously, seventeen wine cellars survive – albeit in the majority of cases without their original houses – that can be visited on special quarterly tours. Dark, damp and deadly silent, they are rather dismal places; it is hard to imagine them bursting with life and brimming with bodies in their prime, so evocative of the cosmopolitanism and conviviality of the brand-new medieval town.

What is most striking, though, is how abruptly the town melts away after St Thomas's Church. By the time you reach the site of Monday Market, you are in rugged fields. You can walk for twenty minutes, feeling like you've left Winchelsea far behind, until you find the ruins of its three hospitals, sorrowful stone shards up-ended in the grass, and all the way to the edge of the dyke, uneasy ruts and bumps where long-vanished houses, stone-vaulted cellars and St Giles's Church once stood. These are Winchelsea's ghost streets. The sight of the seven-hundred-year-old New Gate marooned at the southern end of the old town makes the soul quiver; there it stands forlorn, a stranded portal to a lost world. 'The ancient gates stand near three miles from one another over the fields,' wrote Daniel Defoe in his *A Tour through the Whole Island of Great Britain* (1722), three hundred years ago, 'and the very ruins are so buried, that they have made good corn fields of the streets, and the plough goes over the foundations, nay, over the first floors of the houses,'[92] capturing so beautifully Winchelsea's surreal collision of the agrarian and the urban. He was not the only prolific writer to be drawn to Winchelsea. 'I walked over to survey the ruins of

Winchelsea,' wrote the diarist and virtuoso John Evelyn in 1652, 'finding only the ruins of ancient streets and public structures.' He sees vast caves and vaults – relics of Winchelsea's lost wine wealth – and from the relics of monasteries, mansions towers and a 'sumptuous' church he senses that it was 'once a considerable and large *city*', but now 'all in rubbish, and a few despicable hovels and cottages only standing'.[93]

Evelyn must have seen a handful of the new mansions erected during the Tudor and early Stuart era, but in what was recognised to have been a rural style, as though Winchelsea had ceased to be an urban entity altogether, just as its two MPs would ultimately represent a ghost constituency: it was a notorious rotten borough. Defoe wrote of the 'skeleton of an ancient city' and later in the eighteenth century John Wesley, who preached his final sermon under a tree (since replanted) near the ruined church of St Giles, also described it as a 'poor skeleton', contrasting its lamentable condition with the beauty of its medieval hilltop setting. 'I stood under a large tree,' he recalls, 'and called to most of the inhabitants of the town, "The Kingdom of heaven is at hand; repent, and believe the Gospel!"'[94] It must have been a pitiful contrast with the sermons preached at the inception of the new medieval city in the 1290s, full of fire and hope.

They were all responding, in one way or another, to the dramatic depopulation and decline of New Winchelsea; to the poetic beauty of its slow and torturous ruin. It was a sensation that would turn Victorian Winchelsea into a honeypot for painters, poets and novelists of Romantic sensibilities. What by then really was just a village could count amongst its visitors or residents Joseph Turner, conjurer of tempestuous seascapes, who sketched and painted the town; the pre-Raphaelite painter and poet Dante Gabriel Rossetti; the novelist William Thackeray, who set one of his novels in the smugglers' paradise of late Georgian Winchelsea; and even, for a while,[95] that great observer of darkness within the human soul,

Joseph Conrad, who rented a cottage next door. Rossetti went into raptures about 'the pleasant doziness of the place', delighting in the pompousness of the inauguration of the Sessions ceremony with the mayor and his officials in scarlet robes with ancient silver maces in front of a 'mob' of one girl in the street and, it transpired, with absolutely no cases to hear. 'Everyone is eighty-two if he is not ninety-six,' he adds.[96] But the presence of so many illustrious figures speaks to the allure of ruin, loss and absence, the dramatic counterpoint of what Winchelsea once was and what it had become – a spur to the muse (as indeed an even bigger drowned medieval city would be at just the same time – one to which I would also in time be drawn, on the crumbling Suffolk coast). It is no coincidence that the first real history of Winchelsea was published in 1850, allowing people to flesh out its much-decayed grandeur, and the reasons for it.

———

As the sun sank beneath a mauve sky, I set out to explore the little paths and tracks that once led away from Monday Market, and it was there, in the dying light, that I found Deadman's Lane. At first, I assumed this must have been the site of the gallows or a plague pit – like most Sussex towns, Winchelsea was decimated by the Black Death – but it in fact takes its name from one of the darkest chapters in New Winchelsea's history, one that contributed to its eventual demise.

I walked into a tunnel of overhanging branches, squelching ever deeper into the mud, the wind quiet and slow. The lane seemed to get thinner and thinner and I emerged into the foreground of a bright vista with a forlorn, semi-built house to my side. The track once led away from the churchyard of St Giles's, the second, much smaller parish church in quarter 21 which has long since vanished. In the Middle Ages, churches were understood to be sanctuaries where anyone could seek refuge whether from the law or an enemy, protected by God and the miraculous properties of saints. So what happened in 1360 must have seemed the worst kind of sacrilege. On 15 March, a marauding band of between fifteen hundred and three thousand French soldiers[97] – on horseback and foot – burst into New Winchelsea and charged through the streets, hurling flaming torches into the wooden houses and cutting down anyone who stood in their way. They had meant to land at Sandwich, where they had hoped to destroy Edward III's dockyard and, from there, rescue their king, Jean II, who had been imprisoned at Somerton Castle for four years.[98] But they overshot Sandwich, instead alighting on the banks of the River Rother, and headed for the nearest town in search of indiscriminate plunder: New Winchelsea, whose walls were still only semi-built.

Galloping through the streets, they invaded St Giles's Church, where many of the townsfolk had been attending Sunday mass. The terrified congregants cowered behind statues of the hermit saint, but to no avail. Chroniclers report[99] how women were gang-raped, mutilated and murdered. Everyone in the church – the men, women, children and infants – were put to the sword and eventually dumped in a long, twisting row leading away from the churchyard. This marked the future Deadman's Lane. Though people were cut down elsewhere, it has been argued that the ferocity of the attack in St Giles's in particular suggests that the French saw the invocation of sanctuary as a highly provocative act.[100] Had the pirates of Winchelsea inflicted a similar kind of outrage on Norman coastal towns? We know, for instance, that in 1337 they fired part of Boulogne and hanged twelve French captains of the captured fleet. And in 1378, the combined efforts of Winchelsea and Rye's pirates slaughtered anyone who couldn't pay ransom in Peter's Haven on the coast of Normandy, flinging them overboard to drown.[101] No doubt many of Winchelsea's other attacks upon France went unrecorded.

The invaders plundered stores of wine and wool, sank the king's galley *La Jerusalem* and set fire to much of the town. 'They killed all that resisted them regardless of sex, age or station,' recalled the chronicler Thomas Walsingham. 'It was a barbaric and devilish assault.'[102] As the sun began to set, the Sussex men appeared on the edge of town and the French beat their retreat howling with laughter and suffering only minor losses themselves. Thirty-five Winchelsea grandees and hundreds of inhabitants were murdered that day. Nine women were hauled on to French galleys never to be seen again.[103]

New Winchelsea was already in decline[104] thanks to the Black Death and a diminution in trade with Gascony, but the raid left a terrible legacy. A list of 'decayed rents' from 1363 – two years after the raid – reveals 409 properties in ruins.[105] That was just over half of the town. By the end of the decade hardly any of those houses had been rebuilt. It seems that St Giles's Church was for ever tainted by the atrocity, falling into ruin, fading into oblivion. Plenty more horror lay in store; no one could have imagined that the massacre of 1360 was just the opening salvo in a succession of French and Castilian attacks. Between 1360 and 1389 alone there were seven separate invasions. They were of varying degrees of savagery, but collectively they traumatised New Winchelsea's inhabitants and ravaged her buildings. New Winchelsea, 'which was once well inhabited, but being burned by the King's enemies and much more by the withdrawal of burgesses' had become, by the penultimate decade of the fourteenth century, 'now so desolate and almost destroyed that the proprietorship of vacant plots and tenements can scarcely be known'.[106] In other words it had become a ghost town. But even this needn't have been fatal. Medieval towns could prove resilient. Hastings, Rye, Southampton – all bounced back from various firings and pillaging at the hands of French and Spanish privateers in exactly the same period. There was no reason why Winchelsea couldn't as well.

New Winchelsea's fortunes had always been determined by the sea and yet, just as the city was being ransacked and burned by the

French, its tidal flow became compromised. [107] An accumulation of shingle, amassing eastwards, began to block Winchelsea's harbour. This diminished the power of the tide to clear the harbour of silt. The problem was compounded by the tendency of mooring ships to dump their ballast in the anchorage and the habit of those who lived around the Brede Estuary, including Winchelsea residents, to reclaim parcels of the harbour from the sea for farmland and salt works. It was death by a thousand cuts: every time a skipper flung gravel or sand into the harbour, or a farmer or burgher with a harbourside plot eyed a patch of water, they jeopardised New Winchelsea's future. Royal proclamations against ballast dumping and 'innings' were issued and ignored;[108] gradual economic strangulation was less conspicuous than a climactic spectacular, and easier to ignore. Larger ships that came into currency from the fourteenth century ran into the mud at low tide.[109] And so the sea continued its sorry retreat. Trade, fishing and pilgrim expeditions dwindled accordingly.[110] By 1524, Winchelsea could provide only four ships to the Cinque Port fleet (rather than ten, as it had in 1491); twenty years later, it mustered six hoys. This is suggestive of a rapid acceleration in the silting of the harbour. Over the centuries, the once-sizeable estuary narrowed to the dismal little stream I'd seen in front of my hotel. To this day, the landscape feels desolate, as though the sea has only just beaten its retreat. What weathercocks we are to nature's caprice. New Winchelsea suffered for other reasons: trade shifted from south-eastern ports (London excepted) to western rivals, better placed to trade with the Mediterranean after the outbreak of the Hundred Years' War; the herring trade with Great Yarmouth declined. But other towns like Rye bounced back.[111] Winchelsea did not. The very water that had drowned Old Winchelsea now, in its absence, parched New Winchelsea, slowly reducing it to 'a port of stranded pride'.[112]

Deprived of its *raison d'être*, Winchelsea haemorrhaged inhabitants faster than *clairet* gushing from a hogshead in one of its cellars. The loss was so great that in 1415 the civic authorities decided to shrink the town, guillotining it at 6th Street and reducing the town's size by three-fifths, effectively turning it into a village. It was to be fastened in place by a new stone wall. Many of the north–south and east–west courses were blocked off, particularly those leading to Icklesham, Rye Ferry and the southern villages, bringing a newfound sense of isolation to the hilltop rump. New gates were built; houses were destroyed to make way for the wall. Everything south of the 6th Street perimeter – the houses, hospitals, monasteries, leper colony, church, recreation land, fortifications, even the Monday Market itself – was marooned in a shadowy hinterland between the new walls and the villages to the south. Only, the new stone walls were never built – they were unnecessary for what was fast becoming a provincial backwater.

By 1565, there were only 109 houses – inhabited houses, that is – left, down from 409 in 1363.[113] The town had been reduced to a quarter of its size and the Winchelsea Corporation bemoaned 'the poor and most lamentable state' of the town; thirty years later, at the turn of the seventeenth century, the population had shrunk to 120. It had become a shadow of its former self, a mockery – by 1587 there was only one sailor left in the entire port, one William Bucston, and no ships at all.[114] By this point it was absurd that such a place still had its own lord mayor and aldermen – let alone would continue to send two MPs to Parliament for another 250 years – and this was not lost on town officials, who developed something of a feverish obsession with arcane ritual and civic protocol in the absence of real status and power.

By the time of Elizabeth I's death in 1603 only ninety people lived in Winchelsea's thirty houses, St Thomas's was in ruins, many of the cellars were occupied by smugglers, grass was growing through the cracks in the pavement, and the Monday Market would shortly become a bowling green. All this because, as Evelyn later put it, 'the sea, which formerly rendered it a rich and commodious port, has now forsaken it'.[115] Things never improved and, as Daniel Defoe put it, 'nothing of a town but the destruction of it seems to remain'.[116]

CHAPTER FOUR

THE DESERTED VILLAGE: WHARRAM PERCY[I]

The tower was by far the most haunting part of the ruin, scoured open like a dissected vein and chomped, as it seemed to me, by a beast with many teeth. It collapsed sixty years ago, revealing, through excavations, that a timbered church had stood here in the twelfth century. The sky is keyholed through a succession of Normanesque window frames and at the top of the tower is a small parapet – owing to the irregular shading of its slabs and positioning, it seems to have an eerie otherworldly glow as if from another dimension.

I saw some other visitors – a middle-aged couple hunched

over a guidebook and some parents dragging their teenager on an unwanted day out. There were some rain-splattered signs in front of empty fields, but it was not long before everyone's attention was hijacked by the ghostly church of St Martin looming above the fish-pools. It is the undoubted centrepiece of the deserted village, a true spectacle of devastation and loss. Everywhere I looked, there were tracks rutted into the ground by the load of centuries. A sagging sensation filled the whole site, with everything rolling down to the dale through which the Wharram stream whittles. Beyond that, a shield of trees, and the wider countryside – the Yorkshire Wolds – unfurl.

Wharram Percy is often described as 'Europe's best-known deserted medieval village', but visitors hoping to find a freeze-framed medieval world are likely to be disappointed. All you can really see, at first glance, is a field of lumpy grass, bounded by a ditch, giving way to meadows. Beyond that lie much later buildings: a vicarage, a row of labourers' cottages and a solitary farmhouse.[2]

Established in the late Anglo-Saxon period, between AD 850 and 950, Wharram Percy exists on the site of an earlier Middle Saxon settlement, and was continuously occupied for around six hundred years.[3] It was part of a broader trend – the rise of the village. During the ninth and tenth centuries, many of Britain's dispersed farmsteads, some of which drew upon boundaries that were first laid out by barrows, cairns and other Neolithic structures five thousand years earlier, were beginning to coalesce into larger, nucleated settlements. This was especially true in the parts of Britain with the best arable soil, particularly in south-central and north-eastern Britain.[4] They evolved gradually, over about three hundred years, initially as hamlets of up to eight nucleated farmsteads, and subsequently more, called villages, usually centred upon a church and high street. These were surrounded by large open fields which were divided into strips and worked by peasants, and administered by a manorial court that decided which field to leave fallow each year and what crops would be grown on which strip.[5] They have been described as 'an economic response to food insecurity', allowing 'more people to live off less land',[6] and the manor court system was a manifestation of feudalism whereby landowners rented out land to farmers.

Much of Wharram Percy's topography can be discerned from the turbulent grass up on the plateau, even more so if you have a flying licence. On the site are the foundations of two manor houses, buried in the grass. The north manor, home of the Percy family for over 150 years, commanded the plateau. Its earthworks hint at a large hall, commodious barn and a dovecote. The south manor, thought to have been built around 1166 and inhabited by the Percys until they moved to the north manor in 1254, was at the forefront of a large rectangular enclosure that dominated the scarp and church. It had a stone undercroft that was used as a meeting room – possibly for the manorial court – and a conspicuous chamber perched on top.

Sunk into the grass are the outlines and foundations of around forty peasant dwellings and their barns and outbuildings. Several of these have visible doorways and separate rooms. The tofts (house plots) and crofts (their attached strips of land) are in three well-ordered rows, laid out between 1166 and the late thirteenth century, stratified by peasant status.[7] The villeins (those obliged to work the lords' lands and execute manual labour but with the right to farm common fields too)[8] were to be found in North Row; the cottars (also tied to the lord of the manor but who farmed much less land, perhaps just a few strips in the arable fields, with no holdings in the common fields, and who could sometimes commute their labour obligations for money and pursue manual crafts) in the smaller, croft-less plots of East Row, and free peasants or 'sokemen' (who held their farmable land in exchange for an annual rent to the lord of the manor) dwelled in West Row, which was more organic and muddled with larger longhouses (at least one of these was cruck-framed – that is, with a pair of timbers curving into the roof beam forming a gorgeous arched structure – and with the enormous luxury, for the time, of glazed windows). Unlike at Skara Brae four thousand years earlier, the bulk of the village lay in the shadow of the commanding manor house and was subject to its *diktat*.

The plans of several longhouses – bigger and more spacious than you might imagine – have been marked out on the ground. They look a little like a dismembered part of a maze or labyrinth and I felt a compulsive desire to explore their domestic world, to be there as the people woke to bury a relative, sprang from a straw mattress on a saint's bacchanal, or faced the monotony of tilling the fields. A whole acoustic world – the whirring of the watermills, the pealing of church bells, the chopping of wood, the cattle's bellowing at sunrise, the rumble of wagons, the hiss of spades sinking into soil – now lost to the warbling of birds and the wind.

It appears in the Domesday Book as 'Warran' or 'Warron'; 'Percy' was a later addition to honour the Percy family, descended from influential Norman barons, which would, by the late twelfth century, become the dominant landowners. The residence of this noble family in their manor house brought a measure of prestige and prosperity for two hundred years; but the fourteenth century brought misery and misfortune to the people of Wharram Percy. Until the union of the Crowns in 1603, medieval English kings were frequently at war with their counterparts in Scotland, and between 1319 and 1322 the Scottish threat materialised in the Yorkshire village in a manner reminiscent of the French and Spanish attacks on New Winchelsea. Crops were ripped out, watermills set on fire, many inhabitants put to the sword. These attacks left Wharram Percy in ruins. Records show that a year later, two-thirds of the land was stony, overgrown and fit for nothing. The Scottish raids brought tragedy to Wharram Percy but they were not fatal blows. A local tax assessment from ten years later indicates its valuation was about half the average of fifty villages in the vicinity – not great, but it had got back on its feet, at least. And *another* decade later, between one hundred and two hundred people were living there. So by 1346 at least, Wharram Percy had bounced back.[9] Life continued as ever, guided by the changing of the seasons and the tilling of the land, by births, marriages and deaths, and the observation of religious festivals. No one could have known that the village lay in the 'shadow of annihilation'.[10]

———

The Great Death, or the Pestilence as it was sometimes known, was the most deadly recorded calamity ever to have struck humanity – and may well still be. Between 1347 and 1351 it is estimated to have killed 75 million to 200 million people across the world. It was certainly the worst *naturally* occurring (i.e. not anthropogenically exacerbated) disaster part of the world had ever recorded.[11] It saw 40 per cent – even half – of England's population, and much of Scotland and Wales's, bowled down like skittles in the spring, summer and autumn of 1348–9.[12] This disaster came on the back of the widespread famines and terrible floods brought about by, or at least coinciding with, the deteriorating climate in the 1310s as the Medieval Warm Period gave way to the Little Ice Age. Many thought they were soaking up the last glimmers of the universe's existence. 'So many died', wrote the Italian chronicler Agnolo di Tura, 'that all believed it was the end of the world, and no medicine or any other defence availed.'[13] The disease was a force of unspeakable darkness, billowing through the isles, devastating towns, villages and cities, leaving millions dead in its wake.

It is impossible to say exactly how the inhabitants of Wharram Percy experienced the plague, whether they stared gloomily into their fish-pools, prayed frantically in church, or holed themselves up in their roundhouses, but we can extrapolate from impressions and accounts of those who lived through the epidemic. It certainly felt like there was no escape – 'We see death coming into our midst like black smoke,' wrote the Welsh poet Jeuan Gethin, 'a rootless phantom which has no mercy for fair countenance.'[14] Anyone who could, fled. People poured out of cities, wrongly believing 'the wrath of God' could somehow be contained 'within the walls',[15] and 'timid priests'[16] ran for the hills caring little for the souls entrusted to their care, casting them indeed into an abyss of potential damnation.

Some people resigned themselves to their fate and tried to carry on as normal; others became pious little mice sequestering themselves away in prayer; more nihilistic souls plunged themselves into debauchery 'and would baulk no passion or appetite they wished to gratify',[17] while some people became euphoric, viewing the whole thing as a wonderful chance for redemption and salvation, counting down the hours until they could escape their dark, damned world.

Death came suddenly. You might go to bed well, wake up ill and, in the afternoon, die. Or, as one chronicler put it more optimistically, 'those in the prime and vigour of youth . . . breakfasted in the morning with their living friends, and supped at night with their departed friends in the other world'.[18] At times it seemed like the entire country was playing out a macabre dumb show. Priests dropped down dead at the bedsides of the sick[19] and gravediggers fell into the very pits they had just dug.[20] Some people died mid-sentence.[21] Rural communities like Wharram Percy were shattered, workforces decimated, entire families obliterated in the blink of an eye. Church congregations were peppered with empty places, familiar faces faded to ghosts. There was a daily harvest of fresh orphans: grandfathers might be landed with screaming infants;[22] others were passed from family to family like unwanted dogs. Very rarely did anyone who contracted the Pestilence last longer than five days. Boccaccio recalls how most died within three.[23] 'People who one day had been full of happiness', wrote the chronicler Geoffrey le Baker, 'on the next were found dead.'[24]

The scale of the mortality was unprecedented. Henry Knighton marvelled that (a very precise) 1,312 people died in a single day in Avignon, then the seat of the Papacy.[25] Not everyone was afforded a decent burial. The graveyards, already overflowing with bodies, could not cope, so vast rustic pits were gauged into the earth beyond the town and city walls. Corpses were laid out layer upon layer with a filling of soil between 'as though', in the macabre words of one Italian chronicler, 'one were serving lasagne, with layers of cheese'.[26] Outside villages, smaller pits or trenches were dug for the same purpose, 'burials' usually taking place at night when they stank less. Every day the earth swallowed more. Every day, more. The idea that 'there were barely enough living to bury the dead'[27] had become something of a trope for medieval chroniclers reporting catastrophes, but here it seems genuine. The grim task often fell to a family member. 'I, Agnolo di Tura, called "the Fat", buried my five children with my own hands,' writes one chronicler, a soul-destroying image echoed in England by the Rochester monk William Dene, who describes how 'men and women carried the bodies of their own little ones to church on their shoulders and threw them into mass graves, from which arose such a stink that it was barely possible for anyone to go past the churchyard'.[28]

Others fared even worse. 'You might see the poor distressed labourers with their families', writes Boccaccio, 'languishing on the highways, in the fields.' They crawled into woods and underneath hedges and died 'rather like cattle than human creatures'.[29] In towns and cities, vagrants and criminals were hurled into ditches and moats. Agnolo di Tura writes of corpses 'so sparsely covered with earth that dogs dug them up and gnawed their bodies throughout the city'.

The landscape became wild and degenerate. Lighthouses fell dark. No flames blazed from their upper windows – the keepers rotting within, ghostly presences watching over shipless seas. The wind – the devil's breath, some perceived – blew over cliffs towards juddering windmills: the sailcloth torn, spokes broken and wings cracked, wilting feebly to the ground. Fields went unploughed. Weeds grew high. Crops rotted in the fields owing to a dearth of labour, and because those who remained were beginning to demand higher wages.[30] Livestock careered through strips, trampling crops and dying in furrows, under hedges and in ditches 'in numbers beyond reckoning throughout the land', as the Leicester chronicler Henry Knighton recorded, noting 'a great mortality of sheep everywhere in the kingdom', their bodies so putrid that no animal or bird would go anywhere near them,[31] though whether this was the Pestilence or another disease like anthrax he does not say.

At Wharram Percy, and villages all over Britain, vacant cottages and deserted farms abounded, the doors of longhouses left ominously ajar. Above them, ravens black as ink soared lonely through the sky. From the tip of their beaks right down to their wedge-shaped tails, they formed single, graceful curves now flying, gliding, slinking rhythmically as they craned their necks to the ground. Ravens, monogamous to the end, like to forage as a pair, occasionally croaking to their mate: *Cras! Cras!* They soared above the devastated countryside, wheeling over depleted monasteries and murky, overflowing fishponds, darkened castles and derelict manor houses, strangely deserted fields whose wheat and corn had turned pallid grey and more fields, golden this time, but with ominous splotches of white, pink and brown amongst the crops; the ravens flew over motionless meadows with dovecotes full of pigeons ripped to shreds by swooping kestrels and, as the light faded, over the glowing windows of churches, brilliantly lit by an armada of votive beeswax candles.

Over great cities too the ravens flew, above lurching timber-framed houses and dark, crooked alleys, through cacophonies of bells and choirs of lamentations, over rumbling deadcarts, vast bonfires, and the massacred bodies of dogs and cats in the streets.[32] In the cities – 'places now none dare to enter'[33] – bodies were thrown from the upper storeys of houses, grass straggled through cobbled streets, and in London,[34] at the height of the Pestilence, hundreds of people were thrown into vast lantern-framed craters just beyond the city walls every night, the air heavy with the miasma of death. The acoustic landscape was transformed too. There were crescendos of silence and sound in cities full of death and dying – the lilting cries of street hawkers falling silent while church bells pounded almost without cease, the wails of the bereaved echoing from wooden buildings and absorbed by the street mud. Large, usually bustling villages became quiet as death – once-everyday sounds were snuffed out, replaced by the groans of the dying and the fevered squeals of emaciated cattle.[35] All over the land the pulse of prayer quickened as people contemplated their fate, reciting prayers aloud, singing masses for the dead, chanting dirges. And above their heads, ravens flew. The year was, as graffiti in a Hertfordshire church had it, 'pitiful, savage and violent'.[36] And forever the earth was hungry for more.

In the face of so much horror no wonder language itself seemed to buckle and crack, with chroniclers sometimes throwing down their quills in despair. 'It is impossible for the human tongue to recount the awful truth,' writes Agnolo di Tura; 'I, the writer cannot think of it and so will not continue'; 'I', resolves the French chronicler Jean de Venette, 'will not write of the cruelty.'[37] The trauma was, in essence, unutterable.

It was God's horror show, recompense for a world besmirched by sin.

———

Long had this been dreaded. Since early spring, 1347, wild apocalyptic chatter had filtered into villages via peddlers, tradesmen and travellers from London and England's other major ports. They were tales of biblical proportion from the eastern cusp of the world,

Cathay, relayed via Italian merchants who had ventured beyond the Black Sea and spoken to their Arab, Persian and Tartar counterparts. They spoke of earthquakes, tsunamis, mighty floods and volcanic eruptions, their narratives spiced by the inclusion of elements such as krakens, dragons, fire-breathing mountains, showers of serpents and the like. But in time, one element arose above the fantastical fray, repeated again and again in unrelated sources: 'a pestilence of unprecedented ferocity'. Huddled around tables in the alehouse, by stocks on village greens, in churchyards, alleyways and by the well, villagers drank in reports of an invisible cloud of poison that was being blown across the world from Cathay, felling hundreds of thousands of Mongols, Persians and Turks. At first the Christian listeners may have reasoned that those lands were full of heathens, and once God had rid them from the surface of the earth the cloud would dissipate. But it did not dissipate. It scudded merrily across Asia and hovered above Europe, infecting Sicily, Italy, Spain and eventually France. Then it zoomed north, towards England.

At first it lodged in the ports. Even when the Pestilence struck London in the spring of 1348 people told themselves that the metropolis must have been singled out for especial retribution, since it was a diabolical stew of 'pretty boys, pickthanks, catamites, sodomites, lewd musical girls, druggists, lustful persons, fortune tellers, extortioners, nightly strollers and magicians'.[38] But still it spread; fresh reports flowed in, some wildly exaggerated. The entire population of England had to listen to a letter from their local bishop informing them – as if they didn't already know – that 'the inevitable human fate – pitiless death, which spares no one – now threatens us'. This was meant to encourage prayer and penance but it only heightened people's sense of imminent doom, and hearts were filled with anguish, terror and regret. As the plague hollowed out the capital and spread north, people in places like Wharram Percy began to imagine their well-ordered village as a heap of decaying timbers, stuffed with the dead under a halo of flies.

Pre-emptive measures were taken. Wrestling matches were banned in the churchyard, and churches gleamed like never before with scores of expensive votive candles. Crops, families, doorways, even cattle were showered in holy water, and the Host brandished over the fields. Pilgrimages were made to local shrines, people returning with patently fake relics. Tithes were speedily paid. Queues formed outside confession booths. Carpenters banged out wooden Madonnas like there was no tomorrow. The neighbourly spirit became somewhat diminished. Anyone who was afflicted by an ailment, however minor, was treated with the utmost suspicion. Hospitality went to the dogs. Strangers were forced to spit on the ground to see if there was any blood in their saliva, then chased away with stones. A slew of quacks, freelance preachers, magic men, wizards, prophets, soothsayers and purveyors of yet more preposterous relics streamed through villages like Wharram Percy. Even if most villagers saw them as cynical exploiters, they were loath to shun any opportunity to do *something* to purify their souls and get God off their backs. As news of deaths in neighbouring villages arrived, people clutched images of their favourite saints in little home-made shrines.

As the disease spread across the island, there was a great deal of inquisition and soul-searching. The Pestilence, most people believed, was 'caused' by sinful thoughts and actions,[39] and since it was the clergy's job to relieve people of sin, it fell to the local parish priest to explain the encroaching plague. Moral reckonings took place in churches across the land. At Wharram Percy despair reverberated around the nave and choir of St Martin's Church, and up the tower from which clanged, horridly often, the bells to mark another villager's demise. Disease, the priest reminded them, purifies the soul, and though the scale of the suffering looked horrific, God was in fact performing a benevolent act of kindness, moving them to penance and absolution, so their souls might be saved. But why, people asked, were babies dying in their droves – how could they have sinned? Do not be fooled, replied the priest. By snatching them in their swaddling cloths, God was rescuing them from a life of sin and likely damnation, and if this was not a satisfactory answer then the infants were being punished for the sins of their parents (which hardly seemed fair but was *an* answer, nonetheless). But if God was the author of the Great Death, yet others asked, why then did learned men talk about a malignant alignment of stars and planets poisoning the air? If you must think of this, replied the priest, as some game of cosmic bowls, know that it is God doing the bowling.[40] It was certainly something for Wharram Percy's peasants to ponder as they passed by the swirling fish-pools on their way back home.

Many of the answers failed to satisfy even the priest who was giving them, let alone his parishioners, and some questions were completely beyond his powers of comprehension. If the Pestilence was a punishment for sin, why did so many habitual sinners survive while the spotless perished? What made this generation, as opposed to any other, especially sinful? Why hadn't the killers of Christ been struck down by plague? How could people do adequate penance and be filled with grace if they were keeling over their mattress vomiting and dying? How could anyone really believe something on such a horrifying scale could stem from the benevolent impulse of an all-loving God – surely it was the work of Satan himself? Many a long night did the priest lie awake, his faith drained by doubt.

———

The parishioners of Wharram Percy had been indoctrinated to believe that the deathbed was a battleground for the forces of good and evil as the soul teetered on the brink of everlasting damnation.[41] This was a cornerstone of the Catholic Church's moral policing – best not have *too* much to confess, unless you forget some of it – and a way of bolstering the Church's social power by amassing a repository of sins. To die unshriven was everybody's worst nightmare. Shriving was the process whereby a priest took confession, assigned penance, and absolved a dying person of their sins, before performing the last rites. Dying well was a delicate art – what the dying person said and did on the deathbed could determine the fortunes of their soul (and the options were starkly binary). Venial or minor sins could be burned off in the sulphurs of Purgatory, but mortal sins were of a different order since they drained the soul of divine grace. To be absolved of mortal sins the supplicant had to be truly contrite (God would see through feigned remorse) and confess their sins as close as they could to the moment of death. Should a man, woman or child become belligerent, uncooperative or actively hostile on the deathbed, it was believed they were possessed by an invisible demon who was involved in a tug-of-war with the Holy Church for their soul.

At the very least the Pestilence made an already elaborate process more precarious still. Those who were close to death often became incomprehensible, even delirious, as they thrashed around on their bed, making it a fairly tall order to extract anything at all, let alone a lucid enumeration of their sins accompanied by a sense of heartfelt remorse. Those with the plague threatened to make a sacrilegious farce of the whole process, grabbing the wooden crucifix at the crucial moment and hurling it aside, refusing to swallow the Eucharist or, worse still, taking a bite of the body of Christ and spewing it up, mixing saliva and blood with His crumbs. During the Pestilence, because so many priests died, fled or lost their faith, the Pope, in a bold and unprecedented move, issued a special dispensation allowing the laity to hear confession where there was no alternative. This practical measure posed its own peculiar challenges; how difficult it was for husbands and wives to extract meaningful confessions from their mumbling loved ones, and, potentially, how emotionally hurtful too, all the while trying to ward off an image of the hellfire to which their sick ones were headed if they did not get it exactly right, a hell they had seen a thousand times on the stained-glass window in church, seared into their minds by their priest.

Dying was one thing; burial another. If you were to make it to heaven (via a lengthy stint in Purgatory to burn off any outstanding venial sins) ideally – and this was more practicable for the wealthy elites than for the great mass of humanity – you had to be interred correctly, for burial was the passage out of this world. The body had to be shrouded in the expectation that it would be reborn into eternal life. Then, on the eve of burial, the corpse had to be taken to church on a torch-lit bier and placed in the darkness of the nave, then laid in front of the high altar, surrounded by candles. The next day, in front of the full community, a requiem mass was to be sung and the paschal candle lit (as it had been once before, for the dead individual, at baptism). Following this there were prayers, hymns, special masses, and the body was borne to the grave, sprinkled with holy water and buried in consecrated ground. It must be laid head up with its feet to the east, for it was from this direction that Christ would return, from New Jerusalem, at the Apocalypse when the worthy dead would be resurrected. There it would wait, like a coiled spring, until the Seven Trumpets sounded. In the meanwhile it would degenerate to the dust from which first man had been formed. If burial rituals went awry, one's immortal soul was jeopardised.

———

When a raven turned up to eat at Wharram Percy, or another plague-ridden village, it would, as the author of the twelfth-century *Aviarum* put it, first rip off the corpse's eyelids, peck out the eyes, then claw out the brain through the sockets.[42] Or it would begin at the eardrum or anus, reaching deep into the body to reel out the soft brain matter or intestines before resting in a tree, gorged. The ballad 'The Twa Corbies' is an imagined dialogue between two ravens who discuss how much they would like to eat a knight who has fallen somewhere in the war-torn borderlands between England and Scotland; how sweet it would be, they say, to peck out his bonny blue eyes and thatch their nest with locks of his blond hair, to devour his flesh and entrails so that 'O'er his white banes, when they are bare, the wind sall blaw for evermair'.[43]

With their dark plumage, slouching posture and love of carrion, ravens – kings of crows – have long been associated with death and corpses.[44] To aid them in their quest for carrion, the mysterious black birds were thought to have a sixth sense which allowed them to detect imminent death. Bestiaries tell how, like vultures, they were forever to be seen swirling above battlefields, divining a meal. Sometimes they would arrive days before the battle had even started, a clairvoyance also in evidence whenever a raven croaked outside the house of a sick person, signalling that they were not long for this world. The Romans transliterated the deep cry of the raven as *cras*, Latin for 'tomorrow', and this sense was still alive in the Middle Ages.[45] *Cras* conveyed the raven's powers of prophecy but was also a taunt to the slothful and proud who arrogantly assumed God would grant them another day to do what might easily be done today.

The prospect of our own edibility is profoundly distasteful.[46] We like to think of ourselves as belonging to a privileged, non-bestial sphere of reason and consciousness. Carrion birds shatter the illusion of mankind's non-materiality; in a passage of *Paradise Lost*, Milton describes soldiers encamped before battle as 'living carcasses designed for death' scented by 'ravenous fowl'.[47] We are food – food for lions, tigers and crows – and in death, we are made available to other creatures just as, in life, other creatures have been made available to us. Death rituals, burying the corpse in a coffin or incinerating it and scattering the ashes, try to cloak this inconvenient truth. Personal salvation – breaking free from the corporeal prison and ascending to a spiritual sphere unencumbered by materiality – is the logical culmination of the myth of humanity's supposed dominion over nature; irredeemable sinners were 'food for the worms'. Other cultures think differently. At around the time of the Pestilence, in Asia, Tibetan Buddhists began to practise sky burials, in which corpses are bound in cloth, deposited in a rocky place, then chopped to pieces in preparation for the birds' descent. Far from being an act of unmitigated horror, the Buddhists saw this as a final act of charity, giving back to the world that had sustained them.

If the prospect of being pecked and ripped to pieces after death is unsettling enough today, it was an unimaginable horror for the inhabitants of Wharram Percy. By the Middle Ages, the simplicity of the early Church had been obfuscated by a slew of theological accumulations. Dying well had become an elaborate, mysterious and artful alchemy from which the sin-smirched could take solace in the fact that they were doing *something* at least for the longevity of their soul. Being tossed into a ditch and pecked to pieces by ravens was not just the antithesis of this. For the unfortunate dead, it spelt an eternity of damnation. For the living too, it was an unpleasant thought that fellow Christians were languishing in hell. But worse than that, there was also always the unsavoury possibility that the souls of the dead would return, zombie-like, to haunt the community. One way to prevent that from happening, it has been posited, was to dig up some of the bones, while there were still some left, and smash, roast and mutilate them, then bury them in a different pit where they would hopefully stay dead.[48]

As corpses fell, so, chroniclers tell us, did villages. 'Many buildings, both great and small, in all cities, towns and boroughs, fell into total ruin for lack of inhabitants,' recalls the chronicler Henry Knighton, 'similarly many small villages and hamlets became desolate and no houses were left in them, for all those who had dwelt in them were dead; and it seemed likely that many such little villages would never again be inhabited.'[49] Assessing the impact of the Pestilence – and its succeeding, less deadly waves – it is just these sorts of portraits of pure destruction that recur in medieval accounts. Bishop Edington of Winchester told of 'fruitful country palaces, without the tillers' now 'deserts and abandoned to barrenness'.[50]

And indeed, the impact of the Great Death upon rural communities was profound and, ultimately, unforeseen.

———

Some places struck by the Pestilence indeed never recovered.[51] Tilgarsley, near Eynsham in Oxfordshire, was once a large, thriving village. Before the plague struck, it had more than two hundred residents, including twenty-eight taxpayers, but in 1359 the Exchequer learned that the entire population had vanished, laid low, it is recorded, by the Great Death.[52] This is obviously a slight exaggeration – some tenants would have moved away of their own accord, lured by more attractive tenancies, and several members of prominent local families survived – but the village lay in ruins and the landowning abbot was granted relief from paying any future taxes. That Eynsham, its similarly sized neighbour, survives is testament to the peculiar ferocity with which the plague struck Tilgarsley, and we can by now imagine something of the horrors that unfolded there. Nonetheless, the Exchequer was ever hopeful that the community, or *a* community, would one day return; but it never did. By 1422 it was a lost cause, carved up into agricultural leaseholds. There is no hard archaeological evidence for the exact location of Tilgarsley, but the existence of Bowles Farm, to the west of Cuckoo Lane, gives us a clue. 'Bowles' is a corruption of 'Bolds' – in 1390, the abbot was stockpiling hay at a place called Le Bolde – and, since 'bolds' is a word for buildings, we can pinpoint the deserted dwellings somewhere within the region of today's farm. There was too, in the early nineteenth century, a field called Churchyard Ground to the south of the farm. Here the vicar of Eynsham discovered buried bones and stones. Yet there is no mention of any church ground in medieval records, suggesting a posthumous misattribution. Perhaps it was a plague pit.

One hundred miles north-east of Tilgarsley, Apethorpe Park in Northamptonshire is best known for its Renaissance palace (it has some of the best-preserved Jacobean state rooms in the country). But very nearby, almost in its shadow, is the lost hamlet of Hale. Situated on a ridge of clay and limestone towards Tomlin Wood, it was always tiny – no more than sixty-five inhabitants in 1300, and shrinking. Yet it was not in terminal decline – the hamlet merited an entry in the *Nomina Villarum*, a list of villages and lords of manors compiled in 1316, and rents were still being collected as late as 1344. But by 1356, 'the premises are worth nothing because no one dwells or has dwelt in Hale since the Pestilence'. Never resettled, it was valueless by the time of the Poll Tax in 1381 'because the messuages are wasted'.[53] When the antiquarian John Bridges came to write his *History of Northamptonshire* in 1720, he noted 'ruins of this town, and of the old manor house, with the vestiges of three long streets . . . still visible' in a place called Hale-fields, subsumed into an aristocratic park. He correctly attributed its disappearance to the plague, claiming its 'ancient' church survived the village by one hundred years. In a map of 1778, the field to the north of the deserted village is evocatively called 'grass walls'. But Hale is no longer rutted into the fields for its earthworks were destroyed in 1947; its memory is fast fading.

Sometimes the memory of lost villages can be eclipsed by other historical resonances. We know there was a village called Ambion in Leicester because it surfaces in the historical record at the end of the thirteenth century, but after 1346 it is never heard of again; no doubt it was ravaged and depopulated by the plague. Yet Ambion Hill overlooks Bosworth Field, where Richard III, last of the English kings to die in battle, lost his throne to Henry Tudor in 1485. He pitched his camp on the hill overlooking the deserted village the night before he met his doom, and the haunting ruins of long-houses, ponds, manor house and the overgrown street may well have still been visible below. History is silent on whether or not his troops gazed down upon the mournful sight as they reconciled themselves to the prospect of death in battle. But its memory is rutted into the earth to the west of the visitor centre, on the gentle slope down to the woods. The earthworks, clearly visible in places, cover a wide area, girdled by a boundary ditch on the southern side, with a hollow way running north–south through the heart of the site. Some house platforms are visible as grassy mounds.

In Wiltshire, Cowsfield was valued at zero in 1349 'on account of all the tenants being dead from the plague'. At Calstock in Devon, up to 70 per cent of the population died, and at Duns Tew in Oxfordshire, the corn was left rotting in the fields because after the 1349 harvest there was no one left to wield the sickle. Some deserted villages can be identified as victims of later waves of the epidemic. The village of Standhill in Oxfordshire received tax relief in 1446 following a devastating outbreak of plague. The following year, the local priest told his archdeacon there was no point bothering with regular services any more since there were no parishioners left. Two isolated farms are all that remain. If the Pestilence had never exploded into the British Isles, we can hazard a strong guess that many of these deserted sites would still survive – even flourish – today.

It must be said, however, that the Black Death was nothing like the great exterminator of villages (and even towns and cities) it is frequently made out to be – in popular culture, online,[54] and indeed in the writings of contemporary chroniclers. In 1348–9, 55 per cent of the total population of twenty-two different manors owned by the abbots of Glastonbury perished in the Great Death. In the Forest of Knaresborough in Yorkshire, between 45 per cent and 50 per cent of the peasants alive in 1348 were dead by the time the Pestilence retreated. Sometimes the rate of mortality was significantly higher. As close-knit, largely self-contained communities, monasteries could easily become bubbles of plague – at Meaux Abbey in Yorkshire, thirty-two out of fifty monks perished, and things were worse still at the Cistercian foundation of Newenham in East Devon, where twenty out of twenty-three monks died. And, spectacularly, in the village of Woodeaton in Oxfordshire, all but two of the thirty-five tenants were dead by the early 1350s, a death rate of 94 per cent. Yet all these places went on to survive.

Contemporary chroniclers were not necessarily being histrionic (though they did like drama) – they had every reason to believe that 'many such little villages would never again be inhabited', as Knighton put it. When you are in the middle of a pandemic, or in its bleak aftermath, it can be hard to see the light ahead. And indeed, as the social and economic life of the country ground to a halt, Britain became one great shadowland – but not one that endured. But in reality the vast majority of villages (and all the towns and cities) *did* survive in the long term albeit, in some cases, in shrunken and more fragile form. So long as houses could be renovated, crops cultivated and the church restored, it made no sense to found a new settlement when an existing one could be reoccupied. However much local folklorists and amateur historians like to attribute 'their' ghost village to the Black Death directly, the mass mortality of humans was simply not mirrored in the annihilation of their collective habitats. In fact only around eighteen settlements vanished in this way, settlements where a majority of able-bodied men had perished, or ones established on marginal or unfecund soils during the population boom of the early Middle Ages, unattractive to later colonists.

And yet, in the two hundred years following the Pestilence, thousands of rural settlements *did* vanish from the map. That is not to say the Great Death did *not* have a profound impact on England's topography – it did. It can be linked to the disappearance of thousands of villages, but in a complex and indirect way, one that was certainly not foreseen by the chroniclers. For when the scythe came down upon England's villages en masse in the fifteenth and sixteenth centuries, it came from an unexpected quarter. How then did Wharram Percy, where I began my journey, meet its end, along with thousands of others, and what did this have to do with the *Yersinia pestis* bacterium and its exploding buboes?

———

To the bells of St Michael's, I left my hotel in Malton and set out to find Wharram Percy. It was a seven-mile hike and it rained practically all the way, an incessant, windy drizzle – the small umbrella I'd brought with me was hopelessly unsuited to the task. I walked across the morose River Derwent past empty factories, convenience stores and conservatories behind freshly mown lawns. It was a relief when I finally reached two little bollards that marked the liminal point where suburbia melted into the Yorkshire Wolds, unfurling beneath a chalk-white sky, a mellow quilt of meadows, cornfields, streams and clumps of woodland. I felt like I could breathe again.

I walked along by the edge of the road with my camera, umbrella and thermos flask of powerful coffee. Tulips withered in the undergrowth and lorries passed me, carrying pigs to their doom. I took some respite from the road on a little side path when two people emerged behind me on horseback, trotting briskly by. One shouted, 'Ey-up, lad, fancy a canter?' After two hours I came to the village of North Grimston, glimpsing its pint-sized church through a wooden gate and short row of trees. It felt like a ghost village itself, with a red phone box that looked like it hadn't been used in years, a forlorn village hall, an old blacksmith's shop now someone's house, and a general air of listlessness. The only sign of life was a pub, but even that was near-deserted that lunchtime. A couple of miles on, I veered right on to a smaller road.

Within minutes, the wind had died down, the drizzle ceased, and all I could hear was the hiss and the whirl of distant traffic.

Ever the road forged ahead, scything through green fields under a metallic abundance of cloud. I was walking, I sensed, in a dead-straight line, but the road ahead always seemed to be curving left-ward, and the remote hills, cornfields and snatches of woodland I could see on the horizon seemed like stage sets inching backwards with every step I took. I saw some sheep by the roadside. With their broad muzzles, sunken eyes and horizontally slit pupils in dull yellow corneas, it is easy to take them to be dim and docile clones sprinkled across the landscape, mindlessly following the flock. Aristotle, in 350 BC, believed sheep 'naturally dull and stupid'; in the Bible they recur as emblems of unquestioning obedience and redemptive submissiveness, and these ideas became deeply ingrained; during the Enlightenment in the eighteenth century, the Comte de Buffon, a naturalist, noted how the 'contemptible' animal was 'devoid of every mental quality'.[55] In fact, sheep can meticulously recall past experiences and associations; they can re-member the faces of particular animals and humans for up to a year; and certain breeds, like the Merino, can even master mazes.[56] The 'dull and stupid' sheep staring back at me may very well have been picturing a slaughtered friend, lost mate or retired shepherd. But towards the end of the Middle Ages, the sheep came to accrue an unlikely new connotation, appearing in literature as a devourer of people, pillager of churches and destroyer of worlds. Thanks to these 'man-eating sheep', according to literature and official docu-ments, thousands of villages disappeared for good, as a result of the economic legacy of the Great Death of 1348–9 and its successive waves in the fourteenth, fifteenth and sixteenth centuries.

In 1300, the population of England had been around 7 million; by the 1350s it was 3.5 million. The culprit? *Yersinia pestis*.[57] Demand for labour therefore massively outstripped supply, giving peasants unprecedented levels of bargaining power and allowing them over time to emerge as more independent economic actors.[58] Successive medieval governments were naturally alarmed by this development and so repeatedly passed legislation pegging wages (and, because of inflation, prices) to pre-plague levels (see, for example, the Statute of Artificers 1562). Yet landlords could not let the cycle of agricultural production grind to a halt for that would have spelt manorial ruin, widespread famine and an eruption of lawlessness. Seeds had to be sown, fields ploughed, even if that meant ignoring the legislation and paying higher rates – not dramatically higher, but more nonetheless. So landowners competed with each other to attract labour and, though it was technically illegal in practice, peasants could now move to whichever tenancy offered them the most advantageous terms.[59] This meant that, ultimately, it became more profitable and less labour-intensive for seigneurs to convert their land from open fields where crops were cultivated by scores of newly emboldened and opportunistic peasants to enclosed fields where sheep grazed under the vigilance of a few shepherds at most. In the end, it was about profit not plague. This is how Wharram Percy met its end, along with thousands of other villages.

Back on the road there were hardly any birds, little motion at all apart from the swaying of barley, corn and nettles. I walked with a sense of rising dread – my phone had died long ago – and I wasn't sure I was going in the right direction. But in time I came to a

bathetic signpost saying 'Deserted Medieval Village'. It pointed right, down a prehistoric track. The crop on either side rose to my full height as I descended into a deep dale. Over a tiny stream, through a gate, across a plateau – and there was Wharram Percy with its bleak and fish-less pools; its haunting church ruin; information boards dripping in drizzle; outlines of long-vanished houses in the turf.

The lord of Wharram Percy died very shortly after the plague had reached Yorkshire, in 1349. It took its terrible course, killing a third of the population, and leaving forty-five shaken souls. The death of the lord of the manor resulted in a brief period of direct royal control since the heir was a minor. When *he* died, around twenty years later, the estate fell into the hands of a more distant branch of the Percy family and thereafter the Percys were absentee landowners. By the late fourteenth century thirty houses were occupied, the uncultivated land was sprouting crops once more, and one of the mills had been restored to its former glory even if, by the fifteenth century, the village had shrunk to half its original size.[60] In 1400 the Percys swapped Wharram for a manor owned by Baron William Hilton, who became the new landlord, thoughtfully replacing the upper storey of the bell tower but, it seems, not actually living in the village either. When this new overlord died in 1436, and the village passed on to his heir, Wharram was a distinctly less bustling place – sixteen of the houses were occupied. But by now, as the economic advantages of sheep grazing over cereal farming became more manifest, and across England highly tilled arable land was converted to enclosed pasture, the village was living on borrowed time.

The evictions began in 1458. Gradually, the residents were served their notice, their houses ripped down or left to fester, and sheep moved in. Some, finding more advantageous tenancies elsewhere, left of their own accord; others were flushed out by Baron Hilton. By the dawn of the sixteenth century what few houses were left were occupied by smallholders and a few lonely shepherds. The last arable strips were finally converted to pasture on the eve of Henry VIII's quarrel with the Pope, in 1527, and only a 'chief messuage' – probably a well-preserved medieval longhouse – remained. What happened at Wharram Percy was a perfect microcosm for what was happening nationwide.[61]

The fifteenth-century chantry priest and historian John Rous leaves us an impassioned and detailed account of the sheep enclosures of the mid- and late-fifteenth century which destroyed so many villages in a twelve-page digression in his *Historia Regum Angliae* (finished 1486), written thirty years after the first evictions at Wharram Percy, and composed during the time that Henry VII, the first of the Tudors, came to the throne. Rous says he was 'stirred to rise against [the devastation and destruction of villages] by mouth and pen following the clamour and murmurings of the populace', having presented petitions to Parliament in 1459.[62] The occasion for his invective, within his grand narrative of English kings, is his account of William the Conqueror's Harrying of the North, when the Norman invader laid waste to dozens, possibly hundreds, of villages to bring his northern subjects to heel. That, Rous says, was bad enough. But it is not a patch on 'the modern destruction of towns' which flowed from 'the worship of Mammon' – avaricious landowners putting private gain above the common good by converting arable to pasture without the consent of their hapless tenants. In his history, John Rous gives us a list of villages and hamlets that have been destroyed or 'grievously ravaged' by avarice, as Wharram Percy would be. He lists seventy-eight, all within his home county of Warwickshire. He laments the loss of Church Charwelton on the border of Warwickshire and Northamptonshire, where travellers used to find 'healthy hospitality' on their way to London. At the manor of Great Chesterton, from seventy-nine old holdings, scarcely three survived; at Little Wulfield, from forty-three tenants, now just a few; at Billesley Trussell 'only the manor remains, now everyone has been expelled, a great pity'. Some ruined villages, he says, have been put to unsavoury new uses, like the lost town of Cawston on Dunsmore in the parish of Dunchurch, whose sole surviving farm 'is now a hideout for robbers and murderers'. And at Fulbrook, where there had once been a rectory, 'the church has been destroyed, the townsmen have fled, and only the manor remains'. Of all of Rous's vanished – or

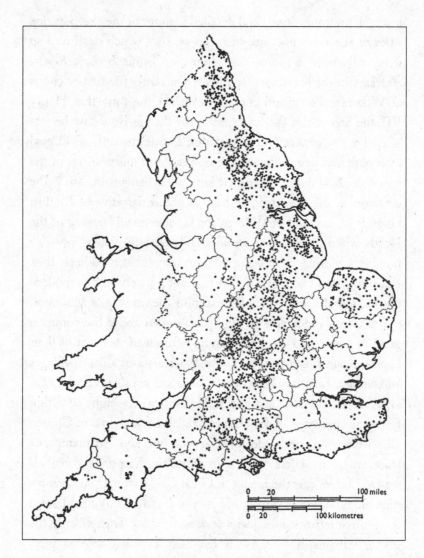

Deserted Medieval Villages

Distribution map of sites located by the Deserted Medieval Villages Research Group up to the end of 1968 (reproduced courtesy of The Lutterworth Press).

vanishing – villages, the vast majority are still deserted today, festering beneath a sea of grass for almost 550 years.[63]

In total, several thousand medieval villages vanished. Thanks to the labours of the Deserted Medieval Village Research Group, and drawing upon sources such as Rous and the *Domesday of Enclosures*, we have a map that plots England's shadow medieval topography, victims of the economic consequences of the Black Death. As the map reveals, the ghost villages were by no means uniformly distributed throughout England, but instead were particularly concentrated in certain counties. Each one of these was potentially a tragedy for at least some of the evicted tenants, and so the landlords attracted much opprobrium and the whole process was seen as a pernicious social ill. John Rous castigates enclosing landlords as 'murderers of the impoverished', 'destroyers of humanity' and 'venomous snakes'. They had showed no mercy to 'the children, tenants and others whom they have forced from their homes by theft', and so could expect 'judgement without mercy' in the afterlife; certainly he would not be singing any masses for the souls of these 'destroyers of towns'.[64]

Worried by the social and economic effects of the enclosures, in 1517 Cardinal Wolsey set up a royal inquiry. The *Domesday of Enclosures*[65] is highly evocative as a symphony of mini-tragedies in which we can sometimes hear – mediated through the depositions – the anguish of the dispossessed.[66] The eighty people evicted from Stretton Baskerville in Warwickshire were 'compelled to go from thence unwilling and unlamented turning sorrowfully to idleness, to drag out a miserable life, and – truthfully – so to die in misery'. 'Truly they have died', it reaffirms, 'in such a pitiful state.' Human stories like these lie behind all the evictions. The new landowner 'wilfully allowed the houses to fall to ruin and turned the fields from cultivation to be a feeding place for brute animals'. Here, as in so many other deserted villages, including Wharram Percy, the abandoned parish church became a terrible symbol of depopulation, a pitiful place where 'animals take shelter from storms and feed among the graves of Christian men in the churchyard, so that it and the church are desecrated and profaned'. Today, all that is left is interlocking earthworks on a ridge between two valleys; a sunken world.

Not long after the villagers of Wharram Percy were driven out,[67] the landscape degenerated. Where once there had been cornfields, blades of grass now straggled; where once peasants had tilled in open fields, sheep – 1,240 of them by 1543 – munched and bleated between thick hedges. The mud-and-wattle cottages were demolished and burned for firewood or were torn down by the wind. Rain washed through untrodden soil and tumbleweed billowed through lonely lanes and roads. In storms, sheep and cows fled to the church, cowering beneath the nave, and when the rain ceased they grazed above the dead to repeated clerical consternation. Eventually, salvagers turned up, reducing some of the church to a sad heap of rubble. At one point a man lay down beside one of the ruined houses' walls and died, rotting away until slates and tiles cracked over his rib-bones. It is tempting to think of this person as the village's final resident, obstinate to the end, but more likely he was a famished vagabond. His bones were excavated in 1964.

But even with its empty streets, tumbledown or destroyed houses and semi-pillaged church, Wharram Percy would not have resembled a ruined village for long. Ever since the settlement had been carved out of thick forest in the Anglo-Saxon period, nature had been biding its time, rumbling beneath the surface, waiting – here, finally, was its chance. Its preferred weapon was grass, the country's residual vegetation. There was no shortage of fertile soil for its blown seed to prosper: soft mud washed through the ruins of houses after every rainstorm. It flowed into hollows and alleys. As retaining walls collapsed, they were trampled into the ground by animals' hooves, and everything was levelled. The grass's whipping green blades were agents of amnesia. In time this little pocket of

Yorkshire dissolved, largely invisible at ground level but marshalled into some sense of order from above. Aerial photography clearly shows the remains of streets, alleys and tracks, like the flight paths of aeroplanes, scorched into a sky of grass.

At the edge of Wharram Percy is a boundary ditch, about eighteen feet below where its houses once stood. It divided the villagers' homes and crofts from the open fields where they toiled beneath the clouds. The slope in between has, over the years, harboured seeds and scrub from which hawthorn and blackberry bushes have sprung, encircling Wharram Percy in a kind of prickly hedge. It is as though nature cannot quite relinquish the memory of the community that once tilled its land and harvested its bounty, felt-tipping its bounds in red and black berries. In spring, buttercups foam from the undergrowth, circling the settlement in gold, a dazzlingly bucolic memento to a vanished world.

On the top of the bank, when I visited, I saw a bull, the silhouette of its head like a ring-girt planet. It looked at me. It was a sign of life in a landscape of loss. By now the other two families had disappeared, scared off by the drizzle. But there would be more tomorrow, and the next day, equally drawn to the lingering remains of a derailed past. I wondered why people were drawn to places like this, to places that to all intents and purposes no longer exist. Wharram Percy and the three thousand villages like it rebuke our sense of invincibility; which of our own villages, we wonder, are going to end up like this, faintly pencilled into the earth? Which of our towns? And would anyone in the future bother to preserve their memory? In the lost village, we see the gently falling sand of the hourglass, or the turning of the earth.

CHAPTER FIVE

THE CITY THAT FELL OFF A CLIFF: DUNWICH

And in 1922, finally, it fell. It fell amid a waterfall of dead men's bones on to the beach below; the lone, windowless tower of a ruined Gothic church that had teetered for so long on the cliff-edge, now overthrown as the sea moved in. Pelvises and thigh bones from the church's graveyard were set into the fallen sods like jelly; cracked, toothless skulls too, their worm-worked eye sockets as gaunt and soulless as the ruins of the beached tower, now just 'playthings for the waves of the North Sea'.[1]

The clifftop wreck made a harrowing image, particularly as a jagged silhouette in the twilight or in the early-morning light. It was much photographed – there was a grim inevitability, but also melancholic beauty, as the cliff-face drew near, and the church inched ever closer to the abyss. It was strange to think that it had

ALL SAINTS CHURCH, DUNWICH.

once been a long way from the cliff-edge, far to the west of the port city and shielded from the sight of sailors by a swarm of stone and timber-framed buildings, but as the sea drew uncomfortably close in the mid-eighteenth century it was declared a lost cause and fell into disuse. By the Victorian period it lay totally abandoned, and in the early twentieth century it would be eaten, in tantalising increments, by the sea.[2] In 1904, its derelict chancel, the east end of the church that had reverberated with choral song for many centuries, crashed to the shore; by 1912, three of the nave's five bays had fallen off the cliff, and those remaining were occupied by bats and owls as the waters spumed over the cliff at high tide and gnawed away at its base, precipitating the landslides; by 1919, only a pitiful shard remained, until, three years later, this too went under. At the four corners of the tower, beneath the swivelling weathervane, could be found salt-sprayed and wind-whipped faces of four archangels, one of whom was blown off in a gust just days before the cliff arrived at the foot of the tower.[3]

Before it fell, All Saints' Church had been one of three medieval ruins on a wooded cliff about thirty feet high overlooking the North Sea. A little to the west stood the fragments of wall and austere pointed arches of Greyfriars Monastery, projecting palettes of vivid light on to the lonely green fields; beyond that were the stone remains of St James's leper hospital. Were it not for the ill-fitting little modern village with its pub, car park, frequently shut museum and small café pounded by the wind and the rain, you would be forgiven for thinking this had been a remote monastic settlement in coastal Suffolk. But the fallen Gothic church was just one of eighteen ecclesiastical buildings in what was once a major port of Saxon East Anglia, a city once the same physical size of the City of London with a population, at its peak in the late thirteenth century, at just the time New Winchelsea was being built, of five thousand, yet which was savagely diminished by two calamitous sea-storms in 1288 and 1328, initiating a process of coastal erosion that would plunge much of the rest of the city off the cliff in the succeeding, sorrowful centuries.

All Saints was the last of the seven parish churches to fall head-long into the waves. Once its angels had abandoned it, the drowned church was doomed to lie in a gulley not far out to sea, a habitat for sponges and crabs, and yet it lives on, unvanquishable; for what has disappeared beneath the sea can rebuild itself in the mind.

———

At ten o'clock on a hot August night in 1876, while the rest of the village slept, an illustrator named Charles Keene sat down on the beach of Dunwich ('a charming, lonely place'), and took out a set of bagpipes to 'skirl away by the sad sea waves' for about an hour or so, the pipes glistening in the moonlight, their blasts vanishing into the dark sea.[4] He was not the only artist drawn to the van-ished city. Thirty years later, in the final decade of his life, a famous American-born author living in Rye was drawn to Dunwich. He paced up and down the coastal path by 'the great church and its tall tower, now quite on the verge of the cliff',[5] and stared out to sea. 'I defy any one,' he wrote in *English Hours* (1905), 'at desolate, exquisite Dunwich, to be disappointed in anything.' Henry James felt that 'the minor key is struck here with a felicity that leaves no sigh to be breathed . . . a month of the place is a real educa-tion to the patient, the inner vision'. Sadness hung in the air like the salt spray of the sea; a sense of squandered potential pervaded everything and yet was somehow uplifting. Keene and James were part of a flock of writers, artists and poets who made a creative pilgrimage to Dunwich, leaving behind letters, essays, pictures and diary entries. The famed city – or rather, the absence of it – in the 'desperate depth of Old Suffolk' put James into a brooding state of mind. Daniel Defoe had been struck by how at New Winchelsea 'nothing of a town but the destruction of it seems to remain' but to

James's mind, the sensation was even stronger when there was virtually nothing left.[6] 'Dunwich is not even the ghost of its dead self,' he wrote; 'almost all you can say of it is that it consists of the mere letters of its old name'; and yet this had once been 'a city, the main port of Suffolk . . . with a fleet of its own on the North Sea, and a big religious house on the hill'. The culprit was the feral sea, or 'the monster', as he later put it. Near where James lived, on Romney Marshes, the sea had receded, leaving reclaimed marshes and grazing land that, as we have seen, led to the decline of the promising city of New Winchelsea in the Middle Ages. But at Dunwich, the opposite had occurred: 'The coast, up and down, for miles, has been, for more centuries than I presume to count, gnawed away by the sea.' The rest of it, aside from the ruined priory and doomed church of All Saints, was in the North Sea, 'a ruminating beast, an insatiable, indefatigable lip'. By any objective measure, the place was dismal and pathetic, yet it was redeemed, he felt, by the power of sadness. The whole landscape was charged with a sense of mystery which 'sounds for ever in the hard, straight tide, and hangs, through the long, still summer days, and over the low, diked fields, in the soft, thick light'. Never can the 'spirit and attitude' of 'the little city submerged' be recovered from the depths. In one of the dozen little cottages to which Dunwich had been reduced, James found an old man who could count on his hands, until he ran out of fingers, all the acres of land he had seen absorbed by the sea; 'he likes to figure that he ploughed of old where only the sea ploughs now'.

For further impressions of the drowned city, James recommended the letters of the Suffolk scholar, poet and translator of Persian poetry Edward FitzGerald, who lived nearby in Woodbridge and came to Dunwich frequently in his lifetime, capturing its 'odd, quaint air'. FitzGerald described Dunwich as 'rather delightful' when he first travelled through it on his way back from Southwold in the summer of 1869. From the mid-1870s, he took to staying – sometimes for entire summers – either at the village inn or with the etcher Edwin Edwards and his wife, where they loved to play dominoes.[7] By then there were only two hundred inhabitants, and, like New Winchelsea, Dunwich had been stripped of all its centuries-old borough privilege, being legislated into obsolescence by 1882. In a commentary on how the village had not been spoiled by the ravages of Victorian tourism, FitzGerald describes it in a letter to a friend in August 1877 as 'the village remains of a once large town devoured by the sea: and yet undevoured (except by Henry VIII), the grey walls of a Grey Friars' Priory, beside which they [the monks] used to walk, under such sunsets as illumine them still'.[8] It was the ruins of this priory, within spitting distance of the cliff-walk, that beguiled the scholar FitzGerald. Most mornings, he would stroll along the cliff-walk, wander towards the ruins of Greyfriars', sit down upon the grass, propping himself up against the flinty shards of the priory ruins, stare out, and write. He was inspired, like so many Romantics, by the fusion of culture (in the form of the ruins) and nature, revelling in the robin 'piping in the ivy' along the priory walls, the 'blackberries ripening from stems which those old Grey Friars picked from'[9] and the 'Dunwich rose', brought by the monks from the North and which blooms on the walls of the priory.[10] In his letters it is as though the ruins summon the past, as though the monks were right beside him, lit by the same sun. There was a compulsive edge to FitzGerald's attachment; he was always reluctant to leave, and sorely missed 'my old Dunwich' when he went home. Its allure was almost magnetic – on one occasion, he hatches a plan to visit Abbotsford, the home of Sir Walter Scott, in the Scottish Borders but readily admits he will probably get no further than Dunwich.[11] In October 1878, his friend Mrs Edwards died, and, encountering her widower the next year, they recalled 'the pleasant days at Dunwich' which 'the tide now rolling up here will soon reach'[12] before, later that month, Mr Edwards himself died. It was a striking convergence of personal and geographical loss, his two close friends vanishing along with the place he most associated them with. 'Those two and their little Dunwich in summer were among my pleasures,'[13] FitzGerald wrote in bittersweet remembrance; the drowned city of Dunwich was his elixir of creativity.

Of all the members of the creative colony that formed in Dunwich, FitzGerald struck up perhaps the warmest friendship with *Punch* cartoonist and midnight piper Charles Keene. In summer 1877, he first encountered Keene while lodging at the village pub, describing him as 'an Irishman, an author, and bookworm' and noting his friendship with Alfred Tennyson and William Thackeray: 'we met every evening and talked belles-lettres, Shakespeare and the musical glasses till midnight'.[14] Keene was scruffy, depressive and unusual; 'little must the reader of *Punch* know what a queer spirit lurks behind those woodcuts of his'. Keene found that one of the best ways to lift his mood was to play his pipes in the lost city; to 'strut on the hard sand and skirl away at "Fingal's Lament" or "The Massacre of Glencoe" . . . out of earshot of a soul'.[15] He liked to have 'a good blow on the pipes . . . every day at Dunwich, which was a great solace'.[16] For such an uplifting place, some of the sights were decidedly morbid. 'All along the base of the sandy cliff (striped with layers of rolled pebbles) you come upon human bones that have dropped from the shallow alluvial soil at the top.'[17] The falling cliff, he noted, also revealed a well shaft. Still, with its quietude, faded grandeur, and cows and horses dotting the green marshes, he fell for it just like his friend FitzGerald. 'I enjoy Dunwich so much, I can't help talking of next year directly I leave it,' he wrote to Edwards in 1864.[18] A quarter of a century later, when he was confined to a chair, he went to spend one last, cold autumn in Dunwich. Four months later, he was dead.

Dunwich was a magnet for Victorian *dreamers*. There was something in the air: a lingering feeling of loss – eerie, gentle and strangely intoxicating. It was a dreamy, gentle place to live or visit, its violent destruction kept at a safe remove. They did not have to contend with entire neighbourhoods crashing into the sea, along with parish churches. But this had not always been the case.

———

Much knowledge would be lost about Dunwich, if it were not for the extraordinary commission of someone who felt a strong personal attachment to the rapidly shrinking port. John Day, who was destined to become one of the most prolific and prestigious publishers of the Reformation, was, in all likelihood, born in the parish of St Peter's, Dunwich, in 1522.[19] Growing up he would have had a view of the central market square and, beyond the townhouses, shops and market sheds, the tower of the beleaguered church of St John's.[20] The neighbouring parish had been fighting a desperate battle to keep the sea at bay. Its church was teetering on the brink of the cliff-edge; with just a tiny bit more erosion, the base of the cliff would be undermined, and the church would plunge into the sea. Ten years earlier, two parishioners left money to build a pier to shield the foot of the cliff to prevent just this scenario. It just about worked for thirty years, the sea swirling within its bounds at the base of the cliff. But in the 1540s the situation became critical, and in 1544 it was decided to sell off the church's treasures in a last-ditch effort to save it by bolstering the defences. Shortly afterwards, the church fell off the cliff and joined the ghost churches that had already fallen beneath the waves. For the next two years, when he made the short walk to purchase a new swordblade, doublet, hot sheep's foot, beef pie or, for that matter, a book, the twenty-two-year-old John Day was treated to a dramatic shopping experience; many of the various stalls and shops in the centre of the market-place were now staring straight into the abyss, and human bones and children's coffins poked out from what was left of the grave-yard. Through the casement windows of his parlour, Day may even have been able to see straight off the cliff. He did not remain in Dunwich for much longer, going on to seek his fortune in London. But he retained a lifelong affection for, and fascination with, the dying city on the cliff, leaving a bequest for a statue in St Peter's Church which, by the time of his death, would barely exist at all.

Day's motto, imprinted on the cover pages of all his books, was *Arise for it is Day*. The pun on his name may well have been intentional but the sincerity of his mission was never in doubt. Day did not just want to fulfil the commercial potential of print – though he was very adept at doing so, with a shop in the heart of London, at Cheapside. In fact, the profusion of publications that rolled off his printing presses was intended to consolidate the Reformation and champion the Protestant cause. In Day's time, printing was still a relatively new medium, and he was easily the most prolific and proficient printer operating in the City of London since the 'Father of Fleet Street', Wynkyn de Worde, William Caxton's more commercially minded apprentice, who opened up shop in St Bride's Churchyard in 1501. Day's predecessor had also used light motifs to promote the merits of his trade, imprinting the sign of a sun on all his publications to equate the printed words with knowledge, enlightenment and a driving out of ignorance. Day was a radical Protestant and he wanted to harness the power of print to the cause. It was fortuitous, then, that his arrival in London coincided almost exactly with the accession of the boy-king Edward VI, himself committed to purifying the English Church of Catholic doctrine and liturgy. The king relaxed the censorship laws and encouraged the production and circulation of Protestant and anti-Catholic publications. It was a fecund environment for Day to flourish by churning out tracts from his lodgings above Aldersgate, just north of Barbican, from which he had a mesmerising view of the sprawling timber-framed city, as well as the suburb of Islington and the recently dissolved religious houses of Holborn towards the village of Westminster.

Day was bound to face the wrath of the authorities on the accession of Mary Tudor, a devoted Catholic who threw the Reformation into violent reverse from 1553. He continued to publish clandestinely, and could quite easily have been burned at the stake – many of his patrons were – and indeed he was arrested at the peak of the Marian persecutions, only to be let off. He may have fled to the Continent, he may have returned to Dunwich, and he certainly stayed in close contact with many exiled Protestants, collaborating with them after the accession of Queen Elizabeth, herself a Protestant on whose watch anti-Catholic tracts were once again in vogue. One of these, John Foxe, a talented historian and martyrologist from Boston, Lincolnshire (who had left Magdalene College, Oxford, because he did not want to enter the priesthood) became a close confidant, who used Day's Aldersgate lodgings as a postal address. While in exile in Germany, Foxe had composed a draft of a Latin history of godly, evangelical individuals – especially Protestants and proto-Protestants (like Lollards) – butchered by the Catholic Church. Now, with Day as his editor and proofreader, he began work on an English version, a vivid and gory account of Catholic oppression and concealment of the truth over the centuries but with a focus on the Marian martyrs, based on horrifying first-hand accounts featuring pregnant mothers burned at the stake, throat-slitting, drownings, rape and murder by Catholic priests, stonings to death and the vilest incest: a litany of horror and injustice that was of existential importance for every righteous Christian in the land. A Herculean endeavour, it was first published in 1563, running to eighteen hundred pages assembled with great technical panache, with a multiplicity of fonts, columns, garish headlines, illustrations and varying type sizes. It had a monumental impact on ossifying anti-Catholic sentiment in the popular imagination – eventually it was ordered that a copy of Foxe's *Acts and Monuments* be chained to every church in the land – and the Protestant martyrs came to supplant the banished Catholic saints of old.

Meanwhile, Day's home city of Dunwich continued to be oppressed by *its* tormentor, the sea. By the time Elizabeth I acceded to the throne in 1558, Dunwich was much diminished. The roving cliff-edge had by then capsized around three-fifths of the medieval city. The parishes of St Leonard's, St Michael's, St Bartholomew's, St Martin's, and former jewel-in-the-crown St Nicholas' had all fallen into the sea, crashing down the cliff-face along with their respective churches. The precipice had advanced as far as the church of St John, formerly right in the middle of the city but now on its perilous eastern cusp, staring the waves in the face. Dunwich's former economic prosperity was in short supply. Most of the wealthy elite had long since fled, leading to a plunge in demand for luxury goods, and concomitant damage to manufacturing; the flourishing shipyards that Henry VIII had impressed to Woolwich to build up the Royal Navy from 1513 had not returned; and, as a shingle bar called Kingsholme drifted further south, it thinned the mouth of the Blythe river, limiting access to the haven. This last greatly advantaged Dunwich's competitors, whose channels could much more easily accommodate more ships.[21] The Dissolution of the Monasteries in the 1530s and 1540s, furthermore, along with the dramatically reduced population, led to a diminution in demand for fish. The fishing fleet, ever a key source of prosperity, dwindled accordingly.

Dunwich wasn't a completely lost cause, not yet. Wealthy Londoners bought up dissolved monastic land;[22] and a healthy number of people still left bequests to Dunwich's churches (which was not a natural thing to do if they were generally believed to be doomed). Yet more butchery at the hands of the sea was to come. Candlemas, in early February of each year, was a festival to remember the purification of Mary by lighting and blessing candles in churches across the land. They did not stay lit for long in Dunwich, where the sea had been planning a purification of its own, rising up with unabated fury on 5 February 1570 in the so-called Candlemas Storm. Many feet of snowfall suddenly thawed on Candlemas Day, causing a terrible flood that coincided with a sea storm. This triggered 'a great rage of water' which stranded people in their houses, demolishing stone walls and buildings and uprooting pews from churches. 'Incredible damage' was done at Dunwich: Southgate was swept away, and what remained of Gildengate crushed.[23] It was another hammer-blow for the town – the county receiver, Thomas Badby, reported that 'the Queen Majesty's town of Dunwich is by the rage and the surges of the sea daily wasted and devoured'. The harbour was 'by diverse rages of winds continually landed and barred, so as no ships or boats can enter in, or ought . . . to the utter decay of the said town'.[24] Elizabeth was moved by the plight of the Suffolk port which 'heretofore hath well and faithfully served her Majesty' both in war and peace. Elizabeth's government decided to try to bail out Dunwich with the proceeds of the bells, lead, iron, glass and stone from the decayed church of Ingate, in Suffolk. It was ostensibly a bond, and she charged the bailiffs and burgesses with making the appropriate arrangements – but it was never repaid.

The more the city disappeared into the sea, the more it grew in the popular imagination. Myths began, portraying the ancient city out of all proportion as an Anglo-Saxon metropolis in its glory days, exacerbated by a lack of information from Dunwich itself as the trade links with London and other ports dried up. As a major player in the book trade and a voracious reader himself, the Dunwich-born John Day had a thorough knowledge of the books that captured the imaginations of the lawyers, artisans, clergymen, merchants, apprentices, well-off shopkeepers and others with the surplus wealth, leisure time and literacy to be able to indulge in reading. At a time when the colonisation of the New World was taking place, when some people were seeking a more scientific understanding of the world propelled by the critical, investigative spirit of the Renaissance, there was an appetite for understanding history anew.

The idea of separating fact from fiction and getting to the truth of what his birthplace, the semi-drowned city of Dunwich, had once been seems to have proved irresistible for Day. Through a mutual patron, Matthew Parker, Archbishop of Canterbury, he knew one of the most esteemed and able topographic historians in the country, John Stow, who had published a series of chronicles of English history and who would later, famously, map the capital in vivid historical detail. A long letter written by Stow survives from 1573 – three years after the Candlemas Storm – and is addressed to one 'Master Deye'.[25] The manuscript is overwhelmingly attributed to Stow.[26] We know that Dunwich piqued his curiosity: in *The Generall Chronicle of England* (an edition of which was published in 1615) he describes 'Dunwich, an ancient city in Suffolk, now decayed, and is supposed more than half swallowed up in the sea'. He goes on to lay out just the kind of myths he debunks, as we will see, in the letter to John Deye, but says these are easily disproved by 'manifest and sound record which I have seen'.[27] He states elsewhere that the ancient splendour of Dunwich 'excited my curiosity of visiting', and his faculties as a researcher meant that he was ideally placed to critically examine the legendary, semi-submerged city. So it seems that the bookseller Day sent the chronicler Stow on an investigative mission. He would see the city first-hand and go through the borough records, examining many documents that have since been lost in his quest to establish the truth.

'I beheld the remains of the rampart, some token of Middlegate', recalled Stow, 'the foundations of down-fallen edifices, and tottering fragments of noble structures, remains of the dead exposed, and naked wells, divested of the ground about them by the waves of the sea.' He also found there 'diverse coins, several millhills and part of the old quai'.[28] Day had some specific questions in mind, which he submitted to Stow in advance in a note. What was the physical extent of Dunwich now and 'in old time past'? What proportion of the original city survives, and how much had sunk? How many churches did Dunwich have of old, and how many now? What of the religious houses, hospitals, chapels and leper colonies? Had there ever actually been a church dedicated to Dunwich's sixth-century Bishop Felix of Burgundy? How many gates had there been? Was there ever, as was frequently claimed, a mint or castle? How many people lived there? When did the mayor vanish? Had it actually been a city or just a big town?

Stow dealt with these forensically, adopting a tone of respect throughout, suggesting an intellectual parity between the two men. The town was two hundred acres within its bounds; and from the quay in the north to the southern limits of Palesdyke, one mile in length, and a quarter of a mile from Middlegate in the west to the cliff in the east. Stow deduced that if Dunwich had been built like other historic cities, then it would have been once as wide as it is now long – a square mile, the same size as the City of London. This meant that either two-thirds or three-quarters of the original city was drowned. He does concede, however, that this is 'gathered and conjectured' for want of surviving sources. Concerning the number of parish churches, he is able to offer a more conclusive answer thanks to 'proof' in the Register of the Bishop of Norwich, as well as 'old evidences and records now remaining in the town of Dunwich'. There were six, four of which – St Leonard's, St John's, St Martin's and St Nicholas' – were 'drowned in the sea'; only two – St Peter's and All Saints' – still stood. A parish rate book showed that St Nicholas' parish was three times wealthier than the others. He confirms the sad destruction of the Maison Dieu and St James's hospitals. He dodges the question of whether there was ever a St Felix's Church (or cathedral), and confirms that there are still five gates leading into Dunwich from the Palesdyke but that there were originally more (he had seen the ancient deeds). He doubts it ever had a mint but acknowledges the testimonies of 'credible persons' who say they have seen coins minted at Dunwich (with 'Civitas Donwic' on them), and defers to Day's judgement; the mayoralty, he believes, became surplus to requirements after 1306. The current, dramatically diminished population he places at around 750; and he relays that old deeds and an indenture seem to support the general opinion that Dunwich had traditionally been a *city*, not a town, but 'wherefore consider of this, as to you shall seem best'. These little asides show how Day considered himself a denizen of Dunwich, with more of an instinctive grasp of the truth than Stow's bookish knowledge; on another occasion he tells Day 'he can judge thereof a great deal better than I'. Something Stow seems to feel uncomfortable entertaining is the 'common fame and report of a great number of credible persons' that Dunwich in its prime around 1250 had no less than seventy parish churches, religious houses, hospitals and chapels, along with a like number of ships and even windmills. This myth would die hard; W. G. Sebald's masterful account of the demise of Dunwich in *The Rings of Saturn*, following the first calamitous storm that swept a chunk of it off the cliff in 1288, talks of 'over fifty churches' toppling over the cliff-face, one after the other. The real number of ecclesiastical buildings, after 1066, was eighteen.

As a record, Stow's letter is invaluable. It is the first genuinely empirical account we have of Dunwich. An anonymous manuscript written twenty years later (in a more legible hand) furnishes us with some extra details.[29] It devotes much more attention to trade, in particular herring fishing, which was a key contributor to Dunwich's early prosperity. By 1300, we learn, it had sixteen 'fair ships', twelve barks and twenty-five fishing barks. Eastwood Forest, in addition, was a site of hunting and hawking before it was 'eaten with the sea'. Intriguingly, the manuscript suggests that buildings were not equally distributed throughout Dunwich, but rather there were clusters of density, the 'chiefest buildings' lying about the marketplace with the rest of the buildings 'scattered'. The manuscript also suggests that it was threatened not only by sea but fire too: 'The town hath been greatly consumed with fire also, so that one quarter of the town remaineth.'

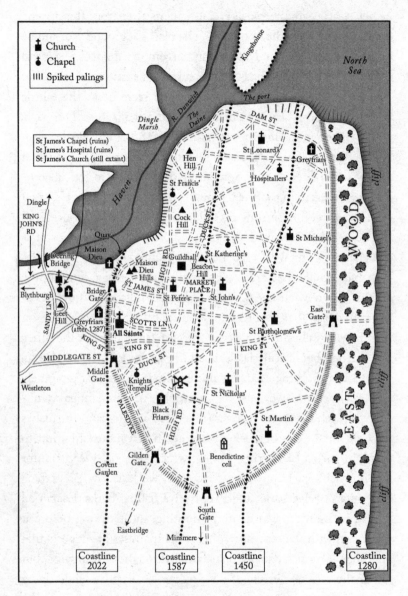

Dunwich's shifting coastline, *c.*1280–2022

The most enlightening evidence, however, comes in the form of a map. The land surveyor and cartographer Ralph Agas, from Suffolk, mapped Dunwich (and its environs) for the first time in 1589. Engraved on fine parchment made from the skin of a calf, Agas's map was part of his failed project to reform and revive the port, whose blockage by the drifting shingle bar Kingsholme had led to such a catastrophic loss of trade. The original map does not survive, but it was copied into Thomas Gardner's eighteenth-century history of Dunwich, and we see a shadow of the city in its high medieval prime before the terrible events of 1288.

Agas was a cartographer rather than a diver, and so could only map what was left – a mere fraction of the original city. However, he does provide a very clear picture of the remaining quarter. The positions of the roads and streets as they reach the sea and are abruptly cut off have allowed historians to interpolate where those streets might have lain in the earlier city. This, in conjunction with medieval records, can help us pinpoint where some of the lost churches (and therefore parishes) lay. The southward-drifting Kingsholme, for example, is sometimes referred to as Leonard's Holme, and a record of a murder reveals that St Leonard's church was on Duck Street, which is heading north-west when it reaches the cliff-face in Agas's map. So we know that that particular church was in the north-east of the drowned city. The position of St Michael's is more unclear. Tax returns from the early 1330s reveal that the parish had lost a fantastic proportion of its houses and land, battered in the storm of 1328, thus inclining us to situate it in the east of the city. But St Michael was also associated with Michaelmas, and therefore fish, so it's also entirely possible that the eponymous parish was in the north near the quay, and the houses had to be abandoned after flooding. Ghost churches are by their very nature elusive.

In the decades following the production of Stow and Agas's representations, Dunwich's predicament became even bleaker, and most artisans left for neighbouring towns, cities and villages, as the merchants had already done. Many of the remainder were impoverished and malnourished, living off the sea-peas that grew around town. In the seventeenth century the fishing trade with Iceland dried up and the herring trade in waters closer to home diminished considerably; countless efforts to revive the port came to nil. As the coastline threatened to sweep further in, people began to move into new, brick-built houses outside the Palesdyke and around Middlegate Street and St James's Street. As ever in the history of vanishing places, there were some stubborn or perhaps overly optimistic souls. In 1631, one Robert Bennett of Westhall signed an ambitious five-hundred-year lease on various houses on St Francis's Meadow, houses that would plummet over the cliff-face before even a fifth of that time was up.

The surviving churches degenerated, along with their parishes. All Saints', 'impoverished by the beat of the sea', and decayed St Peter's, according to a spiritual report in 1652, suffered outbreaks of witchcraft. Eliza Southerne claimed that the Devil himself had assumed the form of a crab, snuck into her bed, bitten her, then forced her to sign away her soul for fourteen years in her own blood. The population continued to fall: the hearth tax returns of 1674 showed only 114 fireplaces, nineteen of which were in houses that lay empty. And then, one night in 1677, came *another* ruinous storm. Waves rolled across the marketplace. The market cross, with its shelter for stalls, was taken down, and all the tradesmen and women began to seek new venues further inland. All the houses north of Maison Dieu Lane were destroyed. In 1688, the east end of St Peter's Church collapsed, and, not long after its bells were removed, its final, pitiful chunk plunged off the cliff, the church where John Day had been born now architecture for the crabs.

When James, Keene, FitzGerald and other Victorian writers and artists luxuriated in the ruins of Dunwich and the void where the rest of the city should have been, they were, in their lamentations and mental resurrections, perpetuating a cultural tradition that stretched back over 350 years. The long century between the 1530s and the 1650s had been one of almost unimaginable pillage and destruction, leaving scars – or works of beauty – on the British landscape that can still be seen to this day.[30] First came the Dissolution of the Monasteries: a violent acceleration of the conflict between Henry VIII and the Papacy and an attempt to remove one of the most conspicuous elements of Catholicism, ruthlessly spearheaded by Thomas Cromwell. The religious orders had first arrived on the island one thousand years earlier, but in the 1530s and 1540s, all of England and Wales's eight hundred religious houses – all its friaries, abbeys, priories belonging to the grey friars, the white friars, the black friars and more – were converted to private houses, retained by the Crown (some of which, like Syon, Sheen and Greenwich, made brief comebacks during Mary Tudor's reign, only to be re-dissolved by Elizabeth), or destroyed and left to fall into ruin. Anything valuable was plundered until all that remained in the main were skeletal shards and battered, windswept ruins. The devastation was particularly intense in Scotland, whose Calvinistic Reformation took on an even more extreme, violent character, resulting in the divinely ordained annihilation not just of its eighty monasteries but of many of its churches and all of its cathedrals too. It was, as even the most radical of Protestant divines put it, 'a wicked age . . . much given to the destruction of things memorable';[31] some of Britain's largest and most beautiful buildings were destroyed by iconoclastic fury, and this was perhaps the biggest transformation of the landscape since the efflorescence of towns and cities in the Middle Ages.

But that was just Act One: the corpses of the dissolved monasteries were complemented, a hundred years later, by the vast architectural destruction of the English Civil War, which broke out between Charles I and his Parliamentary opponents in 1642 and ended with Charles's execution in 1649. Across the land great castles were laid low, either destroyed by Royalist or Parliamentary forces or 'slighted' (deliberately dismantled). The impact – not just religiously, economically and politically, but *psychologically* – of this devastation cannot be underestimated; this widespread sense of loss lingered on through the eighteenth and nineteenth centuries. In Dunwich, of course, this sensation was all the more profound given that the religious houses, by the mid-Victorian period, were essentially all that had survived of the drowned medieval city.

The cultural impact was also immense, but only after a sufficient amount of time had elapsed for the interest not to seem morbid or politically dangerous – anything smacking of the fetishisation of Catholicism would have brought certain risks through much of the Tudor period – and there was a shift in appreciation across the eighteenth century from what the ruins were, to what they could do to you. It began with the antiquarians. The word today has something of a pejorative ring – to say something is 'mere antiquarianism' is to suggest a certain self-indulgence, and this was not unknown then, with the wit and essayist Joseph Addison dismissing antiquarians as 'critics in rust'. Antiquarians surface in the historical record as a distinctive cultural force during the relative political stability, economic expansion and new climate of scientific empiricism of the mid-seventeenth century, coalescing into a London Society of Antiquaries in 1707. They performed a valuable function, seeking to corroborate the grand narratives and arguments of historians by saving material artefacts from the 'deluge of time' and inspired by Renaissance humanism. The objects of their study were physical remains, manuscripts, coins and inscriptions. These they valued not just for the light they could shed on Britain's history but as valuable objects in their own right, relics of the nation's identity worthy of preservation. Ruins fascinated them and they railed against what they saw as a fixation upon both foreign and British classical ruins at the expense of the armoury of more recent domestic ruins that so littered the landscape. Lord Kames in his *Elements of Criticism* (1762) suggested that a Gothic ruin attested to 'the triumph of time over strength', whereas classical ruins were 'barbarity over taste'.

The antiquarians were at the forefront of a broader public interest in Britain's homegrown ruins brought about by significant improvements in communications (roads and transport), the concomitant rise of domestic tourism (in those days you went to a ruin, not the seaside), the influence of the cult of the picturesque[32] and the expansion of the 'middling sort' (people who had the time and money to indulge in such things as leisure pursuits). Significantly, 1726 heralded the publication of *Ruins of Castles and Abbeys in England and Wales*. Beautifully illustrated throughout, it was the first book to take ruins – rather than buildings – as its subject matter, a crystallisation of Britain's newfound interest in its legacy of architectural destruction. That is not to say no one noticed or cared about Britain's domestic ruins earlier – they did, particularly classical ruins which acted as a potent reminder of a lost civilisation – but this was the first time they became subject to extended scrutiny and were considered part of Britain's identity.

The antiquarians identified, analysed, sketched and urged the protection of the Britain's ruins, investing them with meaning that would be articulated and eventually ossified into the tropes and conventions of the 'ruin poetry'[33] that emerged as a sub-genre of eighteenth-century literature. Although interpretations varied, ruins were frequently charged with political meaning. They could be manifestations of – or thanksgivings for – England's deliverance from the soul-threatening doctrines and financial extortions of the Catholic Church; or the political and religious tyranny of Charles I; or as terrible reminders of wanton destruction. For others, they represented the vagaries of political power, especially as many medieval or Gothic ruins elicited nostalgia for a lost, idealised world of honour, piety and chivalry. As history that had been physically embedded into the landscape, they also commemorated the fallen – the words 'monument' and 'ruin' were often used interchangeably. Most powerfully, however, ruins served a morally didactic function that transcended politics and commemoration. They were almost universally interpreted as a powerful metaphors for the evanescence of life – or rather, as landscape gardener Stephen Switzer put it, 'there may be read the instability of all sublunary affairs, and will remind us of the frailty of these our earthly Tabernacles; for if those magnificent piles composed of the hardest and most durable materials of wood and stone, are subject to such casualties; how much easier is it for Providence to destroy this tottering frame of nature, composed only of flesh and blood'.[34] Ruins were memento mori par excellence; and none more so than ruins that were about to fall into the sea.

The empiricism of the antiquarian approach towards ruins, with its love of facts and conclusions, came to be challenged by Romanticism. This cultural movement defined itself against the reason, restraint and objectivity of the Enlightenment (with its esteem for the harmonious classical and neoclassical form), and instead championed subjectivity, inspiration and a capitulation to emotions. Finding its roots in the writings of Rousseau (such as his *Reveries of a Solitary Walker*, in 1764) and others,[35] and emerging as a powerful influence by the early nineteenth century, it was epitomised by the works of Wordsworth, Byron and Shelley, who frequently took their inspiration from the natural world. For a while, this kind of emotionally liberated interpretation was resisted. For William Gilpin, the godfather of the picturesque, ruins were wonderful components of well-curated compositions. 'The ruined tower, the Gothic arch, the remains of castles and abbeys'[36] added *gravitas* to a scene, especially if they were bedecked in ivy and mosses, showing nature's triumph over culture, the crumbling stones and fragmented arches an intoxicating rupture with the monotonous harmony and perfection of the classical form. For him, ruins were more about aesthetic than triggers for reverie; as late as 1760 people sympathetic to 'associative aesthetics' were cautioning against the 'wildest flights of ungoverned fancy'[37]. Yet for the Romantics the value of a ruin was in its capacity to evoke imaginative reverie and sublime sensations, pondering death, longing, absence and mourning. It made the antiquarian approach seem rather dry and unimaginative, for ruins could elicit haunting emotions. They harrow. They awe. They beam us into a mirror universe. Henry James described how in Rome 'the aqueducts seem the very source of the solitude in which they stand; they look like architectural spectres';[38] Flaubert, similarly, likened the moonlit ruins of Thebes to 'a troop of ghosts'.[39] Poetry, with its charged language, free-flowing associations and surprising connections, was seen as the most appropriate vessel for these vivid trains of thought – one could compile several volumes of minor poetry just on Dunwich alone.

———

The tourists of the picturesque saw the folly of earthly endeavour in the ruined Gothic abbeys that they sought out just as, millennia earlier, prehistoric Britons may have seen the idea of earthly permanence itself as hubristic, digging and redigging structures and favouring vast monuments to the dead. It has been said that 'the purpose of structure is delay',[40] to provide a sense of permanence in a natural world that never stands still.[41] 'Ruin' comes from a Latin word for fall, and we certainly tend to think of ruins as fallen states, defining them according to their former utility. The ruin always has to be a ruin *of* something, a ruined castle, a ruined priory, a ruined factory – a ruined city – even if all that is left is a diminutive shadow. They are at once of their time, yet derailments of it, too, bringing the singularity – and fragility – of the present into stark focus. 'The power of ruins relies upon the interplay between', as William

Viney writes, 'what has, what has not, and what could have been.'[42] 'Illustrious Society, can you tamely look on, and suffer our bodies to be basely torn, barbarously mangled, and layed in ruins by a selfish race of unfeeling Goths?' asked one correspondent to the Society of Antiquaries in 1776, emulating the perspective of the 'abbeys, cathedrals and other ancient building of North Britain' themselves! 'Many of us are entirely levelled! Some of us are falling down with Gothic irons! . . . Pity our forlorn situation, and procure us necessary aid . . . or soon! Too soon alas! None of us will be left to groan.'[43] It would be another hundred years before Parliament passed an Ancient Monuments Protection Act.

There is something noble about the death of a giant.[44] Thus Henry James and Algernon Charles Swinburne did not care for Southampton, or Norwich, or Hull, or Portsmouth. Those cities held no allure for them. But they were drawn to Dunwich. Yet no one thought that the destruction of Dunwich was worthy of aesthetic appreciation at the time. Whether in 1287, 1328, 1570 or 1740, the sight of a city vanished into salt spray, its ruins revolving in the waters below the cliff, as W. G. Sebald puts it, was instead met with abject horror and a recourse to prayer. Henry James acknowledged how admiring ruins 'might appear a heartless pastime',[45] and indeed, for them to be appreciated as objects of aesthetic beauty, distance is required. Dunwich became a ruin incrementally, eaten away by the sea and hollowed out as people deserted its vulnerable stretches. Temporal distance provides a safe vantage point to divorce ruins from their horrific context; it took over 150 years for the monastic remains of the 1530s and 1540s to become objects of aesthetic appreciation. The only ruins that are instantly appreciated, perhaps, are the deliberately manufactured structures, follies, popular in the gardens of the elite in eighteenth-century Britain – 'fake ruins' were considered a picturesque way of throwing the beholder back in time, or at least into their own thoughts, filling the gaps and channels created by ivy tendrils and the like.

In French, there is the term *nostalgie de la boue*, literally translatable as 'yearning for mud'.[46] It refers to the sense of being gratified by 'ruin, dissolution or suffering' – and the more violent, the better. There is a guilty pleasure in the art of destruction.[47] For, as one poet would write a decade later just as All Saints' fell, 'beauty is nothing but the beginning of terror'.[48]

———

The skies were heavy, the sea slow. I wandered away from the cliff-edge, through the lifeless village which I was unable to connect with old Dunwich in any meaningful way, towards the remains of Greyfriars'. The priory spread its wings through a lonely, cold meadow. The sun was low in the sky; I longed, as I always did in absent places, for something warming – a quart of mulled cider in the Ship, which was once the Barnes Arms, taking its name from the martial family that once dominated the city's politics. Aesthetics demanded that the ruined nave and fallen arches should be windswept, but they were not. They just stood there. I flanked the

circuit of stone, dead leaves still on the bough tilting gently behind me, and reached a grand arch – once the entrance to the priory – through which could be seen, across a green field, a beautiful block of ruin bathed in golden sunlight, the sky glowing through the four upper window-holes like the vacant eyes of the skulls washed up on Dunwich beach. Looking at what was left of its walls, now standing so vulnerably in the field like a domino, it was hard not to contrast this fragile ruin with its earlier purpose. It was once the refectory, where the monks gathered to eat fish from Iceland and wine from Gascony to the light of a flickering flame, a rare break from their silent symphonies of prayer – now just a heap of stones in a field.

Ruins are time in abeyance. Yet the experience of viewing ruins – whether this be for me pacing about the skeletal cloister of Grey-friars' priory, or the nineteenth-century writers lost in reverie in the shadow of All Saints' Church as it slid ever closer to the cliff – transforms our sense of time. They fetch the past, showing us the roots of our own culture, embedding our history into the ground while portending how our civilisations might end in the future. But, for me, the overriding sense when looking at ruins is of a hovering between thresholds – something beautifully captured by Lord Byron in *Don Juan* when he writes

> A grey wall, a green ruin, rusty pike
> Make my soul pass the equinoctial line
> between the present and past worlds, and hover
> Upon their airy confine, half-seas-over.[49]

Ruins have resisted yet also fallen prey to the 'all-mouldering hand of time'.[50]

———

I walked away from the field with its ruins, opened a gate through an ugly mesh wire fence, and followed a footpath into a little wood where the trees were frail and wispy. I could not help associating this with Eastwood, the forest that had divided the eastern cusp of the medieval city from the sea, which was entirely washed away by the thirteenth century. This was in fact Greyfriars' Woods, which once led towards Dunwich from Westleton and Blythburgh. I found myself on a path where, in the distance, I could see a stone bridge and, beyond that, the sea. Before the coast swept in, this was Middlegate Street, which itself gave way to Duck Street, which in turn curved left up the hill towards the marketplace, eventually opening on to the mouth of the port. It would have been a track busy with carts, riders, litigants come to attend one of the courts, and flocks of geese and ducks – and other livestock – for sale in the marketplace. The only place it led now was the cliff-edge, my destination.

But I was sidetracked by one of the most poignant sights I had seen so far. It was the last surviving gravestone from the church-yard of All Saints'. The gravestone rose like a dead tooth from the barren earth beneath low-hanging branches. The inscription reads: 'In memory of Jacob Forster who departed this life March 12th 1796 aged 38 years.' He was exactly my age. Soon he too will fall to the sea.

I walked to the cliff-edge and looked out to sea, tracing what I imagined to be an area half a mile out. The waters were grey and quivering. The sense of emptiness is haunting and overpowering. 'There is a presence in what is missing,' writes James; 'there is history in there being so little.' One need only stare out at the site of medieval Dunwich to understand that an absence can have more presence than what is present. It was something I felt every day.

———

If Dunwich's resurrection through Victorian visionaries was profound and noteworthy, the same cannot be said for its physical recovery. This is not for want of trying. A series of season-long dives was carried out between 1979 and 1983 but hampered by poor visibility. Discoveries included: masonry remains on the underwater site of St Peter's church (lost in the seventeenth century); a Purbeck marble slab with lettering dated to 1320 from near the site of All Saints' (now in Dunwich Museum); the ruins of some artefacts from the Maison Dieu Hospital (where the car park is today); wood from Eastwood Forest beneath a blanket of mud; and a master mason's plumb bob. The ruins are deep down, covered in crabs and eels. Occasionally, during storms and freak tides, more is visible. The ruins of All Saints' Church lie directly east of the final gravestone in a gully in the seabed. When there is visibility, the tower – the main part of the ruin – can be seen lying across the other ruins. More recently, ultrasound scans of the seabed have been attempted but the results have proved inconclusive. There is potentially an entire underwater world of ruins to explore.[51]

On top of the cliff, it was silent. None of Dunwich's fabled fifty churches rang their bells from the deep. Silence is the music of absence. I climbed down the hill, walked through the car park, and waited for a taxi in the rain.

CHAPTER SIX

THE ABANDONED ISLAND: ST KILDA

The fulmars had been grabbed from the cliffs, roasted on their stone mounds, and eaten in silence. The dogs were all drowned in the bay. The islanders left their crofts with their peat fires burning and Bibles lying open, just as tradition demanded – one at the Book of Exodus. They left their boats and beds behind, their gin traps and horsehair ropes, their birds' bladders and bird-skull lamps which only ever gave out a meagre glow. They hauled their remaining possessions to the quayside in the wild whirling wind and tethered their cows – more valuable than the dogs, and thus salvageable – to a little boat swarming with calves, making them swim out, in the darkness, to a bigger vessel that had been prepared for their evacuation. Their world became a deserted film set.

Most had never, in their entire lives, left their island. Now they would not return: never again would they lay their eyes on the stone cottages lining the unnamed village, the stupendous mountains rising sheer from the sea, the graveyard brimming with infant corpses, nor hear, from the direction of Storm Beach, the bells of the lonely church borne on the wind; never again would they see a fulmar dart into the sunset waves, arising with a mackerel in its bill, nor hear the satisfying crunch as they broke that same bird's neck. They had one final, fitful night's sleep. Then, it was time.

The morning of 29 August 1930 came with a heavy mist and HMS *Harebell* loomed on the horizon like a ghost rig. The corpses of some of the islanders' dogs were bobbing in the water, pecked at and nibbled by the gulls. The islanders were stolid, reconciled to an uncertain future, standing in the freezing air, waiting. There was great public interest in their plight but no press photographers or newsreel operators had been permitted to attend the evacuation, on government orders, save a solitary hack thrashing out his copy in one of the cottage's spare rooms as the wind yowled outside, the windows rattling along to his typewriter. After at least a thousand years of continuous occupation, Hirta, by far the biggest island in the St Kilda archipelago, the remotest inhabitable part of the United Kingdom, was to be abandoned and, from now on, no peat fires would send their plumes of smoke swirling into the sky. Soon, it would be a ghost island.

So silently they stood, the final inhabitants, just thirty-six in number, on the stern of *Harebell* as it receded into a milky-white haze of salt spray and mist. Their home dwindled to a speck in the ocean, then disappeared.

'May God forgive those that have taken us away from St Kilda,' uttered one of the older émigrés, gloomily, as they approached the shores of Scotland.[1]

———

The islanders spied it first from the cliffs and soon all of Hirta was howling: the white fin of a lone wooden boat drawing towards the shore, three years before the turn of the eighteenth century. The boat brought the Reverend John Campbell from the Isle of Harris, sixty miles to the east, to counteract the false teachings of a native called Roderick, who had been claiming to be none other than John the Baptist returned. Also within the drenched timbers of the little boat was a Gaelic-speaking writer from the Isle of Skye, in the Inner Hebrides, called Martin Martin. As the remotest part of Britain, and a domain of pure Highland culture, St Kilda had been the subject of curiosity for some time, and Martin believed the time had come to publish a vivid and enlightening book about the society, culture and natural history of the Outer Hebrides for a wider, English-speaking audience. This was unusual. The ships that appeared on the horizon usually brought administrators or tax collectors; more of these philosophical travellers would roll in during the eighteenth century, and the collection of rocks that were growing bigger and bigger on the horizon would find themselves, for the first time, in the gaze of the public eye. But for the moment, Martin wasn't convinced he was going to make it in one piece.

The whole sixteen-hour journey, he recalls, took place 'to the almost manifest hazard of my life'.[2] Even allowing for artistic licence, journeys to St Kilda seem to have been quite profoundly terrifying given the length of the crossing, the often ferocious weather conditions on that stretch of sea, and the feebleness of the six-oar rowing boat in which they were usually attempted; even three hundred years later, with motorised boats and much-improved navigation, the crossing can still be turbulent, troublesome and altogether trying, if not actually abortive. Later travellers shared Martin's pain. The minister Kenneth Macaulay (great-uncle of the famous historian) found himself caught in a hurricane in 1758 with clouds which 'bursted asunder and tumbled down upon us in violent torrents of rain', and conveyed his crew's astonishment that such a 'small and frail' Highland boat could endure 'such enormous billows without either being overset or dashed to pieces';[3] and for another traveller, E. D. Clarke, writing in 1797, the fundamental terror of the voyage was compounded by an obliterative mist which along with violent gusts of wind and a heavy rolling sea made the voyagers worry that their bowsprit and mast were going to smash violently into the waves.[4] Getting completely lost was *de rigueur*. Without sight of land for hours on end, blinded by whirling mists, and with a tired and despondent crew, successful navigation required a degree of resourcefulness – 'at length one of [the crew] discovered several tribes of the fowls of St Kilda', recalls Martin, 'flying', and the crew used the trails of birds to lead them landward. Before long, the men in the forecastle 'descried the land of St Kilda' and everyone trained their eyes upon the dark silhouettes on the horizon, burning through the mist.

St Kilda was just one of hundreds of remote islands and archipelagos explored and written about in the eighteenth century – not just on the peripheries of Europe but much further afield, in the uncharted waters of the South Seas, Caribbean, northern Atlantic and Asian Pacific. It was an age of discovery that can be likened to the colonisation of the 'New World' in the sixteenth century. Vivid accounts of these places were printed by the newly liberated press, and read and discussed – in coffee-houses and drawing rooms, in inns, walks, book shops and clubs, and the various other spaces of Britain's public sphere.[5] As the empire expanded, trade boomed, towns and cities grew, communications improved, the distribution of wealth thickened, and attitudes towards consumption changed, the ranks of the 'middling sort' swelled, and so more people, beyond noblemen on their grand tours, had the wealth and leisure to travel – or to read about travelling.

One of the main reasons why the emergent genre of travel writing became so popular is that voyages of discovery were also voyages of self-discovery. Then as now travel literature encouraged introspection; as much as authors chronicled the Martian-seeming features of the cultures and landscapes they encountered in the Pacific and Atlantic Oceans, they were also shining a light on the essence of human nature itself, the deep ravines of islands like Hirta leading not just to remote places but also into the deepest recesses of the human psyche. Sailing for days, weeks, sometimes months on end without a glimpse of land against a rarely changing backdrop of sea, sky and sun (or more usually cloud and rain, in St Kilda's case), many travellers were struck by a sense of space folding into time, a feeling they were travelling thousands of miles across the planet but also back to the dawn of society itself. 'The philosophical traveller, sailing to the ends of the earth,' wrote the French *philosophe* Joseph-Marie Degérando, 'is in fact travelling in time.'[6]

These philosophical voyages were important tectonic plates in the intellectual earthquake called the Enlightenment – a European intellectual movement seeking to better humanity by empowering the critical faculties and embracing man's limitless capacity for self-improvement, engineering, ultimately, *un nouveau Adam* (*une nouvelle Eve* was less of a going concern). It was propelled by a tempestuous, long-distance family of intellectuals (or 'Republic of Letters') in western Europe who did not always agree, and who sought to bring about change in their respective countries in different ways, but who worked towards the same goal of collective improvement and intellectual freedom.[7] Published journeys to St Kilda, then, transcended their specific context and were part of a wider conversation. In some senses, it seemed that places like St Kilda were already lost – or adrift, at least – marooned in the margins of time, set apart from the temporal mainstream; the rawer the setting, the purer the human nature on display, for an unspoiled landscape was indicative of bare, essential humanity.

Far away, in lands thought to be largely untouched by the hand of 'civilisation', Europeans sought to meet their mysterious ancestors and, in so doing, a vision of what they themselves could be, or were like, under all the artificial layers of social construction. 'The Tahitian is closer to the origins of the world,' wrote another French philosopher, Denis Diderot, of a remote island in the South Seas, 'and the European to its old age.'[8] Making little effort to discover if his beliefs about Tahitians were correct, Diderot believed the people who inhabited such places lived much closer to nature; nonetheless, encounters between the two worlds would have startling philosophical implications.

———

To evade a storm, Martin's crew had to resort to sheltering beneath the hollow of what, to this day, is one of the loftiest sea-stacks in the whole of the United Kingdom – Boreray – utterly engulfed by birds. There was the fulmar, emblem of St Kilda, a grey-and-white gull, stocky with pipe-like nostrils, ravenous for the fat of fish, and the northern gannet (or solan goose), white, with a long, sharp, slightly crooked bill, and which observed its prey from a considerable height and darted down into the water 'with incredible force', furnishing their nests with whatever they could find, grass, timber shavings, even, Alexander Buchan tells us, 'a red coat, brass sun-dial, arrow and some Moulacca beans'.[9] The birds' excreta gave the stacks a striking white topping that looked, from a distance, like silver frost or the icing of a cake.[10] 'The heavens were darkened by their flying over our heads,' Martin recalls; 'their excrements were in such quantity that they add a tincture to the sea, and at the same time sullied our boat and clothes.' The crew – drunk, having been rewarded with strong brandy – just about managed to drop anchor but were promptly dragged by the fast currents towards the open seas again in the storm, during which they 'laid aside all hopes of life'. There was something intrinsically unreachable about St Kilda, even when you were tantalisingly close, and that made the joy of discovery sweeter still. Even though they were only a quarter of a mile out, they couldn't get anywhere near the shore for the wind and the waves, being compelled instead to plunge through a dark gorge between two immense cliffs. 'All within was dark and horrible,' recalls Clarke. All that could be heard was the smack of wave on rock and the screeching of the sea fowl 'who had there deposited their young'. Into this creek gushed sea-swell like the drool of a kraken suddenly hoisting the boat to stomach-churning heights.

Macaulay recalls how his crew languished for five hours 'in a most distressful condition', soaked through and shivering, thinking they were going to be swallowed alive at any moment. Eventually, distressed crews such as his managed to close in upon the 'smoking settlement' cradled by the high mountains in the distance. Now the crew got a better look at them: vast fangs of rock – one, two, three, more – crash-landed from heaven and soaring from the waves. Behind them loomed a sea-mountain of immense height whose peaks pierced the passing clouds. What manner of man, they wondered, could live on *that*?

———

The nature of primitive man as a subject of intellectual enquiry was not new. Ovid, for example, wistfully evoked a paradisiacal Golden Age, as did the Bible's Garden of Eden – domains of pure innocence in which man and woman lived in harmony with nature until their expulsion condemned humanity to a life of misery and toil. The idea of primal innocence and virtue (before the Fall) underpinned the entire theological basis of Christianity, in which Christ dies upon the cross to purge believers of their original sin, a cornerstone of medieval Catholic belief. Not everyone took the Genesis myth literally but even as metaphor it seemed to imply that primitive man was somehow superior to his fallen albeit more civilised successor, an idea reflected in Tacitus' surprisingly

sympathetic depiction of the 'barbarian' Germanic tribes as foils to the decadence and indolence of the Romanised Gauls.

The idea of primal innocence gained new currency during the Renaissance, with the European discoveries of the 'New World' in the late fifteenth and sixteenth centuries. Columbus relayed how although the Amerindians lived in nakedness and ignorance they were mild, virtuous and intelligent, and in *De Orbo Novo* (1530) the Italian historian Pietro Martire portrays the peoples of Hispaniola as living in a positively prelapsarian state, needing neither laws, books, corrupt judges, clothes nor money to live in a 'golden age'. English explorers reached similar conclusions. For Sir Francis Drake, the aborigines of Brazil were civil and gentle beings; for Sir Walter Raleigh, the tribes along the River Orinoco in South America were wise and of sober judgement. They were also exceptionally beautiful. The implied contrasts with European society are hard to miss, but the first author explicitly and extensively to contrast the life of the New World inhabitants with that of Europeans was Michel de Montaigne. In an essay called 'On Cannibals' in 1580, he described the natives of France Antarctique (a colony in Brazil) as 'blessed with all the native goodness which modern sophistication has destroyed' even though they did rather unsavoury things. Thus, rather than just critiquing Spanish savagery in the Americas, Montaigne cast civilisation itself as a corrosive force upon the innate goodness of man. He had a name for the natives of French Antarctique: *les bons sauvages*, 'the noble savages'. The term did not appear in English for another hundred years – in John Dryden's *The Conquest of Grenada* (1672) – and since cherries were sometimes described as savage too, we can confidently assume the word meant wild in the natural sense rather than *ferocious*.[11]

But then, several generations after Montaigne, the English philosopher Thomas Hobbes hurled a grenade which completely reframed the debate with the publication of *Leviathan* (1651). Man in his natural state, argued Hobbes, was not good – far from it. He was a nasty, violent, sense-driven brute, and life in the earliest times was certainly no golden age but rather 'a war of all against all'; it was 'solitary, poor, nasty, brutish and short'. These last three words have been passed down through the centuries precisely because they *vindicate* civilisation. Absolutist rule was, for Hobbes – who seems to have been influenced by the maelstrom of violence that convulsed seventeenth-century Europe – the only way of holding humanity's destructive impulses in check. It was a straitjacket for man's innate depravity.

In the late seventeenth century, around the time philosophical voyages to St Kilda began in earnest, the pendulum swung again as Hobbes's profoundly pessimistic world view came to be challenged by the philosopher Anthony Ashley Cooper, the Third Earl of Shaftesbury, in his *An Inquiry Concerning Virtue* (1699) which went on to have a formative influence on Enlightenment thought. Man was fundamentally good, he argued, not because God had made him that way, but because virtue was innate, flowing from a sense of shared empathy between fellow human beings. This he called 'moral or natural conscience',[12] natural morality.[13] It chimed with – and gave an explanation for – the observations of the Renaissance explorers who found perfectly moral beings in lands that had never experienced Christianity, or any discernible religion. Throughout the eighteenth century, when Europeans explored over five hundred islands in the scorching South Seas, as well as visiting outposts like St Kilda in their own back yards, stunning opportunities arose to test these writers' conceptions. The intellectual stakes could not have been higher. Pre-existing notions of man's virtue, even the nature of good and evil, could now be checked against a glorious range of reported experience in the form of colourful, *Gulliver's Travels*-esque accounts. The question that had dogged intellectuals since Plato could be settled once and for all: was natural man Hobbes's sense-driven brute or the virtuous creature dreamt of by Shaftesbury and Ovid?

————

Travellers' first impressions of the Hirtans boded well. Macaulay describes how 'with an amazing intrepidity, [they] flew into the water to meet us'. They were selfless – no other race of men, he believed, would attempt this in such treacherous conditions even if their own relatives had been imperilled. In E. D. Clarke's later account, the islanders come across as more suspicious, at first running for the hills and clambering onto the roofs of their huts, 'pointing with great earnestness towards the boat' as it drew into the bay. It was dangerous to disembark and usually the captain would drop anchor and the crew had to languish for another couple of hours and await assistance, soaked to the bone, shivering with cold and sullied by fowl. Macaulay describes quite vividly how, eventually, the 'savage-like men' with their necks banked in freezing cold water gently lifted each member of the crew upon their shoulders and, in two vertical lines with the strongest at the front, carried them ashore, holding each other's midriffs so as not to be swept away by the current. After this, they rushed back in and hoisted the boat – and everything in it – on to the beach.

As soon as they touched down on the sand, the travellers described how the islanders swarmed over to them, along with their beloved dogs – swift, sausage-like creatures with squat legs and tan-coloured faces – who slathered them in saliva and barked their welcome. The Hirtans greeted the crew with 'God save you!', each making their respective curtsies. Anyone expecting to find an 'island mentality' was surprised by the inquisitiveness of the Hirtans, who would fire out questions as 'Whence come ye?'; 'What brought ye to our island?' and, reassured that their crew didn't consist of French or Spanish pirates,[14] 'Oh God Bless you! Come and eat! You shall have what you will of our island,' underscoring, in Clarke's view, the eminence of their hospitality.[15] The islanders were particularly concerned with finding out whether 'it was peace or war' abroad; it was a question newcomers invariably got asked. The minister was the islanders' spokesman; a handful of the others could speak English;

three or four, we are told, were even literate by mid-century thanks to the efforts of the minister; the others expressed themselves 'slowly but pertinently' in 'a very corrupt dialect of Gaelic, adulterated with a little mixture of the Norwegian tongue'. Since literacy was so rare, and outsiders appeared but infrequently, there was little appetite for 'the expensive drudgery' of learning English. It was only really the women who, at least in some accounts, provided a frostier welcome with 'evident looks of distrust and terror',[16] concerned that these boatmen may not have been what they seemed, and, if the location of the islanders' homes were revealed, that the visitors might return under the cover of darkness to slaughter them as they slept, just like the islanders did to the fulmars and gannets on the sea-stacks each year.

The men, we learn, had blond or red hair, leathery faces and curious little beards. They were stout and sturdy but a little ungainly too; 'short of stature', in the words of Macaulay, 'extremely thick and brawny, but rather clumsily made than nicely proportioned'. He notes how they were 'remarkably strong, carry huge burdens, and will tug at the oar for many hours, with an almost undiminished vigour'. The women, though unnaturally (as it seemed to him) muscular, were impressive too; 'most handsome', in the words of Macaulay, 'and their complexion fresh and lively, as their features are regular and fine' – 'there are some of them', he is generous enough to concede, 'who if properly dressed, and gently educated, would, in my opinion, be reckoned extraordinary beauties in the gay world'. The men no longer wore sheepskin but a short doublet reaching to their waists and, around that, 'a double plait of plaid . . . both ends joined together with the bone of a fulmar' reaching to their knees, tied with a leather belt. The women were attired in linen dresses and a head-veil to their shoulders 'and a lock of about sixty hairs hanging down each cheek, to their breasts, the lower end tied with a knot'; both sexes wore identical hats and bonnets. Clarke was pleasantly surprised to discover that the islanders were not filthy yet some sort of 'effluvia affects a stranger's olfactory nerves so sensibly upon entering their little town'. Visitors were also impressed by the islanders' excellent eyesight and by the 'pearly whiteness' of their teeth, a gleaming rebuke to the sweet tooth of the civilised world.[17]

The journals show how St Kilda's population decreased over the course of the early eighteenth century – Martin records 180 people in 1698, yet Macaulay, in 1766, counts only eighty-eight (thirty-eight men and fifty women), the difference accounted for by a devastating outbreak of smallpox. During initial encounters, the islanders (who referred to themselves generally as Hirtans; 'Kildans' or 'Kildians' was more of a travellers' term) were both fascinated by – and wary of – the new arrivals; when strangers were among them, travellers reported, some suffered from a 'boat cold' which blocked their nose and even caused them to spit blood, so many kept their distance. They were not especially parochial; because they had 'a great inclination to novelty', we learn that a number of islanders were always about the mainlanders, admiring their carriage, comportment and cut of their cloth, and the crew would give out little parcels of tobacco and sweets, which were lapped up by the islanders. On one unfortunate occasion, a crewman whipped out a pistol and shot a gannet mid-flight. As it plunged to earth, the male islanders surrounded the minister and the women screamed.[18]

First contact made, visitors were usually taken to the village where all of the hundred or so islanders lived, and it was on this short stroll that they had the chance to appreciate Hirta's extraordinary landscape at a more leisurely pace – that is, without fear of imminent death. The island was, travellers agreed, vast, overpowering, sublime; 'naturally fenced with one continued face of a rock of great height, except a part of the bay,' wrote Martin in 1698, 'well defended generally with a raging sea'. As for the other two bays – Storm Beach and Crooked Bay – anyone who tried to land there would not be long for this world. Village Bay, as it was known, to the south-west, had a sandy beach which was only visible in summer, the sand being washed away by the sea and the rain in winter. Ships could not – and never would be able to – anchor in the bay, because it was so lethal in choppy weather and storms, with ships likely to be dashed to pieces against the rocks. Hirta culminated in several sky-bound spires of rock, like upended icicles. 'The whole island', writes Martin, 'is formed into four high mountains, three of which are in the middle, all thinly covered with black or brown earth.' He describes these mountains (sometimes hills) evocatively as 'ramparts of defence' against the boisterous sea. It was the barest, starkest, most stripped-down landscape that anyone could imagine supporting human life; astonishing. 'Mountains of rocks lay one within the other,' wrote Clarke, lying in 'various fantastic forms, piled against each other'. These island-mountains shot up to prodigious heights, a tight-knit micro-world drenched in the spit of the sea, and their tips were sometimes pleasingly shrouded – as the summits of fantastical islands should be – in ambient white mist.

Some of these rock faces were only accessible to rock-climbing maestros, and even then at their great peril. Everyone was struck by Conachair, the mountain that loomed over the northern edge of Hirta, rising to 430 metres. Here are to be found the highest cliffs in the British Isles by some margin. Of all Hirta's 'frightful precipices', Macaulay singles out Conachair: 'a real prodigy in its kind'; 'a view of it from the sea fills a man with astonishment, and a look over it from above strikes him with horror'. It was sublime, harrowing all who saw it with an overpowering sense of their microscopic place in the universe. Many of the Western Isles, of course, were similarly rugged and precipitous, it was just that Hirta's minute size, remoteness, and relatively higher mountains intensified the effect; an anomaly once seen, never forgotten. The whole island was almost lunar: 'No sort of trees, not even the least shrub grows,' observed Martin, 'nor has a bee been ever seen'.[19] But it was not totally austere. There were beauty spots with white and red clover, daisies, buttercups and dandelion, and the whole island was dotted with the little stone grottoes overlaid with turf. Open to the air, and with the wind whistling through, no dampness could take hold, making them ideal refrigerators for peat, eggs and wild-fowl, without which the Kildans could have starved.[20] Martin reckoned there were five thousand of these 'stone pyramids' all over the island, even at the highest peaks, and, though reduced in number, they are still one of the island's most curious features to this day, now just moribund shells.

It did not take long to reach the village, just a quarter-of-a-mile walk to the east of the island. 'The islanders live together in a small village, carrying all the signs of an extreme poverty,' recalled Martin in 1698, their walls 'rudely built'. They were, rightly put, piles; not the kind of rambling, countryside piles which the middle-class voyagers liked, but, Clarke says, 'a pile of stones . . . raised about three or four feet from the ground, forming a small oblong enclosure'. They had straw roofs, bound with twisted-heather ropes and fastened with a bird's beak. The houses stood in two fairly well-ordered rows, facing one another with a 'tolerable causeway' in between 'which they call the Street'.[21] The village, which held around thirty families by the mid-eighteenth century,[22] was situated in a valley between four mountains to withstand the ferociousness of the elements. The walls Macaulay found reprehensible: 'of rough gritty kind of stones, huddled up together in haste, without either lime or mortar, from eight to nine feet high.' There were stone beds in the middle of them. All the doors of the huts faced north-east to protect them from the horrors of the tempestuous south-west winds,[23] and they were pitched low 'to weather violent squalls and furious hurricanes' – otherwise the first winter storm would have levelled them. This is also why they had to have flat roofs; Macaulay thought there was something of the 'Oriental' about them.

If the travellers' accounts are anything to go on, the domestic life of eighteenth-century St Kilda bore a resemblance to that of Neolithic Skara Brae, on the other side of the Scottish Highlands, two thousand years earlier. E. D. Clarke left a vivid account of going into one of these lowly huts one midsummer's day in 1797. He had to stoop to get into what felt like a fuming oven – the air inside thick and loathsome, it being impossible to see anything for smoke. It was immediately apparent why. In the middle of the enclosure a peat fire burned; there was no hole in the roof, just two tiny apertures in opposite walls which occasionally let the wind in. The fire and smoke helped preserve warmth, particularly in winter when there were only a couple of hours of daylight. Eventually a gust of wind cleared the smell of sulphur, but it was soon replaced by that of manure which had been smeared all over the floor for reasons that escaped the diarists.[24] Now, as the smoke cleared, they came to realise that the Hirtans lived in a kind of feculent splendour. What lay in front of them was a fowlers' forge. Above the fire could be seen a steaming cauldron suspended from bird's-hair ropes, casting a swaying shadow on the wall. It was at midday that the islanders took their main meal, usually fulmar broth with a side of *sloke* – that is, seaweed. The hundred cows that grazed on the island's 'kindly grass' could be cooked into 'sweet, fat beef' but the Hirtans were not permitted to use them, nor grain, for their own nourishment; Clarke claims that it had to be surrendered to the factor (steward), although it is clear from other sources that they *could* barter cows and grain for luxury commodities. So their subsistence upon fulmars, upon their bird soup, was not entirely out of choice, and this would have damaging repercussions in later centuries.[25]

From the ceiling hung the instruments of husbandry – scythes, tillers, a crooked spade – and fowling: ropes, rods, gin traps and other ominous devices that would only make sense once the travellers had ascended Conachair and watched the death-defying prowess of the bird people. On the floor, or rather a carpet of peat, heather and ashes against which one's boot was nearly invisible, a thick rope lay coiled like a python. It was made from salted cows' hide and was infallibly durable, as it needed to be, lined with sheepskin to prevent fraying on the cliff-edge. Each lasted two generations. But of all the assembled instruments of rural autarky, it was the large bunches of fulmars' bladders, perched on a shelf like monstrous bloated grapes, that were most immediately eye-grabbing, brimming with the precious fulmar oil. This the Hirtans used not only to fuel their ghostly lamps, but also to cure, the islanders thought, rheumatism, sprains, swellings and many other ailments; its foul smell belied its miraculous properties. The aroma all travellers' noticed when first stepping ashore came from this oil, and how fitting it was that they should be smeared in the ejaculate of their most precious natural resource: birds. The word fulmar in fact comes from the Old Norse *fúll*, stinking, and *már*, gull; each fulmar yielded nearly a pint of this oil and so precious was it, there was an old island saying, 'deprive us of the fulmar, and St Kilda is no more'.

An arched aperture led into a pitch-black vault 'like an oven, arched with stone, and defended strongly from the inclemency of the weather'.[26] This was their sleeping chamber which, with up to four people stuffed into each 'apartment', visitors found cramped and horrid, with not even enough space for taller people to sit up – a coffin. One sight remained, behind a flimsy wooden partition, near the geese bladders. But visitors rarely ventured in because it was occupied by steaming cows for much of the year; they could sometimes be heard, breathing deeply, and during storms they were known to trample the partition, charge into the chamber and bring forth the very domestic apocalypse. The women of the island had daily assemblies in the centre of the village, spinning wool or flax on their distaffs, chatting, jesting, singing and coming up with poetry on the spot, and men would meet in their 'St Kilda Parliament' to deliberate and decide upon the work for the day.

The minister's manse, with a condensed earth floor, shrubberies, and even cocks and hens – the only tamed fowl on the island – was an improvement, but it was still, to one visitor, 'the throne of wretchedness itself'.[27] Although Martin stayed for around three weeks, most visits were much too brief for any kind of sustained anthropological observation, so we may reasonably assume that much of the (very detailed) information these accounts offer about the islanders' moral conduct comes from the man in the manse. Many no doubt brought preconceptions he was only happy to confirm or deny.[28] It is striking how all the major eighteenth-century voyagers describe the Hirtans' moral conduct as whiter than white. According to Martin, not only was there no fornication or adultery but there had *never been* any fornication or adultery 'for many ages before this time'. Kenneth Macaulay, sixty years later, declared the islanders completely ignorant of laws against suicide or murder, these being 'too exalted', blissfully, 'to lie within the low sphere of their knowledge'. The Hirtans, furthermore, had no knowledge of prostitution, disgrace or misery, making them 'among the greatest curiosities of the moral world', though he did wonder whether much of this was born from an absence of opportunity. He also tells how 'they marry early and their gallantries are generally innocent', and that 'the nuptial tie is always held sacred'. And as for drunkenness, that 'is not yet introduced here' – 'yet' always seeming to be the operative word in these accounts. Alexander Buchan, in 1741, pithily describes the people of St Kilda as 'simple and innocent', 'harborous [not] barbarous'[29] even to British, Continental or Scandinavian crews forced to make an emergency landing. 'To me', Macaulay writes, 'they paid more than a just deference', giving the crew presents of eggs and fowl – which was becoming something of a tradition, although the Hirtans did expect a little something in return.

These commentaries flow into sweeping eulogies of the islanders' unrivalled moral excellence and virtue. Martin proclaims that the islanders are free from 'ambition and pride, and the consequences that attend them' – that is, crime. The islanders exist in a state of 'mutual love and cordial friendship'. It was

Montaignean. It was Lockean. It was positively prelapsarian. None of this reflected particularly well upon the travellers' own societies; 'their morals are,' Macaulay goes on, 'and must be, purer, than those of great and opulent societies, however much civilized'. He declares that Providence had 'kindly concealed' the Hirtans from 'avarice, frauds, extortion'. For an island which he believed to have been originally populated by pirates, exiles and criminals, and given the Highland stereotype, this was quite the coup.

To be sure, it was not a *complete* moral nirvana. There were some shades of grey. The islanders were not averse to pulling the wool over travellers' eyes. Macaulay notes how they were adept at 'dissimulation, or a low sort of cunning, and a trick of lying', a talent they milked to their advantage on the rare occasion a ship pulled in. And the islanders' humanity did not always extend to wildlife. He noted a big, black-winged seabird, detested by every islander, which destroyed other birds' eggs. They called it the imp of hell. If the islanders managed to catch one, they liked to compete with one another to see who could torture it the most, which usually resulted in them plucking out its eyes, sewing its wings together, and casting it out to sea to meet a blind, lonely death. The imp laid the biggest and juiciest eggs on the archipelago but it was considered most 'flagitious' – that is, egregiously criminal – to eat any. Instead, the islanders would scoop the meat from the shell and enjoy the spectacle of the gull pining away on her ghost egg. This did not quite count as living in perfect harmony with nature but that aside, virtually everyone who committed their journeys to St Kilda to paper in the eighteenth century agreed upon one thing: the islanders had what the Earl of Shaftesbury, Montaigne, Drake, even Plato and Cicero said they should have: natural morality, capsizing many centuries of Christian teaching and contributing to a more optimistic view of human nature, where men and women were not held hostage to the idea of sinfulness.[30] Hobbes's being of wicked depravity was nowhere to be seen and the boot of absolutism was absolutely not needed to prevent violence breaking out. The 'savages' were, in fact, joyous manifestations of liberty.

Now it is true that the Hirtans had been converted to Christianity at some point in their habitation of the rock but this never really comes across, in the accounts, as the fountainhead of their virtue. Theirs, firstly, is consistently portrayed as an ancient way of life pre-dating – and largely enduring – the arrival of missionaries. Secondly, the journals give the impression that their spirituality was but a thin veneer of Christianity slathered over a centuries-old accretion of pagan ritual and belief. As a bare minimum, the islanders believed in God and Jesus, and in heaven and hell. They got married just like everyone else; rather boringly, there was no rampant polyamory as *philosophes* like Diderot gleefully reported of Polynesian islands. *Au contraire* – the Hirtans were strict observers of the Sabbath, which for them began at around midday on Saturday, when all work or indeed any kind of endeavour would stop dead.[31] But away from the chapels, staked into the hills, the old gods could still be found, attested to by wind-worn idols and altars. Some of these were perhaps of more practical use than the haughty Trinity. There was an altar to the god of the seasons who could control 'thunder, lightning, tempests and fair weather';[32] another spot, a gorgeous, wonderfully fertile expanse of grass, was dedicated to a god whose name no one could remember yet who was still worshipped anyway and the islanders steadfastly refused ever to turn this land over to farming;[33] there was, also, a large rectangular stone for the 'sportive and placable' god Gruagach, who asked only that cow's milk be splattered here every summer and autumn; and, next to Gruagach's creamy tablet, the 'field of spells and lustrations'.

One might wonder if it was in missionaries' and ministers' interests to exaggerate the 'beliefs of the weak, superstitiously inclined persons', as Macaulay reports it, to justify their own mission and set a benchmark for their proselytising, but secular visitors made similar observations. E. D. Clarke, a man of learning with no formal ties to the Kirk, gave a cursory and abortive sketch of the islanders' religious belief before throwing his hands in the air and declaring, 'It is futile to enumerate all the silly chimeras with which credulity has filled the imaginations of a people so little enlightened.' Macaulay says they believed certain birds were 'feathered prophets', signalling bad weather or the arrival of great men, or fluttering about the head of a reprobate destined for 'the regions of darkness and endless sorrow'. Martin tells us they had their clairvoyant cuckoo too, though none of the travellers ever had the pleasure. The Hirtans, Clarke says, prided themselves on their own gift of second sight and perhaps there was something in the air because in 1797 even the minister appeared to believe it. Part of the reason for the islanders' superstition, it was thought, was their illiteracy. This was bound to limit the impact of the catechism introduced at the start of the eighteenth century, and there was certainly not much, if any, Bible-reading going on. Yet even with only the trappings of Christianity, the voyagers suggest, their virtue and conduct were as pure as the spring water that streamed down their rock.

There were three chapels on Hirta but none of them were big enough to accommodate everybody, so the islanders said their prayers each Sunday morning in the churchyard, which was modest, around one hundred paces in circumference. As visitors peered over its low stone wall, they were greeted with the sad sight of humble mounds marking such pathetically short lives. It was made all the more stark without the softening effect of trees and branches. Travellers write with sadness about how the infants of St Kilda were 'peculiarly subject' to a terrible infant mortality. About five or six days after birth they lost the ability to suckle and were starved of milk; after a week their gums were so tightly clenched together it was impossible to get anything down their throats; soon they were seized by terrible convulsions and, after great suffering, died.

Kenneth Macaulay reported seeing for himself two babies die in such an agonising fashion. He relayed how 'the belief of a destiny, or an unavoidable resistless fate' was one of the strongest articles of their world view, and so such losses were accepted as a fact of life, as fate. The dead were not forgotten, though. The Hirtans 'bewail their relations excessively' and were forever singing death laments.[34] At least until the mid-eighteenth century, whenever the women of the island met with any 'act of cross Providence' they would retreat here, to the gravestone of their departed, and, with tear-stained cheeks, let out a blood-curdling cry which seemed to ricochet from the hills and mountains, reaching every ear on the island, bringing people running to the graveyard.[35]

Inconveniently, for some writers, St Kilda was not an island republic. The entire archipelago was owned by Clan MacLeod, whose territories stretched from the Outer Hebrides to the west coast of Scotland.[36] They were absentee landowners, appearing only occasionally, so all matters of administration were entrusted to their factor (or steward), the main leaseholder, who in turn appointed an officer. The factor or his officer would turn up once or twice a year to intervene in island affairs. With few opportunities for trade, the factor was one of the main conduits between St Kilda and the outside world: he governed them according to the landowner's wishes, dispensed justice (if any needed dispensing), relayed news and sometimes introduced goods, commodities and bewitching articles from the outside world, not to mention stocks of food when the islanders were in dire want.[37] To him the islanders had to pay an annual rent – the greater part in sheep, wildfowl, feathers, oil, and sometimes oats and barley – and here their natural talent for deception came into its own. Macaulay reports how they would habitually lie about how much stock they possessed so they wouldn't have to pay so much tax.[38] This constitutional arrangement might sound innocuous enough, but most of the travellers found it to be pernicious. Inconveniently for their polemical purposes, it showed that St Kilda was not quite the autonomous, self-governing, even utopian community they wanted it to be. But more pressingly, there was no check against tyranny, a fear so characteristic of eighteenth-century Britain with its fixation upon protecting the liberty of its freeborn citizens. The factor 'will always have it in his power', warned Macaulay, 'to monopolise the whole trade of this island . . . or engross every thing it produces'. He could even leave the inhabitants to starve if they were somehow unable to gather their food, or could, along with his well-armed men, turn up and torture the islanders or imprison them without trial. Never mind that this had never actually happened and that the factor in the 1760s would actually relieve the islanders of many burdensome taxes.[39] That it could happen was enough.[40] There was always the minister, of course, but he would prove a wet, unlikely out of 'prudent taciturnity' to go against the wishes of the factor.[41]

The absentee landlord and his factor notwithstanding, St Kilda seemed strangely equal. The Hirtans' passion for equivalence ran through the island's life and economy. Behind the beach, up in the rocks, visitors spied something odd: a 'Commonwealth boat' filled with boulders and stones; the 'greatest of all public calamities', we learn, would be for it to be swept into the sea or dashed against the rocks by a violent wind. So there it sat, beached. It was a strange vessel indeed, 'curiously proportionable to their land and rocks'.[42] Each family was responsible for the upkeep of their section, charged with weaving a part of the flag which visitors thought as a result was a patchwork of aesthetic disgrace. We learn that every Hirtan had a share in the grottoes where they stored their 'peats, eggs and wildfowl . . . in proportion to the extent of land he possesses, or the rent he pays to the steward', and the bounty from the cliffs was shared out equally too.

One of the most distinguishing features of St Kilda, thought the travellers, was a near-complete absence of money, something that was seen to have profoundly shaped the character of the islanders and the nature of their society. They knew about money; they just didn't lust after it: 'they have not touched coin of any kind, I believe before this age,' wrote Macaulay, and even though coins trickled into St Kilda throughout the eighteenth century, this didn't, in the view of those who visited, fundamentally alter the nature of the inhabitants. E. D. Clarke found some, but not much, money on the island – 'they know very little the value of it; and have no other use for it than to buy tobacco and luxuries of the tacksman'. Kenneth Macaulay believed that 'the people there have scarce any wants, and consequently scarce any desires of the pecuniary kind'. As a trope, moneyless societies have traditionally been signs of moral purity – two hundred years earlier, in *De Orbo Novo*, money is described as 'that source of all misfortune'[43] – and the philosophical travellers certainly all portray it as a blessing, a foil to their own shop-window society with its hunger for a dizzying range of material things. Since there was only a very limited circulation of money on the island, a barter economy was in place. Macaulay describes how cows, sheep, grain and feathers were exchanged for imports the islanders could not readily produce – salt, iron and timber – though this was to change as more ships came in.[44]

The Hirtan economy, such as it was, was fundamentally agrarian. There were sheep everywhere; they would occasionally plunge off cliffs into the sea or be carried off by swooping eagles.[45] There were around one hundred 'fat and sweet-fleshed' cows which produced cream 'so luscious, or rather so strong, that some people sickened upon drinking it' and a dozen or so horses on the island that were red and slight, but 'full of fire and very hardy', and had their moment of glory at an annual cavalcade. Travellers were surprised to see that very little of the island, barely eighty acres, had been turned to the plough – or rather 'a kind of crooked spade' – and this was something that would come back to haunt the islanders in the centuries ahead. There were a couple of fields to the southeast, in a valley rebounding with sunlight, where barley and oats were cultivated, and where sheaths of corn grew unusually tall and ripe in summer. It was carved into unequal plots, named after distant ancestors – some with surprising English, even Latin, names, suggesting that all sorts of people had fetched up on St Kilda in the past – as well as the more recently departed, fomenting the sense of a strong island community, unbroken by time. But what was the point of working the land, the islanders wondered, if the factor's officer was just going to turn up and take so much of its bounty away? The salt spray from the sea, which could render the fields infertile, particularly after storms, was another disincentive. Even when they were ordered by the factor to till more of the land, the islanders only made a token effort.[46] It was burdensome. Who cared about corn when each family could consume more than 22,600 gannets a year? And besides, was it not a nobler, more adventurous life, grabbing birds from the cliffs instead of toiling day after day under the sun? Were songs ever sung to heroes of the plough? Tilling the land was of such inferior economic importance that it was largely left to the women. But the waters around St Kilda were bejewelled with cod, mackerel, turbot, herring, pollocks, ling, perches, lithes and more, even if, the Hirtans being bad fishermen, the lion's share went to the birds, none more so than the one hundred thousand or so 'almost insatiably voracious' gannets.

Travel writers went to great lengths to emphasise just how cut off St Kilda was from the outside world. On St Kilda, the quotidian could become the exotic. Take writing, for example. According to Martin, who no doubt is exaggerating for dramatic effect, the islanders were completely and utterly blown away by it: 'They cannot conceive how it is possible for any mortal to express the conceptions of his mind in such black characters upon white paper.' His suggestion that they could learn how to write themselves in as little as two years is met with polite incredulity; neither reading nor writing could be mastered, they thought, within an entire age. In the event, sixty years later three or four of the islanders *could* read and write but only in a cursory and amateur fashion.[47] It wasn't that the Hirtans were fearful of anything new. Far from it – 'both sexes have a great inclination for novelty', observed Martin – it was just that they had no desire to adapt. Smoking was delicious. Fairly ubiquitous in the towns and cities of eighteenth-century Britain, especially in taverns, coffee-houses, on the streets and at home, the 'divine Nicotian weed' was to the St Kildans the very height of luxury. Macaulay observed 'a most violent passion for tobacco'. Modern technology could astound. Clarke rather regretted not bringing fireworks which, he was sure, they would have considered a form of magic, let alone a hot-air balloon for their fowling.

Was St Kilda really as cut off from the outside world as the travel writers would have us believe? One episode is telling. In 1736, Macaulay says, three men and eight boys went to one of the sea-stacks to gather birds and were waiting for the boat to take them back. But the boat never came. They lit bonfires on the top of the rock. But still no one came. It turned out that smallpox had erupted on Hirta, communicated, probably, in someone's clothes, from the isle of Harris. Half of St Kilda died. The fowling party was only meant to have been away for a week. But, as the disease worked its way through Hirta's population, they languished on the stack for the next nine months, from the end of one summer to the start of the next, living off fowl and eggs, making skins from sheep and big birds tacked together with feathers, hopeless and miserable, and in all this time not a single vessel came close enough to aid them. Only once the epidemic had passed were the men of Hirta strong enough to sail to their rescue. That people – most famously, Lady Grange, the 'prisoner of St Kilda' – were occasionally banished to the island also says something about its isolation. Nonetheless, the arrival of a trickle of travel writers and the occasional adventurer was a sign of change – it did not take long for the islanders to clock that they had become an object of fascination; the factor came twice a year; there were emergency landings; and probably slightly more opportunities for trade than the journals would have us believe (though if it had happened without the blessing of the factor it would technically have been illicit) but, still, there is no reason to doubt Macaulay's claim that they were 'neither a fighting or commercial people' – which is exactly what much of the rest of Britain was.[48]

If the Kildans lived such an isolated, outmoded existence, it follows that any trips to 'the civilised world' must have brought on a profound culture shock. And, if we believe Alexander Buchan's anecdotal account of the Hirtan who went to Glasgow, it did. He could not conceive of how there could be so many people on earth, let alone in the same place; mistook a coach for two horses dragging a little house with oddly calm men within; was dumbfounded by mirrors, glazed windows, teapots and hangings; and was flummoxed by a pendant forever swinging back and forth with mathematical exactitude. He missed home, but simultaneously wanted home to be more like Glasgow with its plenteous supply of whisky and tobacco.[49] Martin tells the story of some of the islanders visiting the estate of the MacLeods in Skye. They took it to be an imperial court, but the most astonishing thing they saw? Monster plants shooting from the earth to momentous heights, splaying their arms everywhere, and showering them in mottled light: trees. 'How they grew to such a height above plants', Martin tells us, 'was far beyond their conception.' So enamoured were they of trees, they wanted to lug some all the way across the Isle of Skye, load them on to their boats, and take them back to St Kilda, but prudence prevailed.

———

In one sense, writers needed primitive peoples to be virtuous; if they had turned out to be violent and depraved this would have amounted to nothing more than a vindication of civilisation, and the Enlightenment was nothing if not a critical movement.[50] Of course it helped that they could portray primitive man in this way without undue violence to the truth but, still, the noble savage was in essence a literary stock figure that continued to evolve in the eighteenth century, surfacing again and again in novels, plays, poems and newspaper reports.[51] In a telling passage in his *Confessions* (1763), Rousseau admits that primitive man, as he conceived of him, 'does not now, and in all probability never will exist' but, even so, 'is absolutely necessary to have just notions to judge properly of our present state'.[52] Every 'perfect and true' printed account of travels to far-off lands – including to St Kilda – developed the stereotype and so we might justifiably question the empirical foundations of some of the bolder claims. How could visitors be so certain that no one on St Kilda had ever committed adultery? If drunkenness was unknown to them, how could they 'drink most liberally' on feast days? And if there had never been any crime, why were there laws against striking a neighbour (two-shilling fine), and even stricter fines (4s 6d) for drawing blood?[53] Are we to assume they had never been invoked? And if there was no crime, and everyone minded everyone else's business, why are 'clumsy wooden keys' used by the Hirtans to lock their houses on display in an Outer Hebridean museum?[54]

St Kilda certainly was not the utopian egalitarian commune the travellers sometimes implied it was. Martin mentions in passing three members of the island being ranked as poor (who receive charity from everyone else), confirming hints elsewhere that the land and material resources of the island were not evenly distributed; crofts, indeed, were subdivided between children; more siblings meant less land. The missionary Alexander Buchan could write of 'the richest man in St Kilda' whose fortune consisted of eight cows, two or three horses and eighty sheep. And both the writer Martin and missionary Clarke's descriptions of the fish-out-of-water adventures of Kildans on planet mainland feel fable-esque. Like other Enlightenment travel writers, voyagers to St Kilda were certainly guilty, at times, of seeing what they wanted to see.[55] Nonetheless, so excoriating was the light – however distorted – beamed back, it threatened to undermine the foundations of Old World societies completely. Travels to St Kilda, and like places, were psychologically revolutionary.

Report after report suggested that humans were not living the kind of life nature had intended. Whereas 'savages' like the Hirtans lived a simple, rewarding life in accord with nature, European man had become a 'complicated machine', estranged from his natural impulses through a grim, lifelong process of self-abnegation. Society with all its strictures was rigid and codified, full of protocol and etiquette, materialistic and judgemental. 'Once upon a time there was a natural man,' wrote Diderot, 'but inside him was introduced an artificial one, and within his breast a civil war broke out which will last for the whole of his life.'[56] Hobbes's war of 'all against all' had become one of everyone against themselves. History, then, had taken a wrong turn; was a wrong turn. Outposts like St Kilda showed that another world was possible. In the juxtaposition between 'the infancy of the savage' and 'our present decrepitude' glimmered the fatal path of Enlightenment.[57] But it was precarious, this other world, and observers were not sure how long it could last.

———

E. D. Clarke went to see a fowling party in 1797. It was only after they'd seen the fowlers in action that visitors realised why the women so outnumbered the men on the island.[58] With their ropes slung over their shoulders, a party of men approached the cliffs of Hirta, followed by their dogs. They ascended the hills, passing springs and pagan altars, eventually arriving at a tremendous cliff-edge – Conachair. So precipitous was it, Clarke dared not go anywhere near it unaccompanied; two of the islanders had to prop him up with their arms lest the blood drain from his head. 'I looked over into what might be termed a world of rolling mists and contending clouds. As these occasionally broke and dispersed', he continues, 'the ocean was disclosed below.' Even though he could clearly see the sea spuming over the rocks and gushing into the caverns, the roaring and thundering was completely unheard at that 'stupendous height'.

The islanders put on an even more impressive show than nature, however. Clarke was astonished to watch some of the group approach the slippery brink, sit on the 'extremest verge', and, tied to one other who remained above, climb down the cliff-face, gathering birds and eggs in a stiff cow's-hair noose attached to a slender rod, clambering back out of the crevice with a young fulmar in his hand. Clarke was haunted by the casualness of the man holding the rope, sometimes with one hand, whilst chatting and laughing with the others – and yet this was all that was keeping his comrade from being sent plunging 'headlong into eternity'. Nor did the climber himself seem to be taking it particularly seriously, prancing about on the perilous ledges, capering and shouting, delighting in 'displaying these gambols to a stranger', even dangling off the rope, before reappearing with a necklace of fowl and a fistful of eggs.[59] Dogs were key allies, dexterous at climbing, good at digging out fowl that built their nests underground (such as black guillemots[60] and puffins) and faithfully dropping them at their masters' feet; 'these dogs have a wonderful sagacity', says Macaulay, 'and are so trained, that they neither destroy the fowls themselves, nor part with them till they meet the people of the family to which they belong, in spite of threatenings, flattery or bribes'. The Hirtans were nothing without their dogs.

It wasn't just on Hirta that the 'aeronauts' went about their business. The birds' main habitats were the sea-stacks – Boreray, Stac an Armin – those 'lofty naked rock[s] rising perpendicularly out of the sea' that had made such an impression on the travellers as they sailed in to St Kilda. Macaulay, echoing Virgil, likens the fowl on the stacks to 'an infinite multitude of melancholy ghosts that fluttered about the banks of the Acheron'. The massacres of the gannets and fulmars took place in early spring. The islanders came for them in the night with their buckets and ropes ready for a carnival of slaughter, entire flocks murdered under a wild sky as the sea heaved and moaned. They lowered themselves over the precipices and crept down the crevices of the rocks. On the stacks, brooding birds on either side could clasp fowlers' clothes. The Hirtans either killed the sentinel bird first before it could sound the alarm, or exploited mass avian confusion by thrusting an alien bird into another's nest, or killed one and waited for the birds to 'mourn immediately over their departed friend, with a lamentable tone of voice, examining his body very narrowly with their bills'. Either way, they set about twisting the necks of as many as possible, 'thrusting their heads into his belt' or dumping them in a bucket of shallow blood, killing, in Clarke's estimation, some eight hundred in one night. Only the fulmar could fight back, squirting oil from its nostrils.

The birds were flung from the casting point into the sea or reeled down in a pulley, loaded on to a ship and spirited away to Hirta where they were made into shoes, where their breast grease was distilled into porridge stock, where their precious oil was decanted from their stomachs into little stone lanterns which, in any case, only ever gave out a meagre ghostly glow, and where their stomach linings were wrenched out and turned into containers for the oil which was to be sold to their king across the water. Either that, or they were eaten, along with their unhatched babies.

———

What were Europeans meant to do with their startling conclusions from remote places like St Kilda? Despite Voltaire's jibe at Rousseau that everyone should start crawling on all fours after taking his lessons to heart, no one was saying that people should regress to their primitive state. That was impractical. 'Refined vice under a suit of silk', as Diderot put it, was far preferable to 'stupid ferocity beneath an animal skin'.[61] Civilisation could not be reversed. But it could be improved. Civilisation could salvage what was needed of the savage to emerge as superior moral beings. But they had to move fast because increasing contact with isolated societies like St Kilda came at a cost.

Like the eruption of Europeans into uncharted continents in the sixteenth century, European encroachment into *terra incognita* in the eighteenth was portrayed as a blight, or even a curse, even by those doing so or writing about it.[62] 'They introduce among them wants and perhaps disease that they never before knew,' wrote Captain Cook;[63] 'Weep!', urged a sage old man in Diderot's *Supplément*, 'for the coming and not the leaving of these ambitious, wicked men.'[64] Dire long-term consequences were perceived. Many believed that when contact was first made, it derailed the natural timeline of the primitive societies, spinning them towards the kind of materialistic misery, violence and estrangement that Rousseau believed beset the life of the eighteenth-century European. The old man in Diderot's *Supplément* warns the 'natives' that it is now their calamitous fate to be 'captive' to European 'follies and vices', 'as corrupt, vile and miserable as they are'.[65] As more tokens of the civilised world were introduced, news pumped in and contact increased, some travellers worried that the islanders were being edged into a vortex from which they would never emerge. In what kind of condition might they find the Hirtans in, say, a hundred years' time?

———

No longer did they come on yachts. Now they blasted into Village Bay, still without a quay, 'a ship on fire', as the petrified islanders put it when this first happened, in 1838. A week-long round trip of the 'Romantic Outer Hebrides and Lone St Kilda', full board, first-class cuisine, was £9 a whack, aboard a 240-ton, splendidly fitted steamer, lighted by electricity.[66] From these cruisers spilt up to forty excitable lawyers, clerks, secretaries, teachers, writers, shopkeepers, sociologists and doctors, armed with notebooks and cameras, hungry for spectacle and souvenir. They crawled over every inch of the island, exploring the curious, crescent-shaped row of houses, the stone grottoes that ribbed the turf, the chapels, graveyard, hills and blood-curdling panoramas from the precipices, getting the primitives to caper on the clifftop, dangle off ledges and retrieve a dead bird, poking their snouts into doorways and gawping at the bubbling cauldron of fulmar porridge, shoving cameras into people's faces, making them stand still, and pulling down on the trigger. It was, as one newspaper advertisement put it, 'the only human menagerie in the whole of the British isles'. The tourists left with stories to tell, their satchels bulging with tweed, eggs and jaundiced postcards of a fast-fading world.

One such steamer, the *Hebridean*, carried a special correspondent from the *Glasgow Herald* called Robert Connell. The plight of the Hirtans, he explains in his witty, incisive and evocative reports, subsequently published in expanded book form as *St Kilda and the St Kildians* (1887), had become of much public concern in late September 1885 after a 'message from the sea' – a little toy boat – was found washed up on the Isle of Lewis, one of several western Hebridean shores. In a tiny scrawl, it said that the Hirtans were on the brink of starvation and would all die unless help were immediately sent.[67] This, it turned out, was a gross exaggeration; the letter was written by a schoolboy. Before long, a letter from the minister of St Kilda reached a reverend of the Free Church in Glasgow explaining that although they were not actually starving, a recent storm had destroyed the entire seed for the next year's crop, so they were in need of relief before the winter, when traditionally very few, if any, vessels passed by. A relief mission was hastily organised, funded by an appeal to the public in newspapers – which was met, almost in the space of a single day – and the SS *Hebrides* set off from Glasgow in mid-October loaded with seed corn, barley, meal and potatoes, and the journalist Connell, who had been dispatched to satisfy the *Herald* readership's curiosity about St Kilda, along with the factor John Mackenzie and his son, and the island's new schoolmaster.

Like the philosophical voyagers before him, Connell recalls emerging from the Sound of Harris 'on the great billows of the broad Atlantic' and seeing 'the little speck on the distant horizon'. He recalls glimpsing 'the green slopes of the romantic little island' which they managed to find without getting lost, all the dogs at the sound of the steam-whistle materialising 'like a great company of evil spirits' to the landing place and barking in unison, the islanders streaming from the village 'like bees', hailing them 'with their Gaelic gibberish' and rowing them ashore, asking for gifts and charity, demanding to know, as ever, 'Where is the war raging?', and, he notes irritably, offering them no breakfast until he had shaken hands with every single one of them. They also insisted on relating all the events from their 'little world', various accounts of the weather and 'the doings of the unseen powers'. For the next two weeks, Connell went about his fact-finding mission with great diligence, being careful to express well-observed truths instead of impressionistic snapshots. His work, one of a great number of journalistic accounts of Victorian St Kilda, is a tremendous foil to the earlier accounts of the philosophical voyagers, showing how people of different eras could view Britain's shadowlands in very different ways.

According to his, and other, accounts, the regular presence of tourists was perhaps the biggest difference between late Victorian St Kilda and Georgian St Kilda. Whereas philosophical voyagers appeared only occasionally, steamships came from 1838 and, following the maiden voyage of the *Dunara Castle* in 1875, an annual steamer season emerged, with several vessels making regular trips to the islands well into the twentieth century. The cumulative effect, according to Connell and other writers, was to commodify St Kildan society, making it less authentic and more performative, a simulacrum of an antique way of life crystallised in the grain of photographs, and one which that very same tourism, ironically, was making unsustainable. There is no overwhelming sense the Hirtans resented the eruption of middle-class tourists on to their island; in fact, their presence pandered to their 'talent for dissimulation and cunning' noted by even the earliest travellers, which inclination now intensified in a new context. Reverend Neil MacKenzie, who kept a journal of life on the island between 1829 and 1843, observed how the Hirtans quickly worked out what tourists wanted to see, and colluded with those expectations, to their profit. According to MacKenzie, the wide-eyed islanders would rush on to visitors' yachts and 'mistake' polished brass railings for solid gold; coins for worthless metal; coal for food (expressing surprise they could not eat it); and they screamed when they saw themselves in the ship's magnificent mirror, even though they had shaved in their own looking glasses that very morning.

Performances became even more elaborate the more steamers rolled in. Why bother? Coin. When the philosophical travellers had visited the island in the eighteenth century, currency was scarce (even if the islanders' bewilderment at its value was exaggerated or feigned); by the age of Victorian tourism, this was no longer the case. When they were invited on board to inspect a ship's machinery and weapons, the islanders would first ask for payment. They would often refuse to sit for photographs without being paid for the trouble. And as soon as travellers alighted on the shore, visitors recall, they were besieged with requests ('begging', in Connell's words) for tobacco, lead pencils, a hamper of wine and more. According to Connell, the Kildans seem to have developed an inflated, even prima donna-ish sense of their own worth. Receiving a new boat from well-wishers, on one occasion, they chopped it into firewood 'so that their kind friends in the South might have a chance of giving them a better one'. None of this seems especially unreasonable – the steam cruisers were profiting from St Kilda without compensating its inhabitants, after all – but it disrupted deeply ingrained romantic notions; noble savages were not supposed to be wheeler-dealers yet the Kildans never missed an opportunity to turn a tidy profit; 'Give a man a sovereign for an hour's work in scaling the rocks, and he will tell you that he once got five for a similar performance,' observed Connell. As for the poor pestered tourists, they wanted to get their money's worth too. Norman Heathcote, the nephew of the proprietor of St Kilda, liked to sail out and explore the island with his sister, noting in 1900 how some of the tourists treated the islanders like wild animals in a zoo. 'I have seen them standing at the church door during service, laughing and talking, and staring in as if at an entertainment.' Hirtan women, he noted, particularly hated having their photograph taken.[68]

According to Connell, and many others, the flow of tourists and relief missions fundamentally changed the nature of St Kildan society. On the one hand, this was a positive development. It gave the Hirtans purchasing power, and increased their wealth, making them more independent economic actors. They could now buy from and sell to whoever they liked, independent of the factor. But on the other, 'one cannot be long on the island without discovering the great moral injury that tourists and sentimentalists and yachtsmen, with pocketsful of money, are working upon a kindly and simple people'. Reliant on charity, gifts and money from outsiders, St Kilda was losing its famed self-sufficiency at a time when the able-bodied young were beginning to leave, or think seriously about doing so. This had reduced the Hirtan, in Connell's eyes, to 'a fibreless creature' quite unlike most Highlanders, dependent upon those most undependable of things: the wind and the sea. It was all very well when specks appeared on the horizon. But when they didn't?

Much stayed the same – still the islanders boiled their puffins in porridge for breakfast and lived off the sweet flesh of the fulmar. Fouling remained their primary activity; all the soil gave up, grudgingly, was oats and potatoes. Their passion for equivalence was now their 'communistic principle', and Connell found them to be even more devout Sabbatarians in the chokehold of a miserable minister which, in the view of Connell and other travellers, seriously impeded their productivity.[69] But he also noted some changes, improvements. The houses, rebuilt by a progressive proprietor in the 1860s, were now 'neat and comfortable', a far cry from the smoky huts that were the wretched abodes of their forebears, their roofs covered not in thatch and birds' beaks but zinc.[70] Ever since a schoolmaster had arrived the previous year, children and youths were learning to read and write in Gaelic and English, which made the world beyond their shores much less of a daunting proposition, though for many of the older generation, a feather was a feather, and the strokes and squiggles of the quill remained as mysterious as ever. If St Kilda were turned into a fishing station, thought Connell, it could easily support a population of several thousand – if only the islanders weren't so hopeless at fishing.

Connell considered the infant lockjaw 'the most appalling thing connected with St Kilda'. Of the eighty-four islanders who died between 1856 and his visit in 1886, no fewer than fifty-two died between before they were but one month old, the vast majority of lockjaw. Around half of newborn Hirtans died of this scourge. Whether it was caused by consanguinity, the fetid air in their houses or poor feeding habits (was it really wise to pour port wine and cow's milk down the throat of a one-year-old?), doctors could still not agree. Nowadays we call this illness tetanus, a bacterial disease whereby a spasm of the jaw muscles clenches the mouth shut, preventing swallowing – but Connell was predictably horrified to find 'pious men' from the Free Church who said it was God's ingenious, and inviolable, way of 'keeping the population within the resources of the island', a notion that chimed with the nihilistic fatalism that so many of the islanders, goaded on by the tyrannical minister, still seemed to believe in. Fortunately, at the behest of the proprietor's sister Miss MacLeod, a professionally trained nurse took up residence in 1885, and there had been no lockjaw deaths for a year and a half. Yet there was no guarantee it wouldn't come back, and the islanders still lived in the shadow of this terrible plague, with mothers refusing to clothe babies until they had survived their first few perilous days, wrapped, until then, in coarse flannel, like a shroud.

Victorian impressions of the islanders' morality tend to be somewhat less rose-tinted than their predecessors', to put it mildly. Connell considered the last century's praise of the 'purity and high moral tone' of the islanders greatly exaggerated; how could one grasp the 'inner life of a people in a hurried visit' of no more than a couple of days, he wondered. He perceived 'a glamour about a primitive, patriarchal existence, such as the St Kildans lead blinding the eye of the observer'. He concurred with Kenneth Macaulay, a hundred years earlier, that it was a negative kind of virtue, born of absence. The Hirtans now had better records than in the eighteenth century, with Connell beadily noting that, according to the Registrar General who had kept an official record, there had been five illegitimate children born in the last thirty years, one, in 1876, of adultery.[71] It was not quite the moral utopia dreamt of by the eighteenth-century philosophers.

Whereas the philosophical voyagers had wished to salvage aspects – real or imagined – of the Hirtans' primitive existence to perfect their own humanity, Victorian visitors, it is clear, wanted to save them from a barren, perilous existence that was unconscionable in their modern age. As far as it was still a mirror, St Kilda reflected the shortcomings of the British Empire – living off birds, dying of lockjaw, and pathetically frightened of new technology. Hirtans were in want of something that was the right of all British citizens and subjects: *civilisation*.

Even if, in the winter of 1885, the Hirtans were not in as desperate straits as the 'message from the sea' proclaimed, the subsequent relief mission that brought Connell to the island showed how precarious their food supply was. The staple of the island diet was of course bird flesh and eggs, but the food crops that the SS *Hebrides* had brought were an important complement, and, with a population of only eighty, around half what it was during Kenneth Macaulay's visit one hundred years earlier, an over-reliance on grabbing birds could look precarious. The loss of their boat could spell starvation for the remaining islanders. There were many other ominous signs. The hillsides were being stripped of turf for fuel, further diminishing the space available for pasture. With the islanders increasingly dependent upon charity, state aid and tourist money, much of the produce of the island – feathers, oil, cloth, fish, cheese and cattle – was in decline. Even the fulmar, staple of the islanders' diet and emblem of the island's identity, was beginning to diminish in numbers. *Deprive us of the fulmar, and St Kilda is no more.*

'The romance is gone,' wrote Connell, scrubbed out by 'repeated periods of destitution imperilling the very existence of the community.' Evacuation, many 'sensible people' believed, was the only viable solution. Some islanders had already emigrated – to the almost antithetical climes of Victoria, Australia (which the British had begun colonising one hundred years earlier), christening their landing stretch St Kilda Beach. And now the remaining islanders were better educated, and, thanks to the tourists and increased mail services, more attuned to the world beyond their shores than earlier generations, more emigration was not at all inconceivable. In fact, it is what many Victorian observers, increasingly, wanted for them. Connell believed they would make 'capital colonists' in Australia or another dominion, or could survive well enough on the mainland.

There was of course the small matter of the islanders' opinion on the matter. We might suspect the journalist Connell's impartiality in reporting how eager the islanders were to jump ship, given his rhetorical agenda to present them as in need of rescue, but one would expect the Inspecting Officer of the Board of Supervision to be forensic in his accuracy. In October 1885 he reported, strikingly, that 'with the exception of one or two old men, I found none who were not anxious to be transferred either to the mainland or Australia'. The émigrés wrote letters to their former friends and neighbours telling them how marvellous life was in Australia, exhorting them to join them and sometimes even enclosing money to help them do so. Perhaps, with all the tourists gaping at them, the letters informing them of new ways of life, and the crop failures, the Hirtans now had a greater sense of the anomalousness and precarity of their situation. Connell echoes the Inspecting Officer's conclusions, reporting that 'the opinion in favour of emigration was almost unanimous, the only dissentients being one or two old men, whom it would be folly to ask to go to a new settlement at their time of life'. The minister's housekeeper, Connell reports, describes St Kilda as 'the biggest prison in all the world'. He does concede, however, that such talk was precipitated by the arrival of the mails from Australia, and that the islanders had little stamina for sustained mental focus. They were in favour of emigration one day, but the next seemed to have forgotten about the whole proposition.

A series of haunting postcards capture St Kilda in its twilight, in the decades surrounding Connell's visit, freezing in time both staged scenes and fleeting moments.[72] Cameras were expensive and cumbersome, so late Victorian and Edwardian tourists purchased sack-loads of picture postcards. These were evocative and, as it turned out, elegiac mementos of their travels; they kept some for themselves, and sent others from the corrugated shack that was the St Kilda Post Office from 1901 – no fewer than eight hundred postcards left the island in the final mail of August 1906 alone. In the postcards, we see the misty stacks and mountain peaks of St Kilda, the spherical chimney of the steamships *Dunara Castle* and *Hebrides* pouring black smoke into the air as they drew into Village Bay with the silhouettes of the islanders waiting on the shore; we see puffins peering over a precipice and dangling from a horsehair noose; we see, in 1886, all the members of the St Kilda Parliament ready to decide upon the day's work and five women taking a break from their tartan weaving, two wearing the white headbands that signified marriage, the men of the island packing tweed to sell to tourists, a boy perched atop a bale, an old man snuggled up with a dog (dogs are virtually everywhere, a truly ubiquitous presence in the life of the island); we see, strangely for a picture postcard, the infant graveyard parcelled in by stones where so many victims of lockjaw were sunk into the earth; there are islanders sitting in the street, no more than twelve feet wide, doing not much at all; and in 1884, a group of islanders pose with the new nurse Ann McKinley, radiating warmth, and a rather more apprehensive-looking new schoolmaster Mr Campbell; and a bowler-hatted man sitting on a wall outside the Fairy Cave dangling his legs in the air.[73]

I found looking through the postcards a sobering experience. It made me realise just how much these 'natives', as the captions call them, have been mythologised through the ages. For all the eighteenth century's fixation with the noble savage as a missing part of the modern persona and the nineteenth century's primitive being in need of civilising grace, truly, in the pictures, it can be hard to tell them apart from the tourists, at least at first. Whether they are leaning against houses in the street, posing with the schoolmaster, capturing puffins, showing off their sheep or unloading the factor's smack, the Hirtans look kind, genial, engaged, and contented in their own skin; in many of the photographs islanders are smiling, fairly rare in Victorian photography. In contrast to the eighteenth-century portrayals of them as an indistinguishable mass of inbred 'savages', they come through as individuals. There is one postcard in which four smartly booted, well-dressed tourists thrust themselves uncomfortably close to a woman at her wheel, but elsewhere the islanders do not seem particularly put upon, the tourists keeping a respectful distance. Since the postcards were sold mainly to tourists, it would have been perverse to portray them as looming vultures, but the facial expressions and body language of the Hirtans do not look especially contrived, raising the possibility that the extent of tourist 'exploitation' was exaggerated by moralistic observers keen for compelling reasons to 'save the natives'. Certainly the increase in tourism was not the central medium of oblivion; it played its part, making the locals less self-sufficient and putting their economy on a much more precarious footing, but other factors, such as food scarcities, depopulation by the ablebodied and disease, were of more pressing importance.

Aesthetically, the postcards are powerful, and it is hard not to be moved by them. It looks as though white blood is pooling from the edges of the photographs, slowly blotting out the rocks, mountains, stone houses and sea in a slowly disappearing land. As is common in Victorian photographs, the images lack definition and depth of focus, meaning it can be hard to distinguish between land, water and sky, the ripple-free sea coming across as an endless expanse of mud, or dirty ice, or lunar rock, heightening the sense of a world

melting down and imploding. This is not how Victorian travellers would have perceived it, of course – the glistening sea-stacks, rock-bound shore and colonies of birds would have been crisp and vivid to their eyes. But the postcards strike a particular tone. They are wistful, mournful, spectral. Every inch of them seems to anticipate St Kilda's fate. We gain a sense, too, of just how dwarfed the islanders are by the quailing landforms, by these eruptions of rock that burst through the earth's surface so many millions of years ago. There is an unmistakable fragility to the figures, and, particularly in some later postcards, the preponderance of older to younger islanders is harrowing.

The islanders were sorry to see Connell go. 'Tears were shed', he writes, 'and the hand-shaking exceeded all conceivable limits.' The schoolmaster, his tenure finished, had to kiss all the women one by one. The journey back to Dunvegan, in the factor's smack, was suitably awful, 'as daring a proceeding as even the most seasoned salt could desire'. They experienced a proper Gaelic 'red storm', with the Atlantic rearing into billows 'high as mountains, and our little craft was but a speck on the limitless waste'. Also aboard the vessel, in its mailbag, was a letter from three young Hirtans (two of them married) to the agent of the Victorian government in London applying for assisted passage to Australia.

———

One spring morning in 1918, everyone was horrified by the latest abomination offered up by the sea. From the beach the villagers could have tossed a stone on to its fin but of course they pelted up the hills the second they saw it. Now, looming out of the blue, the whole village seemed to be in the shadow of destruction, the enormous steel whale which the gannets and fulmars were giving a wide berth poised to fire. In fact, Commander Walter Remy of the German Imperial Navy had been pacing beneath the waves for several hours, dreaming of destruction. He had been tasked with destroying St Kilda's wireless station, which was being used to convey news of enemy ship movements in the Atlantic from the lookout posts on the island's mountain peaks to British central command. The submarine was armed with hundreds of shells and a machine gun, now pointing at the island's row of houses. As Commander Remy peered into his periscope, St Kilda faced the prospect of complete annihilation.

The submarine pounded the village for nearly an hour. The cows and sheep rushed from one side of the island to the other in terror. The two wireless masts behind the factor's house were blasted to bits early on in the assault but the German commander turned out to be merciful, warning those islanders still inside their houses, by loudspeaker, to get the hell out or face imminent destruction. More than sixty shells were fired. The church and manse were destroyed, along with two cottages and a storehouse, and two boats were ruined beyond repair. And with that, the ship slipped beneath the waves and disappeared. It could have been a lot worse: the death toll was just one lamb. It was the first time, however, that St Kilda had become embroiled in the maelstrom of violence that had seized the outside world, further relieving them of the notion, if anyone still believed it, that the island could exist as a self-contained entity. Later that year, a solitary mounted gun was installed above Village Bay to be greased and polished by the postmaster each month and such a formidable deterrent it was, it was never once fired.

After the First World War, St Kilda fell into a death spiral. The sixteen sailors on secondment departed, but their stories of life in London, Glasgow and other parts of Britain lingered on in the islanders' imagination, compounding a pre-existing sense of wanderlust. Between 1919 and 1920, a quarter of St Kilda's population was lost to the prospect of employment and a better life on the mainland. That these émigrés were all young was ominous because, as we have seen as far back as the Stone Age, the haemorrhaging of youth from a community is a harbinger of its desiccation and demise. And so the wheel turned. Crops failed. Alien vessels brought disease and conveyed news of the Hirtans' pitiful state to the outside world. In 1926 the whole island was laid low by flu; no fires burned, no dogs barked, and the bells in the chapel fell still. Only the wind kept up its sour lament. On the first day of the outbreak some islanders lit a fire on a hill, but no trawlers passed by. By the fourth day, when the HMS *Hebrides* finally appeared on the horizon, four islanders were already dead. One islander had to wrench planks of wood from an old woman's ceiling to make her a coffin; such was the scarcity of timber.

The man who performed this inventive piece of carpentry was called Lachlan MacDonald. Like so many other young and able-bodied Kildans, he felt trapped. His father had drowned in a climbing accident years earlier and it fell upon him to look after his disabled mother. A trip to the mainland one summer brought home how monotonous was his life. 'There was nothing there,' he recalled, 'no enjoyment . . . just working from one day to another, even nights.' Already the dominoes were falling. A couple of years earlier, William Macdonald (no relation) had become the first Hirtan to remove his entire family, their permanently locked door a dark prognostication of things to come, and one day in 1925 the minister Donald John Gillies upped and left aboard the HMS *Hebrides* for Canada. These prompted a cascade, a flight of the able-bodied. In his report from May 1928, the police constable from the isle of Harris described a community in free fall, with a population now of just thirty-seven, a rump dangerously reliant upon imported food; the fulmar broth and gannet eggs now seemed to yowl of yesteryear. The next year brought a winter of hell. In October 1929, a passing fisherman found the islanders bleeding and itching with blisters brought on by an eczema outbreak. The Board of Health did nothing because they had not heard directly from the official channel, Nurse Barclay, never mind that she was laid low herself.

Mary Gillies, thirty-five years of age, was the mother of the diarist Norman Gillies. She had an expressive face with free-flowing black hair, and in 1930 was pregnant with a daughter. Her appendix burst one day in the spring of 1930. True to form, the government's response was slow. An attempt to rush a doctor to the island in May proved abortive, so a woefully ill-equipped Nurse Barclay had to tend to the ailing woman herself. It took a further two weeks for the government to arrange for a fishery cruiser from Harris to transport Mary to the mainland for urgent medical attention. 'I can remember her being taken off,' recalled her son, 'on to the boat, and me standing near the pier with my grandmother and waving to her and she'd got her shawl round her head and was waving back'[74] – but she died two days later in a ward in Glasgow. Mary's sad end strengthened Nurse Barclay's argument, in a letter to the Board of Health, that St Kilda was no longer fit for human habitation. When the *Henry Malling* rolled in, as spring bloomed in 1930, it found a community in the throes of death, suckling on the sugary provisions that they bore like half-starved animals and devouring sacks of letters and newspapers for some glimmer of hope from the outside world. Some children had spent the winter barefoot and were delighted to put on laced boots. They found that only one islander had bothered to sow crops for the winter, such was the general climate of resignation.

Evacuation was not a new idea but the likelihood of it actually happening had never gained much traction, until now. When it had been suggested the previous year, one old woman declared she would *never* move unless physically forced to do so. Yet one year later, following the tragic winter, the idea of remaining on St Kilda seemed hopeless, masochistic even. 'They have gone through such privations this winter', observed Skipper Quirk, 'that they don't want to face another.'[75] It was these arguments that won the day when, at the factor's house in April 1930, Nurse Williamina Barclay convened a grave tea. The remaining islanders were to discuss the prospect of evacuation. With their autarky in ruins, a grim finality set in. 'Between you, me and the deep sea,' said Williamina at this final summit, 'I think you're on your last legs.' 'We sat down at the table for hours, and one old man with the tears trickling down his face came and put his arm around my shoulder. "We all think God sent you here."'[76] She had told them another world was possible. A world where you do not have to struggle just to survive. A world where the children would have a chance in life. And so there was consent. The minister Dugald Munro sat down, took a piece of scrap paper, and composed a petition – a prayer – to the Secretary of State for Scotland. His request was workmanlike and devoid of elegy. The population was now just thirty-six, he said, of which a significant proportion were determined to leave. There would not be enough able-bodied individuals to tend the sheep, to weave, to look after the widows, to eke out even a meagre existence. Since the island was no longer self-sufficient, they needed the government's help to remove themselves and their possessions and 'to find homes and occupations for us on the mainland'. After two thousand years of continuous oc-cupation, the Hirtans had become shipwrecks on their own island. The petition was signed by all the adults on the island – twelve men, eight women – and handed to the next trawler to appear in the bay. Then they waited and prayed for the wheels of bureaucracy to turn, delivering them from their certain ruin.

Four days before the evacuation, in the dying days of August 1930, the final postcard was sent. Its message, from a tourist called Freda, said, just, 'Last Greetings from St Kilda.' Then the post of-fice shut for ever, the final service was held at church and, bowed by sorrow, the islanders rounded up their dogs, those indomitable hunters and guardians, tied weights around their necks, placed them in sacks, and dropped them from the pier, looking sorrow-fully on as the yelping bundles sank beneath the waves. Then they returned to their houses and waited for HMS *Harebell*.

And up on the stacks of Boreray, from their nests in the cliffs, the birds rejoiced.

CHAPTER SEVEN

THE GHOST OUTPOSTS OF NORFOLK

If you look closely at maps of Britain you can find, in certain parts, roads running towards villages which stop, abruptly, leaving the ghostly outline of a shape within – like veins and arteries leading towards a spectral heart. But unlike blood vessels, these channels convey very little in or out, and run not to a pumping fountainhead of life but a fenced-off wilderness. These military precincts, though they are sometimes bleached out of maps, have played an instrumental if sometimes undervalued role in the defence, or even existence, of the United Kingdom for the last eighty years. Typically taken over for military training, they conceal ghost villages. The 225 residents of Tyneham in Dorset, for example, were 'temporarily' evicted in 1943 'to help win the war and keep men free' and yet none were ever able to return;[1] the public, at weekends, can walk up to the mouldering facades of houses and feel for themselves the skein of the abandoned village.[2] But this is far from the case with the cluster of villages that lie within the Stanford Training Area in Norfolk.[3] STANTA, as it is known, is a fenced-off military zone in Breckland, a sandy heathland stretching from the northern cusp of Suffolk into mid-Norfolk. The whole area is covered in yellow-flowered gorse and is a terrain of eerie beauty spread beneath expansive skies. I had become aware of this shadowy military lair in East Anglia after finding a number of perplexing references, in various newspapers, books and websites, to a 'Nazi village' in Norfolk.[4] It was utterly tantalising.

After an abortive reconnaissance, which only served to demonstrate how well sealed off and guarded STANTA was, I was forced to abandon my plan of sneaking in, taking pictures and writing the whole thing from the perspective of a roving outsider. I got in touch with the Ministry of Defence – or tried to. It had the feel of a wild goose chase. There were bounced-back emails, unanswered voicemails, requests for passport, driving licence and other proofs of identification and residency, demands for ever more detailed descriptions of the precise nature of my interest, trails warming up, trails going cold.[5] Then silence. It left me despondent, but then, quite out of the blue, I received a message from someone who seemed willing to help – or, at least, someone with a great enough passion for the training area to look upon my request favourably. There would of course have to be further checks, but so long as I met the appropriate criteria, I would be granted access; would be guided, by him, on a motorised tour of this ghostly landscape. Nothing prepared me for the world of dissimulation and mirage that I would find on the other side of the perimeter fence. Of all the lost settlements I visited, these were the only ones which, post-oblivion, would adopt completely new identities; over six hundred years earlier, Old Winchelsea had managed to 'become' New Winchelsea, but it was essentially an upgrade, replicating its former identity in a new physical and topographic context. The identities of the STANTA villages, however, were more in flux. What lay beyond the perimeter fence was a place where reality and fantasy existed in an uneasy concord, and where the forces of good could suddenly become evil – rustic villages in Merrie England turning, in the blink of an eye, into chilly outposts of evil empires.

————

With my military escort,[6] I set off to tour the ghost villages of the Stanford Training Area in Norfolk, in the cold, curt days of December. The landscape was wild and untamed, a seventy-year absence of agriculture allowing for a proliferation of flora and fauna, some exotic, showing how man's loss is often nature's gain. In the sparseness of winter we could see for miles, the branches of the trees imprinted upon a bare blue sky. There was a time when the Training Area was home to six flourishing villages and hamlets – West Tofts, Langford, Buckenham Tofts, Stanford, Sturston and Tottington.[7] These are now no more, abandoned since the Second World War, although mementoes of their existence litter the landscape like the forlorn gravestones of the unmourned dead.

As we drove through the lost village of West Tofts, we saw mounds where houses had once been. They were built from clay lump in the late nineteenth century and, once abandoned, as the rain and damp set in, soon fell to rot and decay, eventually melted away. A triangular monument marks the site of the vanished post office and, beyond that, a lone house stands in a coppice of tree stumps, the brick from which it was built ensuring its survival. We drove silently on, past rows of Scots pines planted by the Victorian aristocracy to shield the sandy soil from the ravages of the wind, soil which today is dominated by gorse, broom and heather. It was the rabbits, I learned, who had always presented the biggest threat to the fecundity of the soil, burrowing down and severing the roots from the crops, causing it to degenerate into a sandy wilderness – so much so that these creatures were eventually confined to giant rabbit penitentiaries where they were slaughtered in great number, or starved, and left to rot, the living feasting on the corpses of their departed brethren.[8]

The day was crisp and golden on the heathland – which my companion adored, professing he had the best job in the world because he got to experience this untrammelled wonder of nature. In the distance, through the fields, we could sometimes make out a lonely church shimmering in and out of visibility on the horizon. We drove on, my guide relentlessly cheerful as though there was nothing remotely sad or strange about the landscape, being naturalised to it, to the abandoned village of Tottington whose provenance stretches back to at least the eleventh century.[9]

Above us we occasionally saw, through the branches of the trees, a notoriously shy raptor: the golden pheasant. But it was another, yet more majestic bird with an ostentatious plumage which, by 1942, was flying above the parliament buildings of much of western Europe. The Nazis who took the golden eagle as their symbol had by then sucked around three-fifths of Europe into a churning abyss of war, occupation and genocide, and their plan to extend their dominion to the shores of Britain was well advanced. If Britain along with her allies, the government realised, were to stand a decent chance of defeating Nazi Germany in Europe, they would need to train their troops to fight effectively and victoriously. And that meant that vast swathes of Britain would have to be carved up into 'battle areas'.

A classified communiqué from the Under Secretary of State clarifies the rationale for carving out the battle areas. It was about priming the British Army for the smack of warfare ahead. 'The most serious disadvantage which our army at home suffers in comparison with the enemy', he wrote, 'is that when called upon to operate it will pass overnight from conditions of peacetime training to the stresses and nerve-strain of war.'[10] The forces of the Reich were battle-ready, battle-hardened; the forces of Britain were not. The only way to bridge the gap, to shake them out of their slumber, was to emulate the conditions troops were going to face on the Continent in the most 'lifelike' and 'realistic' way – these two words recur throughout the War Office files, emphasising a fixation upon mimesis that would still be evident within the landscape some eighty years later, a vivid emulation of battle conditions abroad.[11] In part, this was topographical; the chosen landscapes should be similar to what the troops would encounter in northern France at D-Day; preferably it would 'contain beaches that would not be unduly difficult for landing operations, while, on the other hand, the ground inland should be reasonably difficult'. But it was also operational; 'it is essential', the files say, that troops would be able to undertake operations that 'vary wildly in nature and scope'. This meant troops being able to fire their rifles and machine guns liberally, the detonation of up to five thousand grenades, the firing of mortars engulfing parts of the landscape in smoke, helicopters hovering overhead providing cover; ideally, therefore, training areas would be sparsely populated without any railways or main roads. That this – and at such top speed, too – was going to be controversial, outrageous even, was not lost on officials. It was suggested, rather vaguely, that 'measures' be put in place to anticipate and mitigate the backlash.

It was not just in East Anglia that this was happening. The area to the north-east of Thetford was one of six proposed training areas all over the country. The others were around Rothes and Dunbar in eastern Scotland; to the west of Otterburn in Northumberland; east of Wye in the South East; south of Poole Harbour and Dartmoor in the south; and around the Cambrian Mountains in Wales. In total, 20 per cent of the entire landmass of the UK was appropriated in this way.

True, the Ministry of Supply was not going not be too thrilled about the loss of the Thetford area's plenteous supply of timber, but at least the dispossessed, a majority of whom were agricultural workers, were in high demand elsewhere and would not struggle to find jobs. The ends surely justified the means and so the eighteen-thousand-acre area, Whitehall decreed, would be requisitioned under D.R. 51, a little-known emergency power allowing the military to commandeer vast swathes of the country for training purposes.[12] The Stanford Battle Area was born. As the report articulated, the area was mostly heath and woodland and some of it was already being used quite intensively for tank training. There were farms, too, and it was initially suggested that the flocks of sheep be allowed to stay, even as the war games raged around them, with compensation being paid each time one was shot, blown up or crushed by a tank. The same strategy could hardly be pursued for the area's human inhabitants, of which there were 750, living in and around six villages, all of which now stood in the shadow of death.

In June 1942 the inhabitants of the doomed villages were summoned to two meetings with government and army spokesmen, at a blacksmith's in Tottington and a schoolyard in West Tofts, and told the news.[13] It was met with great sorrow, but leavened by a sense that, given the unimaginably high stakes in Europe and the existential struggle for the survival of Western liberty, it was a necessary evil; the landowner Lord Walsingham (himself a retired Lieutenant Colonel) asked his tenants for 'fortitude and courage'.[14] Doubt surrounds the exact nature of the War Office's original proposition. My guide assured me that, contrary to what was commonly alleged, the War Office *never* made any official 'undertaking' that the villagers would be able to return after the war, although he conceded that informal pledges may have been made behind the scenes by junior officers.[15] But whatever the military might claim today, evidence in the National Archives tells a rather different story. The Home Office's files on agricultural damage to the Thetford Battle Training Area (which incorporated the Stanford Battle Area) are peppered with references to what, in one instance, is described as 'definite assurances when evacuation took place that the land etc. would be returned when the emergency was past'.[16] Even more compellingly, an edition of *The Times* in 1947 has a letter from an officer who was officially charged with overseeing the evacuation of the Stanford Battle Area in 1942: 'I was in charge of the arrangements made to remove and rehouse the inhabitants to the villages involved,' he recalled, 'and was present with the GOC-in-Charge Eastern Command at the public meetings . . . Both of us gave the most categorical undertakings that the people *would be allowed to return when the war was over . . .* they were told every care would be made to preserve [the buildings intact against their return' [my italics].[17]

It is fair to say that not all the evictees were entirely convinced by the Army's assurances. In premonition of the forlorn prayer pinned to the church door in the abandoned village of Tyneham four months later, a certain M. G. Griffin, who lived at number 17 on Tottington's main street, affixed a notice to the front door of his house on the day of departure, 1 August 1943. 'These premises were vacated to enable you to have an area for battle training,' it declares. 'The occupants, who with good will have given up their homes for the war effort, hope to return some day. Do not wantonly destroy, damage or remove their property. Don't let them down.'[18] The direct, admonitory tone conveys a distinct scepticism and, though we cannot say if he spoke for all the villagers, it is entirely possible that a sense of mistrust was felt, a mistrust that would have left them in psychological limbo, trying hard to reconcile themselves to their 'temporary' new homes yet forever haunted by the prospect – real or otherwise – of not being able to return to their true homes.

The emergency, in the event, did pass. But, outside of a coffin, the villagers were not allowed back. It was decided that the requisitioned land – which had served its purpose so well – should be retained so that the military could more effectively meet the challenges of the future.[19] The promise, then, was broken. Though there was never any real sense that this had been done out of malice or greed, and, as the note left on the door of number 17 reveals, the banished residents fully understood just how much had been at stake during the Second World War, it would have been surprising if there had not been any resistance or repercussions, particularly when it became clear that the military wanted to increase the size of the battle zone yet further. In 1947 appeared the 'Humble Petition' from the former inhabitants of Stanford, Tottington and West Tofts, and the inhabitants of the parish of Sturston and parts of other parishes within the battle area. 'Free the SBA, see justice done!'[20] it demanded, vowing to make the War Department keep its promises and restore their bullet-riddled homes. 'Sign the petition now for the release of houses and land in the Stanford Battle Area.' The thrust of the argument was that the annexing of the land was not just a betrayal of promises but a criminal waste of resources at a time when there was a dearth of land for food production, and housing. '15,000 acres in the Battle Area could be in cultivation now – instead a further 9,000 acres threatened.' It would also liberate 'the main roads of Norfolk' that had been sucked into the vortex, those that seem to vanish on today's maps. 'Sign the petition! For the RELEASE of the Stanford Battle Area.'

But to no avail. The War Office's plan to annexe and expand the Stanford Battle Area permanently proceeded, to the dismay and disgust, but perhaps not surprise, of its former inhabitants. 'Now it seems that if the War Department has its way a large slice of Breckland will become nothing more than an ugly scar,' decried a letter to one local newspaper, adding, 'They will smash it to pieces.' This was, they continued, 'a sad fate indeed for one of the most delightful corners of Norfolk which came through the period for which it was originally requisitioned comparatively unscathed'. It was, wrote another, 'a devastating encroachment upon the fairest part of Britain'. Correspondents worried that it would become a degenerate landscape with crops of weeds and stocks of vermin and so they took consolation that it would in fact bloom into unnaturally vivid nature, with naturalists finding flora and fauna 'not to be found anywhere else in the British Isles'.[21] Still, the disruption could be unbearable, particularly for farmers. An eyewitness account, published in the *Thetford and Watton Times* in May 1947, described 'heavy gunfire which cracked walls of houses and broke down windows'. 'I have seen seed-beds just prepared for drilling overrun by tanks; and guns, vehicles and troops smashed down our gates, broke our fences and tore up miles of rabbit wire.' Ever the menace, 'the rabbits invaded the arable land and devastated it', for which, as we have seen, they were slaughtered in their thousands[22] so that the area did not fall to barrenness.

In the view of one reporter, in the immediate aftermath of the Second World War, the battle area was eerily empty, but salvageable. Kenneth Pipe, a reporter for the *Daily Express*, visited in the summer of 1947. He found a series of stilled villages in an expansive landscape where nature, wondrously, was beginning to reassert her primacy. 'I am sitting on the dirty, grey stone step of an empty house,' he wrote from 'a deserted village' in the Stanford Battle Area; 'the windows of its six rooms are covered with a form of black-out, and its outdoor buildings are scarcely visible in a weed forest of giant wild parsnip, hemlock, and bracken.'[23] It was once home to a farmer and his family but they, along with all the other residents of the battle zone, had gone, leaving a sense of secluded absence. 'It is lonely here,' Pipe wrote of the 19,000-acre area, fortified with barbed wire, barricades, chained gates and 'No Admission' signs. A whistling warden fails to spot him as he cycles along on a lone patrol – the reporter was technically trespassing, but seems to have found it incredibly easy to get in, unlike me, seventy years later – and his only companions were rabbits, hares and field mice. The 1942 evictions, he reports, led to the abrupt desertion of sixteen farmhouses, two smallholdings, 132 cottages, three schools and two pubs (he curiously omits the handful of abandoned churches), and sent a wave of one thousand people rolling into other parts of England (the figure official records has is 750).[24] Pipe proceeds to conduct the reader on a whirlwind tour of the 'fifteen or sixteen deserted villages and parishes' (there were actually four villages and two hamlets, and Pipe seems at pains to make the requisitioned area denser than it in fact was, possibly for dramatic effect). His visual impressions, though, were reliable, thorough and powerful. He saw 'strong, habitable, empty' houses on the road to Wretham over fertile, bracken-covered land; Bodney Hall and

Wretham Hall standing empty and forlorn; locks of barley and oat on land where aeroplanes used to take off on bombing missions to Germany; and mangolds, peas and cattle elsewhere. The training area was, in Pipe's view, ripe for repopulation; it could house six hundred people and the fecund land would offer up crops in abundance. The houses at Tottington, he thought, were excellent, 'locked and bolted', of course, but 'modern with red brick and solid outbuildings, steel-framed windows' and rooms that were in good condition, though covered in dust.

It was a very different impression from that, forty years later, of Dorothy Spragg. The daughter of a shepherd, she had grown up on a small farm in Tottington but was evicted along with her nine siblings in 1942. She only went back, she told a local radio programme in 1986, to tend the family graves, and it was on these sorrowful occasions that she saw the village in ruins, the 'few bricks that was once her happy home . . . now a pile of rubble'.[25] The only houses still standing were some of the redbrick council houses that Kenneth Pipe had seen forty years earlier but in a much fallen condition, 'now used for street fighting'. Certainly, by this stage, a powerful sense of grievance had taken hold amongst the dispossessed and their children. The broadcast described how 'a broken Army promise forty years ago has bred a deep distrust of the Army among some older Brecklanders', recounting, dramatically, and in the language of war, how 'hundreds of Brecklanders became refugees in their own country when the Army seized their villages to make the Stanford Training Area in July 1942'. As Dorothy Spragg put it, 'We were happy to go if it ended the war more quickly and brought our relatives back from the front. But the promise was broken and people are still bitter about it.' She begrudged the period of economic hardship that followed, not to mention the destruction of a seemingly indefatigable community. Everything M. G. Griffin, Dorothy's near neighbour who left the prophetic scrawl at number 17 in 1943, had feared to lose, he had lost.

Not everybody went quietly into the night. Some held out until there were tanks on their very lawn. Lucilla Reeve grew up in Tottington in the years following the First World War.[26] The daughter of an agricultural labourer and an unknown, absent father – rumoured locally to be someone of very high social standing[27] – she went to work in domestic service in London during the 1930s and returned highly versed in literature, music, politics, art and commerce; she knew how to manage accounts and, as her later writings testify, she had quite the poetic turn of phrase. After a fairly conventional start, her career path took an unusual twist for a woman at the time. Living in her grandmother's cottage in a meadow, she became the secretary to the land agent for the Merton Estate, one of the major landowners in the area, with over eight thousand acres to its name. Soon she was herself the land agent, and by the mid-1930s was in charge of managing the tenancies of the four villages and several farms in the keep of the landowner, Lord Walsingham. She was charged with collecting rents, keeping the houses in good repair, keeping meticulous accounts, and maintaining the pastures, woods, crops and tree plantations. She was not afraid of getting her hands dirty. She milked cows, operated heavy industrial machinery, and shot. Reeve developed a profound emotional attachment to the land, insisting that it was holy and blessed, even alive. Her writings, *The Earth No Longer Bare*, *Farming on a Battle Ground* and *Pheasants Had No Tails*,[28] radiate a demonstrable love of nature, of trees, lakes, plants, and of the animals in her charge, all of which she viewed as individuals with souls. She threw herself into her work, transgressive in almost every regard. She rode her horse with legs astride, not, as was the custom, side-saddle. She was blunt not polite. She hurtled through the estate in a bright-red racing car, driving so death-defyingly fast she was nicknamed 'madcap' (she later owned a motorbike). Her unusual appearance added further spice. She would stride forth looking like something out of a Weimar Republic jazz bar in a tight navy blue or black jacket, a stiffened white blouse unfailingly buttoned to the top, tweed skirt, and stout brogues, with her hair cut very, very short.

Her manner may have been unsettling and aloof, but it was her political views that ultimately alienated her from the community. As the 1930s progressed, she became interested in the National Socialist German Workers' Party and, in Britain, the Blackshirts, also known as the British Union of Fascists. She attended the 'Britain for the British' rally in Norfolk and, though it is difficult to know whether to classify her as a genuine supporter of the racial superiority, anti-democratic authoritarianism, and nationalism that were fascism's ferment, she at the very least flirted with Mosleyite ideology, and this gave her madcap character a sinister undertone, particularly as war with Germany looked increasingly inevitable. A female estate manager was one thing, but how could the Brecklanders put up with a suspected Nazi in their midst?[29] However unfair their characterisations of her (and her brusque manner no doubt exacerbated them), she ceased working for the Merton Estate and felt compelled to move to Bagmere Farm, to the south of the village of Stanford, in 1938. Here she attempted to set up a guesthouse, renovating the dilapidated buildings which had become overgrown with bracken and ragwort, forever putting up wire fences to keep out the recalcitrant rabbits. She failed to attract custom and her timing was, in any case, inauspicious.

On 13 June 1941, her farm was commandeered by the army for tank and troop training. 'The tanks are out on Frogshill Heath,' she wrote, 'my clover ground to dust beneath the wheels of war; I see the wreck of hay and corn, across Spring Breck.'[30] There does not seem to have been any suggestion she would get it back, nor does she seem to have responded favourably to any attempts to rehouse her, so attached was she to the land. As tanks swept through her corn all she could do was mourn, alone. In fact, she faced considerable financial hardship. She sold off most of the machinery and livestock at Eastmere Farm (itself in the shadow of military takeover) as well as her beloved horses, Beauty and Ben. Insisting she stay as close to her beloved land as possible, she planned to move into several plucking sheds on the cusp of the battle area, in Merton Woods. Transporting all her worldly possessions into the dingy outhouses that were to be her new residence proved emotional. 'I drove my car down Frogshall Hill,' wrote Reeve; 'the hour was late, the earth was still. The trees look'd down with pitying eye to see the laden car go by.' She continues, 'My heart was sad and bowed my neck, four years of work and planning wreck, behind me lay, across spring Breck.'[31] In the back of the car were her two dogs; beside her, three ducks in a box; and on her lap, a stray black kitten.[32]

She erected the three poultry huts on a hill overlooking the woods, in a circle of trees. They were hot in summer and cold in winter, but not entirely uncomfortable. There were bookshelves, chinaware and an easy chair where hens had once been plucked.[33] She tried to operate a little farm there, with the juddering of helicopters, blasts of mortars, and rattle of gunfire clearly audible from the battle zone. She was not impervious to the war games, recalling how on one occasion troops suddenly materialised and hacked down all her fences. She tried to expand her modest empire a little, gaining the thirty-two-acre Great Ellingham Farm elsewhere, and she managed to accrue almost a hundred cows, pigs and sheep, each of whom she knew by name. It was well known locally that the last two farmers at Ellingham Farm had taken their own lives, and for a woman with such mystical sensibilities, who prided herself on her dowsing, who saw ghosts 'often',[34] was unable, indeed, at times to distinguish them from real people, the ominousness of this was not lost; 'I felt he wondered if I would be the third!' she wrote of a ghoulish local who imparted the news.[35]

Ultimately, she proved much more adept at managing estates than farming them and, by November 1944, her empire had halved in size, to sixteen acres surrounding her huts. There was no prospect of moving back; by 1943, her old home, Bagmere Farm, lay in ruins, having been pounded by shells, and many of the trees and shrubs she had so assiduously planted were torn up and destroyed. In November 1945, a couple of months after the end of the Second World War, she returned to Tottington and described the 'ruin . . . of a village I had only seven years ago described as lovely'. The sense of loss and destruction was harrowing: 'The dead and staring eyes of the cottage windows where once the geraniums bloomed, and the spotless curtains fluttered, look out on a scene of desolation.'[36] It was as though it were a scene from the pulverised Reich, not a quiet corner of the home front. She was horrified to see that 'the sides of the once tidy road are full of holes made by tanks roaring through . . . and the once lovely hedges of privet, lilac thorns and wild roses are mangled and torn'. 'A silence as of night', she finishes, 'broods over all.'[37] Her old home, she laments, only had one wall left standing. For someone who believed so strongly that the land was holy, the wasteland it had become was not just an act of political vandalism, but sacrilegious too.

Reeve spent her later years back in the plucking sheds overlooking the woods. It was cold and hopeless, the winds roaring over the woods and thrusting into the huts 'like waves of the sea'.[38] Thoughts of returning, of rebuilding a life within the battle area, faded with each day that went by. She had come to embody the land that had been devastated, and took on the suffering *it* had suffered. There could be no conciliation. Alone, and semi-maimed by an accident with a reef hook, she too hanged herself in that godforsaken shed, in 1955. A suicide could have no place amongst the dead of St Andrew's, Tottington, and so her body was placed in unconsecrated ground away from the church; mercifully, the metal fence of graveyard has since been extended so that it incorporates her grave – a grave I saw in the silver afternoon light.

'I hope to live to see the day come', wrote Reeve in 1948, 'when the battle training areas of Britain are again used for the growing of food for man and beast,' but it was not to be.[39] The military were very reluctant to let go of the battle area after the war and it was decided, in 1948, as the War Office had to keep reminding aggrieved farmers, 'that it was essential in the interests of national security that the battle training area . . . should be retained by the War Office for training purposes'.[40] Peace had not magically descended upon Europe and such a nursery of military skill was too valuable to let go until such a time as 'the military picture changed'. The amount of land retained by the military did dwindle, but only by a little, and incrementally: in 1946, 27,500 acres were under military control; by 1952, 25,000; and by 1963, 19,500. So even two decades after the evictions, the area retained by the military had only shrunk by a quarter. Some of the land was returned to agricultural use (including the airfield, as Pipe had noted), both arable and pastoral – in 1956, a young shepherd arrived from the Forest of Dean to take charge of 750 ewes that spent their days 'roaming the lonely fields and woods of this almost forgotten corner of Breckland'. Their liberty was soon curtailed, restricted to a five-thousand-acre region right in the centre of the zone, on account of, as an official order for the intensification of training puts it, 'the execution of military exercises, the erection of encampments, the construction of military works of a non-permanent character, and the supply of water to the persons using the land under the provisions of this order'.[41] The training was, at this stage, using blank ammunition, but this would soon change. The land was cleared for explosives, thousands more rabbits were exterminated and concerns were repeatedly expressed by farmers about troops parading through fields of crops. By the mid-1950s, the area was full of troops, though they were a sparser presence in winter, and the whole area littered with camping huts, some appallingly derelict, and gamekeepers' houses left to rot, too.

As we drove through the sorrowful remains of the STANTA

villages, I wondered if the right to private property, seen as sacrosanct, is in fact profoundly precarious. There are threats facing us in the future: pandemics, climate change, biological weapons and more. The events that took place here in 1942, and indeed on the Hill of Iham in 1288, show that land can be requisitioned at the click of a finger by a compulsory purchase order, whether at the behest of a medieval king or twentieth-century war office.

We carried on down the bumpy track, a little to the north of Tottington towards the vicinity of Eastmere Farm where Lucilla Reeve had worked. Here lay another ghost village. There appeared on the horizon a peculiar conglomeration of buildings which looked like they had been married from completely different parts of the world. My guide, behind the wheel, fell uncharacteristically silent. At first it just looked like a mass of buildings, hard to make any of them out clearly, but as the car slid forwards I could see that it resembled a Continental village – or at least, the part on the left did. The battle area was involved in certain chapters of Britain's history that are not generally known about, my guide told me; key chapters. 'People think that it's just the *Dad's Army*[42] set but

actually', he said, 'it was a theatre of war in its own right, infiltrated and invaded by a formidable enemy in the early eighties'.

———

A newspaper screams: 'Key targets across Norfolk were pounded by air strikes and increasingly ferocious attacks by Soviet Saboteurs yesterday.' 'Losses', it goes on, 'were reported on both sides as enemy forces made an all-out effort to destroy the country's vital installations.' The situation across the Channel was equally menacing. 'Meanwhile the tanks of the Red Army were rolling across Europe, and the Channel ports were subjected to heavy bombardment as the main Warsaw Pact forces crept closer to threatening a full-scale invasion of the UK.' The year was 1985, the month September, and these were not words you would usually expect to find in the *Eastern Daily Press*.[43] A whole swathe of Norfolk had been placed on a war footing, and violence was erupting everywhere. After reconnaissance and probing attacks earlier that week, the 'Soviet Commandos' (in fact five thousand British troops acting the part of soviet infiltrators) had now escalated their operations. Their game, it was assumed, was to reconnoitre the sites that would later be pounded by thousands of enemy troops, the ground, thanks to their efforts, tilled for a full-scale invasion.

'They have launched', reported one commander, 'with great enthusiasm and determination with bombs and guns! Activity has really hotted up! The enemy are chucking everything they have got at us, but we are fighting back nobly.' 'There are machine-gun fights in the woods; unexploded bombs artfully placed; people firing rocket launchers; air raids; men and equipment moved via helicopter or truck . . .' But the hostilities would reach their peak in Breckland, in – a twist of irony here, since it had been designed to prepare British troops for action overseas – the Stanford Training Area. 'We're heading for a jolly good punch-up,' reported a military top brass. 'The troops are being exercised extremely thoroughly. Everyone is certainly getting a fair crack of the whip in defending their locations.' NATO and the British government had long feared this day, and now they were being tested to their limits.

Britain's army, such as it was, so preoccupied with warding off the Soviets' westward advance in Europe, was not sufficient to counter the invasion of highly trained infiltrators nor, given the risk that key parts of it had been 'turned' or even infiltrated by Soviet forces, could it be trusted. So tens of thousands of reservists emerged from their offices, shops and farms to do their patriotic duty – GPs in search of adventure, bored bank clerks, solicitors, secretaries and other part-time soldiers, hidden in ditches, bushes and manure heaps across the countryside. At East Wretham (a small village south-east of Tottington near a disused grass airfield which had been absorbed into STANTA),[44] Tottington and Buckenham Tofts, 130 such reservists guarded their posts, avoiding sniper fire, and assessing in a matter of seconds whether those approaching them were dog-walkers, double agents, a member of a small team of Soviet saboteurs working behind enemy lines called *spetsnaz*, joyriders or harmless passers-by, and whether to open fire. The wrong decision, and they could find themselves incinerated in a fireball from a grenade or lacerated by machine-gun fire from the many enemy craft that seemed to materialise out of nowhere in the sky. It had been like this for two weeks. Near Lucilla Reeve's old home, in the ghost village of Tottington, four men masquerading as joyriders were arrested at a road checkpoint after sniffer dogs indicated the boot of their car was stuffed with ammunition; in another vehicle, at Buckenham Tofts, a ticking 500 lb bomb was discovered and a disposal team had to be wheeled in at top speed to diffuse it; and a camp in East Wretham came under sudden fire until the two Soviet snipers were shot dead. Everywhere, the British had to forge new and effective ways of defending themselves against the wily *spetsnaz* who focused all their energies on crippling, or at least knocking out, key parts of the country's economic and military infrastructure. Resistance could not just be effective; it had to be quick. The Soviet army had coursed through Europe and now it was waiting to launch its full-scale invasion of the UK.

There were of course casualties, fatalities. British reservists were picked off from inside a building near Buckenham Tofts and had to be stretchered away. And some Soviet saboteurs did manage to knock out airfields and factories. There were, as in any war, incidents of 'friendly fire'. British troops guarding a radar station at RAF Weybourne on the north Norfolk coast noticed a helicopter was trying to land without clearance. Their sergeant ordered them to stand-to. They sprang into action, training their rifles upon the pilot, and fired the moment he came within range. It was a British colonel, tragically, who fell to the ground. He had been forced to make an unexpected landing because of poor weather conditions which had reduced his visibility to near-zero. But he did not quite grasp the enormity of what had happened, his demise, so they shouted across: 'I'm afraid you are dead, sir.' But he was not annoyed. They had been absolutely right to kill him.[45] And the military umpires agreed. There they stood, all over Norfolk, betwixt and between the ghost villages of the training area, writing their little notes, reporting upon how everyone had done. It was just a wonder there had not been any chemical, or nuclear, attacks. But even that would not have been out of the question in this sandstrewn landscape of dissimulation and mirage.

After the defeat of Nazi Germany, the Union of Soviet Socialist Republics became Britain's principal enemy and, since STANTA is a mirror of the evil that lies beyond – and sometimes within – our shores (as defined by the government), the Cold War left its indelible mark on Breckland. The 1980s are often associated with a thaw in relations between the West and the USSR, in large part because of the emollient foreign policy and economic reforms of President Mikhail Gorbachev. But Gorbachev did not become

General Secretary of the Communist Party of the USSR until 1985, or president until 1990. With Margaret Thatcher and Ronald Reagan standing shoulder-to-shoulder against the Soviet Union, the earlier part of the decade was in fact a time of escalation. So much so, in fact, that the British government felt compelled to prepare its military for a war in central Europe – the cockpit of the clash between the forces of capitalism and communism – and its reservists, the Territorial Army, and the Home Service Front (a Home Guard-esque military force, created in 1982, a sort of real-life *Dad's Army*), for the very real possibility of the infiltration and invasion of Britain. This would necessitate, they believed, the development and expansion of the United Kingdom's diminished battle area; at the end of the Second World War, Britain had a million acres of training ground but by the mid-1980s, it had shrunk to just 370,000 acres.[46] The Ministry of Defence was looking to build another battle village – not, this time, a mock-up of a village in northern France but, rather, on a different site within the training area, the kind of built-up environment where British forces might find themselves fighting in central Europe. 'The houses are to be used for training troops going to West Germany', reported a BBC Radio Norfolk programme, 'in conditions similar to those on the border with the east.' It would be besieged by land and battered by air, aircraft and helicopters forever lurking in the sky like vultures.[47]

From the outset, it was only really ever the Stanford Battle Area that was in the frame, not just for the proposed battle village, but large-scale anti-Soviet exercises more broadly. And for good topographical reason. 'The Breckland countryside is', as Major General Charles Ramsay of Headquarters Eastern District explained to the *Eastern Daily Press*, 'just like the Northern German plains where NATO forces might expect to fight a future war'. It was 'a setting which is a realistic representation of the continental conditions we would expect to experience' – namely, open farming country, fairly flat with excellent panoramic visibility, with plenty of space for manoeuvres, and a wide range of defence and attack options.[48] Stanford was therefore 'the best training area they had'. The problem with Salisbury Plain – the army's biggest battle area – was that it was *barren* and so was quite unlike the countryside where British troops might fight in central Europe.

The military settled upon Eastmere Farm, where Lucilla Reeve had worked in the late 1930s, which lay to the north-east of Tottington, site of the 'Nazi village' which, by this point, had morphed into a mock Northern Irish village, to prepare British troops for missions and close-quarters combat in Northern Ireland, a row of its houses daubed with IRA slogans for immersive effect.[49] Topographically, this brand-new battle village was, as officers revealed at a meeting at their West Tofts camp, 'intended to be a mockup of the sort of village found on the East German plains';[50] 'The houses are to be used for training troops going to West Germany in conditions similar to those on the border with the east.' Its function was to provide 'tactical training realism' for troops before they were posted to Germany, and in particular 'specialised urban fighting techniques'. The 'Stasi', 'Soviet Army' and Britain's army and air force – all would converge on this forgotten corner of Norfolk. 'Eastmere' would be a distinctive immersive world, built from scratch. But beyond that, there seem to have been several, slightly different blueprints. One scheme projected 'sixteen houses, a church, public house, and other outbuildings' on the cusp of a nature reserve.[51] But Brigadier James Templer of UK Land Forces Headquarters envisaged 'twenty-six skeleton houses and a sewer tunnel'. There were already FIBUA (fighting in built-up areas) facilities in Yorkshire and Hampshire, Salisbury Plain Training Area and Sennybridge in Wales, but a close-quarters fighting *village* would be STANTA's unique contribution, all the more so given that it was near a live-firing area. It would not be in continuous use, General Ramsay assured residents, and, he went on, 'I hope you will recognise that we have taken quite significant, and exceptional, measures to take account of local feeling.'[52]

Eastmere farm, as UK Land Forces point out, was potentially ideal because it was 'screened by trees and most of the activity was confined to inside purpose-built houses'. Helicopters would not, after all, James Templer promised, be used, 'but there would be staged battles using blanks' and perhaps even 'new laser weapons' which were 'far quieter than either blanks or live firing'. But nonetheless, the site wasn't exactly in the middle of nowhere and the MoD's Head of Defence Lands acknowledged that good relations with people who lived nearby were important; 'nobody', he said, 'wants soldiers treading across their back garden or setting up machine guns in their hedges' – exactly the kind of thing, in other words, that had happened to Reeve on this very site forty years earlier. There would, for this reason, be three-hundred-metre buffer zones. The proposal received the green light from Breckland planners in June 1986, though many people who lived outside the training area but near the proposed mock village were not reassured. At the end of November 1986, 'an army of [two hundred] local folk' converged upon a military outpost, decidedly unimpressed by the MoD's assurances over 'compensation, noise, conservation and military traffic'.[53] They tapped into a rich vein of grievance and suspicion, given what had happened in 1943. So, on 13 December, they held a public meeting to protest the planned street-fighting village that so threatened their peace.

Merton was a nearby village, a cluster of farmhouses and barns, just over a mile to the north-east. For the chairman of Merton Parish Council the whole enterprise was a travesty, the firing of machine guns along with the hurling of grenades and people prancing around with handheld projectile launchers frankly intolerable. Wasn't the whole exercise pointless and contrived? 'Where are these twenty-five-house hamlets in the plains to be found in Europe?' he demanded in a furious letter.[54] 'Where they *are* to be found,' he continues, moonlighting as a military strategist, 'the proper tactic would be to blitz them and bypass them, not to go trading small arms house to house.' (He was wrong on this – employing *blitzkrieg* tactics was never seriously on offer, the prospect of a retaliatory nuclear strike notwithstanding.)

Merton's opposition in fact pre-dated the go-ahead for the new battle village, for its residents had been disturbed by other training exercises going on within STANTA. In February 1985, the chairman of Merton Parish Council, Lord Walsingham, sent an angry letter to the Secretary of State for Defence, Michael Heseltine.[55] The chairman had been a member of a commando unit involved in helicopter-borne deployment of troops in the Far East in the 1960s, and he did not want such things coming back to haunt his retirement. He took umbrage at 'low-level helicopter overflights of villages abutting the STANTA', and in particular helicopter sorties thundering above some of the houses in Merton at only 100 or 200 feet altitude, in the middle of the night. Couldn't they do their very low-level helicopter-borne deployments somewhere else in the vast training area? The pilots could catch up on their sleep but the villagers could not. And indeed it must have been odiously surreal to be going about your business in a peaceful rural village in one of the great beauty spots of Norfolk with, practically on your doorstep, a kind of mirror village on a permanent war footing, forever besieged by land and air, ricocheting with the crackle of machine-gun fire and the booms of mortars; a slippage from a less fortunate dimension. Along with many others, this correspondent doubted the military's earnest reiterations of the urgent necessity of the whole scheme: 'They ought not to be subjected to this kind of disturbance (as if the Defence of the West were dependent on just such a disturbance which is surely patently absurd).'

Their pleas fell on deaf ears. The concerns of the residents of nearby villages were made to seem slight, even selfish, when weighed up against the urgent need of protecting Britain against the 'empire of evil' brooding behind the Iron Curtain, biding its time. The military was determined to go ahead with its Soviet-style battle village, and go ahead it did. It was in front of us now.

The car pulled up, and I went for a wander. The 'Soviet village' at Eastmere Farm, unlike the 'Nazi village' at Tottington, was built from scratch in 1986. Accordingly, the buildings did not look decayed and timeworn; they were crisp, fresh. I saw, as I strolled through this strangely leisurely place, wooden houses, a commanding Lutheran-style church (where the British troops learned to co-ordinate and evaluate mock-intelligence of enemy movements), and a leafy main street. The illusion was impressive; I might have been sauntering through a village in Saxony. Apart from being deadly quiet, nothing seemed especially incongruous with the rural, heathland setting.

This set that I was ambling about was part of what, by the mid-1980s, had grown into a busy live-action battle zone, used by up to fifteen hundred troops a day. On the live-firing ranges in the heart of STANTA, one day in three, soldiers (both regular and territorial) roamed through the heathland with rifles, machine guns, grenades, mortars and short-range field artillery, including anti-tank weapons, and all this alongside infantry manoeuvres, aircraft practising ground attacks and helicopters deploying troops and equipment – *busy, loud*.

The whole area – including many of the abandoned villages – was also used for elaborate training exercises, furthering the precinct's rich traditions of military masquerade. Operation Brave Defender, described above, fulfilled all of the theatrical bravura promised – but never delivered – by the 'Nazi village' forty years earlier. 'The exercise is designed to test Britain's ability to defend vital bases and installations in wartime,' a newspaper reported, 'as if Soviet behind-the-lines special forces, knows as *spetsnaz*, had already landed.'[56] It took place at a time of heightened tension between the West and the USSR, following the expulsion of twenty-five Soviet spies. The exercise followed NATO's thinking that in a time of tension Western countries would inevitably be targeted by sabotaging commandos operating under the cloak of secrecy hoping to cripple the country's military and economic infrastructure ahead of a 'conventional', full-scale invasion. It was no secret what was going on – the government wanted Russia to comprehend that Britain's reservists meant business, and, like a coiled spring, were waiting to crush the saboteurs should they dare to strike. Coverage in newspapers was fairly comprehensive, vivid – it was, after all, something of a journalist's dream to bombard readers with sensational, instantly provocative and distressing reports from an alternative reality, to disorientate the reader by presenting fiction as fact, paint lurid, worst-case scenarios, or even give the dead a voice, and the plans for the exercise were also discussed in Parliament earlier in the year.[57]

The main aim of the exercise was to ascertain whether the Home Service Force was up to the job of defending the country against infiltrators. There had of course been well-founded fears of Nazi, Napoleonic/French Revolutionary, Jacobite, even Jesuit infiltrators through the preceding centuries – but this was on a bigger, and potentially more deadly, scale. The exercise progressed from a reconnaissance to a sabotage stage, then full-out assault. It took place over vast swathes of the United Kingdom but reached its climax in STANTA (where three thousand troops were deployed) and in the deserted village of Stanford in particular, the only place where live ammunition was used. There were mock casualties, surprise sniper attacks, and enemy helicopters firing machine guns overhead. The exercise was watched by military umpires drawn from forty countries, some of whom enthusiastically reported the great success of the exercise to newspapers. 'A new concept in defence against Russian *spetsnaz* teams', reported one, 'has been proved correct.'[58]

Eight years later, an almighty bang rolled across a misty Breckland as ten tanks were blown up near the ghost village of West Tofts. It was a condition of the ending of the Cold War, which the events in Germany of November 1989 had made inevitable. By that stage, STANTA had long since emerged as the country's pre-eminent training area 'with thousands of troops full and part-time, and sometimes from abroad, using its unique Breckland vastness', with 'aircraft movements of all kinds'.[59] The explosions had destroyed the turrets, wheels and gun barrels but the corpses of the tanks were left in one piece, so they could be used for target practice in the future. The Soviet Union may have disintegrated in 1991, but God only knew what kind of enemies Britain might have to face in the future.

———

We drove west, along ghost roads, to the other side of the battle area. We passed a disused runway and faded cricket pitch, the abandoned, blast-proof church of All Saints' in the deserted village of Stanford, and, a little further on, by Buckenham Tofts, the stillest, saddest lake I ever saw, a morose pool of tears as though the landscape were mourning its lost.[60] 'Are you ready?' said my guide. 'For this?'

We had arrived at Bridge Carr, *carr* referring to the boggy wooded area around the River Wissey. In the place we had come to see, however, there was not a marsh in sight. It was one of the eeriest, most disquieting places I had ever set foot in. We drove up to the outer barrier, got out of the car, and walked straight into a mouth of darkness. We found ourselves in a cubed maze, open to the elements. Wrought of concrete, in the sparse Breckland moors, it felt like a transplant from another world. We walked past deserted market stalls, foreign-language graffiti and ominous entranceways. The walls were menacingly high and I could imagine the heads of snipers appearing from behind the battlements at any moment, training their rifles on me and my genial guide.

We floated down wide bays, shrouded in shadow, but occasionally pierced by beams of hostile sun, and eventually our section of the maze opened into a bright courtyard, open to the expansive Norfolk sky, completely deserted. There were outdoor tables for butchering fowl and chopping wood, a communal baking oven, basins behind a wall for ablutions, cell-like bedrooms, and alcoves for storage. One of these was a veritable grotto of canned meat, vegetables, sauces, pickles, olives and other non-perishables with garishly coloured labels with a script indecipherable to my eye.

My guide, rapt in admiration, showed me the well on the other side of the courtyard or rather, the well that was not a well, just as the beds were never slept in; the pickles were never eaten. The whole village indeed was a simulacrum of the kind of settlement where British troops would encounter enemy action in the desert plains of Afghanistan. It was one thing to remodel abandoned villages so they better resembled northern European landscapes during the 1940s and 1980s, but it was quite another to build an entire mock village from scratch so it faithfully mirrored – shadowed – Afghanistan's theatre of war. What I found in Norfolk is a tiny synecdoche of the killing zone where, after 2001, the war on terror would supposedly be won or lost. When I visited, everything was deadly quiet. The presence of absence, by now a sensation I was horribly used to, hung in the air like a pall. I had felt it powerfully in Dunwich, but here was different: the framework was still very much intact – it just needed to be animated.

When Ishmara – or the Jackson Wright village,[61] as it is sometimes known, after two of the architectural designer's paratrooper friends lost in action in Helmand – opened in May 2009, it was seething with life – and death – with routine atrocities playing out in the Norfolk countryside. The Ministry of Defence intended that every British soldier bound for Afghanistan – around eleven thousand per year at the time of opening – would undergo intensive training here for around a week. It was, without any shadow of a doubt, STANTA's most ambitious and sophisticated simulacrum yet, where the realism that had characterised the installations reached its apotheosis, with such meticulous attention to detail as to eclipse the 'Nazi village' and 'Soviet village' I had seen earlier.

When Ishmara 'opened its doors', the military went to quite extraordinary lengths to mimic the sights, sounds, smells, tastes – and *feel* – of the kinds of settlements to which British troops would be deployed in Helmand Province.[62] The floor of the compound was strewn with dust, tyres, mangled motorbikes and carts. In the communal courtyards and bazaar, tables were propped up with spare bicycle parts. The kitchens and sleeping chambers were full of pots and pans and bunk beds, and decorated with rugs. The market stalls were well stocked with rice, traditional kaftans, flip-flops and bread. The storage alcoves were a cornucopia of pickled fruits and vegetables. There was a mosque which looked and felt like a mosque. All over the village, the synthetic odour of traditional Afghan food was pumped out along with less savoury notes, such as the stench of meat rotting in the desert heat. Nor was the soundscape neglected – the call to prayer wailed from the mosque and reverberated throughout the compounds during the day, sometimes to be drowned out by the sound of an Apache helicopter overhead, and, in the bazaar, crackly melodies played from the local radio. It was a contained, but convincing, set: 'We've sourced props from all over the world,' the commander of the training area proclaimed in 2009. 'We've replicated everything except for the desert heat, but there's not much we can do about that in Norfolk.' The village, though, was much more than a realistic stage set. It was animate. It was *alive*.

John Pickup lost his leg in a motorbike accident in the early 1990s. Twenty years later he found himself here, in Ishmara, with some fellow actors from Amputees in Action waiting to jump out at troops, clutch the stub of his leg, and scream at the top of his voice.[63] Make-up artists were on hand to recreate the look of a freshly severed leg, which spurted out an immense quantity of fake blood as he yowled in agony, writhed around in the dust, and cried for help. It was the most convincing impression of a femoral arterial bleed most soldiers had ever seen, with Pickup recalling how he had seen troops throw up their meals at his very foot. Then he would go back to 'sitting around in a puddle all day, cold and miserable' like an extra in a budget immersive theatre experience, awaiting his next leap into the limelight. Actors with the ability to play the freshly maimed victim of a suicide bomber convincingly were in great demand in the mock village of Ishmara.

Pickup was just one performer and the aftermath of a suicide bombing just one scenario encountered by soldiers training at Bridge Carr. The amputee actors worked alongside a large cast of Afghan émigrés, and a smaller contingent of Gurkhas, who played the villagers, victims and – villains of the piece – the Taliban and al-Qaeda insurgents with their machine guns and suicide bombs. There were mock soldiers and mock police in this odd theatre of war; mock imams and mock babies, everyone dressed in the appropriate Afghan dress, speaking in Pashto and broken English. It is true that people – usually members of the British armed forces – had played the role of German and Soviet troops and saboteurs in STANTA's earlier battle villages, but nothing this textured or elaborate had ever been attempted; and besides, the very rare double agent aside, those earlier roles had almost always been hostile combatants whereas here, the bulk of the cast played Afghan nationals trying to go about their daily lives in a hopelessly wartorn land, reflecting the belief that Britain's mission was as much about establishing a rapport with ordinary Afghans, winning local consent rather than cowing them into submission through force. The sophistication of the set, variety of spaces, and plenteous supply of actors made for a wide range of scenarios for the troops to master. In the mosque, British troops prayed with village elders and learned about southern Afghanistan's culture and society. In the lengthening shadows of the compound, troops encountered villagers who wanted to barter their bicycles for British guns. In the bazaar, soldiers slowly paced through the crowd, looking for telltale signs of suicide bombers. Beyond the compound, soldiers had to dodge insurgents' bullets in the woodland, crawl for cover, and return fire, attending to injured parties, blood spurting from prosthetic throats through a haze of purple smoke; in another field, they encountered an improvised explosive device by the roadside.[64] And sometimes, from somewhere in the compound, there could be heard a dull boom, then a dirge-like chorus of moans and groans, as troops followed a trail of guts though the maze, towards the dead bomber who had hidden in plain sight in its centre.

The surreal elaborateness of Ishmara reflected a belief that the West was facing a new, and unfamiliar, type of enemy. The Nazis had pioneered devastating new modes of warfare like *blitzkrieg* and the V-1 and V-2 missiles that rained down on British cities, and the Soviets fine-tuned behind-the-lines sabotage techniques, but, although these enemies had launched kamikaze missions, the idea of contending with a seemingly never-ending stock of ideologically motivated suicide bombers who did not particularly care about civilian casualties – indeed wanted to maximise them, as they saw anyone who did not resist the illegitimate, infidel-imposed regime as fair fodder – was new. Unlike Tottington, which mimicked villages in northern France that were yet to be won, the Jackson Wright village represented territory already 'liberated' by the US-led coalition, which was attempting to hold in the hope of crushing the insurgency so that a fledgling democracy – one that would no longer sponsor terrorism – might take root. It wasn't just the nature of the enemy but the whole environment, culture and society of Afghanistan that was substantially different from the sorts of European countries – France, Germany, Northern Ireland and the former Yugoslavia – whose villages Breckland had mimicked before. New techniques would have to be learned against a new kind of enemy – not the military forces of a nation state or empire, but a resilient insurgency practising asymmetrical warfare.

Preparedness was therefore key to the mission's success, and the military were immensely proud of the verisimilitude that had been achieved at the site. 'Eerie' and 'uncanny' are words which recur in the military's characterisations of it: 'The place is magnificent,' declared the commander of the training estates in eastern Britain, Lieutenant Colonel Simon Lloyd, in a newspaper interview. 'I've served in the Middle East and the likeness is uncanny.'[65] For fellow officer Colonel Richard Westley, 'The hairs on the back of your neck stand up. For a minute you are back there. Ask veterans of two or three tours and they will tell you it is genuinely eerie.'[66] The main purpose of the unusually high level of realism was to familiarise troops with an alien environment and desensitise them to the psychological trauma that lay ahead 'so', as Lieutenant Colonel Lloyd put it, 'they get on with saving lives, instead of reacting, when faced with the real life horror of it'.[67] 'It will make the shock of going to war much less,' he added (echoing the mission statement of the original 1940s battle village to prepare troops for the 'smack of warfare' ahead), 'and prepare troops to the very best of their ability.' For General Sir David Richards, the commander-in-chief of the UK land forces, the intricacy of the facility was an act of patriotic love towards 'our excellent fighting soldiers' who 'deserve nothing less', a reciprocation of the insoluble bond between soldiers and their country, giving them 'the very best chance to succeed in today's complex operations and return home safely'.[68]

Their praise was not misplaced. When it was unveiled, the village was a manifestation of a groundbreaking new concept in defence training. Unlike the East German-style street at Eastmere, which was always essentially frozen in time, the mock Afghan village was organic, growing ever more realistic, and quite gloriously interconnected with its host territory for which it served as a stunningly immersive synecdoche for everyone who passed through it, or performed in it, making a tiny but potentially life-saving contribution. Ishmara's reality was bang up to date, fed by the very latest intelligence from the desert plains of Helmand; the Ministry of Defence solicited the help of people who were formerly in positions of authority in Afghanistan – army officers, policemen, governors, even ministers – on all aspects of the setup: the layout of the buildings, behaviour of the 'inhabitants', dramatic scenarios and environment, and more. These consultants retained extensive links with their equivalents in their native country, and stayed in touch with a 'roving team' who travelled through the towns, villages and cities of Helmand actively gathering intelligence. Thus Ishmara was hot-wired into any shifts in insurgent strategy – if the Taliban changed its bomb-making tactics, for instance, the team would feed this information back to their allies in England and it would immediately be incorporated into the training scenarios.[69] Another source of potentially life-saving intelligence was returning soldiers – soldiers who perhaps were looking forward to some respite from the front line, only to find themselves here, in the uber-vivid simulacrum of Afghanistan, mentoring some poor trooper who was about to fly out and experience the real thing for the first time.

There was a pleasing symbiosis to the whole project, with the military obviously keen to equip British recruits with the necessary skills to achieve their objectives in the field. So, too, were the Afghan actors and consultants keen for the exercise to be successful; the more successfully they trained the British soldiers to limit bloodshed, the less their fellow citizens whom they had left behind would suffer, and the brighter the future. The stakes were therefore high. What happened – or didn't – in this remote corner of Norfolk could affect lives that were hanging in the balance some four thousand miles away. STANTA's latest mock village represented a shift towards a more proactive and progressive form of military training, especially tailored to defeat a new kind of enemy. As the Director General of Land Warfare put it in 2010, 'The culture *was* one of waiting to be told. Now we go to theatre [Helmand] and find out'; it was, in the words of Colonel Westley, less about the passive reception of policy, doctrine and funding and more about conveying the fluid reality of conditions on the ground back to this patch of Breckland heath.[70] With virtually all Helmand-bound troops passing through the village between its opening in mid-2009 and the withdrawal of British combat troops from Afghanistan in 2014, there can be no doubt that the training village had a huge impact.

At the same time, it would be remiss not to acknowledge that the battle village was a valuable asset in terms of publicity, and this certainly was not lost on the military or the government. The village was built at a time when public opinion had soured against the wars in Iraq and Afghanistan. In the eyes of many British citizens, there had been precious little to show for so many years of war but the carnage that appeared so frequently on their television screens. For some, the whole American-led enterprise was looking more and more like a fool's errand. There had also been major concerns, vented in the press, that British troops lacked basic kit and so were woefully ill prepared and equipped for combat operations. Whilst there is no suggestion that it was its main purpose, the existence and elaborate workings of Ishmara did at least convey to a domestic audience – not to mention to the Taliban and al-Qaeda – that the Ministry of Defence was going to quite elaborate lengths to prepare British troops for combat operations, and, very much unlike the secret training at the 'Nazi village' in Tottington (which had to be kept secret lest D-Day plans got out), but not without parallels with the 'Soviet village' at Eastmere, which did receive some limited coverage, the opening of the training facility was accompanied by a splash of publicity in major British newspapers including the *Daily Telegraph*, *Daily Mail* and *Independent* as well as in local papers. These articles gave lucid and vivid accounts of what exactly went on in Ishmara and were peppered with superlatives from military commanders – it was 'the best equipped training site in the UK'; its facilities delivered 'the highest possible standard' of military training and so on, claims that would have been particularly satisfying for the predominantly right-wing, and therefore overwhelmingly pro-military, readerships of the former two papers in particular.[71] Some readers, however, considered the whole enterprise unpatriotic, even treacherous. 'I've a feeling that these "volunteers" are paid more than the troops,' wrote one reader. 'Hope I'm wrong, but?' 'What they are *actually* doing', opined another, 'is teaching the Afghans how the British army operate, dumb!' And, in a particularly cynical take, one correspondent suggested that the country 'just send the children of the politicians to fight and die in that hole'. There was the odd flash of optimism – 'It's about time the *Daily Mail* published a story that does not paint the UK Muslim population in an anti-British light. Well done.'[72]

Training still takes place here, I learned, though not as regularly now that Britain's military campaigns in Afghanistan and Iraq have come to an end. Lying empty surrounded by mellow heathland, a lake and marshy woodland, it did indeed feel both eerie (because it was deserted) and uncanny (because it was surreal and unsettling, out of place and out of time). In some senses, I thought of 'Ishmara' as a memento of Britain's misguided military enterprises in the Islamic world, but a reprisal too – a tiny Afghan outpost which had sprouted in Breckland. Britain's invasion of Afghanistan had been folded in on itself; in a microcosmic, surreal sense, the invader had become the invaded, the fictional Islamists having established a tiny foothold in their occupier's homeland.

———

My tour of the battle area was coming to a close. But not before I had taken a closer look at St Mary's West Tofts, the church that had been keeping a vigil upon us, at a safe remove, all this time. My guide got out of the car – the first time he had done so – and unlocked the gate in the wire fence. We wandered about the graveyard, peering at the tombstones, all with their epitaphs seared into grey stone, some weathered so far as to be almost illegible,[73] dating back to a time when the village was in its prime. 'The dead are like the stars by day,' says the tomb of one who died in 1856, aged fifty, 'removed from mortal eye'; 'We are dying day by day,' says another, 'soon from earth we pass away,' as he did in 1886, aged seventy-seven. Some of the most affecting are those of the young, sometimes very young; for Emma, who died aged nine in 1885: 'Had He asked us well we know, we should cry O spare this blow, yes with streaming tears should pray, Lord we love her let her stay'; for William Clowes, just seven days old, in 1853: 'For what is your life? It is even a vapour that appeareth for a little time and then vanisheth away' – just like the village of West Tofts itself – and many more epitaphs to the finitude of life, agonies of loss, and continued presence of the dead.

Wreathed in barbed wire and behind a large 'keep out' sign, it is as though St Mary's West Tofts flaunts its ghost credentials, but the interior confounds them. It is elegant and well preserved; there is nothing forlorn or forsaken about it; it is in fact, my guide told me, one of the finest examples of Pugin architecture in the country,[74] a neo-Gothic masterpiece, restored in 2004. At one end of the church was a stained-glass window with jewel-like palettes of colour. It was like a frozen kaleidoscope pouring plumes of melancholic light upon the high altars and tombs which, I had assumed, had lain unseen for decades. For whom do they gather this musty light?

Every year, a week before Christmas, those with historic ties to the Training Area – the friends, relatives and descendants of the

dispossessed, and those who survive – return for a special carol service officiated over by the minister of a nearby parish. The path of lime trees leading to the church is specially illuminated, and, on those bittersweet occasions, the cadences of their song, the streaks of the choir, the gushing of the air through the bellows of the organ effuse from the glowing nave, soaring over the shards, the mounds and the ruins of the deserted and disfigured villages, transforming them through the redemptive power of sorrow, and resurrecting them in the theatre of the mind.

But that is for just one night. For the rest of the year, the splendour is for the ghosts.

CHAPTER EIGHT

THE VILLAGE OF THE DAMMED: CAPEL CELYN

For the people of the valley, it was just another day – farmers milked their cows, rapids poured down the hills into the creaming turbulence of the Tryweryn river, the tiny schoolroom resounded to the sound of Welsh poetry, and the bereaved laid flowers at the tombstones of the dead – but little did they know, there were aliens in their midst, eyeing the land. On the edge of the village, in the fields, had appeared people no one recognised, men in trench coats and wellington boots sinking their spades into the soil, measuring the depth of rock, photographing the landscape, and making notes.[1] A few people asked them what they were doing but their answers were evasive, and they soon disappeared. No one gave them another moment's thought.

Life continued in the remote rural community much the same as it had done for generations. In the school, Martha Robert Jones translated English sentences into Welsh; in the post office, John Parry Jones swapped gossip with the parcel-wielding villagers; in the chapel, an adolescent, full of remorse, prayed for forgiveness; in the farmhouses, wives prepared a mid-morning snack of toast, tea and currant buns for their husbands in the fields. In some of the farmhouses, a batch of official-looking letters lay unopened, stacked beneath bills and old newspapers. They were soon discarded by anyone who bothered to open them, for they were oblique and full of jargon, concerning some agricultural project which may or may not go ahead. They were stamped, as far as anyone cared, with the bold insignia of the Worshipful Corporation of Liverpool.

Three months passed, and some of the villagers were sitting

down for breakfast. It was five days before Christmas 1955. They glanced at a paper, the Welsh edition of the *Liverpool Daily Post*. There was the usual quota of good news and bad news, sad news, and all other types of news. Wales was to have its own capital, Cardiff. Submissions for the National Eisteddfod were now closed. The robber of Dolgellau had struck again. Then, at the top of page two, something no one was expecting. Their village was to be drowned.[2]

———

Capel Celyn was a request stop; passengers had to inform the guard they wished to get off or they would have ended up in the granite quarry by Arenig Fawr. The sign looked homespun – crooked cream letters crucified on thin planks of dark-brown wood, on stilts, looming over daisies. It felt like arriving at a funfair or Wild West set. The truth was more austere.

Visitors to Capel Celyn found themselves in a broad valley surrounded by dark, undulating hills, in the hill country of Merionethshire, North Wales, about five miles north-west of the town of Bala.[3] White heather grew on the hillside and grouse fluttered through the air, but it was hardly a beauty spot. The terrain was stark and rocky. It was dotted with white-washed farmhouses. Peering through the windows one might have seen a woman in a white apron mashing up rhubarb. There were usually thousands of sheep grazing on the hillside and in the valley – no farmer had fewer than three hundred – and a few hundred black cows too. A faintly rutted track led to the village, past, on a typical afternoon, a young boy and his sister riding tricycles though a meadow of budding daisies, a cadaverous man waving a bucket beneath the nose of a playful cow, and, in the undergrowth, a fox ripping out the throat of a vole.

A gentle slope led to the river, where cows liked to bathe. The water was usually soft and gentle, but the Tryweryn river could be deadly and capricious, prone to wild floods; after heavy rainfall, it could swell to frightening levels, surging into tree leaves and pens and sties, carrying away sheep, pigs, haystacks, tractors and watch-dogs. But usually it bubbled past rocks, trees and weeds without a hint of menace, eventually forking into a second, smaller river, the Celyn, which led to the village.

Over a bridge, a sliver of dark-grey buildings lay on a gently curving road. This was Capel Celyn. With twelve farms spread over eight hundred acres, the valley had a population of just sixty-eight, a small majority of whom lived in the village. There was a post office, a school and a Methodist chapel. There were also around a dozen stone houses. Visitors glancing through the window of one, Rhyd-y-fen, may well have seen a man with a shock of silver hair and angular features sitting, lost in thought, as a huge harp loomed over him. His front room was wallpapered but with bare light bulbs. Here, he handcrafted all manner of harps each evening, after he had finished herding his sheep. There was high demand, for in Cwm Tryweryn, all the farmers were poets and all the poets were farmers.[4] Standing outside the farmhouses after dark, it would have been possible to hear the lilts and tones of Welsh poetry rise into the darkening skies as farmers gathered around hearths to recite verse to harp music.

There was a powerful sense that the mist-swirled hills shielded the village from the outside world. But Capel Celyn wasn't com-pletely archaic – some of the houses had electricity and running water (occasionally radios and the odd television set with terrible reception, too); there were pylons in the fields, and beetle-backed cars parked outside some of the houses. But many of the residents still lived lives of rustic antiquity, with no running water and no electricity. The county patrol shepherd lived behind the graveyard. Each day he walked nearly twenty miles over the mountains and hills to find sheep that were sick, stolen or strayed, immediately recognising them by the variously cut nicks in their ears and by their wool, which subtly changed at fifteen-mile intervals owing to minute fluctuations in the climate. And in the western part of the valley, above a slate quarry, lived John Jones, father of fourteen and giant of a man who, each summer, could be seen cutting back the growth on every last inch of his land with a spotless scythe.[5]

A small cottage with heavy oak beams was the post office, the village's main interface with the outside world, from the stone porch of which a terrier watched the world go by with fear in its eyes. Inside could be seen, on a typical day, an elderly woman cheerfully thwacking a parcel on shuddering scales whilst a few customers milled about, chatting (everyone knew each other in the valley). Nobody could have predicted that years on it would be the final outpost in a war against a faceless enemy.

Next door, rising from black railings on a slight slope, was an unprepossessing triangular building: the school. There were just sixteen sitting at the desks inside. Like many traditional rural communities in North Wales, the valley was relatively poor and suffered from a chronic lack of social and economic opportunities. Rural depopulation was rife across Merionethshire, with families and their young children being sucked into the industrial cities of England in particular, leaving behind an ageing population.[6] Inside the school, English was taught as a foreign language, like French, and for many of the pupils it was the only place they'd ever need to speak it; in fact, one would have been hard pressed to hear anyone speaking English in the valley. It was one of the sole surviving predominantly Welsh-speaking enclaves in the land.

The village took its name from the Methodist chapel, which was a modest affair – everything in the village was a modest affair, on the outside at least – no ostentatious spire or cross, just a rectangular building with a steep roof and slender sash windows. In spite of slightly dwindling attendance, it was still the fulcrum of the community (there was no pub, note) and it was here in the bleak midwinter days of early January 1957 that we find the entire community gathered together to discuss the dark cloud that had unexpectedly appeared on the horizon, threatening to destroy their whole way of life.

———

They sat on the pews, their faces white and horridly curious, as their enemy's strategy was uncloaked.

Liverpool, the great industrial city of the North West, was running short of water. The Corporation of Liverpool had calculated, with great mathematical exactitude, that to sustain industrial output, facilitate economic expansion, and meet its obligations to provide water for Merseyside, it was in dire need of a new reservoir.

The Corporation had originally pinpointed six potential locations, but this was soon whittled down to two, both safely across the border in Wales.[7] It had been decided, after great deliberation, that the most efficient option would be to impound the Tryweryn river by turning the valley – which had one of the biggest watersheds in Wales – into an enormous reservoir and dam. The Corporation fully realised this would mean flooding the village and a dozen of its outlying farms, dispossessing some sixty people, but they would be amply compensated and they were sure there would be no hard feelings because Great Britain was a 'tight little island' and this was a 'just' and 'necessary' measure.[8]

The congregation – not just the valley folk, but concerned parties from nearby communities – sat through these astonishing revelations in silence, incredulous, and almost grimly entertained by the audaciousness of such a proposal. Then, a blizzard of questions whose answers they collectively pieced together from recent newspaper reports.[9] *Was this legal?* Potentially, yes. The Corporation was planning to bulldoze a private members' bill through an English-MP-dominated Parliament to obtain a compulsory purchase order.

Did they not have to take Welsh opinion into account? No. *Were they going to pay for the water?* No. *Don't they need planning permission?* No. *The first some of the villagers had heard about this was when they read about it in the newspaper. Did Liverpool Corporation not have a shred of moral integrity?* Seemingly not. *What would happen if the villagers simply refused to leave their homes?* They were probably going to find out. *Did the corporation not realise Capel Celyn was much more than a village, but a bastion of Welsh tradition and culture?* Its actions would suggest otherwise.[10]

And what were the people of the valley meant to do? Sit back and watch as the Corporation of Liverpool buried their village and everything it stood for under 68 million tonnes of water? Not a chance, they would fight them tooth and nail, with every fibre of their being. But how?

This was the most urgent question, attracting the attention of Elizabeth Watkin Jones in particular.[11] She was a stout, kind-looking woman in her mid-fifties who epitomised the family values of the community, and who grew up in the post office. The eldest daughter of Watkin Jones, a lynchpin of the community, she selflessly returned home from university after her mother died tragically young in 1924 to look after her four siblings. A woman of considerable intellectual talent, she became an auxiliary teacher at the village school and, like pretty much everyone else, she learned to play the harp, piano and organ. Eventually she ended up moving to Bala to work in the primary school but remained fiercely loyal to her roots, for ever the girl from Capel Celyn. She put herself forward as the secretary for the Capel Celyn Defence Committee, and proved herself to be a woman of Herculean diplomatic prowess, a letter-writing powerhouse instrumental in winning over local councils, chapels, churches, trade unions and eventually Welsh politicians, not all of whom had instinctively felt there was much point in challenging Liverpool's proposal.

She was friends with Gwynfor Evans, the leader of the Welsh

nationalist party Plaid Cymru. A passionate advocate for cultural nationalism, particularly the protection of the Welsh language, he was naturally very keen to take on – hijacking, some thought – Tryweryn as a *cause célèbre*, describing it as 'the most important of all our battles'.[12] Over the months and years ahead, in large part thanks to Gwynfor Evans and Elizabeth Watkin Jones, the iniquities of Liverpool's scheme were debated and denounced not just within the valley but all over Wales and far beyond, in letters, pubs, chapels, societies and even on the startling new medium of television. Many of Britain's lost towns, cities and villages disappeared with barely a whimper. Capel Celyn was different. It wouldn't be fading from any map without a monumental life-or-death struggle.

The odds were against them. It was a tiny rural authority against the full might of the Corporation of Liverpool; in essence, a small-town David versus a corporate Goliath. 'May God guide your throw', urged the *Star* newspaper, 'to keep the hymns of Capel Celyn, and the ballads of Bob Tai'r Felin from being murdered by the devil's dam.'[13] In time, the Committee plotted a march on Bala, a conference in Cardiff, and a show of strength in Capel Celyn itself. But most of all, they encouraged people to write, and write they did, in their thousands. The red dragon of Wales had roared back to life and was ready to breathe fire.

———

Tryweryn was always about much more than a dam and a village; it was a painful reminder of Wales's perennial lack of independence and political autonomy, its powerlessness to shape its own destiny. No doubt this is why the many hundreds of letters sent to the Corporation of Liverpool and Department for Welsh Affairs in Whitehall seethe and boil with rage, the vividness of the voices sometimes leaping from the page to smack me in the face when I visited the Meirionnydd Record Office in Dolgellau on one of those mid-February days that can be so grey and sullen.[14]

'My advice to the people of Tryweryn,' says one, 'is to shoot the first devil that puts his foot in the valley. You dirty selfish creatures, you want to rob the Welsh people – and if I were them, I'd see you in hell and damned, before you get 1 gill of their water.'[15] 'It is to your eternal disgrace', writes a vet from Carmarthen, 'to even suggest such a gross violation of human rights. How dreadfully un-British of you!'[16] 'Yes – England!' screams a third, 'your days are over . . . Hands off Wales!'[17] Others promised the wrath of God and violent curses in abundance. The scheme itself is colourfully described as 'a wicked plan', 'a barefaced atrocity', 'daylight robbery', 'sacrilegious plundering', 'a piece of most damnable impudence and impertinence', and 'a criminal assault in the eyes of the whole world'.[18] The councillors of Liverpool Corporation, for their part, were 'haughty, high-handed' and 'corrupt',[19] 'damnable hypocrites', 'snakes in the grass', 'skunks',[20] 'greedy capitalists'[21] and 'a gang of planners'.[22]

Most of the letters came from Wales; some from England; a tiny minority from America, Australia and Canada. The arguments deployed were many, but the writers all agreed, firstly, that it was a profoundly undemocratic and outrageous transgression by a slippery and mendacious council, and, secondly, that much more than a remote village and valley was at stake. Tryweryn is repeatedly described as a 'fortress' or 'bastion' of Welsh language, culture and tradition – 'Some of our greatest traditions were, and are, nurtured in this locality, which you now propose to drown.' Its destruction, therefore, would be 'a great national loss', 'a tragedy', and 'a further erosion of our already imperilled traditions'. They were thinking of the Welsh-language lessons at school, of the poetry jams, of the harp recitals, of the hymns in the chapel, of the sheep-shearing and rhubarb mashing.[23] Wasn't the preservation of an ancient way of life and rich folk culture much more 'essential to the flowing of the human spirit'[24] than ruthless urbanisation?

The tone of the correspondence was informed by a widespread sense that the Welsh language – and hence, according to one letter, 'the continued existence of the Welsh nation'[25] – was gravely imperilled, and in this the writers certainly had a point. Half the population of Wales – a million people – had spoken Welsh in 1911; by 1950, that figure had fallen to 29 per cent, and it would continue to fall. With the arrival of English-language cinema, radio and the greater provision of non-Welsh newspapers in the 1920s, the immigration of English-speakers to the more densely populated and industrialised south, and television, the idea of speaking Welsh began to look less useful; pointless and counter-productive, even.[26] Another factor to contend with was rural depopulation, particularly in the Welsh-speaking north-west, robbing the young, procreative and able-bodied, draining towns and villages.[27] Within living memory, children had been caned in schools for speaking their own tongue, and it would be many years before the Welsh language was on equal footing with English in public life.[28] 'We in Wales are fighting to the last ditch to defend our language and our culture,' writes a man from Swansea. 'We dread to think that a power like Liverpool Corporation has the freedom to walk into our country and steal our water and our land in this tyrannical way.'[29] If an English city could casually annihilate a centuries-old way of life, what did that say about the perceived worth of that culture?

There were other arguments. Was it not inhuman to flood a graveyard containing people's relatives? Did anyone actually believe Liverpool needed the extra water for boiling kettles and running baths? Weren't they in fact trying to profit from it in some way, 'greedy capitalists' as they were? Why couldn't they find a source of water closer to home, in the Lake District or Merseyside, for example? Had they completely forgotten their debt of gratitude to the Welsh, who took in so many families during the Second World War? 'There may be another War again some day', one letter suggests darkly, 'and the people of Wales will remember then.'[30] How could they vandalise 'the unspoiled beauty of the valley, destroying rivers, streams, beauty and farms, land and homes, roads and railways and churchyards?'[31] And was the land really suitable for a reservoir? Wasn't the Tryweryn valley prone to flooding? Might not the dam burst and drown the nearby town of Bala, as foretold in the old prophecies?[32]

How, for that matter, would England like it if Wales came to steal its water – drowning Stratford-upon-Avon, perhaps, or some other quaint quintessence of Englishness?

And this was the nub of it, the iniquity of England 'taking' a Welsh village, as one letter put it, in terms redolent of a military invasion.[33] When, twenty-five years earlier, twenty-four houses, some of notable architectural pedigree, in the nearby village of Trawsfynydd – just ten miles to the west of Capel Celyn – had been drowned by a Welsh council for a new hydroelectric power station, precious few people kicked up a fuss; the new lake was regarded as a force for good, lighting up North Wales, for a time servicing another, nuclear power station, the drowning fully consented to by the Welsh authorities, not foisted upon them by an alien corporation. Still it exists today, the lake, still powering electricity, flanked by barren hills.

Something that all the letters agree on, if sometimes implicitly, is that Tryweryn was but the latest episode in an age-old saga of Wales's oppression at the hands of its more powerful neighbour, England – which gave it such resonance, and 'aroused the nation's feeling to white-hot indignation'[34] as the local MP put it – and although the actual dam hadn't been built yet, bitter cultural memories were already beginning to amass in the mental reservoir of the Welsh people. It wasn't as though Wales hadn't benefitted at all from being absorbed into England (1284 and 1536) and ultimately the Union (in 1707 and 1801) – it had, in myriad ways – but because Tryweryn fitted into this sorry saga, it encouraged the protesters to think of the last thousand years of Wales's history in a profoundly negative light, as one of perpetual struggle.

Welsh nationalism was arguably grounded in the hurts done to the country and its people since the Norman Conquest, but there was also an awareness of an older culture linked to the Celts of Europe.[35] The Welsh language has been spoken for longer than any other on the island of Britain; in its oldest form, it may have been spoken here since the Bronze Age. The Welsh, as some of the protesters saw it, had a special connection to the island, being descended from the Celtic tribes who were amongst the earliest inhabitants of Britain. These people had a distinctive culture and Brythonic language, and, in time, led many rebellions against Roman rule (AD 43–410). After the disintegration of the Roman Empire, they had inherited some sophisticated elements of Roman civilisation but remained distinctively British, and their tribes co-alesced into kingdoms that eventually covered the surface of Great Britain. Then came the 'waves' of Anglo-Saxon 'invaders'. The first colony was planted in Kent in the fifth century, and after that the Anglo-Saxon presence seeped exponentially outwards, like an ink-blot, eventually inundating Brythonic kingdoms as far away as Bryneich (Northumbria) and parts of Dumnonia (present-day Devon and Cornwall).

In the 1950s it was perhaps a badge of honour amongst nation-alists that the Brythonic kingdoms that had survived beyond the eleventh century were in Wales (though the concept of a unified Wales would have been alien to most medieval Welsh people). The sense that Wales was a distinctive if fragmented entity was enhanced by Offa's Dyke, a long scar rutted into the earth from near the mouth of the River Wye to the Dee, built to mark Wales's frontier with the formidable Anglo-Saxon kingdom of Mercia in the eighth century. But whereas the Anglo-Saxon kingdoms even-tually coalesced into a single (if feuding and unstable) political unit – England – in the ninth century in great part to ward off the Viking threat, Wales remained war-torn and divided, with the individual kingdoms – Gwynedd in the north, Powys in the east, Gwent in the south, and more – sometimes enlisting the help of individual Anglo-Saxon kings in their own conflicts, which set a dangerous precedent; the ninth-century King of Wessex, Alfred, for example, became overlord of Wales.

Ultimately, their relative cohesion, not to mention size, gave the English an edge over the Welsh, setting the scene for a protracted drama of conquest, assimilation and marginalisation, one which, as the Capel Celyn protesters saw it, had never really ended, however stealthily it might be carried on in the twentieth century. It began with William the Conqueror, who, as we saw earlier, thrust the Welsh border westwards and presided over the growth of that shadowy, sometimes lawless zone called the Marches, a nest of feuding warlords. But it was King Edward I, who ruled between 1272 and 1307, who built on this unwholesome legacy and launched the conquest of Wales in earnest. Crushing the rebellion of Llywelyn ap Gruffudd, the prince of Gwynedd, he built castles across the coastal landscape, and grew *bastides* around them – Conwy, Beaumaris, Caernarfon and more – which he stuffed full of English and Gascon colonists after banishing the local population. However could the medieval Welsh look upon places like Caernarfon Castle with its pretentious Byzantine-style land walls, golden gate, and imperial eagle without feeling like strangers in their own land, without seeing 'magnificent badges of our subjection'?[36]

Not content with territorial acquisition, the English nobility proceeded to do all it could to scour away the skin and bones of Welsh nationhood. Under the terms of Edward's Statute of Rhuddlan (1284), the *coup de grâce* of his conquest, Wales was helpfully informed it was 'no longer a kingdom, a country or a principality' and that its lands west of the Marches were going to be carved up into English-style shires. He also supplanted much of the Laws of Hywel Dda, Wales's distinctive legal system, one founded on mercy, reconciliation and compassion, with something as brutal and retributive as the invaders themselves: the English legal system.

Its laws emasculated, language became the standard-bearer of Welsh identity; but here, too, the Brythonic language – ancient tongue of the British Isles – was systematically suppressed, castigated as 'sinister' by Henry VIII's ministers, and relegated to the status of a useless, backward tongue. The language, which the Welsh believed to have produced some of the finest epic poetry in Europe, was described as unnatural – 'nothing like, nor consonant to, the *natural mother tongue* used within this realm', according to the wording of the Act of Union – and accordingly banished from law courts, schools and palaces and mansions, compelling Wales's landowning classes, and anyone who wanted to get ahead, to learn and speak English.

This Act – in fact two acts, passed in 1536 and 1542 – stemmed from a newly emboldened Henry VIII's desire to rule over a truly sovereign state, one free from alien 'rights, usages, laws and customs', now he had cast off the yoke of Rome. Its language was insultingly imperial, claiming that Wales had only ever been subject to the 'Imperial Crown of this Realm' and fawn as it might over the 'amicable concord and unity' between England and Wales, in truth the Welsh never had any say in the matter and could only look on in silence as Welsh-speaking territory was incorporated into the English counties of Shropshire and Herefordshire. In 1707 and 1801 when Great Britain and the United Kingdom were forged, the Scottish and Irish parliaments, highly unrepresentative of their national populations, had been complicit in their own destruction, willingly voting to cede sovereignty to Westminster. Wales had never even had its own parliament, and at the time it seemed as if it never would; ever its destiny would be decided elsewhere.

And what of the great Welsh leaders who had come within a whisker of unifying the Welsh kingdoms – Rhodri the Great, Gruffudd ap Llywelyn, Llywelyn ap Gruffudd? Llywelyn had ended up dismembered, his head mockingly crowned in ivy and placed on a spike above the gate to the Tower of London.

Yet, against the odds, parts of Wales had survived into the twentieth century with the old language and culture intact, due in no small part to the impact of the Protestant Reformation, Methodist Revival and a revolution in grassroots schooling, which sought to save souls by increasing literacy amongst ordinary people. All of which made it so much more of a tragedy, thought the protesters, that the essence of traditional Welshness – its culture, close-knit rural way of life and especially language – found itself under threat, once again. Could Wales survive the vanishing of its language, the haemorrhaging of its population, and the stagnation of its rural economy?

Not all the correspondents would necessarily have been thinking of these particular historical episodes, but they had passed into the bloodstream of the nation; still to this day, the Welsh national character can be defined by, as Jan Morris puts it, 'a sense of indefinable loss'.[37] And was not England was up to its old tricks? Had not swathes of Wales been commandeered by the MoD during the Second World War and never given back?[38] All those hundreds of thousands of people who left Wales – where had they gone? Whose economy had profited? Had not, indeed, one Welsh-speaking village already been drowned by Liverpool Corporation, at the end of the nineteenth century?

It was true. The Corporation had played exactly the same trick before – in the 1880s – when it drowned the village of Llanwddyn, about an hour's drive from Capel Celyn, to make Lake Vyrnwy, again to augment the city's water supply. On that occasion, there was hardly any opposition recorded at all; the villagers migrated to a new village further south, and so far as it was mentioned in the press at all, it was as a wondrous feat of engineering. But by the late 1950s, a usually dormant volcano of anti-English sentiment was threatening to erupt, fuelled to some extent by nationalist ideas but also by a bleak economic outlook, demographic decline, and a new, post-war climate of opinion that embraced 'positive' state intervention (spending on the welfare state, for example) and abhorred anything that smacked of imperial aggression in an age of decolonisation. The letters bubble with international comparisons, urging the Welsh to stand firm against English oppression. 'We decry the Soviet blood-bath in Hungary,' writes one, referring to the Soviet Union's massacre of Budapest civilians in 1956, 'but this red-handed attempt to seize vital water supplies and strangle a rural community is equally to be condemned.'[39] As the British Empire disintegrates, writes another, might not Wales be the next to break away from its imperial overlord?

How would Mr Cain of Liverpool Corporation's Water Committee feel if he experienced *his* country 'being sucked away from you, as it were by a voracious swallowing wind into the hands and possession of another country and civilization'?[40] England had annexed their nation, beheaded their princes, abolished their laws, impoverished their language, flooded their villages, stolen their youth, diluted their culture and gagged their voice; was it really now going to go ahead and drown – in the face of overwhelming opposition – one of the last remaining strongholds of Welsh language and traditions in the land?

It was. The Corporation of Liverpool, with great tenacity and clear-headedness of purpose, vowed to rise above the popular clamour, to crack on with the scheme undeterred by all the rants that were every day landing on the desk of the Liverpool town clerk. Nothing must impede the flow of progress.

But there were going to be consequences. Plaid Cymru might stay within the line at constitutional opposition, but not everyone felt the same way. One letter arrived in a dainty little envelope with a red stamp of a very youthful-looking Queen and a beautiful 'post early for Christmas' graphic. Inside was a piece of blunt menace, fist-scrawled in block capitals violently intersecting the ruled lines with diagonal disdain: 'THEY TRY', it warned, 'AND WE GO DOWN FIGHTING THE ENGLISH ANY PLACE. OUR FRIENDS THE IRA ARE COMING TO HELP US. THIS WILL BE A LONG WAR.' It was signed 'THE WRA' – the Welsh Republican Army.[41]

'This is the beginning of a Crusade which your Council does ill to ignore,' warned another; 'the voice of Wales no longer cries in the wilderness.'[42] But the Corporation, with steel unbounded, was not cowed by the threats. It would prevail. The Capel Celyn Defence Committee, meanwhile, realising these little missiles of vitriol raining down on the stout civic buildings in Whitehall and Liverpool were having little effect, decided to strike at the heart of enemy territory.

———

Liverpool, November 1956. Steamers roll into the harbour. Grime-black terraces vanish into a smoggy swirl, multiple families squeezed into some of the houses, cold, hungry and with no running water. Rats are rife. The destitute dig through bins. Factories litter the fabric of the city, black smoke pouring from tall chimneys, workers clocking in at six o'clock in the morning and leaving ten hours later, broken, famished and exhausted. All was not well, either, for the factory owners and the social elite. Water was the lifeblood of industry, and Liverpool was running out of it. If they didn't secure a new source soon, jobs would be lost, living standards would fall, disease would break out, the slum clearance programme would falter, and a wave of crime, suicide and homelessness would roll in; it would be chaos, and if there was one thing the Corporation of Liverpool didn't want on its hands, it was chaos.

Such were the arguments rehearsed in the Grand Council Chamber in Liverpool on a bleak November morning in 1956. Now the Labour MP Elizabeth 'Bessie' Braddock, a tireless socialist campaigner, was highlighting some stark facts: post-war

Liverpool, with its population of 750,000, had some of the worst slums in Britain. In order to improve sanitation and advance economic development, 65 million gallons of water a day were needed. Over the past ten years, the average demand had gone up by a million gallons a day thanks to a rising population, the expansion of industry and the expansion of domestic luxuries like baths and washing machines. The previous March, the Corporation's agents had visited ten dam sites in North Wales to find a source capable of supplying Liverpool with 60 million gallons per day. Tryweryn was by far the most efficient. It would channel water into the River Dee, which could then be extracted at Chester, eliminating the need for fifty miles of pipelines, saving millions. It would still cost around £16 million, but it was worth it to ensure the future prosperity of the city, and the twenty-two other local authorities it was obliged to provide with water. All it would take would be a couple of dry summers and Liverpool would die of thirst. They needed Tryweryn, and fast.[43]

A lot of people had sent letters, it's true, but equally many more had not. And why would they? Liverpool and Wales had a deep-rooted bond and relations were usually amicable. Had not Liverpool welcomed a constant flow of economic migrants from Wales with open arms over the last two hundred years? Were there not in fact infinitely more Welsh in Liverpool than in the remote little village itself – citizens who would benefit immensely from an increased water supply and concomitant flourishing of employment opportunity? Would the displaced villagers not welcome the opportunity to move into modern houses with all the latest mod cons? No, with adequate compensation (which the Corporation would provide) they expected the valley could be washed away with a minimum of fuss.

Around midday, Bessie Braddock's husband, Alderman John Braddock, the leader of the Council, got to his feet and moved the floor to vote. The result, he assumed, would be a foregone conclusion. But what was this? Some ungodly sing-song rising in the air, floating through the windows of the Grand Council Chamber. Wasn't that the tiresome man from the remote little village, that fool who'd heckled the Corporation only three weeks ago? And what about everyone else? They might as well have drowned the valley already – the entire population seemed to have turned up on its doorstep – every man, woman, child and baby, a mass of bumpkins.

———

They'd left as the sun appeared in a black midwinter sky.[44] The school was shut for the day. Only the postmaster, a one-year-old baby, and two farmers remained. Capel Celyn was silent, a ghost village. The rest of the valley's inhabitants, who ranged in age from three to seventy-six, piled into three coaches and zoomed across the English border. They were fighting for the life of their valley. They drank tea on the way, and were merry.

They arrived two hours later, singing a Welsh hymn, 'Cofia'n gwlad' ('Remember Our Land'), amongst empty parked cars, not a soul to hear them, and unfurling a banner, *Please, Liverpool, be a Big City not a Big Bully*, before marching through the cold, misty streets, escorted by an excessive number of police. They had wanted to appear dignified – the young boys in new boots, the older boys and girls in long trousers, the women in winter coats and felt hats, the farmers in tweed flat caps – and although it wasn't quite the 'yokels' day out' of the mean-minded *Manchester Guardian*'s fancy, it did have about it something of the prim, of the Sunday School outing, about it, and as the villagers moved gingerly through Liverpool's imperious streets, conspicuous against the stark industrial blocks and scaffolding, the ever-changing urban landscape a foil to their own, there was indeed a sense that they were out of place and out of time.

They had planned to drive up and down the streets with a loudspeaker, booming their cause to office workers and shoppers. But they were only allowed to use it in the tunnel out of the city, and, in any case, no one could remember how to turn it on. So they marched along with their placards. 'Capel Celyn Must Live!' announced one. 'Does Liverpool Want this Spectre in its Water?' asked another, surreally depicting a glass of water with a ruined house at the bottom.[45] Leading the crowd with a kind, self-assured smile was Gwynfor Evans. It was his second visit to Liverpool in as many weeks. The first had not ended well. After Liverpool refused to admit any deputations from Capel Celyn he'd snuck in, with two others, to the gallery of the Council Chamber when they were first debating Tryweryn. At the appropriate moment he leapt to his feet and, quite contrary to established protocol, exhorted them to spare the valley. No one had taken kindly to this, least of all Bessie Braddock, a great big woman with double chins, an abrasive manner, and deep, masculine voice, as he portrayed her in his memoirs.[46] The youngest of the children to march that day was Eurgain Prysor Jones; she recalled (clearly drawing on other people's reminiscences since she was just three at the time) an 'absolutely vile' reception. 'There was a councillor there called Bessie Braddock, the spitting image of Ena Sharples on *Coronation Street* [a big battle-axe of a woman, her face scorched by time] and she was spitting at us and throwing rotten tomatoes.'[47] But hindsight can play tricks on the mind, and Bessie made a perfect cartoon villain (the rotten tomatoes are suspicious). She'd had a fit, smashing her fists on the desk, cowing Gwynfor Evans into submission before he and his fellow saboteurs were bundled out by the police as the chamber filled 'with the roars of hell's pit'. Today, they were attempting a greater show of force, parading the human face of what would be lost if the Corporation's scheme went ahead in front of the very noses of the people who stood to gain. *Your homes are safe, save ours, do not drown OUR homes.*

But if that was the aim, by all accounts it didn't work. Elwyn Edwards, a boy from Frongoch who had played in the valley as a child, was thirteen when he skived off school to go on the march. He remembered 'toothless women . . . shouting and spitting at us. Others were cursing us mercilessly and calling us all kinds.'[48] Another, older marcher, Harriet Parry Jones, remembers ambivalence and apathy from the spectators who thronged balconies and doorways to peer at them.

They reached the Council Chamber building and sang 'Hen Wlad Fy Nhadau' ('Land of My Fathers'), and then a special 'battle hymn' composed by the absent postmaster, Mr Parry Jones. Eventually, smudged white faces appeared in the upper windows of the Town Hall and the Corporation agreed, apprehensively, yet with *great magnanimity* and in *no way influenced* by the presence of journalists in the crowd, to give Gwynfor Evans a fair, fifteen-minute hearing. This time, they clapped him in. He spoke of the sacredness of the valley, its importance to Welsh language and culture, and its potential necessity as a spur to industrial development in North Wales. The Lord Mayor of Liverpool stood beside him, gently nodding. If it went ahead, Evans warned, Liverpool could expect a tsunami of opposition, and likely parliamentary defeat. And so persuasive was his argument, so well thought-out and articulate, so impassioned and clear, the councillors gave him a thundering ovation. Then they voted 94–1 to go ahead with the scheme anyway.

The little Welsh village had lost to the big English city. The whole thing had been Gwynfor Evans and Elizabeth Watkin Jones's idea; hardly any of the villagers had wanted to go, worrying that they'd just end up making fools of themselves. And hadn't they? Hadn't the whole thing been, as the *Manchester Guardian* sneered, 'inescapably pathetic'? The villagers retreated to the car park, dejected. They had to be back in time to milk the cows.

———

There was one last hope: Westminster. English MPs outnumbered Welsh ones by 280 to 46 but if the Welsh MPs could make a powerful enough case, Liverpool's bill might yet founder. The scheme came to be debated in the House of Commons in July 1957.

Tryweryn's local MP, Thomas Jones, spoke first, asserting (a little histrionically) that 'the people of Wales have never felt so intense on any subject this century'.[49] He went on to argue that the proposal was unjust, unwarranted (because Liverpool could easily find water sources closer to home – like the Mersey), inimical to North Wales's industrial prospects, conjectural (how could Liverpool be sure it would need 65 million more gallons daily to meet demand in fifty years?) and a dereliction of Parliament's duty to defend the weak against the powerful.

But most of all, he argued that the scheme was mendacious and greedy because the extra water was patently not for domestic consumption but industrial resale; commercial gain, in other words. Between 1920 and 1955, he pointed out, daily industrial consumption had increased by 12 million gallons whereas household consumption had only risen by 4 million – was it not obvious the Corporation was in this adventure for the sake of profit, he asked, to a loud cheer in the House. Another Welsh MP warned against the monopolisation of such a valuable resource as water by a single municipality, ominously declaring that 'for every gallon that flows from the Welsh hills, 10 million gallons of good will flow with it';[50] another claimed 'over-centralised industrial units' were draining North Wales of its youthful population. At what cost would industrial Britain thrive? Wasn't the whole thing ill-considered, wondered the MP Tudor Watkins, when 40 per cent of rural Welsh districts didn't even have running water; 75 per cent in his own constituency of Montgomeryshire, to the east of Merionethshire?

The first MP to speak in favour of the scheme was Sir Victor Raikes, member for Liverpool Garston.[51] In a wide-ranging speech, he batted away many of the Welsh MPs' more logistical objections.

The distinction between 'commercial' and 'industrial', he argued, was bogus since the sale of water would provide employment for the people of Liverpool (with its sizeable Welsh community); the majority of the income, he might have added, would be pumped straight back into public services, into housing, welfare, sanitation and so on, not the mindless accumulation of wealth. Merseyside, he reminded the House, was a vast industrial area covering a hundred square miles with a population of over a million; Liverpool, furthermore, had obligations to provide water to twenty-four areas – it would be madness not to plan ahead, especially as demand was rising. If they continued to rely on their existing source at Lake Vyrnwy, and a couple of dry years came along, there would be a deficit of 7 million gallons a day. Tapping the muddy, sewer-like Mersey for drinking water was a preposterous idea and prohibitively expensive, nor were any of the alternative schemes, however elaborate and well meant, remotely viable. It had to be Tryweryn.

English MPs were not completely tone-deaf to what was at stake for the Welsh. Henry Brooke, a few days into his new job as Minister for Welsh Affairs, had promised he wouldn't just sit in London reading about the remote province but actively immerse himself in Welsh society 'to understand Welsh thoughts, Welsh needs and Welsh hopes'. Now, during the debate, he grasped – or purported to grasp – that the scheme was seen as an 'English intrusion . . . upon Welsh nationhood and cultural life' at a time when those very things were in danger of 'eventual disappearance through absorption into all the rest of British life'.[52] Taking a stand on Tryweryn, he understood, greatly transcended the social and economic fallout of uprooting a tiny community; it was about the battle for Wales's soul; it went far beyond some cost-benefit analysis.

But ultimately, it didn't, not for him or any of the other English MPs. As the Westminster light began to fade outside the chamber, he ended with a threat. If members were to reject the Bill, they would 'saddle themselves with a very grave responsibility for water shortages which might occur in the next few years on Merseyside . . . I cannot believe the preservation of the Welsh way of life requires us to go as far as *that*,' he concluded adding, with rhetorical flourish, that to do so would be to banish the Welsh from 'the brotherhood of man'.

Most of the arguments advanced by English MPs were, like this one, coldly utilitarian. Sir Victor Raikes got to the crux of it when he rose to his feet at eight o'clock and declared, 'If it is decided that in the interests of a large number of people the rights of a very small number of people are affected, then, subject to proper safeguards for the minority, the right of the majority must prevail.' It was mathematically judicious – the dispossessed would get 'precisely equivalent land' and 'precisely equivalent houses', completely failing to take into account how to 'weigh up' the value of culture and tradition – but even the speaker acknowledged this was essentially unfair. Yes, the population of the big city dwarfed that of the little valley, but not of Welsh-speaking Wales, and if Welsh language and culture slowly vanished, was *that* the greatest good for the greatest number?

Finally, the nemesis of Tryweryn took the floor.[53] She was dressed in black, wearing her trademark thin pearl necklace, and spoke in grave, considered tones. Liverpool, said Bessie Braddock, had, after many years of 'devastating unemployment', finally attracted industries that had delivered almost full employment. These needs must be met. She then launched into a string of justifications – all hotly contested by the residents of Capel Celyn – suggesting that the Corporation had not been as haughty and high-handed as had been suggested. Liverpool's plans had always been perfectly transparent, she said, and the Corporation had kept all affected parties – the tenants and Merionethshire county council – in the loop every step of the way, writing them letters, even sending officers to interview them in person; the Corporation had been, now that she thought about it, a veritable model of diplomacy. To halt the whole scheme in its tracks *now*, to threaten the future prosperity of Liverpool for the sake of some people's attachment to their ancestral land, well, it simply wasn't worth it. 'Everyone deplores the fact that in the interests of progress sometimes some people must suffer,' she said, 'but that is progress.'

The Ayes had it: 166 voted in favour; 117 against. Of the Welsh MPs, 24 of 36 voted against; the rest either abstained or didn't turn up. Only one Welsh MP joined the Ayes, the member for Cardiff North. The spectacle of England's MPs passing a law that would adversely affect another part of the United Kingdom against the express wishes of its population and politicians was deeply unfortunate – a spectre indeed that still haunts British politics to this day – but constitutionally, there was nothing illegitimate about it at all because Wales and England had been part of the same country for four hundred years, since the sixteenth-century Acts of Union. But because it *felt* a summary execution, it intensified calls to restore Wales's ancient political independence.

At the end of the month, the Bill passed at its third reading by an increased majority of ninety-six with no further debate, and received the royal assent the next day. The rain would continue to fall on the hills of Merionethshire but much of it would now flow to England, and Capel Celyn and the Tryweryn Valley found themselves in the shadow of oblivion.

———

Work on the lake began in November 1959. Plaid Cymru never gave up, continuing to produce ever more elaborate schemes to prevent the drowning, but few of the residents had time for these pipe dreams. It was bad enough to be on death row, even more so to cling to the remote prospect of a last-minute reprieve.[54]

In 1961, a woman and a man in long overcoats – Mabel and John

Evans – posed for a final photograph on their porch. John had
lived in this house, Garnedd Llwyd, since he was three months old;
his wife for thirty years. Along with their little sheepdog, they repaired to a farm that Liverpool Corporation had bought for them
in the hills above Bala where, at night, they could see glimmering
headlights on the new road across the valley, which made them
feel a little homesick. But they were enjoying having thirty-four
acres of land, pleasant neighbours and, excitingly, electricity, which
they'd not had before. No question it had been a wrench to leave,
they told the *Liverpool Daily Post*, but they were reconciled to their
new life, and had refused to sign the petition of protest against
Liverpool Corporation.[55]

Some years later, they were both dead. Killed in a car crash. It
was suggested by some, darkly, that this was God's judgement for
the alacrity with which they had reached generous terms with the
Corporation. Another couple who had lived in the valley for sixty-
one years found themselves in an agreeable terraced house in the
nearby village of Frongoch, 'within sound of the valley, which we
shall never forget'.[56]

As families trickled out, life ground to a halt and, piece by piece, Capel Celyn was dismantled and detached from the outside world.[57] The first casualty was the railway. The last passenger train to go through the valley left Bala one cold black morning on 2 January 1960.[58] A crowd of around two hundred had thronged on to the platform, many wearing black neckties, some with cameras, others with binoculars, all leaning in and craning their necks to get a good look at the doomed train as it drew in. A local brass band was in attendance. When the moment came, the bandmaster raised his wand, the guard waved a green flag and, as the train lurched forwards, the band played a Welsh funeral hymn and the crowd chanted, 'Last train to Capel Celyn. If you miss this one, you will never get another one.' The two guards smiled wistfully out of the window as the train vanished into the morning mist, trundling into oblivion. No more would trains coast along the sinuous, single-track railway between blue hills, streams pouring down the glistening slopes; no more would passengers gaze out of their windows and see farmers harvesting hay hundreds of feet below; no longer would the much-loved guards, Moss and Jones, toss copies of the *Daily Post* out of their window for the valley's residents.[59] A year later, both request stops disappeared and the tracks were removed from the embankment, leaving a curious mound.

The following June, clay for the dam's core was first laid down and, not far from the village, gravel was dug from pits to cover the surface. Construction works began in earnest; a grotesquely ironic sign went up on the dam site saying 'Trespassers will be prosecuted', and the valley degenerated into a dust-ridden wasteland.[60] Eurgain Prysor Jones was nine when the Corporation began clearing the valley. She remembered a happy village where everybody knew each other, and where children used to play on the roads and in the fields. Overnight, she recalls, it turned into a frightening alien domain with lorries and machines incessantly digging up the earth and throwing up enormous clouds of dust which clogged up their lungs. But in the early mornings, without the farmyard noises, it was deadly quiet.

By the spring of 1963, only three families remained in Capel Celyn. Of these, the Parry Joneses held out the longest, holed up in their ghost post office, taking mournful turns in the empty village gazing out at the lorries crawling over the landscape like caterpillars. They were finally ejected on a bright morning in May 1963 and were still in sight of their old home as the bulldozers moved in.[61] By then the school's class size – there was only ever one class – had shrunk to fourteen. Many of the children were haunted by a sense that the waters could rise at any moment, gushing into the classroom mid-lesson, carrying them off, and drowning them deep in the valley.[62] One exhibit at the Royal Cambrian Academy of Arts was painted by a girl from Capel Celyn. The valley, with its stark black hills, is unmistakable, and the Tryweryn stream has accrued an ominous new significance, coming across as a great slithering snake, ready to poison the landscape.[63]

The school finally closed its doors one summer's day in 1963. All the children posed for a final photograph with their teacher, Martha Robert Jones. She had been the schoolmistress for nine years, though she was from Bala herself, which she claimed gave her a valuable external perspective to gauge the toll of anxiety in the valley. She tried to keep the subject out of school and carry on as normal, hard enough in such a close-knit community, but even harder when a JCB smashed into the school roof mid-lesson, tearing off slates.[64] On their final day, the children received a cake from Plaid Cymru with thick dollops of icing addressed 'to the children of Tryweryn' – an apt metaphor, some thought, for the feebleness of the official nationalist resistance.[65] Shortly afterwards, the bulldozers moved in. By the end of the summer, the school was a hollow wreck of a building, a shell. Only a chimney stood, forlorn, the whole resembling a ruined monastery lost in an arid landscape.

The final church service – called, with excruciating poignancy, the Dissolution Service – took place a year before the waters came, beneath silvery plumes of cloud. It was a pitiful echo of the villagers' assembly seven years earlier when they had formed the failed Defence Committee. This time everyone wore hats, many dressed in black, inconspicuous against the churned-up surroundings. With two long queues of parked cars outside, this was perhaps the most crowded the chapel had ever been, attracting people from miles around, scrunched together in the pews, squeezed into doorframes, and spilling into the antechamber. The ceremony was conducted by the Reverend G. R. Jones, who had preached at Capel Celyn every single year since 1921; he spoke of loss, resilience and hope. Afterwards, the visitors' book lay on a coffin for people to sign, and the chapel's Bible was entrusted to a representative of Anglesey Church. Outside, after the service, there was a funereal cheerfulness with people smiling and laughing and beaming with pride – they were on camera, of course, and wanted everyone to see the best of Capel Celyn to highlight the tragedy of what was being lost, but they also wanted one last image for themselves, of mutual respect, companionship, and close community spirit, for it was precisely these things which were being obliterated.

Eight months later, the deconsecrated chapel was stripped bare and knocked down. First, the complicated interlocking wooden banisters that made up the preaching pulpit were chopped out and the pendant lights yanked out of their sockets. For a while, there was debris everywhere, a strange eruption of chaos into the minimalism of the Methodist aesthetic. Next the roof was swiped off and for a while the walls and gables stood erect, though in time these too were smashed away and the open air, and eventually water, rushed in. The fulcrum of the community had been reduced to ruins. Some of the chapel's stone blocks were used to help build the gloomy memorial chapel overlooking Llyn Celyn; others were insultingly used in the construction of the dam itself,[66] meaning that stones that once enclosed a sacred space allowing parishioners to commune freely with the Lord and, if he allowed, be saved, now shored up the very thing that had obliterated it, the mighty dam, the dark-grey flagstones saturated in hymn and prayer now grinding against millions and millions of gallons of water destined for a secular power; a woeful appropriation, if you asked the villagers (which no one did).

On a bleak misty day, the agents of the Corporation went to the graveyard and dug up the dead. The cobwebbed coffins were dusted down, labelled and loaded on to a truck to be transported to their designated cemeteries; the once well-ordered graveyard became a giant rabbit warren of ditches and mounds. If their families preferred, the dead could be left in their graves, snug beneath a blanket of concrete, marked by a lonely underwater plaque.[67]

The valley became starker by the day. Slate was ripped from the roofs of houses and sold. All the trees were chopped down, in case they blocked the floodgates; the hedges too. What buildings were left stood like lonely dominoes. By 1964, all the features of the landscape – all the houses, hedges, trees, sheds, horses, livestock, lines of rail and mounds – had been scoured away, the empty stone cottages that once stood forlorn in barren fields reduced to heaps of rubble, dead stumps replacing trees, and when the grouse and swallows flew across Cwm Tryweryn now, they looked down upon an eerie lunar landscape, devoid of life. Only the wall of the cemetery and two stone bridges remained. It was a scene of pure desolation. The older people were devastated, recalled Martha Robert Jones: 'You could see it in their faces.'[68] Eighteen people died during the devastation of Tryweryn – over a quarter of the valley's population – their hearts weighed down by sorrow.[69]

The valley was ready for drowning. In September 1964, the basin's floodgates were closed and the river dammed for the first time. Now the rainwater flowing down the Merionethshire hills, finding its path to the sea blocked, amassed in the shorn valley as the lake came into being. Some stood and watched as the remains of their old homes melted into the lake. Aeron Prysor Jones was twelve when his parents' twenty-acre farm was lost to the waters. 'I remember the flooding,' he recalled in 1995. 'It was such a tremendously wet September . . . it wasn't a slow process at all. One day you were looking at a particular spot and the next day, it was gone beneath the water.'[70] He never moved away, living on a farm overlooking Llyn Celyn, which was a daily reminder, he said, of 'the most dreadful deceit ever perpetrated on this nation'.[71]

Finally, by autumn 1965, it was complete: a magnificent reservoir two and a half miles long and a mile across, a depth of 43 metres, with a capacity for 16.4 million gallons of water. Since they had spent £18 million on it, it was only right that the Liverpool Corporation should come down to admire their handiwork. And not only that – they would have a grand opening ceremony followed by an official five-course luncheon.

Gwynfor Evans had seen this for what it was and had written to the Corporation urging them to reconsider. No, came the response, that would be impractical; the wheels were already in motion and it was not the will of the Corporation to flaunt its victory over the valley but to pave the way for a mutually beneficial partnership, while marvelling in a feat of modern engineering. And besides, the Corporation enjoyed cordial relations in the valley, did it not?[72] The date was set: Thursday 21 October 1965. Tactlessly, invitations were sent not only to local councils but anyone with family links to the valley, including those who'd fought the hardest the save it, and the dispossessed. One was sent to the chairman of the Defence Committee, Dafydd Roberts, who didn't have to suffer the indignity of opening it since he'd died ten days earlier, foretelling how 'echoes of songs and praise' would for ever rise from the deep of the lake 'to the crest of the waves above'.

Gwynfor Evans had been right. The prospect of an opening ceremony was widely perceived as the final insult, the last dirt shovelled on the coffin of Wales. Accordingly, on a strangely muggy autumn morning, hundreds of protesters amassed on the edge of the reservoir.[73] They awaited the arrival of around four hundred guests from Liverpool who would have to drive straight past them to reach the marquee by the power station down below. There were students in sunglasses, grandmothers with walking sticks, young children, mothers with babies, intellectuals with neatly swept back hair, and smart grandfathers all brandishing placards full of re- proachful words, crisp against the livid-blue lake: 'GO HOME THIEVING SCOUSE'; 'HANDS OFF WELSH VILLAGES'; 'GWLAD! GWLAD!' (Country! Country!) It was not the villagers who were protesting – they had moved on with their lives – but people from all over Wales who had commandeered the anti-English cause. One banner even said 'CRUSADE AGAINST ALL CRUELTY TO ANIMALS', another 'PREVENT FOREST FIRES', showing that Tryweryn had become a lightning rod for all manner of injustices. At eleven o' clock, the cavalcade appeared, twisting around the hillside road, and soon the mood turned dirt-ugly.

The protesters formed a quivering tunnel, bearing down upon the convoy, thwacking roofs with placards, bashing bonnets with their fists, and thrusting loudspeakers into wisely wound-up windows.

They blotted out windscreens with banners, rolled boulders into the road and tried to capsize the cars. They ripped off aerials, smashed wing-mirrors, kicked in side panels, leapt on boots. Some even threw themselves in front of cars, suffragette-style. Some people stood back shielding their eyes from the sun, smiling and smoking, watching a middle-aged woman wielding her placard like an axe, glaring at a councillor over the rim of her glasses; a man next to her in a suit tilting the sign 'Stop Robbing Wales' straight on to a windscreen, his mouth wide open in chant; a grandmother lurching forwards with a giant Red Dragon, crashing its claw into a car's headlights; a child in shorts and a beanie hat squirting a water pistol, ecstasy on his face; a policeman spread-eagling himself on the side of the car, trying to prevent contact, a lean and grizzly look on his face. Still the cars rolled on, the drivers desperately avoiding eye contact as women yelled through the windscreens. The atmosphere was so hot it was a wonder the water of the lake did not boil over the basin.

Midway through the pandemonium, the protesters, now numbering five hundred or so, spied the VIPs from Liverpool Corporation arrive in coaches on the *other* side of the reservoir, scuttling towards the marquee in all their finery. Furious, they broke through a police cordon, poured down the dam's steep escarpment, and converged on the marquee where the ceremony was due to take place.

On the grandstand were the three arch-villains of the piece: Mr J. Haughton, Liverpool's Chief Constable; Alderman David Cowley, the Lord Mayor in his ridiculous golden chain; and Alderman Frank Cain, chairman of the dreaded Water Committee. They were met by a blizzard of boos and a cacophony of plaintive chants. At first they listened in respectful silence – not realising the words to one song meant 'all English are arseholes' – and waited for the crowd to pipe down, but it never did. Taking the microphone, the Lord Mayor tried to give thanks for the reservoir but could only be seen 'blabbering like a goldfish';[74] the microphone wires had been cut.

The bombardment of booing, jeering and chanting – amplified through loudspeakers – reduced what was meant to be a forty-five-minute ceremony to a three-minute travesty. One dignitary ended up with a flagpole in his eye. The Lord Mayor had to duck a brick. The engineer of the dam was struck on the shoulder by a chunk of slate. At one point a side of the marquee mysteriously collapsed. Three young guns from the Free Wales Army attempted to burn a Union Jack, bringing petrol for the purpose, but it refused to light. In the end, they trampled on it in a foaming frenzy, and threw it in the reservoir. The tattered and sullied flag ended up drifting across the surface of the lake.

Someone yelled something about poisoning the lake with cyanide. That wouldn't make any difference, shouted back another, everyone knows Scousers drink only beer, and never wash. Alderman Frank Cain of the Water Committee got to his feet. The booing and chanting reached a crescendo. 'This is not a function to celebrate the fact that we are taking Welsh water,' he began. '*Go Home English.*' 'It is not a function—' '*Robbers!*' '—that is intended to rub salt in the wounds of Wales.[75] It—' '*Traitors!*' '—is a function to establish the balance—' '*Hands off Wales!*' '—that will heal the friction of the past and lead to an amicable future for all of us.' '*You fascist Scouser.*' 'I—' '*You fascist Scouser bastard.*'[76]

Raising his voice, Cain went on to explain that Liverpool Corporation had nothing – *nothing!* – to feel ashamed of. It had put its case to the Welsh people and to Parliament and had been given the authority to go ahead. It was, therefore, a *privilege* and a *pleasure* to declare the Llyn Celyn reservoir open.

He yanked on a lever, sending millions of gallons of water spurting from the stilling basin into the river below, drowning out the rousing tones of 'Land of My Fathers' in a monstrous, obliterative gush just as they, earlier, had drowned him out. The protesters fell silent and listened to the roar of the water. It was a harrowing moment and the symbolism was lost on no one – here, once again, was the Welsh way of life being drowned, here was Welsh culture being diluted, here was Wales's most precious natural resource being drained, here, pissed upon, was the spirit of the Red Dragon, dissolved into tiny particles of water at the hand of an English oppressor.

The councillors bid adieu to the querulous mob. They were much looking forward to sinking their teeth into some succulent Welsh lamb.

———

One cloudy afternoon, sixty years later, I set out from my guesthouse in the hills overlooking Bala to find Llyn Celyn. It was a five-mile walk. The day was grey and the tips of the hills were shrouded in mist – it was hard, in fact, to tell where the mist ended and the skies began; the sun was puny behind a thick veil of cloud. By the side of the road I saw clumps of daffodil shoots, ready to burst to life, and a flattened fox shrouded in its own fur. Finally, I arrived at the eastern end of the reservoir, by the dam. Above the road, in front of an electricity pylon, was a squat stone building spray-painted with the words *Cofio Celyn* – Remember Celyn – along with the spider-like insignia of the Free Wales Army.

The dam itself is an earthwork rampart that meshes spectacularly with the green fields beyond, falling concavely away until it rises into the mountains and vanishes into the mist. Visitors are often struck by the restfulness of the lake, marvelling at how the tranquillity belies so many years of turmoil, but that's not how it presented itself to me. When I visited, the water seemed restless, imprisoned, pent up. Little waves strove for the shores, annihilated by bare cubes of rock around the perimeter, and the whole surface quivered under a low, leaden sky. In the distance, I could see headlands creeping into the water and, not far from the southern shore, a lonely concrete structure that looked like a prison watchtower. (It was the drawing-off tower, I later learned, the orifice through which the Corporation siphoned off its water.) There was a certain beauty in the deadening air. There were white gulls whirling against livid-blue water. One dived towards the surface but finding no fish flew off, into the gloom.

According to Welsh folklore, birds will not fly over any lakes that have witnessed death or drowning, or which are haunted by ghosts – so not, one would have thought, this one.[77] One fable tells how, after a young prince of Gwynedd was drowned by his cousin in a secluded lake, all the birds vacated its shores; it is known as Llyn Idwal today, silent and still as ever. A lake can be a repository of the unknown, a leveller of the landscape, a womb-like space associated with birth and renewal, and a portal to mesmerising fairy kingdoms. But it is impossible to gauge the true depth of a lake with the naked eye and lurking at the bottom are devils, ghouls and monsters, planning abominations. Unlike their close cousins the sea monsters – the krakens and leviathans, multimillion-year-old creatures who are free to roam the fathoms of the sea – they are usually confined or imprisoned, and bitter. Some of Wales's lakes are said to be occupied by mutant eels, one-eyed fish and, in one case, a dragon with a death stare that can only be thwarted by flapping cockerels. Others are abodes of giants, cursed owls, and predatory fairies. In Snowdonia can be found dark mountain pools, the blacker the more dangerous. One of them, Llyn Lliawn, is said to fire out huge waves, reeling in passers-by; at Llyn Crymlyn, all it takes is the slightest speck of spray. Other lakes can play havoc with the senses. If you fall asleep by Llyn Cau near Barmouth, you will wake up mad, blind or a poet; quite the roulette.

Wicked cities, debauched courts, vile villages – they can all be found beneath restful Welsh waters as punishment for their sins. The most famous of Wales's fabled sunken cities lies beneath

Llyn Tegid, or Bala Lake, which I could see from the window of my guesthouse. Long ago, goes the story, when Wales was a free land, there lived an old harper called Robyn. One day, Robyn received an invitation from the prince of Gwynedd to play at a banquet to celebrate the birth of his son. But the prince was a wicked prince, slaying whom he pleased, seizing their treasure, and laying waste to their farms. He ravished maidens, drank prodigiously, and gorged on enormous pies. When Robyn arrived, he was struck with wonder for never a more gluttonous meal did he see, the courtiers munching through the skeletons of baked birds, smearing their hands in beef grease. As he was strumming his harp, a little bird hovered above his harp singing, 'Dial a ddaw, dial a ddaw,' in a reedy voice, beckoning Robyn with his wing. The words mean 'vengeance is coming' and lo, there was a sense of menace and dread in the perfumed air. In the midst of the feast, Robyn laid down his harp and followed the bird out of the palace. On they walked, the singing bird and he, past grottos and labyrinths, watchtowers, gates and gallows, over bogs, and up into the hills. If ever Robyn paused to catch his breath, again the bird would sing, 'Dial a ddaw, dial a ddaw.' On the way up, Robyn lost the bird in the darkness. At that moment, the wind roared and a great tempest flared. The earth shook for hours on end, swallowing hills, houses and fields. Terrified, Robyn lay down in a ditch and prayed. He awoke to find that a great calm had descended over Gwynedd. He looked down the hill towards the palace but there was no palace, only a silent lake, with his harp floating on the water. Bala Lake, then, pours from the wrath of God; I wondered what sins the inhabitants of Capel Celyn had committed to deserve being drowned – other than finding themselves on the wrong side of progress.

At Llyn Tegid, fishermen have reported seeing the quivering reflection of the palace's ivory towers and golden baubles crushed and in pieces at the bottom of the lake, and, as at Dunwich, hearing the muffled sound of its bells rising from the deep. So too the ghost of Capel Celyn sometimes stirs, emerging wreath-like from the dark waters. Since the drowning of Tryweryn, the ghost village has re-appeared at least five times, during the droughts of 1976, 1986, 1989, 1995 and 1998, and each time people came to the valley to see the ruins of the houses, school, chapel and the graveyard, relishing the sense of unaccustomed liberty that allowed them to walk through a usually underwater world, across parched, cracked mud and past twisted tree stumps grinding into the earth like fossilised taran-tulas.[78] It was particularly painful viewing for one woman whose eighteen-year-old brother still lay buried in the graveyard. With the lake shrunk drastically, the drawing-off tower found itself ma-rooned on a mud plain as though it had landed from outer space. An underwater bridge resurfaced. Skull-like blocks stood in a heap of rubble and the bridge that once led to the village was now a bridge to nowhere, sweeping across a trickle of water into a muddy wasteland. Everywhere were ruins, a Golgotha of stubs, roots and waste.

'We were able then to walk along the old road that ran through the village,' recalled Gwyn Siôn Ifan in 2001. 'We could see broken crockery from the farmhouses still lying on the ground. The feeling of the community had not gone away.'[79] For those who had grown up in the valley, the experience was especially painful, and many could not bring themselves to revisit their fallen home. In 1989, Welsh Water laid down slate plaques identifying the individual houses on their foundations, further accentuating the sense of loss. Mysteriously, when the ruins of the village rose up from the waters, some had garish slogans spray-painted on their sides, graffiti like 'ENGLISH GO HOME', 'DROWNED BY ENGLISH PIGS' and 'WE WILL REBUILD'.[80] Some people were convinced these had survived underwater for over thirty years; others (rightly) suspected they were of more recent vintage, but in any case they reinforced the sense that the ruined village was a major stain on the conscience of

Liverpool Corporation, a secret that could never be buried.

But these ghostly apparitions were not necessary to sustain the memory of the village, which became etched into the Welsh consciousness. The word 'Tryweryn' has become both a byword for courageous resistance to an act of tyranny and a rallying call for the protection of Welsh language and identity.[81] In the 1960s and 1970s, when the campaign to protect the Welsh language reached its peak, you could see the words *Cofiwch Dryweryn* (Remember Tryweryn) all over Wales, daubed on bridges, tunnels, buildings and rocks. Now, most of them have vanished, with one striking exception. By the side of the A487, overlooking the seaside village of Llanrhystud some sixty miles from Llyn Celyn, is a derelict stone wall. It is spray-painted with the words *Cofiwch Dryweryn* on a bruise of red paint. First daubed in the early 1960s, it has been anonymously restored and repainted in the dead of night ever since. In Merionethshire at least, the memory is still poignant. In the archives, one woman told me she lived near the lake and had called her daughter Celyn. There is apparently a cluster of children called Celyn, all perpetuating the memory of the vanished village.

———

The opposite bank seemed so far away as to be quite out of my reach but I carried on, determined to get as close as possible to the exact spot where the village had vanished over fifty-five years ago, to look down, as the villagers had done, into doom-laden waters.

By now it was deep twilight and the reservoir was fading into an abyss of mist. On the horizon I could see an ominous black spot – the water tower where I'd begun my journey two hours earlier, a journey which it seemed was now coming to an end. I called up some taxi numbers, imperiously assuming they would materialise in a flash. They didn't. They didn't appear at all. By now the rain was getting more aggressive, the wind was excoriating my face, and I was numb to the bone with cold. Very soon it would be pitch black. The only option was to hitchhike.

I can't say how long I was standing by the edge of the road but, with each car that blazed past, I was plunged ever further into the darkness. Soon, all I could make out were the suggestions of promontories ahead and the shimmering of car headlights on the winding roads, like a network of lighthouses, luring me onwards. Roadside pigs stared at me and I wondered whether, by some diabolical machination, I was going to be swept into the reservoir myself, cast down among the bones of the Capel Celyn dead.

In May 1964, the Corporation pledged to cover the costs of digging up the dead (so long as it didn't exceed £35 per grave). This they announced on four sheets of A4 pinned to a crooked board in front of a pile of rocks. 'Notice is hereby given, pursuant to Sub-Section (5) of Section 64 of Liverpool Corporation Act, 1957, that, in accordance with an arrangement made with the appropriate relatives, the Liverpool Corporation intend to remove from the above burial ground the remains of the deceased persons mentioned below and to reinter them in the Cemeteries indicated.'[82] It was followed by a neatly tabulated list of the soon-to-be-dug-up dead and their designated cemetery, signed and dated by the town clerk of the Corporation. There it stood, ravaged by the wind, the insensitivity of English bureaucracy laid bare.

Five cars swept by. The sixth, a white van, stopped. Its driver agreed to run me back to Bala without ever questioning what I was doing on the edge of nowhere. He was a builder who had moved to Wales from Birmingham. His soul was suffering, he told me, from a lack of light.

———

Capel Celyn did not go under in vain. It bolstered Wales's long-dormant impulse to fight for the survival of its unique culture, language and traditions. It meant that English plans to drown other Welsh valleys – which, believe it or not, did emerge from time to time – never got off the drawing board. It inspired people to teach their children Welsh (the number of Welsh speakers is currently rising) and contributed to the establishment of a Welsh-language BBC channel in 1964. It led, too, to the establishment of the office of Secretary of State for Wales in 1964.

No doubt some of these developments would have happened anyway, but Tryweryn gave them a fillip, and its memory was frequently evoked. Whether there is a much of a link between the drowning of the valley in the 1960s and the inauguration of the Welsh Assembly (now the Welsh Parliament, or Senedd Cymru), affording the nation a measure of self-government, in 1999 is less clear-cut – the Welsh overwhelmingly rejected the very same thing in a referendum in 1979, and Tryweryn is rarely evoked by Plaid Cymru, still a relatively minor force in Welsh politics, today. But we can say at the very least that the 'white-hot indignation' fomented by Liverpool's handling of the affair revived and galvanised the age-old quest for Welsh independence, even if that quest played out in various complex ways.

In 2005, Liverpool Corporation finally apologised for the 'hurt of forty years ago' and the 'insensitivity by our predecessor council'. 'What happened to the people in the valley was wrong', said the city council leader.[83] But for those who remembered the drowning, this was too little too late. Elwyn Edwards, who had gone on the Liverpool march as a schoolboy, was twenty-two when the river was dammed. He had enjoyed happy weekends fishing and playing with his cousins on their Tryweryn farm. 'I remember the water coming out,' he recalls; 'there was nothing left – not a tree, a hedge, no sheep, cattle or birds singing. It was deathly quiet, like a funeral.' 'We lost our heritage,' he says; 'we lost everything.'[84] For him and his family it is not a lake at all. It is a graveyard.

Cofiwch Dryweryn.

CODA

Imagine your favourite city, your favourite street, as a wasteland. The cathedral fluttering with bats, the subway underwater, grass straggling through cracked pavements, the city pitch black at night, and silent as death: a heap of mournful rubble, neglected until the windswept reverie of some aesthete many centuries later. It's uncomfortable. We do not wish to think of our own towns and cities in this way any more than we want to think of ourselves in coffins or as ashes sunk into the earth. I have seen paintings from the nineteenth century which imagine London in ruins. They seem to be projecting it as a vast imperial seat, destined for decay. It seems a strange kind of ruin porn, to project into the future like that, fantastical in the context of the time, not something that necessarily weighed heavily on people's minds. But then, such a prospect would have seemed equally far-fetched to the inhabitants of Capel Celyn or the Breckland villages, let alone Dunwich or Winchelsea. How could they have known that the demise of their homes was just around the corner? It's reassuring to think of these sorts of places as being at the safe remove of history. But it could very well be that many of the places we know and love will soon fall to ruin and obsolescence. And perhaps sooner than we think.

Many of our communities, it is unpalatable to say, are ghost-towns-in-waiting. In amongst the tales of human perseverance, obsession, resistance and reconciliation, and in the pleasure that can be found in the ruins of lost places, this book has contained its fair share of horror. But it only goes up to 2021. A sequel, on the shadowlands of twenty-first-century Britain, would be darker still. That – unless we see major global breakthroughs on climate change, the replacement of the capitalist creed of perennial economic expansion with a more sustainable economic model, reformations in diet and lifestyle, and green industrial revolutions everywhere – could be an apocalyptic volume indeed, with swathes of Britain potentially more shadow than land.

Many of the mediums of oblivion explored throughout the book are still with us. We have recently experienced the devastation of a new pandemic, even if its death rate thus far has been mercifully too low to have wiped any communities off the map. Some rural villages are being hollowed out due to demographic shifts and economic migrations, their demise augured by the closure of the village post office, buses, footpaths and pubs;[1] many pubs, too, simply failed to reopen in the wake of coronavirus, further hastening their decline.[2] Who knows what land the military may need to requisition to prepare its forces for conflicts over scarce natural resources? Other places are threatened by grand projects to keep up with the pace of modernisation, recalling Capel Celyn's struggle with the Corporation of Liverpool: the building of Heathrow Airport from 1944 already put paid to the farming hamlet of Heath Row, and now nearby Harmondsworth is in the shadow of the possible construction of the third runway.[3] The most devastating force, however, is water – one that will only become more destructive in the decades ahead. Barely a month goes by without news about a village slowly sinking into the sea, or in danger of going that way: 'hopeless long to stand', as Old Winchelsea was described in its thirteenth-century twilight.[4]

Britain has some of the fastest disappearing cliffs in Europe, and many stretches of its eighteen thousand kilometres of coast are acutely vulnerable to flooding and landslide.[5] Erosion is nothing new – cliffs have always been pounded by the rain, wind and waves, as we have seen – and it would be wrong to paint man-made climate change as its first cause. But with warmer temperatures, rising sea levels, and an increased likelihood of extreme weather events, the scientific consensus is that it is expediting the process, dramatically in places, just as, to a lesser extent, climate change in the transition between the Medieval Warm Period and Little Ice Age very probably contributed to the ferocity and frequency of the storms that laid waste to Old Winchelsea, Dunwich and others.

Skipsea, in the East Riding of Yorkshire, lies on the fastest-eroding coastline in northern Europe.[6] Over the last twenty years, many of its houses have been washed away in scenes reminiscent of Dunwich's fate, though on a smaller and less lethal scale. Twenty-four seafront houses will, before long, go tumbling in too. At Skipsea, waves smack against the cliff, cascading high into the air, showering saltwater upon the grass, and residents have reported how, when the tide comes in, they can feel the walls of their houses physically sliding towards the cliff-edge.[7] Harrowing aerial photography shows the back gardens of the houses chomped away, revealing the brown sods of the cliff below, and the destructive path of the sea. Many residents have reluctantly moved away, but others seem determined to stay – like the Dunwich inhabitant who signed a leasehold for five hundred years even as the cliff-face edged steadily closer. But what else can they do? Moving out would mean demolishing their houses at the cost of thousands of pounds, and there is no rebuilding compensation offered by the council. They cannot put their trust in sea defences, since there are none – within four or five years, most Skipsea residents fully expect the threatened houses to be in the ocean.

On the other side of the island stands Fairbourne, a small town with a thousand residents on the north-west coast of Wales.[8] By 2013, the outlook was grim. To have any chance of warding off the sea, the cost of coastal defences would skyrocket and so the council, lacking funds, has embarked upon a policy of managed retreat. After 2025, Gwynedd Council plans to stop building or strengthening sea defences altogether and there are no plans to transpose the village, New Winchelsea style, elsewhere – Fairbourne's residents will be dissolved into other communities across North Wales, in an echo of Capel Celyn's fate, or of St Kilda's in Scotland. Meanwhile, the village's houses have become practically worthless, with people seeing their life savings eviscerated overnight and the young unable to secure mortgages for the dirt-cheap housing. Bleak, stultified, with its young drained away, Fairbourne is a ghost-town-in-waiting. By mid-century it is entirely possible it will be completely underwater, like so many others.

These towns and villages are just the tip of the fast-melting iceberg. The Environment Agency estimates that eight hundred homes and buildings in England and Wales could fall into the sea in the next twenty years alone,[9] and the Committee on Climate Change predicts, as a worst-case scenario, that within the next sixty years more than a hundred thousand properties may be at risk from coastal erosion, along with roads, railways, bridges and other infrastructure, and a further hundred thousand properties at risk of coastal land sliding.[10] Some of our major coastal or riverine towns and cities, too, face the prospect of severe flooding or even semi-submersion in the decades ahead, depending on how much greenhouse gas emissions are mitigated. Places such as Portsmouth, Hull, Cardiff, Chichester, Blackpool and Great Yarmouth face sepulchral incursions of seawater. And also the capital.[11]

It's enough to drive one to distraction, to stare into such a crystal ball, to accept that a child born tomorrow may very well find lower-lying parts of London regularly flooded or even entirely submerged by the time they reach their middle age, let alone that the entire species, as scientists warn, may face the prospect of extinction if temperatures rise by more than 5.5°C.[12] It is natural to doubt that such an apocalyptic reckoning could ever take place when, looking out of the window – in Britain at least – so much of the time nothing much seems to be changing; the clouds gather, the rain falls, and night follows day. The Welsh poet Jeuan Gethin likened the progress of the Pestilence to 'black smoke' billowing through society. But then, people were falling all around him. The threat from climate change is more like an invisible, odourless gas, a menace far from people's minds until it manifests with brutal devastation, like the first storm that sent Dunwich on its inexorable path of decline in 1288.

It would be foolhardy to try to divine our future with too great a degree of certainty from the minutiae of our past. And yet it is hard not to see the shadowlands of Britain as a cautionary tale. Their stories may not be able to tell us what we should do but they can at least provide us with perspectives on how we might contend with our fragile future. How will people respond to the threat of destruction? We will no doubt see stubborn individuals like Lucilla Reeve, who would rather die than accept defeat; resisters who will mount campaigns to stave off oblivion like most of the residents of Capel Celyn; more stoical communities like those of the STANTA villages that recognised their eviction was for the greater good; desperate groups which, like the inhabitants of Old Winchelsea, will beg the government to rebuild their settlements elsewhere; and those, perhaps, like the Hirtans, who will be grateful to leave.

Out of all the places on my itinerary of destruction, Orkney and the Outer Hebrides left the most indelible impression. I had peered into the structures that represented a settled domestic world at Skara Brae as my own one crumbled. At St Kilda, I saw a vision of the sort of brutally self-sufficient society to which humanity might regress in the wake of environmental collapse, a third world war or some other, unforeseen catastrophe. The journey to that desolate sea-mountain, a place so shorn and stripped back, allowed me to probe what lay underneath the emotional turmoil and bereavement that characterised the period of writing this book. If a shadowland is a hinterland between places or states, haunted ghosts and spirits, then it was that which I occupied throughout. When I started the book, I was married. My father was ailing but seemingly had time. Life was comfortable. By the end, all was gone, and outside my window the world was torn apart. Yet in spite of this, much of the restlessness of the intervening years seemed somehow to have abated. Whether it had genuinely diminished or I'd simply reconciled myself to it, I am not sure. Having toured and meditated upon so many ruins I had somehow emerged less of a ruin myself.

Sometimes parts of us have to melt away so other parts can exist, a sensation manifested on a national level by Capel Celyn, the ghost villages of STANTA, and Wharram Percy. It is this fluidity, I came to realise, that defines the country's form and boundaries in the long term. Present-day maps are manifestations of success, hiding the false starts, dead ends and sacrifices that allow Britain to look how it does. Today's map is tomorrow's curio. A map of the British Isles in 2175 (if there is anyone left to record it) will look starkly different from one of 1275, just as that map is very far from being a carbon copy of 1975's. Yet those lost places have left their mark. They are still with us. This is as useful a metaphorical truth as a geographical one. We are defined by our failures and losses as much as by our successes.

ACKNOWLEDGEMENTS

It is life-affirming to think of all the people who have contributed to the writing of this book. My agent, Chris Wellbelove, articulated a powerful vision for the project and made it happen; Mark Richards helped to incubate the idea. At Faber, in Laura Hassan I have found a transformative and empathetic editor; in Ella Griffiths and Mo Hafeez judicious line editors; in Sam Matthews a copy editor of assiduity and patience. I would also like to thank my editor at W. W. Norton, Matt Weiland, for his enthusiasm, Huneeya Siddiqui for her hard work, as well as the teams at both publishers.

Special thanks must go to the archivists and librarians who proved so helpful; to Mark Condren for invaluable research for various chapters; and to Dr Ian Mortimer for going through the text in forensic detail and delivering hours of glorious feedback, and indeed all the authors who were generous enough to read and endorse my work; any mistakes and infelicities are on me.

Of my family, I thank all those who have taken an interest in the book and borne its gestation with such understanding, especially my mother; of my friends, I must single out Duncan Brown, Keiran Goddard, David Heales, Edward and Alex Shawcross, Will Dorling, Hannah Parham, Anthony Hurley, William Kherbek and Thomas Warham for stimulation; and also Adam Wieclawski for his recitals of early drafts, curious letters, and devastating critiques, Alexander McCutcheon for his beauty and wonder, and exhortations to improve; and, especially, William Gardner for being the first person to read the manuscript, setting some of it to music, and for providing a preternatural level of inspiration, now and always.

NOTES

INTRODUCTION

1 W. G. Sebald, *The Rings of Saturn*, trans. Michael Hulse (2002), p. 155.

2 See, for example, https://www.theguardian.com/environment/2011/mar/14/rising-seas-new-york-london.

3 This is widely reported in newspapers. But on the inextricability of the coronavirus pandemic and the climate crisis, see also Andreas Malm, *Corona, Climate, Chronic Emergency* (2020), which tells us 'the virus emerged from human interactions with animals whose habitats had been ravaged'.

4 Michael J. Alexander, *The Earliest English Poems* (2006), pp. 30–2.

5 It is the references to 'wide streams' welling 'hot from source' and 'baths . . . hot at hall's hearth' as well as other topographical descriptions that incline historians and literary scholars to identify the ruined city as Bath.

6 It is true that more general, panoramic studies have been written, usually under the canopy of 'Britain's lost villages', and while these can be fascinating as repositories of information and syntheses of research, and impressive in their geographical range, what is gained in thoroughness can be lost in emotional impact as the layers of detail become overwhelming and the narratives become – heresy for such sudden and unanticipated twists of fate – predictable. See, for example, Richard Muir, *The Lost Villages of Britain* (1982); Henry Buckton, *The Lost Villages: Rediscovering Britain's Vanished Communities* (2008).

7 That is not to say that there aren't Roman forts, towns and other settlements that *did* amount to naught, and whose ruins can still be seen within the landscape – the walled shell of Silchester in Reading, or the grassy defence ditches of Richborough in the East Kent Marshes, both haunting presences – but they have been evocatively written about elsewhere and so spatial constraints have have denied the lost settlements of Roman Britain a place in the pages that follow. See especially Charlotte Higgins, *Under Another Sky* (2013).

ONE: THE HOUSES BENEATH THE SAND

1 *The Illustrated London News*, 7 December 1850, prints a narrative from 22 November, evoking the storm which smashed the *Edmund* to pieces off Kilkee at around midnight on Tuesday 19 November. One of the fullest

accounts is in *The Spectator* of 30 November 1850, which reports in quite gruesome detail 'many fatal disasters at sea . . . as the consequence of last week's storms'. For the death toll figure of ninety-six at Kilkee, see Joseph Irving, *Annals of Our Time, 1837–68* (1869), p. 194.

2 For the modern history and geography of Orkney I am indebted to Caroline Wickham-Jones, *Orkney: A Historical Guide* (2007); William Thomson, *The New History of Orkney* (2008); Lloyd Laing, *Orkney and Shetland: An Archaeological Guide* (1974); Alexander Fenton, *The Northern Isles: Orkney and Shetland* (1978); and the website Orkney Jar (http://www.orkneyjar.com).

3 For the best narrative accounts of the discovery, excavation and evaluation of Skara Brae, see Vere Gordon Childe, *Skara Brae: A Pictish Village in Orkney* (1931); V. Gordon Childe and D. V. Clarke, *Skara Brae* (1983); Alexandra Shepherd, 'Great Sites: Skara Brae', in *British Archaeology*, 55 (Oct. 2000); and, more than anything, the wonderfully authoritative David Clarke, *Historic Scotland: Skara Brae* (2012). For shorter, colourful accounts: Bill Bryson, *At Home: A Short History of Domestic Life* (2011); Simon Schama, *A History of Britain, Vol. 1: At the Edge of the World* (2000).

4 Childe, *Skara Brae*, p. xiii.

5 Bryson, *At Home*, p. 61.

6 Sally Green, *Prehistorian: A Biography of V. Gordon Childe* (1981), pp. 143–4.

7 This is the recollection of Professor Charles Thomas, who knew him, written in 1992. *The Archaeology of V. Gordon Childe*, ed. David R. Harris (1994), p. 134.

8 See Green, *Prehistorian*. He was described after his death as 'ugly, awkward and shy'. Stuart Piggott, 'Vere Gordon Childe', in *Proceedings of the British Academy*, 44 (1958), p. 310.

9 In the 1860s, the Orcadian antiquary George Petrie publicised the site and its artefacts in a series of sometimes illustrated articles in archaeological journals. See, for example, 'Notice of ruins of ancient dwellings at Skara, Bay of Skaill, in the parish of Sandwick. Orkney, recently excavated', *Proceedings of the Society of Antiquaries of Scotland*, 7, pp. 201–19.

10 John R. Tudor, *The Orkneys and Shetland: Their Past and Present State* (1883), p. 310. *Weem* is Scots for a cave or cavity in the ground.

11 Green, *Prehistorian*, p. 69; Bryson, *At Home*, p. 58. The merry party included the distinguished geologist and archaeologist Professor William Boyd Dawkins, who really should have known better.

12 Childe, *Skara Brae*, p. 5. And quotes below from pp. 1, 6, v.

13 Stuart Piggott, *The Neolithic Cultures of the British Isles: A Study of the Stone-using Agricultural Communities of Britain in the Second Millennium BC* (1954).

14 Shepherd, 'Great Sites', p. 13. Unlike Childe's narrower dig in the 1920s, the emphasis fifty years later was on uncovering the age of the site, its economic life, and the wider environment in which it existed. The findings appeared, firstly, in Childe and Clarke, *Skara Brae*, then subsequently in David Clarke and Patrick Maguire, *Skara Brae: Northern Europe's Best Preserved Prehistoric*

Village (1989) and ultimately in David Clarke, *Skara Brae* (2012), which is available at the site museum.

15 This extensive description of the houses and structures of Skara Brae is informed by my visit to the site and secondary sources such as those listed above.

16 House 9 is the best-preserved structure from the earlier period; House 10, in contrast, is almost completely ruined. Childe may have habitually called them huts but later historians and archaeologists are more comfortable with 'houses' and for me, it is more appropriate.

17 On the midden, see Childe, *Skara Brae*, pp. 6, 27, 67; Clarke, *Skara Brae*, p. 25.

18 In the later years of the final village, the houses were more than half-buried in the midden.

19 Clarke, *Skara Brae*, p. 19. He notes that, as far as limited excavation can tell, none of the other Neolithic villages whose traces remain on Orkney had roofed passageways. This was the case with Braes of Rinyo on Rousay, for example, whose features have only partially been disclosed by limited excavations before and after the Second World War. Some of those other villages *did* have contrasting features, however: some were likely to have been bigger or smaller, and some had much larger buildings for social assemblies and religious rituals.

20 Joshua 6:26 (KJV). Professor Childe believed this was very likely an expression of the ancient belief that 'a wall will not stand unless there be a spirit, provided by a corpse interred beneath it, to keep it up'. Childe, *Skara Brae*, p. 142.

21 Although impossible to prove, there is much that could be construed as evidence of prehistoric foundation sacrifices. In 2017, Korean archaeologists uncovered two skeletons from the fifth century AD under the walls of the Moon Castle in Gyeongju, South Korea. They believe them to be victims of foundation sacrifices: http://benedante.blogspot.com/2017/05/foundations-laid-in-human-sacrifice.html. It has even been argued that the modern idea of a haunted house derives from ancient foundation sacrifices. See https://daily.jstor.org/someone-buried-under-floor.

22 Clarke, *Skara Brae*, p. 21.

23 Francis Pryor, *The Making of the British Landscape: How We Have Transformed the Land, from Prehistory to Today* (2010), p. 82. Estimates range, sometimes wildly, from historian to historian, underlining the continued uncertainty.

24 See, for example, Richard Bradley, *The Past in Prehistoric Societies* (2014), p. 57; Clarke, *Skara Brae*, p. 54.

25 The axes were presumably used to slaughter animals and to cut bark from (or to cut down) what few trees existed on the island.

26 Clarke, *Skara Brae*, pp. 42–3.

27 Jessica Smyth, *Settlement in the Irish Neolithic: New Discoveries at the Edge of Europe* (2014), p. 9; Barry Cunliffe, *Britain Begins* (2013), p. 260; Clarke, *Skara Brae*, p. 32.

28 Euan Wallace MacKie, *The Megalith Builders* (1977), pp. 22–4, 187.

29 Shepherd, 'Great Sites', p. 13; Clarke, *Skara Brae*, pp. 32–3.

30 A Neolithic track connected Skara Brae to those sites, going as far as the chambered tomb of Maeshowe.

31 This section on the arrival of agriculture is informed in particular by Graeme Barker, *The Agricultural Revolution in Prehistory: Why Did Foragers Become Farmers?* (2009); Alan Simmons, *The Neolithic Revolution in the Near East: Transforming the Human Landscape* (2011); Vere Gordon Childe, *Man Makes Himself: Man's Progress Through the Ages* (1951); Bryson, *At Home*; Peter Ackroyd, *The History of England, Vol. 1: Foundation* (2012); Pryor, *Landscape*; Nicholas Crane, *The Making of the British Landscape: From the Ice Age to the Present* (2016); Laing, *Orkney and Shetland*.

32 Pryor, *Landscape*, pp. 28–32, 35. Pryor cautions, however, that Mesolithic settlements were not necessarily as flimsy as one might imagine.

33 Pryor, *Landscape*, pp. 28, 30–2, 45; Crane, *Landscape*, pp. 28–31; 'Star Carr', Historic England, https://historicengland.org.uk/listing/the-list/list-entry/1401425.

34 Bryson, *At Home*, p. 57.

35 For fire, see Stephen Pyne, *Fire: A Brief History* (2001); Johan Goudsblom, *Fire and Civilization* (1992).

36 Crane, *Landscape*, pp. 79–80. 'By 3900 BC', he writes, 'the ways of the "house people" had been adopted wholly or in part across south-eastern Britain.' This process was exacerbated from around 3800 BC when, perhaps within a couple of generations, 'new landforms flooded west and north'.

37 That is not to say the inhabitants of Skara Brae only ate husbanded animals. Their diet was complemented by cod, eel, red bream, trout and a plethora of shellfish. They gathered birds too, particularly in the twilight of Skara Brae, as the coast drew near and the productivity of farming was reduced by the encroachment of salt spray and sand. The remains of forty-six different species have been found at the site, including ducks and plover (now a gourmet food) along with their eggs. They hunted red deer for venison, wild boar for pork chops, and both beasts for their skins. They liked the odd hazelnut and beached whale. But it is clear from the proportion of remains in the midden that husbanded animals were their staples; no fishing material has been found, suggesting it was of auxiliary importance, though they may have ordered their hounds into the waves. Their diet, then, was a meaty one, and it is also possible that the cows provided milk and cheese. The quality of life was probably as good as it got in prehistoric Britain.

38 It is notoriously difficult to cite population figures for Neolithic Britain with authority. 20,000 in 2500 BC is cited in W. G. Hoskins, *Making of the English Landscape* (1955), p. 20; 2 million by 2000 BC is cited in Michael Reed, *The Landscape of Britain* (1990), p. 52; and, as noted, 250,000 in 2000 BC in Pryor, *Landscape*, p. 82. See also Bryson, *At Home*, p. 57 (20,000 by 3000 BC). Many general histories perhaps wisely do not even try to give a figure.

39 Causewayed enclosures were an important form of architecture that appeared all over southern Britain, and perhaps elsewhere, from around 4000 BC until 3300 BC – just a hundred years before Skara Brae came about. 'In terms of the development of the prehistoric landscape', argues Francis Pryor (*Landscape*, p. 56), 'it would be hard to overestimate their significance.'

40 Pryor, *Landscape*, pp. 55–60; see also his fascinating paper 'Abandonment and the role of ritual sites in the landscape', *Scottish Archaeological Review*, 9–10 (1995), pp. 96–109.

41 A desire to brew beer may have been the driving force behind the cultivation of cereals (Li Liu et al., 'Fermented beverage and food storage in 13,000-year-old stone mortars at Raqefet Cave, Israel: Investigating Natufian ritual feasting', *Journal of Archaeological Science: Reports* (Oct. 2018), pp. 783–93).

42 Bryson, *At Home*, p. 63.

43 Gordon Childe, *Man Makes Himself* (1936).

44 Mansel Jones, *A History of Kenfig* (2011). On sand's capacity to bury and preserve and the philosophical implications of its status as the 'antithesis of form', see Gordon Osborn, *A Handbook of Sand* (1984); Michael Welland, *Sand: A Journey Through Science and the Imagination* (2009), p. 115 (on Kenfig); and Robert Kaplan, *The Nothing that Is: A Natural History of Zero* (1999).

45 Childe, *Skara Brae*, p. 42.

46 Shepherd, 'Great Sites', p. 13.

47 Clarke writes: 'With house walls standing several metres high, it seems improbable that just half a metre of sand would cause the inhabitants to flee rather than just dig out the sand,' positing that the sand probably poured through the roof over a long period of time, and therefore is not remotely indicative of the reasons for the abandonment (*Skara Brae*, p. 45).

48 Clarke, *Skara Brae*, p. 45.

49 Schama, *History of Britain, Vol. 1*, p. 26.

50 Clarke, *Skara Brae*, p. 45.

51 This is the theory of Sigurd Towrie who runs the Orkney Jar website. See http://www.orkneyjar.com/history/skarabrae/abandon.htm.

52 Clarke, *Skara Brae*, p. 55.

53 For the self-senicide rituals of the Comanche and Arapaho tribes, see the Ethics of Suicide Digital Archive, https://ethicsofsuicide.lib.utah.edu/region/americas/north-american-native-cultures/.

54 G. J. Barclay, 'Neolithic Buildings in Scotland', in *Neolithic Houses in North-west Europe*, ed. Timothy Darvill and Julian Thomas (1996), pp. 61–76.

55 A Neolithic enclosure from *c.*3500 BC once stood on the site of the stupendous Iron Age hillfort, Maiden Castle, for example.

56 https://tradingeconomics.com/united-kingdom/urban-population-percent-of-total-wb-data.html.

TWO: THE LOST CITY OF TRELLECH

1 Much of this narrative comes straight from the horse's mouth: Stuart Wilson, whom I interviewed on Zoom. But I have also drawn upon various newspaper reports of the extraordinary story of the excavation of Trellech: Steven Morris, 'Archaeologist defies sceptics in pursuit of lost city of Trellech', *Guardian*, 3 Jan. 2017, https://www.theguardian.com/science/2017/jan/03/lost-city-of-trellech-uk-archaeologist-stuart-wilson-defies-sceptics; Kerry Walker, 'The quiet Welsh village sat atop a forgotten medieval city', *Telegraph*, 15 Feb. 2019; Caroline Mortimer, 'Man finds ancient medieval city on border of England and Wales', *Independent*, 4 Jan. 2017; Gurpreet Narwan, 'The history buff who dug deep to make a medieval discovery', *The Times*, 4 Jan. 2017, https://www.thetimes.co.uk/article/the-history-buff-who-dug-deep-to-make-a-medieval-discovery-v6d5w6xc3; 'Lost Welsh city found after 700 years', *Wales Online*, 14 Aug. 2004, updated 31 March 2013, https://www.walesonline.co.uk/news/wales-news/lost-welsh-city-found-after-2426041; Steph Cockroft, 'The lost city of Trellech: History fan spends his £32,000 life savings buying a field on a hunch – then is proved spectacularly right when he digs it up to discover the remains of a medieval town', *Mail Online*, 3 Jan. 2017, https://www.dailymail.co.uk/news/article-4083716/History-fan-spends-32-000-life-savings-buying-field-digs-discover-lost-medieval-city.html; and the notably more critical investigative piece by Avi Selk, 'A "militant archaeologist" is famous for finding a lost city. Some say he just stole the credit', *Washington Post*, 17 Jan. 2017, https://www.washingtonpost.com/news/speaking-of-science/wp/2017/01/17/a-militant-archaeologist-is-famous-for-finding-a-lost-city-some-say-he-just-stole-the-credit/; 'Conversations: Field of Dreams', including interview with Stuart Wilson, *Archaeology*, 59/5, (Sept./Oct. 2006).

2 Julia Wilson, 'Trellech: A New Location for an Old Town', *Archaeology in Wales*, 38 (1998), pp. 67–70.

3 Wilson is at pains to point out, during our interview (see below), that drawing definite connections between archaeological remains and the historical record can be a fool's errand; it is instructive, he tells me, but very hard to prove definitively.

4 The official website for the Lost City of Trellech project is https://www.lostcityoftrellech.org.

5 Trellech, and Wilson's quest to dig it up, frequently crops up in television documentaries too. A whole television series, though frequently mooted, is yet to materialise.

6 See in particular Raymond Howell's 'Excavations at Trelech, Gwent, 1991–1993: An investigation of a decayed medieval urban settlement', *Monmouthshire Antiquary*, 11 (1995), pp. 71–86; 'Excavations at Trelech: 1996–1999', *Monmouthshire Antiquary*, 16 (2000), pp. 131–46; *A History of Gwent* (1988); 'A Report of the Excavation of a Medieval Industrial Site in Trelech, Gwent', *Medieval and Later Pottery in Wales*, 11 (1989), pp. 62–80; S. Clarke et al.,

'Medieval Iron-working at Trellech: A Small Salvage Excavation', *Monmouthshire Antiquary*, 4 (1981–2), pp. 45–9.

7 Selk, 'A "militant archaeologist"'.

8 Wilson's ultimate aim, he told me, is to establish a permanent presentation centre on the site of his dig, to enlighten, inform and entertain the public. The one at Caerphilly Castle is an inspiration to him.

9 Selk, 'A "militant archaeologist"'.

10 https://twitter.com/Kasuutta/status/816709052516405248, 4 Jan. 2017. The previous year, in November 2016, David Howell posted on Twitter 'One manor house does not a "city" make. Personal agendas cloud archaeology.' https://twitter.com/Kasuutta/status/800466118464794624.

11 Selk, 'A "militant archaeologist"'.

12 'Good for you mate', writes one *Guardian* correspondent in the comments beneath Morris's article, 'for keeping on track and trusting your own judgement rather than the snobby naysayers'; 'a great story', says another, 'of one man's vision trouncing the experts who were looking elsewhere'. Readers find Wilson's story uplifting: 'If he'd invested in a house,' a commentator points out, 'I'd never have heard of him . . . but he dared to dream.' The 'professionals', in contrast, are often criticised; one commentator writes that 'they should swallow their pride and work WITH him'.

13 The story sparked imaginations. One reader suggests the whole thing was worthy of a movie in which there could be a high-speed car – or cart – chase between the academics and Wilson past the pub, churning up the dig site, and weaving through the village's ancient stones. Was he in it for the money, with his dreams of a tourism centre and television series? Of course not, wrote Wilson, 'but yes, I would like some money. Academics get paid, so why not me? After fifteen years of free labour that is not unreasonable to ask.'

14 The Historic Environment Report of Monmouthshire, https://www.archwilio.org.uk/her/chi1/arch.html?county=Monmouthshire&lang=eng.

15 All these images are taken from Gerald of Wales, *The Journey through Wales; and The Description of Wales*, translated [from Latin] by Lewis Thorpe (New York, 1978), pp. 93–4.

16 Gerald of Wales, *Journey and Description*, p. 114.

17 During the Harrying of the North in 1069–70, villages, crops, cattle and of course potentially rebellious northern subjects were destroyed. It has been estimated that tens of thousands of people died as a result of the campaign and the famine it precipitated. James Aitcheson, 'The Harrying of the North', *History Today*, 12 Oct. 2016, https://www.historytoday.com/history-matters/harrying-north.

18 Orderic Vitalis, *Historia Ecclesiastica*, ed. and trans. Marjorie Chibnall (1983), 4, pp. 138–9.

19 Nicholas Crane, *The Making of the British Landscape: From the Ice Age to the Present* (2016), p. 290.

20 Images and details from Gerald of Wales.

21 Gerald's *Journey* paints a picture of a never-ending cycle of violence, blood feuds, revenge murders and counter murders. 'Sometimes by the local inhabitants at the expense of those in command of the castles, and then, the other way round, the vindictive retaliations of the castle-governors against the locals.' Gerald singles out Ranulf Poer, Sheriff of Herefordshire as someone responsible for terrifying atrocities 'in our own times' at the instigation of Henry II (pp. 109–12). 'We should note, however, that the *Journey* was written in the late twelfth century, around a hundred years before Trellech reached its prime, by which point the extent and intensity of the violence had abated somewhat. I am grateful to Ian Mortimer for alerting me to this.

22 This horror took place at the Massacre of Abergavenny (1175) when William de Braose, pretending peace, summoned three Welsh princes (one of whom he held responsible for his uncle's murder) and looked on as they were slaughtered on his orders.

23 See the story of the ambush of Richard de Clare in the Forest of Dean, below. Many of these images are imaginative interpolations from the many contemporary accounts – for example, from Gerald of Wales and Orderic Vitalis – of the guerrilla warfare and political conflict that took place in the Marches. See E. A. Rees, *Welsh Outlaws and Bandits: Political Rebellion and Lawlessness in Wales, 1400–1603* (2001). One of the reasons Henry VIII wiped the Marches off the map under the terms of the Acts of Union (1536–43) was because he felt that bandits and felons who operated there were an affront to his authority, bribing the Marcher lords to gain safe passage to Wales to evade English justice. Amongst other intriguing details, Gerald of Wales describes felons, bandits, slinking wolves and murder squads lying deep in the woods and clairvoyant Flemings telling the future by boiling the right shoulder blades of rams in their little wattle huts.

24 It is thought that Richard Fitz Gilbert may well have been a childhood friend of William of Normandy as his father tutored William. Richard Mortimer, 'Clare, Richard de (1030x35–1087x90)', *ODNB*.

25 Richard Fitz Gilbert's de Clare lands were by no means his most important holding. His other lands lay in Surrey and Kent, clustered around Tonbridge. Collectively these lands were worth a flabbergasting £873 (*ODNB*).

26 Clive H. Knowles, 'Clare, Gilbert de (1243–1295)', *ODNB*.

27 Davis, *Three Chevrons Red*. Davis claims that Richard de Clare had, by 1260, become 'easily the richest and potentially the most powerful baron, next to members of the immediate royal family, in the British Isles'.

28 His chronicle covers 1066 to 1289. *The Chronicle of Thomas Wykes*, quoted in Davis, *Three Chevrons Red*, p. 231.

29 When we scan the peaks of the high politics of the Middle Ages, Gilbert the Red is frequently to be seen. He joined the baron Simon de Montfort's rebellion against Henry III in 1264, capturing the king's brother Richard of

Cornwall in a windmill at the Battle of Lewes, and sat on a special council of nine whose job it was to dictate terms to the king. Gilbert the Red also changed sides five times between 1262 and 1267, abandoned the de Montfort cause, and secured a peaceful end to the civil war.

30 Knowles, 'Clare, Gilbert de', *ODNB*.

31 The de Clares' income from the regality of Glamorgan alone rose from £359 in 1265 to £1,276 fifty years on. Davis, *Three Chevrons Red*, p. 231.

32 Rhys ap Maredudd, mentioned later, had a de Clare mother.

33 The local Welsh prince Morgan ap Maredudd, for example, despised Gilbert the Red as he had deprived him of his ancient seat at Caerleon.

34 Crane, *Landscape*, pp. 319, 321, 323.

35 Crane, *Landscape*, pp. 319, 321–2; Pryor, *Landscape*, pp. 315, 325–6; Beresford, *New Towns*, pp. vii, 5, 377. Crane believes that, by 1300, one in five of Britain's population lived in towns, half in urban settlements of 2,000 or fewer.

36 On the technology that facilitated the rise of multi-storey houses, and hence greatly bolstered the process of urbanisation, see Crane, *Landscape*, pp. 308–9.

37 The measure of self-determination took the form of municipal self-government, aldermen and an annually elected lord mayor, watchmen, rubbish collectors, clinks and guildhalls.

38 Trellech first surfaces in the historical record in 1231, during the troubled reign of Henry III (1216–72) when England slid into civil war. Henry's government could be impuissant, with baronial rebellions, and even a year-long exile; real power latterly resided with his son, Edward I, who had the ambition, relative competence and military prowess his father so conspicuously lacked. It appears as a small settlement by a wooden fort that had been built after the Norman invasion of Wales.

39 The valuations and burgage assessments of Trellech over subsequent years can be found in TNA SC6/920/18, SC6/1247/21, SC6/925/30; C6/927/2; 1247/29; NA C133/77/3; NA C134/43.

40 TNA SC6/1247/21; SC6/925/24.

41 These figures are all from the same, or surrounding, decades. They can be found in Maurice Beresford's magisterial *New Towns of the Middle Ages: Town Plantation in England, Wales and Gascony* (1988).

42 There is no way of proving this but it does seem plausible given the rapid pace of urbanisation before 1288 and the increased demand for iron as a result of the wars and rebellions of the 1290s. It would have entailed an expansion from 378 to 422 burgages within the space of eight years, which is ten per cent growth.

43 If this is true, it would call for some truly radical revisionism; most urban and landscape historians believe Wales had very few towns of more than two thousand people in the thirteenth and fourteenth centuries, and Trellech is never listed as one of them.

44 Richard Britnell, 'Commercialisation and economic development in

England, 1000–1300', in *A Commercialising Economy: England 1086 to c.1300*, ed. Richard Britnell and Bruce M. S. Campbell (1995), p. 10.

45 It is thought that the population of London had risen to 80,000 by 1300, although the Black Death would reduce it by up to half by mid-century. See *The Oxford Encyclopaedia of Economic History*, vol. 5. (2003), p. 356; Rosemary Horrox and W. Mark Ormrod, eds, *A Social History of England, 1200–1500* (2006), p. 145. https://www.vrc.crim.cam.ac.uk/vrcresearch/london-medieval-murder-map/london-XIV-cent.

46 'Mapping the Medieval Countryside: Properties, Places and People', University of Winchester and King's College London, http://www.inquisitionspostmortem.ac.uk.

47 Christine Carpenter, 'Introduction', in *Calendar of Inquisitions Post Mortem Preserved in the Public Record Office XXII: 1422–1427* (1–5 Henry VI), ed. Kate Parkin (2003), pp. 1–42; *The Fifteenth-Century Inquisitions Post Mortem: A Companion*, ed. Michael Hicks (2012); *The Later Medieval Inquisitions Post Mortem: Mapping the Medieval Countryside and Rural Society*, ed. Michael Hicks (2016). I am very grateful to Dr Paul R. Dryburgh, Principal Records Specialist (Medieval Records) at the National Archives, with whom I corresponded by email, for clarifying my thinking on these complex sources.

48 *The Cambridge Urban History of Britain, Vol. 1: 600–1540*, ed. D. M. Palliser (2000), pp. 525, 700–1, 702. In his essay on the Welsh Marches the contributor Ralph Griffiths helpfully clarifies that there was no nationwide borough return, and that we must rely to some extent on the caprice of fate, since the best type of evidence – the inquisitions post mortem – would only happen at the death of a seigneur (a feudal lord). Michael Hicks, in *The Fifteenth-Century Inquisitions 'Post Mortem': A Companion* (2012), argues that such documents are, in fact, largely empirically accurate.

49 Rebecca Solnit, *River of Shadows: Eadweard Muybridge and the Technological Wild West* (2003); Mark Binelli, *The Last Days of Detroit* (2013); S. Lee Johnson, *Roaring Camp: The Social World of the California Gold Rush* (2001); Eric L. Clements, *After the Boom in Tombstone and Jerome, Arizona: Decline in Western Resource Towns* (2003).

50 Ray Howell, 'Excavations at Trellech: 1996–1999', *Monmouthshire Antiquary*, 16 (2000), pp. 131–46; 'Excavations at Trelech, Gwent, 1991–1993: An investigation of a decayed medieval urban settlement', *Monmouthshire Antiquary*, 11 (1995), pp. 71–86; 'The Roads of Trellech: Investigation of the Development of the Medieval Town', *Monmouthshire Antiquary*, 21 (2005) pp. 45-63.

51 This imaginative section is interpolated from general knowledge and a wide range of sources, but see in particular: Stephen Moorhouse, *Medieval Iron Production* (1980); Larissa Tracy, *Torture and Brutality in Medieval Literature* (2015); Jim Bradbury, *The Routledge Companion to Medieval Warfare* (2004).

52 For some lucid explanations and illustrations of medieval nails, see John Steane, *The Archaeology of Medieval England and Wales* (2014), p. 221.

53 Middle Rainton in Sunderland received sentence of death and withered away in the 1970s. Now there's just a nature reserve left but at one time there would have been rows of terraced houses, a pub and a saw mill; mention of coal outcrops were made as early as 1531 and an open cast mine was opened in 1604. There is a revealing interactive map of the 'Category D' villages in County Durham online: https://mattjamessmith.com/content/the-category-d-villages-of-durham.

54 A decade later, in 1304, only 271 burgages were recorded; in 1314, the number had fallen to 265.

55 Edward Lhuyd, in Camden's *Britannia* (1695 edition). Lhuyd (later, keeper of the Ashmolean) was particularly interested in the curative properties of the well, and baffled by the three stones.

56 See, e.g., *Gloucester Journal*, 29 Aug. 1796; *Hereford Journal*, 31 Aug. 1796.

THREE: THE OBLITERATED PORT

1 Barbara Ross and Eleanor Searle, eds, *Accounts of the Cellarers of Battle Abbey, 1275–1513* (1967), p. 41. The abbey bought prodigious quantities of beef and cooked a whole pond's worth of fish for the pleasure of King Edward. The first petition from the inhabitants of Winchelsea asking for help was sent to Henry III in 1236.

2 The contemporary source for this is Holinshed's *Chronicle* (1587), http://english.nsms.ox.ac.uk/holinshed/texts.php?text1=1587_3499, p. 272. Departing from Dover, says Holinshed, 'the Prince visited the sea coasts, punishing diverse of the inhabitants within the precincts of the Cinque Ports, and putting them in fear, received diverse to the king's, his father's, peace. The inhabitants of Winchelsea only, made countenance to resist him; but Prince Edward, with valiant assaults, entered the town, in which entry much guilty blood was spilt.' Prince Edward attacked Winchelsea with a fleet recruited mainly from Yarmouth and the East Coast and with almost six hundred Welsh archers. The leading citizens were 'put to the sword', but the majority spared. They had supported the Barons in their war against King Henry.

3 Edward's slaughterous appearance really did add insult to injury. In 1265 his father, Henry III, had tried to win the townspeople's support and, failing, set his army loose on their precious wine cellars.

4 This description comes from Thomas Pennant, *A Journey from London to the Isle of Wight* (1801), vol. 2, p. 30.

5 The first known reference to Winchelsea is from 1131. So there must have been a fishing community here at least by that point. Jill Eddison, 'The Origins of Winchelsea', in *New Winchelsea Sussex: A Medieval Port Town*, ed. David and Barbara Martin (2004), p. 3.

6 On the size of towns, see, for example, Peter Ackroyd, *The History of England Vol. 1: Foundation* (2012), p. 138.

7 In the absence of first-hand accounts of the rise of Winchelsea, we might take, as a parallel, evidence presented by a Grimsby jury to Edward I in 1290 about the new town of Ravenserodd, for the origins of Winchelsea are likely to have been similar. Ravenserodd materialised, and rapidly grew, after the sea cast up a sandbank 'in the utmost limits of Holderness between the sea and the Humber'. The jury revealed 'a certain island was born which is called Ravenserodd. And afterwards fishermen came to dry their nets there and men began little by little to dwell and stay there, and afterwards ships laden with divers kind of merchandise began to unload and sell at the town. And now, inasmuch as the island is nearer the sea than Grimsby and as ships can unload there more easily, nearly all ships do stay, unload and stay there.' Proximity to the sea was the key co-efficiency, and it would suffer a similar sad fate. Beresford, *New Towns*, p. 513.

8 It has been suggested that *Wincel-ēg* is Old English for 'island by a river bend' (*Dictionary of British Place Names*, ed. David Mills (2011), p. 501), but 'island on a bend' seems more likely, from *wincel*, bend or corner; *ēg*, island, and because it was the coast that changed course not a river.

9 The Royal Navy would not come into existence until the early years of Henry VIII's reign at the start of the sixteenth century.

10 Winchelsea merchants paid £62 whereas Rye's paid only £10. Eddison, 'Origins of Winchelsea', p. 3.

11 We know that King Edward visited Winchelsea in person, on 2 July 1276, because three writs exist, from 1276 (relating to an infringement of the Bishop of Ely's liberties), which were tested (i.e. heard) by 'The King at Winchelsea' (William Prynne, *The History of King John, King Henry III, and the Most Illustrious King Edward I* (1670), p. 182). Also, two items of business on Membrane 17 of the Calendar of the Patent Rolls, from July 1276, are marked as having been transacted at 'Romney', which was a neighbour of Old Winchelsea, and this proximity is indicative of the king's presence at the sinking city (*Calendar of the Patent Rolls, 1272–1281* (1971), p. 178; William Durrant Cooper, *The History of Winchelsea* (1850)).

12 Giant (by our standards) meatballs in jelly were a medieval delicacy. See Ian Mortimer, *The Time Traveller's Guide to Medieval England: A Handbook for Visitors to the Fourteenth Century* (2009), p. 180; Melitta Weiss Adamson, *Food in Medieval Times* (2004), pp. 62, 68, 100.

13 In the hierarchy of falcons and hawks white goshawks, although not as noble as gyrfalcons and peregrines, were nonetheless highly prestigious. Edward I adored falconry, building the Royal Mews at Charing early in his reign, and, in the same year he visited Winchelsea, sending agents to Scandinavia to buy the finest birds. Robin Oggins, *The Kings and their Hawks: Falconry in Medieval England* (2004), pp. 22, 16, 83.

14 Mario Damen, 'Giving by Pouring: the Function of Gifts of Wine in the City of Leiden, 14th to 16th centuries', in *Symbolic Communication in Late*

Medieval Towns, ed. Jacoba Van Leeuwen (2006), pp. 83–100. In medieval European cities, Damen argues, wine acted as a social lubricant, a token of respect, and as a sign of recognition for services rendered in the past or future. Prestigious visitors were handed tin jugs inscribed with the city's insignia and the quantity, type and quality of wine reflected the status of the visitor. Rulers might be offered up to five hundred pints of exquisite wine!

15 Beresford, *New Towns*, pp. 3, 14.

16 Eddison, 'Origins of Winchelsea', p. 5.

17 Edward issued this writ at his chancellor's castle of Acton Burnell in Shropshire, where he held a parliament in 1283; abridged and translated by John Docwra Parry in *An Historical and Descriptive Account of the Coast of Sussex* (1833), p. 275.

18 These are the words of the chronicler William Camden, reproduced in William Somner, *A Treatise of the Roman Ports and Forts in Kent* (1693), p. 58.

19 Matthew Paris, *English History, from 1235 to 1273*, trans. J.A. Giles, vol. 2 (1853), pp. 391–2.

20 Paris, *English History*, pp. 391–2.

21 Paris, *English History*, pp. 472–3.

22 Jill Eddison argues that the sea coursed a small but stable channel through the shingle spit in 1086 as there are references to one hundred salt works in Domesday; this became a permanent breach in 1180, resulting in the formation of an outer spit. It was this outer spit that was swept away in 1250. Eddison, 'Origins of Winchelsea'.

23 TNA C 53/61. The charter roll is dated 6 Nov. 1271. It is reproduced and translated in *Calendar of the Charter Rolls Preserved in the Public Record Office*, vol. 2 (1906), p. 214.

24 The port tolls fell from £87 in 1272 to £33 in 1273. Beresford, *New Towns*, p. 15.

25 *Calendar of the Patent Rolls Preserved in the Public Record Office* (1901), p. 151. It was one of many grants issued to Winchelsea citizens during the thirteenth century.

26 Parry, *Historical Account*, p. 274.

27 *The Historical Works of Gervase of Canterbury*, ed. William Stubbs, vol. 2 (1880), p. 293. Eddison states that this was written by a continuator of the chronicle ('Origins of Winchelsea', p. 6); Somner attributes it to 'an ancient French chronicler' transcribed by a Canterbury monk (*Treatise*, p. 57).

28 Hubert Lamb, *Weather, Climate and Human Affairs* (1988), p. 78. Lamb pioneered the study of historical climate change. He describes these storm-flood disasters as 'among the worst recorded in human history anywhere in the world'.

29 Brian Fagan, *The Little Ice Age: How Climate Made History, 1300–1850* (2000), p. 65.

30 The main evidence for this shift in climate comes from tree rings (which reveal historic temperature fluctuations), excavations of ice cores (where

volcanic ash is trapped), written historical records (extreme weather events, for example, attract the attention of medieval chroniclers and others) and a more sophisticated understanding of climate data in the present day. Few historians or climatologists deny that the Medieval Warm Period happened, though some rightly question how widespread and constant it was.

31 Fagan, *Little Ice Age*, pp. 9, 28, 39.

32 See, for example, Lamb, *Climate*, vol. 2 (1977), pp. 120–6; Basil Cracknell, *Outrageous Waves: Global Warming and Coastal Change in Britain through Two Thousand Years* (2005), passim; Fagan, *Little Ice Age*, p. 54, where he states, 'By 1400, the weather had become decidedly more unpredictable and stormier.'

33 Hubert Lamb, *Climate, History and the Modern World* (1995), pp. 166, 176, 198.

34 Richard Comotto, 'Digging into Winchelsea harbour', *Rye News*, 29 April 2015, https://www.ryenews.org.uk/culture/digging-winchelsea-harbour.

35 Cracknell, *Outrageous Waves*.

36 His theory centres around the North Atlantic Oscillation Index, a northern equivalent of the atmospheric pressures that produce El Niño in the equatorial Pacific, and whose workings are still not fully understood. Fagan, *Little Ice Age*, pp. 46–8.

37 It would be highly unfortunate to claim, as some have, that because medieval global warming was not man-made, neither is ours. Fluctuations in solar radiation have contributed to past global warmings, so could it not be the driver in the twentieth and twenty-first centuries? Plainly observable scientific facts simply do not bear this out. NASA's Fifth Assessment Report makes this clear: 'If the warming were caused by a more active sun, then scientists would expect to see warmer temperatures in all layers of the atmosphere. Instead, they have observed a cooling in the upper atmosphere, and a warming at the surface and in the lower parts of the atmosphere. That's because greenhouse gases are trapping heat in the lower atmosphere.' The dramatic extent of temperature increase over the last hundred or 150 years cannot be explained by increases in solar radiation nor by decreases in volcanic activity. If we overlay CO_2 emissions, there is an alarmingly precise correlation, from which we can infer – a 95 per cent chance, according to the IPCC – that carbon emissions are the decisive motor of global warming today.

38 This was from a quitclaim of 1295 – the formal relinquishing of a claim to properties 'within the new *and old* towns of Winchelsea'. British Library, Add. Ch. 20169. This is a collection of deeds relating to lands in Sussex between 1200 and 1760.

39 British Library, Add. MS. 15776, ff. 175–220.

40 'Because of the rapidity of the removal of shingle barriers and the speed of coastal changes,' writes one geographer, 'it is unlikely that any of the materials of the old town survived in place for long after 1280 when Old Winchelsea was submerged.' Eddison, 'Origins of Winchelsea', p. 2.

41 Barry Floyd, 'A Geographical and Historical Study of an Ancient Town and Port in Sussex' (unpublished dissertation, Gonville and Caius College, Cambridge, 1948–9), in possession of the Winchelsea Museum as a PDF file.

42 Beresford, *New Towns*, p. 509. Tantalisingly, New Sarum was built perhaps on the very site of the lost Anglo-Saxon *burh* of Searisbyrig, a once-consequential town with a mint and which in 960 played host to a *witenagemot* (a 'wise man's meeting' sometimes portrayed as an embryonic parliament), but of which there is no trace today; it would, in this case, have been something of a 'penitent's return'.

43 The aggrieved residents of nearby Wilton complained that New Sarum, contrary to its charter, which licensed only one, was having markets every day of the week save the Sabbath. They were potentially exaggerating. But we can be in no doubt that the new city prospered, to Wilton's cost.

44 Beresford, *New Towns*, pp. 506–9.

45 The image of rabbits being trapped underground is extrapolated from a range of contemporary evidence. 'The king, in the eighth year of his reign, issued a commission to Ralph of Sandwich, his steward, authorising the purchase of a rising hill or piece of ground containing 150 acres, which was then a rabbit warren, called Iham, within the parish of Icklesham. The purchase was completed, an arrangement was made with the vicar to pay him 10l in lieu of tithes, and the "inhabitants of Old Winchelsea took to it by little and little and builded it."' *Penny Cyclopaedia of the Society for the Diffusion of Useful Knowledge*, vol. 23 (1833–43), p. 347. See also Cooper, *History of Winchelsea*, p. 29, on which he says that 'the spot was principally an uneven sandstone rock, fit only for, and used as a rabbit warren'. A contemporary writ from the eleventh year of Edward I's reign, additionally, mentions that 'the inhabitants had begun to build at Iham, which, before that period, had been called a rabbit-warren'.

46 The original rental rolls, in Latin, are housed in the National Archives (TNA Patent Roll, 11 Edward I, m.7; TNA Rentals and Surveys, SC11/674). A full transcription can be found in F. A. Inderwick, *The Story of King Edward and New Winchelsea: The Edification of a Mediaeval Town* (1892), pp. 153–219. More practically, there is a great online rendition drawing upon the above, at http://users.trytel.com/tristan/towns/florilegium/community/cmfabr28.html.

47 It was drawn up by the mayor, the king's twenty-four jurats and by the Lord Bishop of Ely, acting on behalf of Edward I.

48 TNA E372/150/m. 32d. The full rent, as assessed in 1292, was received each year until 1297; later taxation revenue (1298–1306) appears in Add. Ch. 18963. The Pipe Rolls show the full 1292 evaluation, £14 11s, arrived safely and swiftly at the Exchequer from Jan. 1293.

49 On the topographical history of the urban grid-plan, see Spiro Kostof, *The City Shaped: Urban Patterns and Meanings Through History* (1991); Dan Stanislawski, 'The Origin and Spread of the Grid-Pattern Town', *Geographical*

Review, 36/1 (1946), pp. 105–20; T. F. Tout, *Mediaeval Town Planning: A Lecture Delivered at the John Rylands Library* (1916).

50 This design is usually credited to Alfred but excavations by archaeologists at the University of Oxford have suggested an earlier, mid-ninth-century provenance. *Winchester: A City in the Making: Archaeological Excavations between 2002 and 2007*, ed. Ben Ford (2011). Francis Pryor is wonderfully judicious in his distinction between a 'grid-like' street plan and a 'grid' lay-out. The former can be applied to early tenth-century Winchester; the latter to thirteenth-century Salisbury and New Winchelsea. Pryor, *Landscape*, p. 324.

51 Kostof, *The City Shaped*, p. 121.

52 Beresford, *New Towns*, p. 177.

53 Beresford, *New Towns*, p. 194.

54 Conway is the best surviving example of a Welsh *bastide*. It has an imposing castle that dominates the river, and the town, which is shaped like a Welsh harp, has long, straight streets.

55 https://www.nationaltrust.org.uk/features/a-lost-castle-at-winchelsea.

56 Wyke caught Edward's attention on a visit to Berwick. In November 1292, he eyed it up, ordering a valuation of the entire town, and then, within three months, he had acquired it from Meaux Abbey (in exchange for other lands which they believed would be of 'great profit' but, in the event, actually yielded less in rent – along with the right to build mighty broad approach roads). Edward's aim was 'to increase the fitness of the port for ships and traffic'. Beresford, *New Towns*, p. 511.

57 In 1346, two-thirds of Ravenserodd was washed away; two hundred houses had been lost within just over a decade; and the borough's tax assessment plunged by two-thirds. Truly it was a sinking ship because twenty years later, there was nothing left to tax at all. TNA SC8/6/284; 68/3380; 87/4306; 156/7763.

58 'It is a handsome city, but distractingly regular. After walking about it for an hour or two, I felt that I would have given the world for a crooked street' (*American Notes* (1875), p. 107).

59 The Anglo-Norman monk and chronicler Nicholas Trivet provides a vivid eyewitness account of entering the freshly minted city of Winchelsea as part of his story of the king's near-death experience in his *Annals of the Six Kings of England*. The evocation that follows owes much to Trivet's beguiling description, but is also based on the rent rolls, later maps, my own tours of the site, the wonderful model of the town in Winchelsea's museum, and other eyewitness accounts. The passage is quoted in David and Barbara Martin, 'The Defences', in *New Winchelsea Sussex*, pp. 41–3.

60 Trivet, *Annals*, cited above.

61 'One of the most unusual customs of the Greyfriars was to keep a live eagle in captivity in the grounds.' George Goldsmiths Carter, *Forgotten Ports of England* (1951), p. 186.

62 TNA SP 12/75/70. Quoted in Beresford, *New Towns*, p. 16.

63 These are taken from the wonderfully detailed and exact rental roll of 1292 (Cooper, *History of Winchelsea*, pp. 44–53). See also the online list and analysis, cited above.

64 The rental rolls suggest that many of the tenants on the south side of the Monday Market were prostitutes. A visitor to Winchelsea Museum had deduced this from their names, and I am grateful to the curator for passing this on. This was the closest thing New Winchelsea had to a red-light district.

65 Trivet tells us there were 'very many' windmills in the town. Modern scholars and archaeological experts on Winchelsea believe this account, stating that the spot which to this day is called King's Leap would be exactly the kind of place from which such a mishap might occur.

66 Thirty-three survive and are accessible; the locations of eighteen others are known; others have been destroyed.

67 David and Barbara Martin, 'The Winchelsea Cellars', in *New Winchelsea Sussex*, pp. 105, 107. The Alards occupied half of block 8's twelve plots, including the three rectangular ones with dual street frontages; overall their buildings overlooked all four sides of the block. Beresford, *New Towns*, p. 20.

68 David Sylvester, 'The Development of Winchelsea and its Maritime Economy', in *New Winchelsea Sussex*, p. 12. New Winchelsea (and probably Old Winchelsea in its twilight, too) must have been somewhat cosmopolitan. Gascon vintners liked to take up residence for several months of the year to enjoy the tax privileges afforded to the Cinque Ports, and the presence of alien wine merchants is recorded right through the fourteenth century (David and Barbara Martin, 'Winchelsea Cellars', p. 124).

69 Susan Rose, *The Wine Trade in Medieval Europe, 1000–1500* (2011). Rose argues that by the eleventh century it was 'probably' the most widely traded commodity in Europe.

70 Rose, *Wine Trade*, p. 148.

71 Rose, *Wine Trade*, p. 80.

72 This poetic description is taken from Henry d'Andeli's poem *La Bataille des vins* (1225), in which a judge assesses and ranks a series of European wines so that only the finest can be served to the French king. Bordeaux wine was fruitier and had more zap than the northern whites it superseded, and it tasted best within a few months of the harvest. Cited in Rose, *Wine Trade*, p. 15.

73 The authorship of *Liber Vinis* is disputed. While it was once attributed to the Catalan physician Arnaud de Villeneuve, recent textual scholarship has favoured one Maestro Silvestre. It was written at some point in the 1320s. See José Rodrígez Guerrero, 'El Origen del Pseudo-arnaldiano Liber de vinis, Obra del magister Silvester (*c*.1322–8), y su Tradición Manuscrita en el Siglo XIV', *Azogue*, 7 (2013), pp. 44–74.

74 Quotations taken from the erroneously titled *The Earliest Printed Book on Wine by Arnald of Villanova*, ed. Henry Sigerist (1943).

75 Rose, *Wine Trade*, p. 116.

76 Rose, *Wine Trade*, p. 138.

77 Melitta Weiss Adamson, 'Infants and Wine: Medieval Medical Views on the Controversial Issue of Wine as Baby-Food', *Medium Aevum Quotidianum*, 50 (2004), pp. 18, 20. These questionable pieces of advice were imparted by the physician William of Saliceto and Padua physician Michele Savonarola, grandfather of the famous Florentine ascetic demagogue Girolamo Savonarola.

78 Pietro de' Crescenzi, *Ruralia commoda*, quoted in Rose, *Wine Trade*, p. 17. This text drew heavily upon the first-century manual on Roman agriculture *De Re Rustica* by Columella.

79 Rose, *Wine Trade*, p. 131.

80 *Wine, Beer and Ale, Together by the Ears* (1629). Although a later pamphlet, it expressed ideas found in medieval and classical literature on wine.

81 *Earliest Printed Book on Wine*, p. 41.

82 *Earliest Printed Book on Wine*, p. 41.

83 Geoffrey Chaucer, 'The Pardoners Tale', in *The Canterbury Tales*, trans. David Wright (2011), p. 331.

84 *Wine, Beer, Ale and Tobacco: Contending for Superiority: A Dialogue* (1658), p. 4.

85 David and Barbara Martin, 'The Winchelsea Cellars', in *New Winchelsea Sussex*, pp. 122–3.

86 On this episode, see C. Platt, *Medieval Southampton* (1973), p. 107; Peter Murphy, *The English Coast: A History and a Prospect* (2011), p. 141.

87 Norman Longmate, *Defending the Island: From Caesar to the Armada* (2001), p. 273. These are probably not the direct words of de la Cerda; his intention is extrapolated from two proclamations sent by Edward III to both of his archbishops, in his instructions to mobilise divine support. De la Cerda was the son of a Castilian prince. But he had grown up in France and his brutal acts of piracy against the English were directed by the French; he was richly rewarded with titles for his bellicosity at sea.

88 All the quotations below are from Froissart, *Chronicles of England, France, Spain, and the Adjoining Countries*, ed. Thomas Johnes, vol. 1 (1808), pp. 197–9. Some additional details are furnished by Longmate, *Defending*.

89 This would have been seen as valuable experience. 'A youth must have seen his blood flow and felt his cheek crack under the blow of his adversary,' wrote the chronicler and courtier Roger of Hoveden in the twelfth century (cited in John Marshall Carter, *Medieval Games: Sports and Recreations in Feudal Society* (1992), p. 32).

90 *Sussex Depicted: Views and Descriptions, 1600–1800*, Sussex Record Society, vol. 85 (2001), p. 337.

91 The arrival of the garrison doubled Winchelsea's population.

92 Daniel Defoe, *A Tour through the Whole Island of Great Britain*, ed. Pat Rodgers (1986), p. 146.

93 *The Diary and Correspondence of John Evelyn*, ed. John Forster (1854), p. 279.

94 *The Journal of the Rev. John Wesley*, ed. J. Kershaw (1827), p. 483.

95 Another resident was the writer Ford Madox Ford, who naturally featured Winchelsea in his *A History of the Cinque Ports* (1899) and married the daughter of a local doctor. He was Conrad's neighbour for a while too.

96 *Dante Gabriel Rossetti: His Family Letters, Vol. 2*, ed. William Michael Rossetti (1895), pp. 189–92. The letter, to his mother ('Antique'), was sent in 1866.

97 Graham Cushway, *Edward III and the War at Sea: The English Navy, 1327–1377* (2011), p. 171.

98 Longmate, *Defending*, p. 276.

99 Many of the disturbing details of this assault are recounted in Thomas of Walsingham's *Historia Anglicana*. See Dan Cruickshank, *Invasion: Defending Britain from Attack* (2001), and Cushway, *Edward III and the War at Sea*, p. 171. See also *Knighton's Chronicle: 1337–1396*, ed. G. H. Martin, pp. 174–5.

100 Cruickshank, *Invasion* , p. 29.

101 Cooper, *History of Winchelsea*, pp. 69, 91.

102 Quoted in Cruickshank, *Invasion*.

103 Knighton, *Chronicle*, p. 175: '. . . and they took away with them nine beautiful women from the town and violated them in a manner horrible to relate.'

104 The 1358 Schedule of Decayed Rents declares 184 properties as 'waste and uninhabited'. This also reflects the impact of earlier, less catastrophic raids.

105 Cruickshank, *Invasion*, p. 31.

106 This is from a letter patent dated 3 March 1384. *Calendar of the Patent Rolls Preserved in the Public Record Office: 1381–1385, Richard II*, vol. 2 (1897), pp. 425–6.

107 David and Barbara Martin, *New Winchelsea Sussex*, pp. 21–2. The Calendar of Patent Rolls reveals complaints against ballast dumping in the harbour, lodged in 1336 and 1357; see also another essay in the collection, Sylvester, 'Development of Winchelsea', p. 18. In 1400, Henry IV issued a proclamation against 'mariners both native and foreign . . . filling up and obstructing the channel of said port . . . with stones, sand and other ballast'. He set aside safe ballast-dumping grounds, which were ignored.

108 See, e.g., the 1548 Act renewing prohibitions against ballast dumping, which would not have been necessary if the previous ones had been heeded.

109 By 1433, the harbour could still accommodate vessels of up to 200 tonnes, but bigger and heavier vessels were very much at risk.

110 In 1400, international merchant vessels were present and Winchelsea was a major point of embarkation for pilgrims to Compostella. Not so by 1500.

111 Rye capitalised upon Winchelsea's decline by improving its water flow and stealing some of its rival's lost trade.

112 Coined by a local historian: Malcolm Pratt, *A Port of Stranded Pride* (1998).

113 David and Barbara Martin, *New Winchelsea Sussex*, pp. 101, 206; Cruickshank, *Invasion*, p. 31.

114 Roy Millward and Adrian Robinson, *South-East England: The Channel Coastlands Part Two* (1973), p. 165. That the state papers of 1587 feature an inquiry into Winchelsea show that its sad decline was of national concern.

115 Evelyn, *Diary and Correspondence*, p. 279.

116 Defoe, *Tour*, p. 146. New Winchelsea's story doesn't end here exactly. Its nineteenth- and twentieth-century history had distinctive chapters which, although nowhere near as dramatic as its medieval rise and fall, were nonetheless meaningful for the tiny population it had left, and for the local historians who have studied them in forensic detail since. The ancient port enjoyed a moderate economic revival during the early nineteenth century thanks to an influx of French refugees who set up weaving workshops in the old wine cellars. There, they cultivated flax and wove cambric, linen and lawn. Yet the rebirth of Winchelsea as an industrial centre was another false start; by 1810 the remaining weavers had repaired to Norwich, by then the epicentre of textile manufacturing in England. It ceased to be a rotten borough in 1832 and by the later nineteenth century, if it was renowned for anything, it was smuggling (David and Barbara Martin, *New Winchelsea Sussex*, pp. 18–25).

FOUR: THE DESERTED VILLAGE

1 This chapter offers a bird's-eye view of Britain at a time when much of its landmass degenerated into a shadowland. This is the focus as much as the individual abandoned settlement of Wharram Percy in Yorkshire.

2 The eighteenth-century vicarage is the fourth to stand on the site since the 1330s and the row of labourers' cottages dates from the nineteenth century.

3 Apart from my own impressions, my account of Wharram Percy has been informed by Stuart Wrathmell, ed., *A History of Wharram Percy and Its Neighbours* (Wharram Settlement Series) (2012), Simon Mays, ed., *The Churchyard* (Wharram Settlement Series)(2007); Philip Rahtz and L. Watts, eds, *The North Manor Area and North-West Enclosure* (Wharram Settlement Series) (2004). There is also a good general work co-authored by Maurice Beresford, the country's leading authority on deserted medieval villages: Maurice Beresford and John Hurst, *English Heritage Book of Wharram Percy, Deserted Medieval Village* (1990). For rather shorter guides which are more accessible to the non-specialist reader: Susan Wrathmell, *Wharram Percy, Yorkshire* (1996) and Alastair Oswald, *Wharram Percy: Deserted Medieval Village* (2013).

4 The relative dearth of villages in the South East during this period may be because of the resilience there of woodland (Nicholas Crane, *The Making of the British Landscape: From the Ice Age to the Present* (2016), p. 286).

5 Francis Pryor, *The Making of the British Landscape: How We Have Transformed the Land, from Prehistory to Today* (2010), p. 252. This was known as the champion system. See also Crane, *Landscape*, pp. 286–7.

6 Crane, *Landscape*, p. 286.

7 English Heritage have distilled decades of research into a lucid website that illuminates the topography of Wharram Percy: https://www.english-heritage.org.uk/visit/places/wharram-percy-deserted-medieval-village/history/description.

8 https://mercedesrochelle.com/wordpress/?p=1422.

9 See the surveys listed above, and the English Heritage entry on the history of Wharram Percy, at https://www.english-heritage.org.uk/visit/places/wharram-percy-deserted-medieval-village/history/#A16.

10 This phrase is from W. G. Sebald, *The Rings of Saturn*, trans. Michael Hulse (2002), p. 23.

11 Writing was only invented around 3400 BC. It's possible that earlier civilisations suffered worse outbreaks whose existence we know nothing of. And of course, since *Homo sapiens* has existed for, on recent estimates, at least five hundred thousand years, it is extraordinarily likely earlier natural disasters were even more deadly, per capita (the global population at the end of the last Ice Age is thought to have been no more than 10 million).

12 To put the horror in perspective, Covid-19 (in this age of modern medicine) has a mortality rate of around one per cent, compared to the medieval bubonic plague's 50 per cent, the pneumonic plague's 75 per cent, and septicaemic plague's 100 per cent. All were forms of the Black Death, although bubonic, being the first stage, was the most prevalent. Surviving manor records suggest that a death rate of between 40 and 60 per cent was common, and the highest proportion of manors experienced a death rate between 45 and 55 per cent. Of course, we have no way of knowing what the rate of infection was, so the 'mortality rate' essentially means how many people died rather than what proportion of those infected died. But if the pandemic did, as historians think, reduce England's population by half and the death rate was around 50 per cent, then this would mean virtually everyone must have been infected, which seems unlikely. It is telling, however, that multiple chroniclers mention that hardly anyone who caught the plague survived, and this suggests that the proportion of those infected who went on to die was potentially closer to 100 per cent than 50 per cent, just that only around half the population caught it. The picture is complicated by much historiography which extrapolates conclusions about the Black Death from late Victorian outbreaks of *Yersinia pestis*. But significant immunity may have built up by then, so what was true in the ninteteenth century was not necessarily true in the fourteenth. It is a conundrum. There are simply no clear answers. See especially John

Hatcher, *The Black Death: An Intimate History* (2008), p. 152.

13 The quotations from Agnolo di Tura, a Sienese chronicler, are from John Larner, *Italy in the Age of Dante and Petrarch, 1216–1380* (1980), p. 265.

14 Quoted in Philip Ziegler and Colin Platt, *The Black Death* (1998), p. 197. 'Woe is me of the shilling in the armpit,' he goes on to say. His classic account was first published in 1969 and has been much reprinted since for its clarity, concision and vivid drama.

15 Giovanni Boccaccio, *The Decameron; Or, Ten Days' Entertainment of Boc-caccio*, trans. Walter Keating Kelly (1867), p. 3. In this work, Boccaccio, a fourteenth-century Italian writer, set out 'a mournful remembrance of that most fatal plague, so terrible yet in the memories of us all'; it is one of the most harrowing first-hand accounts of the Pestilence in Europe. Some of the most detailed contemporary reports of the Black Death are written by European rather than British authors but, since it was the same disease, they warrant inclusion here.

16 *The Chronicle of Jean de Venette*, trans. Jean Birdsall, ed. Richard Newhall (1953), p. 49 (Jean de Venette, of peasant origin, was a French chronicler and Carmelite friar, recording events *c*.1340–68).

17 Boccaccio, *Decameron*, p. 3.

18 Boccaccio, *Decameron*, p. 6.

19 See Ole J. Benedictow's authoritative, magisterial and indeed enormous study *The Complete History of the Black Death* (2021), p. 111.

20 Hatcher, *Black Death*, p. 155. Hatcher offers a singular take on a much-studied subject by imaginatively interpolating scenarios, internal monologues and even dialogue from the unusually well-documented experiences of a village in Suffolk. Imaginative yet empirically grounded, it is in my view a successful attempt to go beyond the sources.

21 'They would swell beneath their armpits and in their groins, and fall over dead while talking' (Agnolo di Tura).

22 Benedict Gummer, *The Scourging Angel: The Black Death in the British Isles* (2014), p. 64.

23 'Nearly all died the third day from the first appearance of the symptoms' (Boccaccio, *Decameron*, p. 2).

24 Quoted and translated by Rosemary Horrox, *The Black Death* (1994), p. 81. The Oxfordshire clerk's chronicle spans 1303–56. Horrox is a useful source-book of key Black Death texts.

25 Quoted and translated by Horrox, *Black Death*, p. 76. Knighton was an Augustinian canon of Leicester who wrote his chronicle in the final years of his life, in the early 1390s.

26 This terrific image was conjured by the Florentine chronicler Marchionne di Coppo Stefani. Quoted in Chiara Frugoni, *A Day in a Medieval City*, trans. William McCuaig (2005), p. 69.

27 Gummer, *Scourging Angel*, p. 211.

28 Quoted in Horrox, *Black Death*, p. 70. William Dene captures the horror of the plague with some élan.

29 Boccaccio, *Decameron*, p. 5.

30 The Rochester chronicle (attributed to William Dene) observes that there was such a shortage of craftsmen and agricultural labourers that 'the humble turned up their noses at employment, and could scarcely be persuaded to serve the eminent unless for triple wages' (Horrox, *Black Death*, p. 70).

31 Quoted in Horrox, *Black Death*, pp. 76–7.

32 Although the Pestilence was generally attributed to God, people did consider what the instrument of his vengeance might be, and often, especially in cities, it was dogs and cats that got the blame and, accordingly, were slaughtered in great number.

33 The Rochester Chronicle, quoted in Francis Aidan Gasquet, *The Great Pestilence, Now Commonly Known as the Black Death* (1893), p. 107.

34 For an imagined physical journey through London during a later plague visitation (for which there is much more source material), see Matthew Green, *London: A Travel Guide Through Time* (2016), pp. 161–241.

35 Horrox, *Black Death*, pp. 33, 78, 127.

36 This was the church tower at Ashwell. One of the inscriptions, scratched into the inner wall of the tower, can be translated from the Latin as: '1350, miserable, wild and distracted, violent the dregs of people alone survive to witness'. David Short, *Guide to St Mary's, Ashwell* (n.d.), p. 11. There is a later description from 1361 which mentions a tempest the parishioners perhaps understood as clearing the air of plague. See also Richard Muir, *The New Reading the Landscape: Fieldwork in Landscape History* (2000), p. 40.

37 William M. Bowsky, *The Black Death: A Turning Point in History?* (1971), p. 14.

38 *The Chronicle of Richard of Devizes Concerning the Deeds of Richard the First* (1841), p. 60.

39 In October 1348, the Bishop of Winchester wrote of 'a multitude of sins' – stemming from, yet surpassing original sin – 'which have provoked the divine anger, by a just judgement, to this revenge.' Quoted in Horrox, *Black Death*, p. 118.

40 These questions are based on surviving medieval sermons that take the form of a dialogue between the priest and his parishioners. See Hatcher, *Black Death*, pp. 160–2; Gerald Owst, *Preaching in Medieval England: An Introduction to Sermon Manuscripts of the Period, c.1350–1450* (1926).

41 For this section on death and burial, I am indebted to Gummer, *Scourging Angel;* Anu Lahtinen and Mia Korpiola, eds, *Dying Prepared in Medieval and Early Modern Northern Europe* (2017); Christopher Daniell, *Death and Burial in Medieval England 1066–1550* (2005).

42 *The Medieval Book of Birds: Hugh of Fouilloy's Aviarum*, ed. and trans. W. B. Clarke (1992), p. 117.

43 The English version of the ballad, 'The Three Ravens', was first written down

in 1611; the Scottish version, 'The Twa Corbies' was recorded later, in Walter Scott's *Minstrelsy of the Scottish Border* (1849). But both existed in oral form long before this, and may well have been contemporaneous with the Black Death.

44 This section is indebted to Boria Sax, *Crow* (2003) and Thom van Dooren, *Vulture* (2014).

45 Sax, *Crow*, pp. 52, 71.

46 For this discussion of edibility I have drawn upon the ideas of Val Plumwood, *The Eye of the Crocodile* (2012), and Buddhist thought more generally. Plumwood developed much of her philosophy of edibility after nearly being eaten by a crocodile.

47 *Paradise Lost*, X, 276–8.

48 https://www.sciencedirect.com/science/article/pii/S2352409X1630791X.

49 Quoted in Scott Waugh, *England in the Reign of Edward III* (1991), p. 85.

50 Richard Muir, *The Lost Villages of Britain* (1982, updated 2009), p. 118.

51 The examples below are cherry-picked from Muir, *Lost Villages*; W. G. Hoskins, *Making of the English Landscape* (1955); Crane, *Landscape*; Pryor, *Landscape*; Henry Buckton, *The Lost Villages: In Search of Britain's Vanished Communities* (2008); and, above all, Maurice Beresford, *The Lost Villages of England* (1954).

52 See Muir, *Lost Villages*, pp. 130–2 (and 2009 edn, pp. 104–13); Crane, *Landscape*, pp. 329–31; Keith Allison, Maurice Beresford, John Hurst, *The Deserted Villages of Northamptonshire* (1966); Keith Allison, Maurice Beresford, John Hurst, *The Deserted Villages of Oxfordshire* (1965); W. G. Hoskins, *Essays in Leicestershire History* (1950); *Deserted Medieval Villages: Studies*, ed. Maurice Beresford and John Hurst (1989). English Heritage's website has details on many of the villages lost to the plague.

53 A messuage is a medieval term for a dwelling place along with its land and subsidiary buildings.

54 See, for example, this highly mendacious *Guardian* article which claims the Black Death and subsequent plague epidemics were responsible for 'most of' Britain's ghost towns and vanished villages, especially in Suffolk and Norfolk. It is riddled with factual errors. https://www.theguardian.com/travel/2020/may/23/historic-ghost-villages-tyneham-dunwich-imber.

55 Tellingly, the singular form in English is the same as the plural; branding someone a 'sheep' is to say they mindlessly follow the crowd. But away from the individualist West, sheep are considered creatures of vast mental acuity. See Alan Butler, *Sheep: The Remarkable Story of the Humble Animal that Built the Modern World* (2010); Phillip Armstrong, *Sheep* (2016); Thomas More, *Utopia* (1516).

56 The experiments were carried out at the University of Cambridge. In one, scientists showed a sample of rams and ewes fifty photographs of sheep faces, aligned to various food rewards, and observed that all could identify all

fifty faces with 80 per cent accuracy, even two years later (Armstrong, *Sheep*).

57 Ole J. Benedictow, *The Black Death, 1346–1353: The Complete History* (2004), p. 383.

58 Virtually all the authorities on the Black Death highlight this phenomenon. See John Hatcher, 'The Aftermath of the Black Death', *Past & Present*, 144/1 (Aug. 1994), pp. 13–19, 20–3. Langland describes how, in the later fourteenth century, labourers began to demand hearty chunks of meat, fried fish, delicious wheat bread and fine ale rather than the vegetable slop, coarse bread and cheap ale which had been the more common repast earlier in the century (*Piers Plowman*, ed. Attwater, p. 58).

59 The phenomenon was somewhat offset by inflation. Gummer, *Scourging Angel*, pp. 283–4, 344, 371.

60 Those who remained in Wharram Percy had better holdings, more land and were generally more prosperous.

61 I am indebted to the argument laid out by Alastair Oswald. https://www.english-heritage.org.uk/visit/places/wharram-percy-deserted-medieval-village/history/.

62 At this time, the Parliament sat in Coventry.

63 John Rous, *Historia Regum Angliae*: E Codice MS in Bibliotheca Bodlejana (1745), p. 121. I am extremely grateful to Edward Thicknesse for translating the medieval Latin text for me, a good eighteenth-century edition of which is online: https://archive.org/details/joannisrossiantoorousgoog/page/n7/mode/2up?view=theater. All of the translated quotations are taken from the invective-filled digression on pp. 113–23.

64 Rous, *Historia Regum Angliae*, pp. 115–16.

65 Landowners suspected of enclosing their lands and driving out their tenants were called up before a jury and subjected to interrogation. Since they employed a range of ingenious ways of obfuscating, or prevaricating, or simply by just lying, e.g. by blaming the gutted population upon earlier outbreaks of the plague, the inquiry had little effect on checking the shift from arable to pasture.

66 Royal Historical Society, *The Domesday of Inclosures 1517–18* (1897), pp. 431–2.

67 This section draws upon some of the specialist works on Wharram Percy listed at the start of this chapter's notes.

FIVE: THE CITY THAT FELL OFF A CLIFF

1 *Daily Chronicle*, 8 April 1904. The journalist who wrote 'The Death of a City' (whose vivid imagery inspired some of the opening of the chapter) recalls finding a skull of one of Dunwich's former residents on the beach. Following a little landslide, they count 'a score of fragments of human limbs, there a thigh bone, there a part of a pelvis, and there, perched on a mound of earth and masonry, a broken, toothless skull'.

2 Between the late eighteenth century and Victorian period, the church of All Saints was occasionally used for christenings, weddings and funerals. The chronology of Dunwich's decline and fall is soberly yet effectively rendered in Nicholas Comfort, *The Lost City of Dunwich* (1994).

3 Allan Jobson, *Suffolk Miscellany* (1975), p. 164; Comfort, *Dunwich*, p. 99.

4 *The Life and Letters of Charles Samuel Keene*, ed. George Somes Layard (1892), pp. 232–4.

5 Henry James, *English Hours* (1905), pp. 320–30. All the quotations below are taken from this wonderful piece of writing on the 'desolate seaport' of Dunwich.

6 See p. 116. Defoe visited Dunwich too, noting how it is supposed to have had fifty churches in its prime when it was 'equal to a large city' but describing it by the 1720s as 'eaten up by the sea . . . and the still encroaching ocean seems to threaten it with a fatal immersion in a few years more'. Daniel Defoe, *A Tour through the Whole Island of Great Britain*, ed. Pat Rodgers (1986), pp. 80–2.

7 Edwards believed that everyone should carry a set of dominoes at all times to alleviate the pressure of having to make conversation all the time.

8 FitzGerald to C. E. Norton, 21 Aug. 1877, in *Letters of Edward FitzGerald*, vol. 2 (1894), p. 223.

9 FitzGerald to C. E. Norton, 28 Oct. 1877, in *Letters* (1894), p. 229.

10 FitzGerald to C. E. Norton, 2 July 1878, in *Letters* (1894), p. 253.

11 FitzGerald to J. R. Lowell, 28 Feb. 1878, in *Letters* (1894), p. 235.

12 FitzGerald to S. Laurence, 22 Sept. 1879, in *Letters and Literary Remains of Edward FitzGerald*, ed. William Aldis Wright, vol. 1 (1889), p. 447.

13 FitzGerald in a letter to Wright, *Letters* (1889), p. 447, note.

14 *The Life of Edward FitzGerald*, ed. Alfred McKinley Terhune (1947), p. 337.

15 Keene to Joseph Crawhall, 27 Aug. 1877, in *The Life and Letters of Charles Samuel Keene*, ed. George Somes Layard (1893), p. 257.

16 Keene to Joseph Crawhall, 20 Aug. 1878, *Life and Letters*, p. 273.

17 Keene to Crawhill, 27 Aug. 1877, *Life and Letters*, p. 257.

18 Keene, *Life and Letters*, p. 94.

19 There is a debate on this point, but to my mind the weight of the evidence suggests he was from Dunwich: Day owned a house in Dunwich later in his life (see below), left a bequest to St Peter's in his will, had strong connections with Norwich, and, in my view, it was he who commissioned an incredibly detailed report from one of the country's leading topographers as described below. Nicholas Comfort, who has written an authoritative account of Dunwich, is in no doubt Day was one of its denizens. See also the following scholarly monographs: Christina Garrett, *The Marian Exiles: A Study in the Origins of Elizabethan Puritanism* (2010), p. 142; James Raven, an authority on the history of the English book trade, says that Day 'came from Dunwich' in *The Business of Books: Booksellers and the English Book Trade 1450–1850*

(2007), p. 359; and John King, who contributed the essay 'John Day: Master Printer of the English Reformation' to Peter Marshall and Alec Ryrie, eds, *The Beginnings of English Protestantism* (2002), accepts the tradition, referring to 'Day's hometown of Dunwich' (p. 186). Even if he was not born there, he had strong ties to the vanishing city. Other scholars are more circumspect. Andrew Pettegree, Professor of History at the University of St Andrews, states that his subject 'may have been born in Dunwich' (*ODNB*). Elizabeth Evenden, however, who has written a PhD and monograph on Day, is much more critical of Day's Dunwich birth tradition, pointing out that the parish records of St Peter's in Dunwich have not survived and that his name does not appear in the local subsidy returns from 1549–1600, though there could have been good reasons for this, and taxation assessments are far from perfect, as we have seen in Trellech (Elizabeth Evenden, *Patents, Pictures and Patronage: John Day and the Tudor Book Trade* (2016), pp. 3–4, 145).

20 Details of John Stow's biography are taken from Comfort, *Dunwich*, pp. 142–4; A. Pettegree, 'Day [Daye], John (1521/2–1584)', *ODNB*. Christopher Oastler, *John Day, The Elizabethan Printer* (1975); *The Unabridged Acts and Monuments Online* or *TAMO* (HRI Online Publications, Sheffield, 2011) (featuring the unabridged texts of the four editions of the *Book of Martyrs* in 1563, 1570, 1576 and 1583), http//www.johnfoxe.org; and the older books on Dunwich, cited above.

21 Walberswick, for example, began trading extensively with Ipswich and Lincoln around 1500.

22 In 1552, the Lord Mayor of London, Sir George Barne, purchased some dissolved monastic land in the borough of Dunwich (his descendants would remain major landowners, dominating Dunwich's politics in later centuries).

23 Francis Blomefield, *An Essay Towards a Topographical History of the County of Norfolk*, vol. 3 (1806), p. 295; Comfort, *Dunwich*, p. 144.

24 Derek Wilson, *A Short History of Suffolk* (1977), p. 99.

25 'A Letter to John Dee describing the destruction of Dunwich by the sea in 1573', British Library Harley MS. 532, ff. 53v–60r, https://www.bl.uk/manuscripts/Viewer.aspx?ref=harley_ms_532_f053v. The quotes below are taken from this wonderful source.

26 Alfred Suckling, who published a full transcription of the manuscript now in the British Library, in *The History and Antiquities of the County of Suffolk: With Genealogical and Architectural Notices of Its Several Towns and Villages* (1846), pp. 245–52, claims it was probably written by John Stow, and later historians have largely accepted this. See, for example, Elizabeth Evenden, 'Patents and Patronage: The Life and Career of John Day, Tudor Printer' (PhD thesis, University of York), p. 24.

27 *The Annales, or Generall Chronicle of England Begun First by Maister John Stow, and After Him Continued and Augmented with Matters Forreyne, and Domestique, Anncient and Moderne, Unto the End of His Present Yeere 1614*

(1615), pp. 62–3. He writes: 'The common fame, and report of the inhabitants is, that before the town came to decay there belonged thereunto two and fifty divine houses . . . But certain it is, as appears by manifest and sound record which I have seen . . . four . . . parish churches are now swallowed up in the sea, and but two of them remaining on land . . . Saint Peter's and All Saints.'

28 Contrary to what many historians claim, this transportive section does not appear in the manuscript letter. It is an extract from Stow's chronicles. Quoted in Suckling, *History and Antiquities of the County of Suffolk*, p. 73.

29 'A Description of the town of Dunwich [co. Suffolk] and of the coins in King Athelstan's time, AD 924, continued down to 31 Aug. 1590', British Library, Add. MS. 23963.

30 For this section on the cultural impact of the Dissolution and rise of anti-quarianism in Britain, I am indebted to the rich and diverse collection of essays published by the British Library: Dale Townshend, Michael Carter and Peter Lindfield, eds, *Writing Britain's Ruins* (2017); and William Viney, *Waste: A Philosophy of Things* (2014).

31 John Bale, a Carmelite monk who transmogrified into a hot Protestant reformer (Michael Carter, 'Introduction: The Making of Britain's Ruins: Monasteries and Castles, 1536–1650' in *Writing Britain's Ruins*, p. 13).

32 The artist, cleric and author William Gilpin conceived of the picturesque in terms of landscape as 'that kind of beauty which is agreeable in a picture'; it was later often set up as the 'rustic' third to the terrors of the sublime land-scape and the pleasures of the classically beautiful.

33 Dale Townshend, 'The Aesthetics of Ruin', in *Writing Britain's Ruins*, p. 100. He defines ruin poetry as 'topographical poems written in, about and to ruined Gothic piles across the British landscape'. This he describes as a dis-tinctive sub-genre in eighteenth-century verse. It drew upon and developed earlier traditions; note Shakespeare's reference to 'unswept stone besmeared by sluttish time' in Sonnet 55.

34 *Ichnographia Rustica; or, The Nobleman, Gentleman, and Gardener's Recreation* (1718).

35 Addison penned an essay as far back as 1712 arguing that architecture built on a grand scale opens 'the mind to vast conceptions, and fit it to converse with the divinity of the place. For every thing that is majestic imprints an awfulness and reverence on the mind of the beholder, and strikes in with the natural greatness of the soul' – but he thought classical structures did this better than the Gothic. 'On the Pleasures of the Imagination, Paper V', *The Spectator*, 26 June 1712; collected 1841, p. 475.

36 William Gilpin, *Three Essays: On Picturesque Beauty; On Picturesque Travel; and On Sketching Landscape* (1794), p. 46.

37 Townshend, 'The Aesthetics of Ruin', p. 88. See, for example, Alexander Gerard, *An Essay on Taste* (1759), p. 127.

38 Henry James, *Foreign Parts* (1883), p. 126.

39 In a letter to a childhood friend. Quoted in Christopher Woodward, *In Ruins* (2002), pp. 72–3.

40 This is from Ann Rae Jonas's poem 'Structures', in *A Diamond Is Hard But Not Tough* (Washington, DC, 1998).

41 For this section on the philosophy of ruin, as well as thoughts that have been incubating in my mind for years, I am indebted to Midas Dekkers, *The Way of All Flesh: A Celebration of Decay*, trans. Sherry Marx-Macdonald (2000); Dylan Trigg, *The Aesthetics of Decay: Nothingness, Nostalgia and the Absence of Reason* (2006); Viney, *Waste*; Woodward, *In Ruins*.

42 Viney, *Waste*, p. 129.

43 Quoted in Joan Evans, *A History of the Society of Antiquaries* (1956), p. 156.

44 Dekkers, *The Way of All Flesh*, ch. 2.

45 Adrian Harding, Annick Duperray and Dennis Tredy, eds, *Henry James's Europe: Heritage and Transfer* (2011), p. 113.

46 Trigg, *Aesthetics of Decay*, pp. 57–8.

47 'To delight in the aspects of sentient ruin might appear a heartless pastime, and the pleasure, I confess, shows the note of perversity.' Quoted in Harding et al., *James's Europe*, p. 113.

48 Rainer Maria Rilke, 'The First Elegy', in *The Duino Elegies* (1923). Trans. A. S. Kline, *The Poetry of Rainer Maria Rilke* (2015).

49 *Don Juan*, Canto X, 61. Byron was of course a hugely influential figure in the European Romanticism that so revered ruins as a source of poetic inspiration.

50 Joseph Heely, *Letters on the Beauties of Hagley, Envil and the Leasowes*, 2 vols (1777), i, pp. 172–3.

51 Jean and Stuart Bacon, *Dunwich, Suffolk* (1988) focuses in particular on the underwater exploration of Dunwich. See also Jean and Stuart Bacon, *The Search for Dunwich, City Under the Sea* (1979); D. A. Sear, and others, 'Cartographic, Geophysical and Diver Surveys of the Medieval Town Site at Dunwich, Suffolk, England', *International Journal of Nautical Archaeology*, 40/1 (2011), pp. 113–32; the Underwater Dunwich project, led by Professor David Sear from the University of Southampton, http://www.touchingthetide. uk/our-projects/underwater-dunwich.

SIX: THE ABANDONED ISLAND

1 Tom Steel, *The Life and Death of St Kilda* (1988), p. 25 (these mournful words were spoken by Finlay MacQueen, nearly seventy years of age, to a much younger man, Neil Gillies). Originally published in 1975, Steel's *Life and Death* remains the classic work on St Kilda, even though revisionist historians have recently challenged some of Steel's arguments and themes, in particular the idea that the Kildans were forever involved in a

'battle against nature' which, eventually, they lost.

2 All quotations from Martin Martin in this chapter are from *A Voyage to St Kilda*, 1698.

3 All quotations from Kenneth Macaulay in this chapter are from *The History of St Kilda* (1764).

4 All quotations from E. D. Clarke in this chapter are from *The Life and Remains of Edward Daniel Clarke*, ed. William Otter (1824). Clarke's voyage to St Kilda was a highlight of his tour of certain Scottish islands.

5 This time around there was a much bigger, more socially diverse audience to read about and debate newly discovered societies following the final lapsing of pre-publication censorship in England and Wales in 1695 (fifteen years later in Scotland) and ensuing eruption of print that triggered a news mania in coffee-houses, taverns and elsewhere.

6 Joseph-Marie Degérando, *The Observation of Savage Peoples*, trans. F. C. T. Moore (1969) [Fr. orig. *Considerations sur les diverses méthodes à suivre dans l'observation des peuples sauvages* (1800)], p. 63.

7 French thinkers, known as *philosophes*, embraced the concept of philosophical time travel with especial gusto as it promised to reveal humankind in its true colours, beneath the twin evils of Catholicism and an unenlightened monarchy.

8 *Diderot: Political Writings*, ed. John Hope Mason and Robert Wokler (1992), p. 40.

9 Alexander Buchan, *A Description of St Kilda* (1741). A Molucca bean is a drift seed from Caribbean vines, transported by the Gulf Stream to Britain.

10 The cake analogy is Clarke's.

11 The *OED* records an instance of 'a salvage cherry' from 1697!

12 John Ashley Cooper, *An Inquiry Concerning Virtue* (1699), p. 127. The very similar idea of 'natural morality' was advocated by the German thinker Christian Wolff, who controversially praised Chinese morality. Like so many of the *philosophes* he wasn't really interested in an empirical study of Chinese culture, more in a 'universal morality that derived its authority from the idea of a shared, universal humanity, rather than from scripture or divine command' (Anthony Pagden, *The Enlightenment and Why It Still Matters* (2013), p. 280).

13 In one of his most controversial conclusions, Shaftesbury argued that Christianity was *not*, contrary to what had been taught for over a millennium, the ultimate source of morality; nor were humans, as the Bible would have us believe, born sinful and in need of redemption.

14 The quotes are from Martin and Clarke. In one of the accounts, the island's missionary concedes he had been half-worried that they might have been French or Spanish pirates. Also Clarke reports that the minister was 'a little alarmed, thinking you might probably belong to some privateer'.

15 Even though they don't seem sequestered in a way that we might associate

with an island mentality, the islanders do seem reasonably attuned to the wider world: pace Clarke's claim in 1797 that the inhabitants had no idea their island had been written about before – by either Macaulay or Martin. He also says they have no books, but this seems unlikely given the presence of the minister.

16 The quotations in this paragraph are from Clarke, Martin, Macaulay and Clarke again respectively.

17 Hirtans were strangers to sugar and honey.

18 This is Clarke's account. It has the whiff of farcical exaggeration, but may be entirely true. We just don't know.

19 Martin is very keen to present Hirta as treeless. He tells, at some length, an anecdote about the utter stupefaction of the few islanders who make it to the mainland when they see trees. Most historians of St Kilda corroborate the idea that the islands were completely treeless, unlike Skara Brae where there *had* once been trees. However there is a curious passage in Macaulay's 'Story of St Kilda' in which he claims trees once grew on the hill, but had, by 1765, fallen off and now lie buried in the sea.

20 Kenneth Macaulay tells us that 'every St Kildan has his share of them, in proportion to the extent of land he possesses, or the rent he pays to the steward'.

21 Kenneth Macaulay tells us, disdainfully, in 1764.

22 The figure of 'thirty or thirty-two families' is cited by Alexander Buchan in 1741. But note that Clarke, in 1797, mentioned one hundred people divided in twenty-two families of, on average, six people.

23 The descriptions in this paragraph are from both Martin and Macaulay.

24 Clarke tells how ashes from the peat fire are smeared over the floor, diluted, covered with heather, mulched together and preserved for manure.

25 Clarke considers fulmar broth the principal food, while acknowledging the supplementary role of the carcasses and eggs of gannets.

26 Descriptions in this paragraph are from Clarke, Macaulay and Martin respectively.

27 This is from Clarke, who mentions that the minister has, over ten years, passed on a slight knowledge of English to 'a few' of the inhabitants. The point about husbanded animals comes from Buchan, *Description*. Ministers brought their families with them. In 1797, the minister, or 'King of the Island' as he was sometimes known, lived in the manse with his wife, mother and three children.

28 It seems plausible that the islanders (at least those who could speak English or Gaelic that was intelligible to the travellers) might point out features of their economy, land ownership and absentee government, but one cannot readily imagine them volunteering that they never murdered anyone or committed fornication or adultery.

29 Buchan, *Description*.

30 Like, supposedly, the Haitians, like the tribes of the Orinoco, like the Amerindians, they had 'natural morality'.

31 This is highlighted by Martin in 1698 as 'an ancient custom delivered down
from them by their ancestors' and in the mid-eighteenth century by Kenneth
Macaulay, who describes them as devout. Indeed they were to become even
more so in the decades and centuries ahead.

32 This is Macaulay. Since he was a proselytiser from the Society for Propagat-
ing Christian Knowledge, the degree to which they had turned their backs
on the ancient gods may have been exaggerated.

33 So fearful were they of this faceless god that anyone who tried, as missionaries and ministers wanted, to turn the field to farming could expect to pay a
very high price indeed, Macaulay darkly suggests.

34 This is from Martin, who also commented in 1698 that they believed that 'all
events, whether good or bad, are predetermined by God'.

35 Buchan, *Description*, p. 34. The minister claims he has rid the Hirtans of this
'foolish' and 'superstitious' practice.

36 Dunvegan, a village in the north-west of the Isle of Skye where the
MacLeods had their ancestral castle. The MacLeods of Skye were distinct
from the clan's other branch, the MacLeods of Lewis, who had lost their
land to rival clan the Mackenzies in the seventeenth century. Both branches
claim descent from Leòd, a Highland warlord who lived in the thirteenth
century.

37 The political arrangement was not necessarily a burning grievance for the
islanders themselves; the islanders did rely upon the officer, the factor and
the laird, and they were not necessarily always as unwelcome as the writers
would have us believe.

38 The grievousness of the taxes goes some way towards morally exculpating
the islanders for their deceit, in Macaulay's view.

39 Relations were certainly not always cordial. Kenneth Macaulay reports that
the steward has the potential, as in times past, to act in a tyrannical way. But
he is rather vague on the specifics.

40 Clarke, in 1797, paints a starker and certainly exaggerated picture, describing
the 'rapacious avarice of distant tacksmen, who have nothing more to do
with their island, than to visit it once or twice a year to plunder the inhabitants of every thing they possess'.

41 This wonderful phrase is Macaulay's.

42 This is an amalgamation of Martin, Macaulay and Clarke's accounts.

43 *De Orbo Novo*, trans. Francis Augustus MacNutt (1912), vol. 1, p. 135.

44 This is contradicted by Clarke who tells us they didn't eat salt.

45 The descriptions in this paragraph are from Martin, Macaulay and Buchan.
Macaulay reckoned that St Kilda's fleet of sheep were the 'bedrock of their
riches' but this seems rather a misguided impression given their relatively
low numbers and the lack of opportunities to trade livestock.

46 Macaulay recalls how there was more fertile ground in the north-west of the island which the factor compelled them to sow, but the experiment was unsuccessful, and in any case the islanders preferred to keep the grass for cattle. According to him, cultivating more crops 'would contribute very little to the happiness of the St Kildans'.

47 According to Martin and Macaulay.

48 Most trade, at this stage, was usually an adjunct of the philosophical sightseeing voyages.

49 Buchan, *Description*, pp. 20–1.

50 The *philosophes* wanted to recast civilisation to mould better human beings; they did not wish to do away with it altogether.

51 For instance, see Daniel Defoe's *Robinson Crusoe* (1719), Baron de Montesquieu's *Persian Letters* (1721), Voltaire's *Candide* (1759) and Jonathan Swift's *Gulliver's Travels* (1726), in which Swift's Houyhnhnms – horses with luminous intelligence – are so superior to the bestial Yahoos (humans) that the narrator, returning home, cannot bear to speak to his own kind.

52 Jean-Jacques Rousseau, *A Discourse upon the Origin and Foundation of the Inequality among Mankind* (London, 1761) [translator unknown], p. xlix.

53 Buchan, *Description*. It was at the discretion of the factor whether these punishments were actually carried out or not.

54 Madeleine Bunting, *Love of Country: A Journey through the Hebrides* (2017), p. 269. The museum is on the island of South Uist.

55 Far-off worlds could be distorting mirrors. In his notebooks, Captain Cook observed how Tahitians would routinely smother illegitimate children; in the published version, however, this is purposefully omitted to make their conduct seem more palatable. James Cook, *Journal: First Voyage* (1893), p. 95.

56 *Supplément au Voyage de Bougainville* (1776) in *Diderot: Political Writings*, ed. and trans. Mason and Wokler, p. 71.

57 The direct quotes are Diderot, from Pagden, *Enlightenment*, p. 201. Rousseau wrote of 'fatal enlightenment' in *Discourse upon Inequality*.

58 Women's fowling was limited to hunting puffin with dogs far away from the clifftops.

59 This is an amalgamation of Macaulay and Clarke's accounts.

60 These devilish black birds were known as scrabers on St Kilda, according to Martin.

61 Quoted in Pagden, *Enlightenment*, p. 204. 'That the savage state is preferable to the civilized state,' Diderot went on to write, 'that I deny!'

62 'An unpolluted, harmless infant world' was how Montaigne described the New World, 'ruined through our justice, discipline and magnanimity'.

63 Dorinda Outram, *The Enlightenment* (2019), p. 68.

64 Diderot, '*Supplément*', pp. 41–2.

65 Diderot, '*Supplément*', p. 42.

66 This sales pitch is blended from various postcards, handbills and newspaper

advertisements promoting cruises to St Kilda on, for example, the SS *Hebrides* and *Dunara Castle*. See, for examples, Bob Charnley, *Last Greetings from St Kilda* (1989), pp. 14–20.

67 All quotations taken from *St Kilda and the St Kildians* (1887).

68 Norman Heathcote, *St Kilda* (1900), p. 70.

69 The miserable minister was called John MacKay. According to Connell, he excommunicated people for falling asleep in church and insisted that absolutely nothing be done on the Sabbath, nor on Wednesday evening prayer night.

70 Their houses were rebuilt by a progressive proprietor in the 1860s, 'certainly a long way in advance of the average crofter's house in the West Highlands', in Connell's view.

71 An official register had been kept on the island for the thirty years since Connell visited in 1887 (Connell, *St Kilda*, p. 107).

72 Bob Charnley collected more than five thousand Hebridean postcards and photographs, including seventy from St Kilda. He published many of these in a mesmerising little book, now very hard to find, called *Last Greetings from St Kilda* (1989). This is the main source material for this section, although there are many more photographs and postcards of late nineteenth-century and early twentieth-century St Kilda to be found online, with new ones occasionally surfacing.

73 The Fairy Cave or House of the Fairies was an earth house of considerable antiquity, believed by former generations of Hirtans to have been populated by magical beings. In the nineteenth century it became a must-see for archaeologists and many tourists (Charnley, *Last Greetings*, p. 47).

74 *Guardian*, 29 Aug. 2009.

75 Steel, *Life and Death*, p. 194–5.

76 Steel, *Life and Death*, p. 193, 195.

SEVEN: THE GHOST OUTPOSTS OF NORFOLK

1 These are from the hand-written words of a note pinned to the church door by one of the departing residents, Evelyn Bond. The note begs the army to treat the church and homes 'where many of us have lived for generations' with care in the interregnum. 'We shall return one day,' it concludes, 'and thank you for treating the village kindly.' Neither came to pass. Patrick Wright, *The Village that Died for England: The Strange Story of Tyneham* (1995), p. 210.

2 Since the ghost villages of STANTA have hardly ever been written about in any kind of detail (quite the opposite of St Kilda), this chapter is based primarily upon archival research, primarily in the National Archives (TNA) and Norfolk Record Office (NRO), and my first-hand experience of touring the training area. However, monographs do exist on certain of Britain's other

villages commandeered by the military in the Second World War, never to be returned, some vivid. On Imber on Salisbury Plain in Wiltshire, see Rex Sawyer, *Little Imber on the Down: Salisbury Plain's Ghost Village* (2010) and an especially poignant book on Tyneham in Dorset, mentioned above, Wright, *Village that Died*. See also Bridgett Elliott, *A 1940s Childhood in Breckland and Norwich* (privately published, 2012; a copy can be found in the Norfolk Records Office). In more general books on the military takeover of the land, cited below, the abandoned villages of the Stanford Training Area are only briefly if at all mentioned.

3 There are a few studies of the STANTA villages, but they are rather limited in detail and scope: *Stanford Battle Area* [assorted authors] (1979), much of which deals with animals and plants; Hilda and Edmund Perry, *Tottington: A Lost Village in Norfolk* (1999), useful for its detail and narrative thrust, yet inimically partisan, even histrionic, in some regards (comparing the military takeover of Tottington, and the other STANTA villages, to 'a lesser version of what the Nazis and Soviets did').

4 References to this fabled 'Nazi village in Norfolk' can be found in the *Daily Telegraph*, 1 May 2009; *Independent*, 11 March 2010; Sadia Qureshi, *Peoples on Parade: Exhibitions, Empire, and Anthropology in Nineteenth-century Britain* (2011), p. 281.

5 This is not to say the Ministry of Defence was being deliberately obfuscatory. Part of the problem was that it took a long time to get through to the right person.

6 I am very grateful to my very genial and generous military consort, who had a near-encyclopaedic knowledge of the UK Defence Training Estate, for an extremely enlightening, and moving, tour of STANTA, beginning at West Tofts Camp, Thetford. Some of what follows comes from our discussions.

7 They are listed from west to east. Of these, Buckenham Tofts and Sturston were technically hamlets.

8 The minutes of a meeting from April 1952, for instance, show that a staggering 2,663 rabbits were killed in the first three weeks of March by the nine warreners employed by the Ministry of Agriculture to combat the burrowing menace. TNA MAF 147/97. The rabbits were generally confined in expansive warrens (the area has the highest concentration of medieval warrens in Britain) with perimeter banks of up to two metres high. Whereas they had once been sold for meat and fur, now they were eradicated so that the new trees planted by the Forestry Commission to address the nation's dearth of timber would not be undermined (*The Warrens of Breckland: A Survey by the Breckland Society* (2010), http://www.brecsoc.org.uk/breckland_warrens%20 FINAL.pdf, pp. 55–6).

9 The village appears in the Domesday Book of 1086 as 'Totintune' (probably 'estate associated with a man called Totta').

10 All the quotations on this page are from the War Office documents on the

Battle Training Areas, 1942–3. TNA WO 199/808.

11 WO 199/808 (in particular the secret letter from the Under Secretary of State); NRO AUD 1/1/7. This wallet of documents in the Norfolk Record Office is described as a transcription of two BBC Norfolk reports on the Stanford Battle Area, broadcast in 1985 and 1990, but it consists primarily of press cuttings and copies of private correspondence.

12 In a secret letter written in May 1942, the Under Secretary State at the War Office declared 'After careful consideration . . . I have decided to apply for large areas of land to be requisitioned under D.R. 51, completely evacuated by the civil population and made available to the army for battle training.' WO 199/808.

13 This was described as 'an elaborate procedure to mollify the inhabitants' by the Minister for Home Security. See O'Donnell, 'Breckland Exodus: The Forced Evacuation of the Norfolk Battle Area 1942', https://www.bbc.co.uk/history/ww2peopleswar/stories/62/a3258362.shtml.

14 O'Donnell, 'Breckland Exodus'.

15 In an email dated 4 Jan. 2019, my guide told me that the banished believed, as they left, that they could return after the war and yet no one in the military ever made such a promise.

16 TNA HO 207/1183.

17 Letter entitled 'Stanford Battle Area', *The Times*, 2 June 1947. This was from Lord Cranbrook, the deputy regional commissioner for Eastern England, who accompanied General Anderson, the GOC-in-Charge Eastern Command, to the fateful meeting that day. link.gale.com/apps/doc/CS85542082/TTDA?u=oxfshlib&sid=bookmark-TTDA&xid=63616134. Accessed 3 July 2021.

18 NRO AUD 1/1/7. This richly informative file in the Norfolk Records Office contains press cuttings relating to the Stanford Battle Area. The note pinned to Mr Griffin's door comes from the *Eastern Daily Press*, accompanied by a striking photograph.

19 MAF 147/97. A letter dated 26 Oct. 1955 from D. Heathcoat Amory to a Breckland resident confirms, 'It was essential in the interests of national security that the battle training area itself, together with the two assembly areas, should be retained by the WO for training purposes.'

20 NRO AUD 1/1/17.

21 NRO AUD 1/1/17. Often these articles exist as press cuttings without a title, so it has not always been possible to identify the particular newspaper, though the one featured most frequently is the *Eastern Daily Press*.

22 *Thetford and Watton Times*, 31 May 1947.

23 *Daily Express*, 20 Aug. 1947.

24 WO 199/808.

25 13 December 1986. AUD 1/1/17.

26 On Lucilla Reeve, see Hilda and Edmund Perry, *Tottington: A Lost Village in*

Norfolk (1999), pp. 260–5; Brian Short, *The Battle of the Fields: Rural Community and Authority in Britain during the Second World War* (2014), p. 192; and Reeve's autobiographical writings, introduced below, especially *Farming on a Battle Ground* and its preface, written by Edmund Perry.

27 Then, and still, to this day, as comments on local history websites testify, it was rumoured to be the landowner Lord Walsingham himself.

28 *Farming on a Battle Ground* (1950) is an autobiographical account chronicling her battles with adversity between 1938 and 1948. *The Earth No Longer Bare* (1950) is a collection of her essays and articles for the *Eastern Daily Post* and *Farmers Weekly*; *The Pheasants Had No Tails, and Other Tales* (1950) contains her short stories and poetry. The latter two are out of print; *Farming on a Battle Ground*, which is vivid and illuminating, was reprinted in 2000 with a preface by Edmund Perry.

29 'Truly my enemies were more numerous than friends; and annoyed, no doubt, that I had not been interned with other people who had supported Sir Oswald Mosley in his plans for Britain for the British.' Reeve, *Battle Ground*, p. 27. She denies, in her writings, any Nazi sympathies.

30 Reeve, *Battle Ground*, p. 110.

31 Reeve, *Battle Ground*, p. 110.

32 Reeve, *Battle Ground*, p. 75.

33 Reeve, *Battle Ground*, p. 76.

34 Reeve, *Battle Ground*, p. 18.

35 Reeve, *Battle Ground*, pp. 89–90.

36 Reeve, *Earth No Longer Bare*, p. 107.

37 Reeve, *Earth No Longer Bare*, p. 108.

38 Reeve, *Earth No Longer Bare*, p. 107.

39 Reeve, *Earth No Longer Bare*, p. 107.

40 MAF 147/97.

41 MAF 147/97. The order is dated 8 Dec. 1955.

42 Much of *Dad's Army* was filmed in Breckland.

43 Operation Brave Defender took place on 2–13 Sept. 1985. Many of the details below are from *Eastern Daily Press*, 16 August 1985; 3, 4, 6, 10, 12, 16 September 1985.

44 East Wretham is now generally known as Wretham.

45 Press cuttings from various local newspapers reporting Operation Brave Defender. NRO AUD 1/1/7.

46 AUD 1/1/17.

47 Transcript of a news item on BBC Radio Norfolk, undated, about a proposed new battle village at Eastmere. NRO AUD 1/1/17.

48 Letter from General Ramsay of Headquarters Eastern District, published in the *Eastern Daily Press*, 12 Dec. 1987. NRO AUD 1/1/17.

49 I am grateful to Simon Knott, author of the acclaimed Churches of East Anglia website, for bringing this detail to my attention. 'When I visited in

2004,' he wrote in an email, 'these houses survived, but had been adapted in the 1970s to represent a Northern Irish village, again for training for door-to-door fighting, complete with IRA graffiti, which I saw, but was politely asked not to photograph.'

50 *Eastern Daily Press*, 12 June 1986.

51 This was the abortive Wretham Plan, which faced stiff opposition from Norfolk county councillors on the grounds it would be hugely detrimental to wildlife. NRO AUD 1/1/17.

52 NRO AUD 1/1/17.

53 *Eastern Daily Press*, 29 Nov. 1986.

54 Letter from the chairman of the Merton Parish Council, June 1986. NRO AUD 1/1/17.

55 8 Feb. 1985.

56 *Eastern Daily Press*, cited above.

57 It was discussed in the House of Commons on 25 Feb. 1985 and 14 Jan. 1986 and in the House of Lords on 11 Dec. 1984, 21 March 1985, 24 April 1985 and 29 July 1986. Written answers were supplied in the Commons on 24 Jan., 18 March in the Commons and 29 July 1986 in the Lords.

58 *Eastern Daily Press*, cited above.

59 *Eastern Daily Press*, 18 Jan. 1990.

60 Today this is called Stanford Water.

61 It is also sometimes known as Sindh Kalay.

62 Much of the detail of this chapter came from my guide but also a number of newspaper and journal reports accompanying, and following, the opening of Ishmara: *Daily Telegraph*, 1 May 2009, https://www.telegraph.co.uk/news/newstopics/onthefrontline/5256219/MoD-builds-Afghan-village-in-Norfolk.html; *Mail Online*, 1 May 2009, updated 24 Jan. 2011, https://www.dailymail.co.uk/news/article-1349944/Helmand-village-Norfolk-British-troops-trained-Afghans.html; *Independent*, 11 March 2010, https://www.independent.co.uk/news/uk/this-britain/welcome-to-afghanistan-no-norfolk-1919462.html; *Legion Magazine*, March–April 2011, pp. 12–14; *Daily Record*, 20 May 2012, updated 3 July 2012, https://www.dailyrecord.co.uk/news/uk-world-news/soldiers-train-for-war-in-norfolk-replica-878367.

63 *Independent*, 11 March 2010. Despite repeated attempts, I haven't been able to track down John Pickup and interview him myself. Amputees in Action was a casting agency for amputee actors, role players and special effects make-up artists for military medical training, film productions and war games. They won a contract from the Ministry of Defence to help bring realism to military training. As well as being an amputee actor, John Pickup was the company director. See also *Army Technology*, 11 July 2012, https://www.army-technology.com/features/featurearmy-simulation-exercises-amputee-interview.

64 Details taken from my tour, and the sources listed above.

65 *Daily Telegraph*, 1 May 2009.

66 *Daily Telegraph*, 1 May 2009; *Independent*, 11 March 2010.

67 *Daily Telegraph*, 1 May 2009.

68 *Daily Telegraph*, 1 May 2009.

69 *Independent*, 11 March 2010.

70 *Independent*, 11 March 2010.

71 Lieutenant Colonel Simon Lloyd; General Sir David Richards. Both from *Daily Telegraph*, 1 May 2009. After this initial splash of coverage, documentation of Ishmara becomes scantier.

72 *Mail Online*, 24 Jan. 2011.

73 The Norfolk Record Office has a deeply moving transcription of all the headstone epitaphs and memorial inscriptions from the STANTA graveyards. The 'Monumental Inscriptions' are part of the Churchyard Surveys collection.

74 This is the opinion of the esteemed architectural historian Nikolaus Pevsner too; he considered it an ambitious masterpiece, one of the finest examples of the Gothic Revival architectural style in the country, which makes its concealment for 364 days a year all the more tragic. Nikolaus Pevsner and Bill Wilson, *The Buildings of England: Norfolk 2, North-West and South* (2002), pp. 141, 770–1.

EIGHT: THE VILLAGE OF THE DAMMED

1 The lack of consultation with the residents of Tryweryn (including its local authority) was rocket fuel to the villagers' ire. Martha Robert Jones, the schoolmistress at Capel Celyn school from 1954 until its closure in 1963, mentioned the appearance of people 'surveying the ground and making boreholes'. 'The locals didn't know what it was about', she continues, 'and thought it was something to do with agriculture' (*Western Mail*, 21 Aug. 1995). Einion Thomas, the author of *Capel Celyn: Ten Years of Destruction: 1955–1965* (2007), tells me that 'when they saw men on their land apparently doing a survey, they gave evasive answers when challenged' (email from Einion Thomas to the author, 14 Feb. 2007).

2 *Liverpool Daily Post*, 21 Dec. 1955. The headline appeared in the top right-hand corner of the page: 'Big new dam near Bala planned, £16,000,000 city scheme'. 'To augment the Liverpool area's water supply,' it went on, 'Liverpool Corporation Water Committee yesterday decided to promote a Parliamentary Bill for powers to dam the River Tryweryn valley in Merionethshire.' At no point does the article say that the scheme, if it went ahead, would destroy Capel Celyn. But the implications were evidently not lost on the villagers. Gwynfor Evans, leader of Plaid Cymru, writes in his memoirs that 'the first the people of Capel Celyn and its Valley knew of the plan to

drown their homes was when they read [of it] in the *Liverpool Daily Post*, towards the end of 1955'; the schoolmistress Martha Robert Jones, in a later newspaper report, recalls, 'One day' – quite out of the blue – 'we saw a notice in the *Liverpool Daily Post* saying the valley was to be drowned.' The tenants consistently claimed they were never consulted; nor, according to Evans, were Penllyn or Merioneth Councils (Gwynfor Evans, *For the Sake of Wales: The Memoirs of Gwynfor Evans*, trans. Meic Stephens (1996), p. 126; *Western Mail*, 21 Aug. 1995).

Liverpool Corporation disputed this version of events, at least at the time. Bessie Braddock, the formidable Liverpudlian MP, claimed that a letter was sent to every tenant in the area where borings were to be taken, informing them that 'Liverpool Corporation was doing some exploration with reference to water and did not want to do anything without the personal agreement of every individual in the area' (Hansard, HC vol. 572, cols 1218–21 (3 July 1957)). But this seems disingenuous. Only a fraction of Tryweryn's residents would have lived on or owned land where boring holes were made and the phrase 'exploration with reference to water' is downright ambiguous, even mendacious, given that the valley was prone to flooding when the Tryweryn river was in spate. There is no evidence any tenant ever received any such letter or, as Braddock also claimed, were visited by representatives of the Corporation to explain the plan. 'The inhabitants of the valley always argued that Liverpool had kept them in the dark', Einion Thomas, author of *Capel Celyn: Ten Years of Destruction* (2007), tells me, 'as to what was going on . . . It was in the press before Christmas 1955 that the inhabitants of the valley found out exactly what Liverpool were after' (email from Einion Thomas to the author, 14 Feb. 2017). The Corporation's retrospective apology in 2005 for the 'wrong' done cast further doubt on their claims to have consulted widely.

3 This section draws heavily upon the enormous, mesmerising collection of black-and-white photographs taken by photojournalist Geoff Charles, which capture in vivid detail the grain of everyday life in Capel Celyn before, during and after its battle with Liverpool Corporation. It would be impossible to list every single image that has informed my descriptions, but the entire collection is freely available online, easily browsed by searching for the keyword 'Tryweryn' (https://www.library.wales/discover/digital-gallery/photographs/geoff-charles).

4 As the secretary of Plaid Cymru told that fateful edition of the *Liverpool Daily Post*, 'The Tryweryn Valley is at the heart of a district where many would acknowledge that Welsh culture is at its finest and strongest and where the arts still flourish among ordinary people' (21 Dec. 1955).

5 Watcyn L. Jones, *Cofio Capel Celyn* (2007). This is a wonderfully revealing chronicle of life in the remote rural community through the years of physical and emotional tumult. I am grateful to Elinor Stephens for her translation.

6 In the Commons debate of 3 July 1957, Clement Davies, MP for Montgomeryshire, mentions an exodus of young people who go 'to Liverpool and to Manchester and to Birmingham'. Does Wales exist merely so Liverpool etc. can flourish, he asked? See also Geraint H. Jenkins, *A Concise History of Wales* (2007).

7 Liverpool Corporation had expressed interest in making a dam at Dolanog. But this would have drowned the home of Ann Griffiths (1776–1805), a celebrated Welsh hymn-writer, and they backed down. Gwynfor Evans expresses the widely held belief that this was a ruse, to make a show of cultural sensitivity, before placing what they really wanted in their crosshairs: Tryweryn (Evans, *For the Sake of Wales*, p. 126).

8 As Alderman Sefton said to Gwynfor Evans at the opening ceremony, 'In Great Britain we are in a tight little island . . . Interests of individuals cannot be divided up by a border between Wales and England . . . If we are to succeed . . . we must act as one' (*Daily Post*, 22 Oct. 1965).

9 See in particular *Liverpool Daily Post*, 21, 22 Dec. 1955.

10 Sadly no transcript of this chapel summit exists. This passage is an evocation of the meeting based on pertinent concerns expressed elsewhere: in letters, diaries, newspaper interviews, petitions and photographs.

11 Elizabeth was the elder sister of Watcyn L. Jones, the author of *Cofio Capel Celyn*. His reminiscences furnish us with much fascinating detail about Elizabeth.

12 Evans, *For the Sake of Wales*.

13 These wonderfully Gothic lines are from the poem 'The Valley of Tryweryn', first published in *The Star* on 29 Dec. 1956. Capel Celyn would, and still does, inspire much poetry. Some particularly good examples are printed on pp. 10–11 of Einion Thomas's book, one by Gwynlliw Jones which describes Wales' culture lying cold 'under the weight of the water's sepulchre', the sun blacked out by 'foreign interference' (Thomas, *Capel Celyn*).

14 In this section I have tried to distil the essence of the hundreds of letters of protest against Liverpool Corporation's proposal to flood the Tryweryn valley and drown Capel Celyn in a reservoir. Letters sent to the Wales Office in the Ministry of Housing and Local Government, Whitehall, are in the National Archives (TNA BD 24/174), and the letters sent directly to Liverpool Corporation, including some of the most vituperative invectives, can be found in the Meirionnydd Record Office in Dolgellau (one of two branches of the Gwynedd Archives) in the Capel Celyn Defence Committee Archive and the Tryweryn Archive. These were usually addressed to the Town Clerk, Lord Mayor or Chairman of the Water Committee. Some of Liverpool Corporation's replies are collected here, and make for fascinating reading. Extremely rarely we find a letter sent from Wales in favour of Liverpool's proposal, and not all correspondence sent to the Capel Celyn Defence

Committee pledged support, with some worried that Tryweryn was being made into too much of a political campaign, distorting the original, local issues. The Caernarfon Record Office has typescripts of letters of protest in support of the Capel Celyn Defence Committee (Z/M/4822/21).

15 Letter from A. M. Kissack, Wirral, to Liverpool Corporation, 2 July 1956.

16 Letter from 'a vet from Carmarthen' to Liverpool Corporation, 24 Nov. 1956.

17 Letter from Alwyn Ganadoc, Glamorgan, to Liverpool Corporation, 11 Oct. 1956. The letter is ominous, threatening that 'as a last resort many Welshmen have pledged their lives in the cause for preventing further molestation of Welsh resources.' 'I, therefore, advise you to withdraw your scheme', he concludes.

18 These descriptions are all taken from especially acerbic letters to Liverpool Corporation from, respectively, Evans G. Jones, West Merionethshire, 24 Dec. 1956; Bobbi Jones (a lecturer in Welsh), Caerfyrddin, 3 Jan 1956; J. Barrett, Neath, 16 March 1957; G. David Williams (a volcano of fury), 22 Nov. (n.y.); A. M. Kissack, Wirral, 2 July 1956.

19 Letter from G. David Williams to Liverpool Corporation, 22 Nov. (n.y.).

20 'Damnable hypocrites', 'snakes in the grass' are from A. M. Kissack's particularly furious letter to Liverpool Corporation, 20 Dec. 1956; 'skunks' from his earlier broadside of 2 July 1956.

21 Letter from John Parry, branch secretary, Welsh Nationalist Party, Planning Branch to the Minister for Welsh Affairs (n.d.). MRO: Capel Celyn Defence Committee Archive.

22 A rare letter of support from an inhabitant of Liverpool: Anthony Cooney, of the Liverpool Anti-Debt League, to the President of the Capel Celyn Defence Committee, 3 Oct. 1956.

23 It is one thing to talk about 'Welsh culture' in the abstract, quite another to understand what it entails. Although about a different rural community in North Wales – Montgomeryshire, about thirty miles to the south of Tryweryn – Alwyn David Rees's *Life in a Welsh Countryside: A Social Study of Llanfihangel yng Ngwynfa* (1950) is highly revealing of the unique expressions and manifestations of Welsh culture in the decade before Tryweryn was drowned.

24 Letter from Janet Rownsley to the Mayor of Liverpool, 30 Dec. 1956.

25 Letter from 'two doctoral holders' to the Department for Welsh Affairs, 28 Nov. 1956.

26 Geraint H. Jenkins, *A Concise History of Wales* (2007); Wyn Thomas, *Hands off Wales: Nationhood and Militancy* (2013).

27 Thomas, *Hands off Wales*.

28 Hansard, HC vol. 511, col. 377 (9 June 2010); Janet Davies, *The Welsh Language: A History* (2014).

29 Letter from Timothy Lewis, Swansea, to Whitehall, 1956.

30 Letter from H. Williams to Liverpool Corporation, 24 Nov. 1956.

31 Letter from E. M. S. Roberts, Colwyn Bay, to the Minister for Welsh

Affairs, Whitehall, 27 Nov. 1956. This is one of the fiercest letters in the whole collection, full of underlinings and double-underlinings. In an animated hand, on pale blue paper, Miss Roberts hurls accusations of treachery at the Minister.

32 A village elder purportedly – the phrasing is ambiguous – told the reporter he would not want to live in Bala, below the dam, because of an old prophecy. Apparently Old Bala lay at the bottom of the lake because of the debauchery of its prince, and present-day Bala would suffer the same fate, being engulfed up to and including (the prophecy is very specific) Llanfor, a village three-quarters of a mile away where the devil appears as a pig (*Country Quest*, Spring 1963).

33 Letter from Mrs G. P. Evans to the Minister for Welsh Affairs, 28 Nov. 1956.

34 T. W. Jones, Hansard, HC vol. 564, col. 1012 (11 Feb. 1957).

35 For this section on the history of Wales and England, which at points is filtered through the sensibilities of the Tryweryn protesters and Welsh nationalists, I have drawn upon, in particular, Geraint H. Jenkins, *A Concise History of Wales* (2007); John Davies, *A History of Wales* (2007); Davies, *Welsh Language*; Kenneth Morgan, *Rebirth of a Nation: A History of Modern Wales 1880–1980* (1987), and the unparalleled Jan Morris, *Wales: Epic Views of a Small Country* (1998, repr. 2014).

36 These are the bittersweet words of the Welsh antiquarian and travel writer Thomas Pennant in his *Tour in Wales, Vol. 2: The Journey to Snowdon* (1781), p. 214. A modern reprint was issued by Cambridge University Press in 2014 with the same page numbering. He is an excellent counterpart to the medieval Gerald of Wales.

37 Morris, *Wales*.

38 Undated letter from T. Lowry-Roberts to the Minister for Welsh Affairs, Whitehall.

39 Letter from an engineer living in Meirionnydd to the Wales Office, Whitehall, 9 Dec. 1956. 'It must be resisted at all costs,' he declares, 'or it will be the beginning of what will mark the end of a Wales as a country.'

40 These are the words of the Welsh philosopher J. R. Jones, who was Professor of Philosophy at the University of Swansea. He is credited with providing a firm philosophical foundation for the crusades of the Welsh Language Society in the 1960s. Quoted in translation in Geraint H. Jenkins, *A Concise History of Wales* (2007), p. 263.

41 Anonymous letter to the Minister for Welsh Affairs, Gwilym Lloyd George, 14 Dec. 1956.

42 Letter from R. Williams, Australia, to Liverpool Corporation, 17 Dec. 1956. Joyfully, a reply from Liverpool Corporation survives: 'Before expressing yourself in the language used in the 2nd para,' it begins, 'I feel it would have been better if you had taken the trouble to ascertain both sides of this question.' The Corporation emphasises that the scheme would only go ahead with parliamentary approval, that there would be

compensation for those 'injuriously affected', and rehousing for the dispossessed (at Frongoch). 'The facts must, I feel sure, have been unknown to you when you wrote to me on the 17th,' it concludes, sourly.

43 *The Times*, 22 Nov. 1956; *Liverpool Daily Post*, 22 Nov. 1956; Evans, *For the Sake of Wales*, pp. 128–30; Thomas, *Hands Off Wales*, pp. 4–6; Liverpool Records Office: Liverpool Corporation Water Committee Minutes, 352MIN/ WTR/1/59. At the end of the month Alderman John Braddock helpfully announced that the council only cared about the citizens of Liverpool and that 'Wales is part of our country' (*Liverpool Daily Post*, 1 Dec. 1956).

44 My account of the villagers' Liverpool mission draws upon the memoirs of Gwynfor Evans, the Geoff Charles photography collection, and, especially, a range of newspaper reports. Those that appeared in the national press are decidedly derogatory and sneering as though the villagers' cause was pointless and foredoomed. See in particular: *Guardian*, 22 Nov. 1956; *The Times*, 22 Nov. 1956; *Western Mail*, 22 Nov. 1956.

45 'Protest in Liverpool attempting to stop the flooding of the Tryweryn Valley', 21 Nov. 1956, the Geoff Charles Collection, National Library of Wales, online (image 10), http://hdl.handle.net/10107/1493899.

46 'She banged the lid of her desk up and down with a noise like thunder, and the other councillors followed her example. It was evident that she had put in a lot of practice at it' (Evans, *For the Sake of Wales*).

47 The reminiscences of Eurgain Prysor Jones and others (including Elwyn Edwards and Jane Charters) are printed in the *Denbighshire Free Press*, 21 Oct. 2015. See also Thomas, *Hands off Wales*, p. 4, fn 22.

48 Thomas, *Capel Celyn*, p. 57.

49 Hansard, HC vol. 572, col. 1170 (3 July 1957).

50 Hansard, HC vol. 572, col. 1183 (3 July 1957).

51 Hansard, HC vol. 572, cols 1184–9 (3 July 1957).

52 Hansard, HC vol. 572, cols 1206–13 (3 July 1957).

53 Hansard, HC vol. 572, cols 1218–21 (3 July 1957).

54 Some of the farmers were in fact not averse to moving into more modern housing. See, e.g., an article entitled 'Life Starts Afresh for Some of Tryweryn's Displaced Villagers' (MRO: press cuttings).

55 *Liverpool Daily Post*, 13 March 1956; MRO: miscellaneous press cuttings.

56 Thomas, *Hands off Wales*, p. 5, fn 25.

57 The following section on the disembowelment of Capel Celyn is based upon a wide range of local and national newspaper reports, official documentation from both Liverpool and Whitehall, eyewitness accounts, and, more than anything, the vast and extraordinary bank of black-and-white photographs in the National Library of Wales, especially the Geoff Charles collection, which capture so vividly – harrowingly – a community in its death throes and a world soon to be lost to the waters.

58 *Liverpool Daily Post*, 28 Jan. 1961; MRO: press cuttings.

59 Jones, *Cofio Capel Celyn.*

60 Watcyn L. Jones, in his memoir, describes the incessant noise from lorries rolling by and the thunk of heavy machinery passing the little school, sending clouds of dust into the air.

61 *Country Quest,* Nov. 1980.

62 *Western Mail,* 21 Aug. 1995; Thomas, *Capel Celyn,* p. 83.

63 *Guardian,* 6 Dec. 1960.

64 *Western Mail,* 21 Aug. 1995.

65 Thomas, *Capel Celyn,* pp. 82–3.

66 Watcyn L. Jones recalls how, after the chapel was demolished, the large stones were used to strengthen the dam.

67 MRO: Tryweryn Archive, document 51 and accompanying photograph; Watcyn Jones, *Cofio Capel Celyn.*

68 *Western Mail,* 21 Aug. 1995.

69 *The Times,* 21 Oct. 1965.

70 *Western Post,* 21 Aug. 1995.

71 *Daily Post,* 13 Oct. 2005.

72 Thomas, *Hands off Wales,* pp. 91–2; Thomas, *Capel Celyn.*

73 The account that follows draws upon some of the secondary sources listed at the beginning of this chapter's notes and, in particular, vivid first-hand newspaper reports from a range of local and national papers, especially *Daily Mail,* 22 Oct. 1965, 8 Nov. 1965; *Daily Telegraph,* 22 Oct. 1965, 24 Oct. 1965, 31 Oct. 1965; *Daily Post,* 22 Oct. 1965; *Western Mail,* 21 Oct. 1965, 22 Oct. 1965; *Liverpool Weekly News,* 28 Oct. 1965; *Liverpool Daily Post,* July–Aug. 1963, 1 Oct. 1956; *Western Mail,* 19–20 Aug. 1964, 4 Nov. 1965.

74 Evans, *For the Sake of Wales,* p. 133.

75 Thomas, *Capel Celyn,* p. 125.

76 For pertinent details, see the rather haughty and belittling reportage of, in particular, *Guardian,* 22 Oct. 1965, and *Liverpool Weekly News,* 28 Oct. 1965.

77 This section on lakes and Welsh folklore draws upon Morris, *Wales;* T. Gwynn Jones, *Welsh Folklore and Folk-Custom* (1930); John Rhys, *Celtic Folklore: Welsh and Manx,* 2 vols (1901); Beryl Beare, *Wales: Myths and Legends* (1996); Frank Ward, *The Lakes of Wales* (1931); Benjamin Radford and Joe Nickell, *Lake Monster Mysteries: Investigating the World's Most Elusive Creatures* (2006).

78 *Wales on Sunday,* 18 June 1995; *Daily Post,* 10 Aug. 1995, 20 Sept. 1995, 21 May 1997, 23 June 2000.

79 *Guardian,* 27 Jan. 2001.

80 Extraordinary photographs of the ghost village re-emerging from the muddy wasteland are printed in *Cambria,* Jan.–Feb. 2016.

81 In 2005, there was a rally on the banks of the lake by Kurdish representatives who were worried that a giant new dam in Turkey was going to force 25,000 people from their homes.

82 A copy of this official proclamation can be found in the Meirionnydd Record Office in the Tryweryn Archive.

83 A copy of this apology is reproduced in Thomas, *Capel Celyn*. For Aeron Prysor Jones, the apology came too late for the traumatised, who were either dead by 2005, or too old to grasp the significance. Ironically, the apology came just days after the death of Gwynfor Evans.

84 *Independent*, 16 Oct. 2010; *Guardian*, 26 Oct. 1999.

CODA

1 Richard Askwith, *Lost Village: In Search of a Forgotten Rural England* (2008), p. 232. Across the country each year, eight hundred village shops are shutting, one hundred plus churches of all denominations are closing, and seven rural schools are shutting.

2 Altus Group, '37 Pubs a Month Vanished in 2020', 11 Jan. 2021, https://www.altusgroup.com/property/insights/27-pubs-a-month-vanished-in-2020/.

3 Esther Addley, 'We feel betrayed', *Guardian*, 25 Oct. 2016.

4 This is how Old Winchelsea was described in 1275 (p. 80).

5 This is the case in some places more than others: England's east coast, being made up of soft clay and sand, is highly erodible – on the Yorkshire coast, land is eaten up at a rate of around four metres a year, and the stretch between Easington and Aldbrough is expected to recede by around eighty metres in the next two decades; the western coast, in contrast, is characterised by harder rock which can better resist erosion.

6 Josh Halliday, '"It's a monster": the skipsea homes falling into the North Sea', *Guardian*, 18 Jan. 2020; Colin Drury, 'Fastest collapsing cliffs in northern Europe leaves Yorkshire coastal homes on brink of falling into sea', *Independent*, 30 Jan. 2020; Sean Smith, 'Fairbourne residents may have to pay £6,000 towards the demolition of their own houses', *Independent*, 28 April 2021.

7 Camilla Hodgson, 'Britain's disappearing coastline: "Right now we abandon people"', *Financial Times*, 9 Aug. 2020.

8 'Legal action threat over coastal retreat of Fairbourne', BBC News, 8 March 2014; Tom Wall, '"This is a wake-up call": the villagers who could be Britain's first climate refugees', *Guardian*, 18 May 2019.

9 Damian Carrington, 'Almost 7,000 UK properties to be sacrificed to rising seas', *Guardian*, 28 Dec. 2014.

10 Committee on Climate Change, *Managing the Coast in a Changing Climate*, Oct. 2018.

11 See Climate Central's coastal risk screening tool for land in Britain projected to be below annual flood level in 2050 (https://coastal.climatecentral.org).

12 David Wallace-Wells, *The Uninhabitable Earth: A Story of the Future* (2019), pp. 3–4, 96–7, 215–16.

INDEX

Numbers in *italics* refer to pages with illustrations.

Cain, Frank, Alderman, 269, 286–7
Calstock, Devon, 135
Campbell, Mr (schoolmaster), 212
Campbell, Reverend John, 174
Capel Celyn (*see also* Tryweryn valley):
    chapel, 258–9, 282–3, 291; dam, 283,
    288; Defence Committee, 260–1,
    270, 282, 284; graveyard, 263, 283,
    291, 293; landscape, 256–8; language,
    258, 262; letters of protest, 261–4; life
    in, 255–8; mass protest of villagers
    in Liverpool, 272–4; memory of,
    292; news of drowning, 256, 259;
    population, 257, 272; post office, 255,
    258, 260, 281; protesters at reservoir
    opening ceremony, 284–8, *285*; rail-
    way, 256, 280; reappearances during
    droughts, 291; school, 255, 258, 260,
    272, 281, 291
Cerda, Carlos de la, 104, 105
Charles I, King, 164, 165
Chaucer, Geoffrey, 101
Childe, Vere Gordon: arrival on
    Orkney, 10–11, 14; arrival at Skara
    Brae, 12–13; career, 10–11; character,
    11, 45; death, 11, 39; descriptions of
    Skara Brae, 13, 18, 25; excavation
    of Skara Brae, 11, 13, 26; 'Neolithic
    Revolution' theory, 33–4; political
    beliefs, 10, 27; theories about Skara
    Brae, 22, 27, 34–6; writings, 13, 33–4
Cicero, 190
Cinque Ports, 74, 101, 102, 107, 108, 115
Civil War, English, 163–4
Clare family, de, 56–8, 60, 62, 65–6,
    69–71, 72, 85
Clare, Gilbert de (the Red), 57, 65–6,
    70, 72
Clare, Gilbert de (son of above), 57, 71
Clare, Richard de, 56, 59, 61, 65
Clarke, E. D.: arrival on St Kilda,
    182–3; description of fowling party,
    200–2; descriptions of islanders'

mainland visits, 199; journey to St
    Kilda, 175, 178; on economy of St
    Kilda, 187, 195; on houses, 187; on
    landscape, 185; on population of St
    Kilda, 184; on religion of islanders,
    192; on technology, 197
climate change: coastal erosion,
    296–7, 298; global warming after
    Ice Age, 33; man-made, 5, 82, 297;
    medieval, 5, 37, 81–2, 297; prospect
    of, 1, 5, 234, 295; storms, 297
Columbus, Christopher, 180
Connell, Robert, 204–11, 214
Conrad, Joseph, 112
Cook, Captain James, 203
Covid-19, 5, 296
Cowley, David, Alderman and Lord
    Mayor, 286–7
Cowsfield, Wiltshire, 135
Cracknell, Basil, 81–2
Cromwell, Thomas, 163

D-Day, 222, 251
Dad's Army, 234, 238
Daily Express, 227
Daily Mail, 44, 252
Daily Post, 280
Daily Telegraph, 44, 252
Day, John, 152–5, 156–9, 162
Defoe, Daniel, 110–11, 116, 148
Degérando, Joseph-Marie, 177
Dene, William, 123
Department for Welsh Affairs, 261,
    276
Deserted Medieval Village Research
    Group, 143
Dickens, Charles, 90
Diderot, Denis, 177, 191, 200, 203
Doggerland, 29
Domesday Book, 100, 120
Domesday of Enclosures, 143
Drake, Sir Francis, 180, 190
Dryden, John, 180

Stanford Battle Area (*cont.*): foundation, 223; 'Humble Petition' for release of houses and land (1947), 227; inhabitants removed, 224; land retained after war, 225–6, 233

STANTA (Stanford Training Area) (*see also* Stanford Battle Area), Norfolk: anti-Soviet exercises, 238–9, 242–4; battle village at Eastmere Farm, 238–42, 249, 251; chosen for battle training, 222–3, 235; chosen for simulated Soviet invasion (1985), 235–7; country's pre-eminent training area, 244; inhabitants removed, 224–5; Ishmara (Jackson Wright village, Afghan simulation), 245–52; landscape, 220–1, 233–5; live-firing ranges, 242; local opposition to battle village, 240–2; 'Nazi village', 219, 239, 242, 246, 247, 251; press coverage of anti-Soviet exercises, 242–3, 251; press coverage of Ishmara (Afghan simulation), 251–2; 'Soviet village', 242, 246, 247, 251; territory, 219, 223, 226, 233; tour of, 220–2, 224, 234–5, 244–5, 253; villages, 221; villages seized, 228; visiting arrangements, 220

Star Carr, East Yorkshire, 29

Star newspaper, 261

Stenness, Orkney, 26, 37

Stone Age (*see also* Mesolithic, Neolithic, Palaeolithic), 13, 28–9, 33, 216

storms: (2500 BC), 34–6; (1250), 78–9; (1252), 79; (1288), 159, 161; (1287–8), 80, 147; thirteenth century, 1, 78–81; (1328), 147, 161; (1362), 81, 82; fourteenth century, 1, 81, 82; (1570, Candlemas Storm), 155–6, 157; (1677), 162; (1850), 9–10, 12, 35; (1924), 12, 16

Stow, John, 157–9, 161

Stretton Baskerville, Warwickshire, 143–4

Sturston, Norfolk, 221, 225

Sturt, Fraser, 81

Swinburne, Algernon Charles, 163, 168

Switzer, Stephen, 166

Tacitus, 179–80

Tavistock, Abbot of, 98

Templer, Brigadier James, 239–40

Tennyson, Alfred, 151

Thackeray, William Makepeace, 111, 151

Thatcher, Margaret, 238

Thetford and Watton Times, 226

Thetford Battle Training Area, 224

Thomas (English flagship), 104, 105

Thomas of Walsingham, 114

Tilgarsley, Oxfordshire, 133–4

Times, 224

Tottington, Norfolk: abandoned, 222; anti-Soviet exercises, 236; descriptions (1947, 1986), 228; 'Humble Petition' for return of village (1947), 225–6; Lucilla Reeve's life and death, 229, 232, 234, 236; 'Nazi village', 239, 242, 251; removal of inhabitants, 224, 225, 228; simulation of northern French village, 248

travel writing, 176–7, 181–2, 196–7, 200

Trawsfynydd, drowned village, 264

Trellech: attacks (1291, 1295), 42; boom town, 64, 71–2; borough status, 59; burgage assessments, 63–4; burgage plots, 60–2; castle remains, 61; controversy, 43, 45, 47–51; decline and disappearance, 72; excavations, 42, 44, 47–8, 64–5; growth, 61–4; iron manufacture, 65–6; iron mining, 64; 'lost city', 41–2, 45; population, 47, 51, 60, 62–4, 65; power base of de Clare family, 57, 65, 71; rediscovery, 40; St Anne's Well, 68–9; site, 40, 41–4, 47–9, 51, 59; size, 46–7, 51, 61–2; three stones, 40, 67, 67–8; village today, 67–9; weapons factory, 69–71

Trivet, Nicholas, 91

Tryweryn valley (*see also* Capel Celyn): battle against reservoir, 261–4; dam, 283, 288; debate over reservoir plans, 271–8; devastation of, 280–3; drowning of, 283–4, 291; farmers and poets, 257; memory of, 292, 294; population, 283; protests against reservoir plans, 261–4, 272–4; reservoir opening ceremony, 284–8, *285*; reservoir plans, 259, 271, 278; river, 255, 256–7, 281; river dammed, 283–4; today, 288–9, 292–3

Turner, Joseph, 111

Tyneham, Dorset, 219, 225

Venette, Jean de, 125

Viney, William, 167–8

Voltaire, 202

Wales: coastal erosion, 297, 298; dissolution of monasteries, 163; Edward I's policies, 57, 66, 76, 90; Edward I's rule, 96, 266–7; English border, 2, 40, 41–2, 52, *see also* Marches; Free Wales Army, 287, 288; harp music, 257, 262, 290; history, 52–6, 264–8; kings and princes, 53, 54, 57, 58, 65, 267, 269; lakes, 289; legal system, 266–7; military training areas, 223, 239, 268; new towns, 58, 59, 73, 76, 90; population, 121, 258, 263, 268; relationship with England, 261–9, 278, 285–7, 294; reservoirs for Liverpool, 259, 268, 271, 287–8; ruins, 165; rural depopulation, 258, 263, 275; settlement shrouded in sand, 34; Trellech, *see* Trellech; Welsh language, 261, 262–3, 265, 267, 269, 274, 277, 292, 294; Welsh nationalism, 264–5, 268–9, 281; Welsh Parliament (Senedd Cymru), 294

Walsingham, Barons, 224, 229, 241

Walsingham, Thomas, 114

Warwickshire, lost villages, 141

Washington Post, 48–9, 50

Watkin Jones, Elizabeth, 260–1, 274

Watkins, Tudor, MP, 275

Watt, William, 12

Wesley, John, 111

West Tofts, Norfolk: Camp, *234*, 239; 'Humble Petition' for return of village (1947), 225–6; inhabitants removed, 224; lost village, 221; St Mary's church, 253–4, *254*; tanks blown up, 244

Wharram Percy: Black Death, 121–2, 124, 126–8, 137; evictions, 140, 141, 144; houses, 119–20; landscape after evictions, 144–5; lords of the manor, 119, 120, 140; manor houses, 119; occupation, 118; population, 121, 140; remains today, 118; St Martin's church, 117–18, *117*, 127, 144; Scottish raids, 120; search for, 137, 139, *139*; sheep enclosures, 140; site, 118–19

William I (the Conqueror), King, 52, 53–4, 56, 141, 266

Wilson, Julia, 41, 42

Wilson, Stuart: appearance, 45; calculating size of Trellech, 62–4; career, 41–2; first Trellech site excavations, 42; interviewed by author, 45–8; media presentation of, 49–50; purchase of field, 42–3; second Trellech site excavations, 44–5, 60; view of earlier Howell excavations, 47–8, 49

Winchelsea (Old and New): Black Death, 112, 114; burgage plots, 85–6; churches, 73, 77, 79, 93, 94, 108, 109–10, 112–14; cloth trade, 75; construction of New Winchelsea, 84–91, 93, 107, 147; decline of New Winchelsea, 111–12, 114–16, 148–9, 150; destruction of Old Winchelsea, 5, 80–1, 82, 115; entrance, 91–2; ferry, 91; flooding, 73, 75, 78–80;

Winchelsea (Old and New) (*cont.*):
French attacks, 113–14, 120; Greyfriars, 92, 109; grid plan of New
Winchelsea, 85, 87, *88*, 89–91, 92–3,
108, 109; harbour, 77, 86, 93, 95, 106,
107, 115; houses, 93–4, 116; King's
Leap, 95, 109; king's visit, 75–6; loss
of harbour, 115; Monday Market,
73, 94, 103, 109, 112, 116; naval battle
(1349), 104–7; New Gate, *110*;
piracy, 73, 96, 98, 102–4, 107, 113;
population, 73–4, 86, 107, 111, 112,
115–16; port, 73–5, 77, 79, 82, 87, 102,
115–16; prosperity, 74–5; relocation,
76–8, 84, 220; rotten borough, 111,
116; sea defences, 79; search for
Old Winchelsea, 82–4; shingle
spit, 73, 74, 79, 82–3, 87; site, 74,
76–7, 84, 87; size, 107, 115–16; Spanish attacks, 114, 120; storm (1250),
78–9; storm (1252), 79; storms (1287,
1288), 80; 'village' today, 107–10;
wine cellars, 95–7, 101, 109, 111, 116;
wine trade, 75–6, 91, 97, 98–9, 101–2,
109, 111
Winchester, 46, 62, 89
Windmill Hill, Wiltshire, 31
wine: consumption, 99–101, 208;
French raids, 113; Gascony trade, 90,
75, 90, 96–7, 101, 114, 170; piracy, 98,
104; taste, 98–9; voyage from Gascony to Winchelsea, 97–8; warfare,
104–7; Winchelsea cellars, 95–7, 101,
109, 111, 116; Winchelsea trade, 75–6,
91, 97, 98–9, 101–2, 109, 111
Wolsey, Cardinal, 143
Woodeaton, Oxfordshire, 136
Worde, Wynkyn de, 153
Wordsworth, William, 166
Wykes, Thomas, 57